Scars That Speak

Rochelle Murray walked onto the pages of my life as a student some years ago. She quickly became an inspiration and a daughter in the faith as I witnessed her courage and perseverance while she searched relentlessly for answers and truth about a blurry past. I can testify that *Scars That Speak* is the honest outpouring of her courageous quest. Rochelle is a gifted poet, composer, and communicator and she uses those gifts to shed light and clarity into the darkness of the long-term effects of unaddressed abuse. Her extraordinary ability to articulate her journey of healing has gifted us all with precious insight into the wounded soul and the immeasurable, mighty power and grace of our wonderful God. I am profoundly humbled and blessed to have had my student become my teacher and a cherished friend.

Terri Fanning

I was emotionally overwhelmed when reading *Scars That Speak*, the personal account of my patient, Rochelle Murray. Her book helps one to understand self-destructive behavior and shows that the path to healing the soul comes through understanding the trauma and courageously enduring the pain of healing. When this occurs, ultimately life will be elevated to a healthy and spiritually fulfilled state.

Arun Patel, M.D.

I have known Rochelle for ten years. I first met her when she was a student. She had intimated to me, as her preacher, some of the struggles that she so graphically writes about in this volume of her life. Not being qualified to help her with some of these issues, I recommended her to a skilled clinician who continues to work with Rochelle. Her faith is the only anchor that I can determine held her steady until she could reach the threshold of her healing. God has since blessed her with all of those wonderful things that she so desired. I am proud to know Rochelle, and I am thrilled to see her faith that sustained her through that dark chapter in her life. There are times when you will cringe in disbelief at her pain when you read about her life. But you will hear her faith as she struggles through each issue. Take the time to read and share this book with others.

Gerald P. Jackson, Evangelist

Rochelle Murray's book, *Scars That Speak*, is a genuinely candid view into the struggles that many people battle daily. She attacks multiple difficult topics that are often perceived as too painful, taboo, or personal to discuss, with the same open and honest sincerity that I have consistently come to know in my friend. Her boldness to share this story about her own harm and damage cannot help but to stir compassion at the same time that it enables a better understanding of the challenges of recovery. That knowledge empowers me to share support that is more meaningful for others in a similar situation. When I first met Rochelle I was drawn to her resolute spirit, gentle heart, and love for God's Word. She rapidly became a comfortable friend who approaches every challenge with an organized and fierce determination to triumph. Now, I delight in observing her continuing awareness and ongoing efforts to remain within the joyful realm of her recovered life. I challenge you to enter her lesser-known world of hurt and pain, open your heart and mind to the challenges of a hurting world, and celebrate in the promise of redemption.

Shannon Sanford, BSN, RN, IBCLC, RLC

Scars That Speak
One Woman's Battle with Self-Destruction

BY
ROCHELLE MURRAY

Scars That Speak

BY
ROCHELLE MURRAY

Copyright © 2011 by Rochelle Murray

Published by Lucid Books in Brenham, TX.
www.LucidBooks.net

All rights reserved. No part of this publication may be reproduced, stored in a retrieval system, or transmitted in any form by any means, electronic, mechanical, photocopy, recording, or otherwise, without the prior permission of the publisher, except as provided for by USA copyright law.

First Printing 2011

ISBN-13: 9781935909156
ISBN-10: 1-935909-15-0

Special Sales: Most Lucid Books titles are available in special quantity discounts. Custom imprinting or excerpting can also be done to fit special needs. Contact Lucid Books at info@lucidbooks.net.

Scriptures taken from the Holy Bible, New International Version®, NIV®. Copyright © 1973, 1978, 1984 by Biblica, Inc.™ Used by permission of Zondervan. All rights reserved worldwide. www.zondervan.com.

The "NIV" and "New International Version" are trademarks registered in the United States Patent and Trademark Office by Biblica, Inc.™

Dedication

To the little girls in my life.
This journey, this healing is for you.
And to my husband,
who brought joy to my journey.

Contents

Foreword... 11
Introduction... 13

1—Me... 17
2—Clues.. 25
3—Cutting.. 31
4—Scars.. 41
5—Therapy.. 47
6—Compulsion... 51
7—Mental Illness....................................... 57
8—Depression... 69
9—Tears.. 77
10—Pain.. 79
11—Hurt.. 83
12—Anger... 93
13—Anxiety... 97
14—Thoughts.. 99
15—Alone.. 107
16—Family... 111
17—Shame.. 115
18—Fear... 121
19—Mom.. 127
20—Boundaries & Image................................. 135
21—Letters.. 139
22—Revelation... 153
23—Joy.. 159
24—Raw.. 175
25—The Little Girl.................................... 185

26—Babies	201
27—Violation	219
28—Truth	239
29—Grief	253
30—Time	265
31—Becoming Whole	269
32—Forgiveness	291
33—Treachery	307
34—Abuse	325
35—Holidays	349
36—Goals	363
37—Breakthrough	373
38—Blame	395
39—Papa	409
40—Courage	419
41—Trust	435
42—Face-To-Face	449
43—The Big Picture	463
44—Victory	499
45—Freedom	529
46—God	559
47—The Future	563
Epilogue	569
Note from Josh	573
Acknowledgments	575
Appendix A	577
Appendix B	579
Appendix C	583
Endnotes	587

Foreword

The reader of this book is embarking on a compelling and dramatic venture into the depths of human dysfunction and the fierce battle to regain mental wellness. There are several unique aspects to this book. For example, this is an actual account of therapy as it unfolds session by session. Rochelle writes this journal in the midst of her daily struggles and with uncertainty as to the final outcome. One sees her desperately clinging to spiritual and therapeutic principles, the overarching principle being that "truth will set you free."

Her story demonstrates the profound depravity and, in some cases, the perceptual neglect of family members who should have protected her in childhood, the long-lasting effect of child abuse, the connection between abuse and subsequent self-abuse, and the emergence of an array of dysfunctional defense mechanisms.

At different points in therapy Rochelle presented me with the "final document" only then to discover, as a mountain climber does, that a perceived hilltop is just the base of another more daunting challenge. This meant that many subsequent chapters were added to this book.

I applaud Rochelle for her courage and determination to find wellness. Her story gives hope that the human soul can triumph over the horrendous abuses that innocent children may experience. Others will find courage and inspiration never to give up and never to surrender, no matter what the cost or how long the road. As the reader will discover in the following pages, the blessings and rewards prove worthy of the fight.

I thank the Lord and Rochelle for allowing me to have a part in this journey. I have learned much and have witnessed the triumph of the Lord's eternal truths. This book is also a reminder to my mental health colleagues that long-term therapy still has a place, that psychiatry plays a crucial part in achieving wellness, that a variety of therapeutic approaches may be needed, that art can facilitate progress in visual clients, that the spiritual concepts of sin and forgiveness need to be addressed, that patience is needed, and finally, that one never give up on the client.

G. Gary Walker, PhD
Clinical Psychologist

Introduction

Scars that speak,
like a
muted whisper,
barely giving
voice
to the words;
or,
like words said
plainly,
clearly,
distinctly;
or,
like a command,
emphatic and
resounding,
making crystal clear
the meaning and
intent;
or,
like a
scream of terror,
wailing with
grief
and fear
and pain,
shrieking out all the
anguish and
despair
of one's soul.
Scars that speak.

This is the story of a woman and her battle with self-destruction. This is not a novel. It is a true story. It's my story. Although I have a bachelor's degree in psychology and some graduate hours, I am not a clinician in any sense of the word. I am a teacher. I am a student of life. I am a writer, a poet, a musician. I am a Christian. I am a cutter.

I remember vividly the first time I hurt myself. It was 1993. I was twenty-three years old and had just spent four weeks in a psychiatric hospital for depression. I had been out only about a week when I ran into an old acquaintance. Memories of my childhood came crashing in on me, and when I got home that evening, I was a mess inside. At one point I picked up my scissors, opened them, and placed the blade against my left forearm. I don't know what made me think to do that. I had never heard of anyone doing such a thing. I just knew it was what I had to do. I started scraping. I scraped and scraped until my forearm was raw. And I felt better.

Over the next ten years, that one incident escalated to the point that I was cutting my body with razor blades many times every day. But in July 2003 I began working with a therapist who saved my life. He urged me to take the vast number of pages I had written in my journal, the countless poems and pictures I'd produced, and the wisdom I've gained and turn them into a resource to help others struggling with the same self-destructiveness. He urged me to let my scars speak. After much time and courage, energy and tears, cutting is no longer part of my life. The last time I cut was September 6, 2005. Cutting can be overcome. If you are fighting the battle of self-injury, I am writing this for you. My prayer is that my struggles, how I moved past them, and what I've learned along the way can help you to move past your struggles as well.

Portions printed in a different font are journal entries, poems, or songs I have written along the way. I've also included a number of pictures I've drawn or painted. Some of what you'll read and see is intense. I have never been one to mince words and I haven't here. I've changed most names and some details to protect people's privacy. As you read my story, please be patient. This book chronicles my therapeutic journey. The picture you get of me in the first chapter is enhanced with details and explanation as my story unfolds. When I began writing, I did not know the ending. I wrote my story as it progressed.

I mentioned that I am a Christian. One wouldn't think that Christians would have the kind of problems described in this book. But we live in a sinful, fallen world. And Christians do have major struggles. I hope my story can help others as they live their lives, trying to be the people God wants them to be. Even if you are not a Christian, I hope you'll keep reading. My scars may speak to you as well.

On my bookshelf sit fourteen books about cutting. So why write another? Because this is not a clinical book written by a clinician. It also isn't a book just about cutting. Cutting is only one way people react to the deeper issues in their lives. This is a book about pain written by someone who has experienced great pain in her life. This is not a self-help book. It's a book written about how God helped one person overcome her destructive upbringing and her own problems and brought her out of the darkness of despair into the light of a joyful life.

This book is a window to my soul. If you are struggling with cutting, depression, anxiety, fear, abuse, mental illness—whatever your pain—please, step up to the window and look. You might see part of your own story. Step up to the window and listen. You might hear words of comfort whispered to you. You might hear something that speaks to your heart. You might hear screams that echo your own battle. And when you hear my scars speaking, you might find your own voice. Then, like me, you can one day hear shouts of victory.

1
Me

Me,
like a trapped animal,
like a slit wrist,
like a dark cavern,
like an abused child,
like a demented soul,
like a severed limb,
like a rabid wolf,
like a bloodthirsty shark,
like a lost puppy,
full of
fear,
anger,
aloneness,
shame,
numbness,
confusion,
hurt,
purging,
sadness,
hatred,
anxiety,
scars,
perversion,
and pain.
Crazy.
Me.

What would cause a woman to cut her body with razor blades? Often it has something to do with the family. Mine was not your typical mom and dad, two kids, and a dog kind of family, although we did have a dog. When my mom first met my dad, he was a married man. But over the course of about a year, he got divorced and my mom got pregnant. Then they got married. Six months later, my father put my very pregnant mother on a plane and sent her home to her folks. My mom and I lived with my grandparents. No one ever talked about my father, and I was sixteen before I met him for the first time. We met for two hours. I had no other contact with him until I was twenty-three.

My family lived by certain "rules" set by my mother. "Rules" such as:

- Family loyalty is primary
- No airing of dirty laundry
- Everyone is expected to act as if nothing is ever wrong
- Appearances must always be maintained
- Don't rock the boat
- Be perfect
- It is not okay to talk about problems
- There should be no boundaries between me and the rest of the family

I was a very angry little girl. And fearful. And depressed. I have struggled with depression since I was ten or eleven years old. At the age of twelve, I was acting out and getting into trouble with my mom and at school. At the school's urging, my mother took me to see a counselor. After the first session, the counselor worked exclusively with me. We did a lot of play therapy, and during some of the sessions my intense anger would come out. He had foam bats and we would pretend we were sword fighting. But it quickly went beyond play for me, and I would start swinging wildly with my bat. My rage would get out of control as I pounded with my bat. The counselor would then grab me in a bear hug and hold me tight while he talked quietly to me and calmed me down. I don't know if this was good therapy or not, but clearly, I was angry. In fact, when I was an adult, this same counselor told me, "You were an incredibly angry little girl. You had more anger than just having an absent father would account for."

When I was in high school, I went back to see the same counselor at my own initiative because I was suicidal. My mother was angry with me for seeking counseling. Why, I did not know. When I went away to college, I was in counseling at the university for the better part of all four years. I continued counseling while I attended graduate school, and during that time I was hospitalized for three days because I was suicidal again. When I was released, my mom drove to where I was living and took me back to my hometown, where I admitted myself to a Christian psychiatric hospital. It was May 25, 1992. I was there for six weeks. I was twenty-two years old, and I was breaking one of my mother's rules. I was rocking the boat.

I was rocking the boat because of what I believed had happened to me when I was a little girl. Because of many clues, I believed that my grandfather had sexually abused me. During my hospitalization, I made the accusation to my family about what I believed my grandfather had done. And instead of getting my mother's support, I got her anger.

In February 1993, almost a year after the first hospitalization, I was hospitalized again for another four weeks. This time I actually attempted suicide. Right after this hospitalization the self-injury started. I was twenty-three. For the next nine years I struggled with it, but it never went beyond scraping my forearms or my thighs with scissors or a knife, probably because I was living at home with my mom. There were still no boundaries in our family, making it incredibly difficult to hide, so the scraping was infrequent and I always had an elaborate story to explain the raw places on my skin. But I did continue to seek counseling, which I was able to keep secret from my mom.

During those nine years I worked with four different counselors. Still, my heart was shackled by chains. I worked diligently at breaking down the walls I had built around my heart, but it seemed impossible. I never got very far. Sometimes I was better than other times, but overall I felt as if I were spinning my wheels in counseling. I was in an impenetrable, inescapable fortress. I wondered if I would ever find healing in my life. The depression came and went, and I even went two years without scraping myself. Was I healed? For two years I thought so, but near the end of those two years I made a huge change. I moved out of my mom's house and to another city to go back to school. For the first time in my life, I was truly on my own, alone. I was thirty-two.

And not five months later the cutting started again, this time in earnest. This time with razor blades. Now I could cut whenever, however, and wherever I wanted. I was alone. I would often sit at my kitchen table with absolutely nothing on, my razors and tissues spread out on the table before me. It gradually got worse. About three months after the cutting started again, I began seeing Dr. Patel, a psychiatrist. He put me on medication for depression. Around the same time, I began working with yet another counselor. Twice he had me sign a "Contract to Live," promising not to hurt myself. Each time I agreed to this for a period of about a month. I broke both contracts. I felt compassion from him, but he ended up referring me to a Christian psychologist, Dr. Gary Walker. Gary saved my life.

The week before I started working with Gary, my psychiatrist hospitalized me in order to stabilize my medication. Up to that point the medications he had tried for the depression really hadn't helped. Now, though, Dr. Patel said he was pretty sure he knew what my problem was and what medication I needed. He wanted to be able to change and increase the medication in a controlled and quick manner, so he hospitalized me for a week. While there, I was diagnosed with bipolar II disorder and borderline personality disorder. With bipolar II, the depression is much more persistent and pronounced, and the manic episodes are much less severe than in regular bipolar. During that week the depression finally lifted a little. The lithium was working.

I was discharged on a Friday and I saw Gary for the first time the following Monday. In that first session, I told him as much about me, my family, and my problems as I could in one hour. I was open and honest, even about the cutting. I signed a contract with him, but unlike the previous therapist, Gary had *me* write out the contract. He wanted me to write it so it would be a contract I could live with, one I could keep. In it, I did not say I *wouldn't* cut. I said I would "make every effort" not to cut. This was a contract I could keep. He also told me that he thought one of my biggest problems was not the depression or even the cutting. He said it was my mother. That scared me. It scared me because I wasn't ready to deal with her. Besides, the cutting was all-consuming at that point. I needed to get the cutting under control. So that's where we started.

Before I began working with Gary, the cutting had gotten out of control. I was cutting myself many times every single day. I would cut my upper and lower arms, my breasts, my stomach, and my thighs. And there was a method to my cutting. I wasn't just making random cuts, although there were plenty of those. I was writing a book on my body. My scars were speaking loud and clear because I was cutting words. Often I would cut over the words I had already cut. I was sure I was crazy.

Am I crazy, deranged, insane?
Am I mentally ill, demented, mad?
Am I a lunatic, unbalanced, unsettled, unsound, sick, daft, deluded, obsessed, nutty, loony, nuts, loco, wacko, derailed, batty, bonkers, unglued, nutty as a fruitcake, off my rocker, cracked, bananas, not playing with a full deck, idiotic, off the deep end, out to lunch?

Well, let's see...
   I cut my body with a razor blade and leave scars all over it.
   I cut and carve words into my body.
   I cut over the same words again and again.

Currently I have the following words cut into my body:
   sad, ugly, why?, shame, bitch, rage, hurt, fear, no, stupid, help me, me, fat, confusion, fear, pain, hurt, confusion, dirty, sad, shame, numb, hope?, sex-pervert, slut, despair, help, alone, self-hate, anxiety, anger, loco, sad, φoβoς (Greek for fear - phobos), σεληφιαζo (Greek for insane - selephiazo)

These words are cut on my arms, my breasts, my stomach, and my thighs.
Would a sane person do these things?
Am I sane?
Would a sane person cut herself on purpose?
Would a sane person carve words into her body?

CHAPTER 1: ME

Only a crazy person would cut herself on purpose.
Only a crazy person would carve words into her body.
The jury is back.
The verdict is in.
The defendant is guilty as charged: CRAZY.

That was my conclusion: I was crazy. I began working with Gary to prove otherwise. I told him that he had his work cut out for him because, over a seven month period, I had made over 530 new cuts on my body, not to mention the many times I cut over existing cuts. I was a mess. I even drew two pictures of what my body looked like with all the words cut into it. I entitled the first one *Deserving* because I felt I deserved all of that. I tried to show how some of the scars had faded, but I was constantly cutting over the old cuts, so in the second picture I tried to show all the cuts.

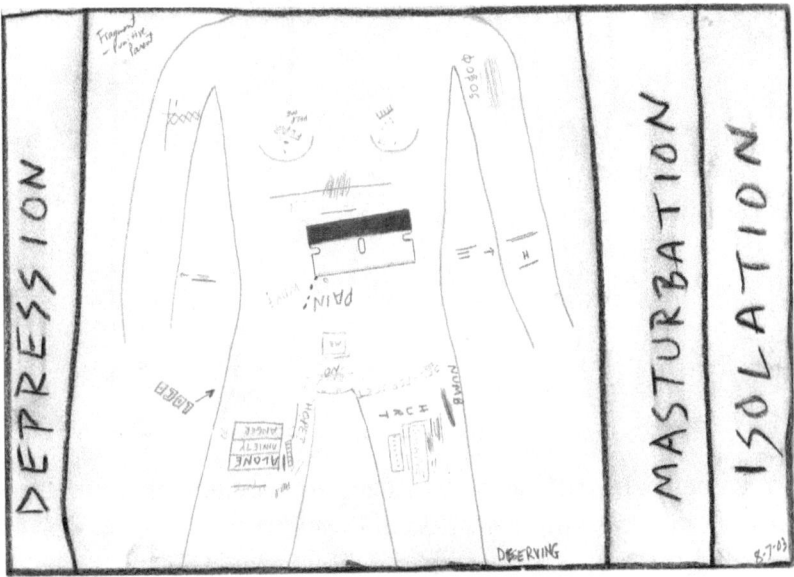

One incredibly wonderful thing happened through all of this. During this time I became friends with, began dating, then fell in love with and married my husband, Josh. He has been such a blessing to me because he knows everything about me and he still loves me. Josh is my soul mate and my strength, my stability and my best friend. He's shown me what true, sacrificial, Christian, *agape* love is like, the kind of love that is described in 1 Corinthians 13. His love for me has helped me see what God's love for me is like. And Josh can do something very few people can do. He can make me laugh! In the midst of an overwhelming depression, in the midst of this horrific experience, God brought me joy by bringing me Josh.

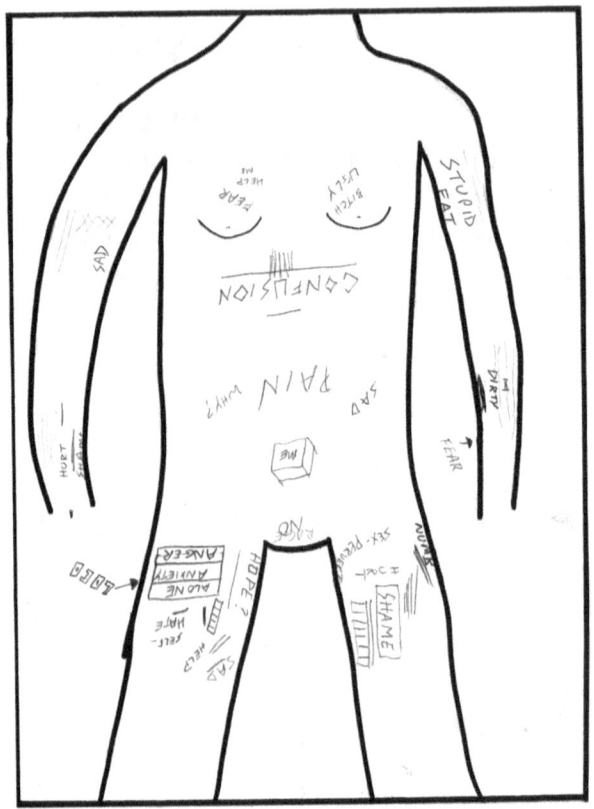

Another thing that has been a huge part of helping me work through all this is my relationship with God. If it weren't for God and His people who helped me, I'm not sure where I'd be today. I would probably be dead.

2
Clues

Clues,
like a
small leak
in the pipe
telling the
plumber
where to look for the
flood;
or,
like red splotches
on the skin
giving indication
of further disease
within;
or,
like a sound
far off
that builds and grows
stronger
and louder
and harsher
as the charging army
crests
the hill;
or,
like a trickle of blood;
all small,
all pointing to something
big,
all to be feared.
Clues.

When I was in college and my friends would talk about their childhood experiences, I realized that I had no such recollections of my own. In fact, I had no real memories of anything that happened before 1978 when I was in the fourth grade. Other than a few vague memories here and there, my first real memory from childhood is the death of my grandfather. It was a few days before Thanksgiving. The EMS workers were at our house and their stretcher filled our small hallway. I was taken to the den in the back of the house where I lay on the loveseat with my face buried in an orange pillow. I was terrified. After the EMS team left for the hospital around one a.m., I remember standing next to my mom's bed, buttoning my long-sleeved, psychedelic-patterned, seventies-style shirt and asking her what was going on. She told me that my grandfather had had another heart attack, his fifth, and the EMS was taking him to the hospital where they could take care of him better. I sat in the waiting room all night. They never let me go in to see him although I begged repeatedly. I learned later that they had been unable to revive him. But I still would have wanted to go in and see him.

The next few days were a blur of activity with people coming and going, expressing their condolences, and bringing flowers and food. I kept myself out of the way by drawing ocean scenes on the oversized chalkboard in my bedroom. No one paid any attention to me except the preacher from our church. He looked at my ocean drawings, talked with me, asked me how I was doing, and hugged me. On the day of the funeral, as we drove to the gravesite, I sat on the preacher's lap and just cried and cried. One of those heart-wrenching, uncontrollable cries. I was nine. That was my first real memory.

Most people have memories of their childhood. I did not. I didn't remember the big things or the little things. I didn't remember eating at the dinner table or playing with my friends. I didn't remember toys I liked, games I played, or TV shows I watched. I didn't remember my elementary school, my classmates, or my teachers. And despite the photographs, I didn't even remember my birthday parties. Everything from before my grandfather's funeral was just missing.

This huge chunk of time missing from my memory was the first clue that something was wrong, really wrong. Since just before my first hospitalization, I've worked at gathering data about my childhood, and I've slowly remembered details and events from my childhood. I've never had a therapist or counselor hypnotize me or push me to remember

CHAPTER 2: CLUES

anything. In fact, when I would bring up the lack of memories, the clues, and my suspicions, most of them would warn me away from "Pandora's box" and encourage me not to push it. Gary told me, "*If you are going to remember, the memories will come when the time is right.*"

Even as a little girl, it seems I had buried memories of my childhood. I recently found an autobiography, *Little Stink-O-Roo*, that I had written for school when I was in the fifth grade. As I read it, I was struck by several things. I wrote about when I was born and a number of things I did when I was three, four, and five years old. Six of the eight events I recounted were negative, or, as I actually said in the paper, shameful. Those six events were things any creative, mischievous child would have done, like pulling all the ribbons off the packages at Christmas, running outside naked at age four, or making a mud puddle at the bottom of my slide and sliding down into it. Not shameful things and yet that was the word I used to describe myself. These were the things my mother always made sure to tell about me. I'm not sure I've ever heard her describe my childhood in anything but negative terms. I've always heard her talk about me being a difficult child, a stubborn child, a "rotten kid." Always negative, never positive.

The thing that struck me the most about what I wrote was what I did not include. I wrote about what I did at ages three, four, and five. I wrote about what I did during the fifth grade when I was ten. The years in between were missing. I was totally silent about those years. I included lots of photographs in my paper, but none from ages six through nine. Again, those years were just missing. This autobiography provided me with another clue.

Of course, the lack of memories was the biggest clue, but there were others. In photo albums from my childhood, there was a noticeable change in my smile around the time I was six years old. It went from an open, happy, genuine smile to a closed, forced, sad one. The open, happy smile returns in photographs in fifth grade. One photograph haunts me. It was taken of me with my grandparents at a studio. I think I was seven. No one is smiling and the look on my face shows that I am uncomfortable and afraid.

There were other clues. As a child, I had frequent stomachaches. I wet the bed until I was a sophomore in high school. In elementary school, I would often wet my pants or soil them. I was terrified of bedtime and I remember often calling out in a whisper for my mother. I was afraid that someone other than her would hear me. A huge clue was that I began acting out sexually with boys at the very young age of eight or nine. I began compulsively masturbating around the same time.

Also as a child, I had a number of dissociative episodes, one of the few things I recall from before fourth grade. In these episodes, I would spiral up to the ceiling in my bedroom or in the hallway outside my bedroom door where I would float while my body remained below, but I couldn't tell you what was happening with my body. I experienced these episodes a number of times while I was a child.

I also had a recurring dream as a child. My grandparents had twin beds in their bedroom, which seems odd to me. Every time I slept in my grandfather's bed, I had the same dream. In the dream, my mother and I would go to some lady's house. When we went inside, they would take me to a room to play while they went away to talk. Every time I would go into the totally brown room, it would start tilting and spinning. I would fall to the far corner of the room. I could never get out of the room, and I was always terrified. The fact that I would always have this same dream whenever I slept with my grandfather was definitely a clue.

There were clues from my grandfather as well. I've been told that his personality changed for the worse when he started having heart attacks. I've also been told that he would leave the room if anything came on the TV about child abuse, which was a red flag to me.

All these clues from my childhood spoke volumes to me, but there were clues from my adulthood as well. The sexual behavior and the compulsive masturbation that started when I was so young continued, becoming more and more addictive and more and more masochistic through the years. I had recurring fantasies of being raped and then rescued. I continued to struggle with anxiety and major depression. I was hospitalized three times and attempted suicide. Numerous other times I wanted to kill myself, once even lining up a hundred pills in groups of ten, but didn't go through with it. And then there was the cutting. I was cutting my body with razor blades many times every day. This was a major clue, as I discovered when I began reading books about cutting, looking for help. As Marilee Strong points out in her book, *A Bright Red Scream: Self Mutilation and the Language of Pain*, "There are many roots to cutting, but the single, most common causal factor is childhood sexual abuse."[1] As I thought back over my teen and young adult years and what little I remembered of my childhood, I realized I had been self-injuring in various ways for many years. I would bite my fingernails to the quick, chew on my fingers, pick at scabs and not let them heal, pick at pimples, leaving scars on my face, and poke myself with straight pins. I did this in middle school and high school. I would see how many I could put into my skin at one time or how deep I could poke them before it hurt too much. When I played sports, I was extremely aggressive, throwing my body to the ground, diving for balls, slamming into racquetball walls, etc., often leading to injury.

I was waging a battle against cutting because of what I couldn't remember. Over time, many memories have returned. More memories may surface as I continue to heal and get stronger. Sometimes I've felt like a detective investigating a crime. I've asked thousands of questions and looked at numerous pictures and items from my childhood. I had the clues. And my clues were pointing to exactly what I had suspected, to what I had feared. Why did I have no memories of my childhood? Why did I cut? I had lots of clues.

3
Cutting

Cutting,
like a laser beam
piercing
through the
dark, dank
blackness;
or,
like a river of
lava
slicing through the
countryside,
leaving a wake of
destruction
and despair;
or,
like a roaring
tornado,
tearing through
the land,
destroying
home,
and livelihood,
and life.
Cutting.

The counselor I worked with before Gary had me sign two different "Contract(s) to Live", neither of which I kept. They were very official and quite specific about what I agreed to: "no cutting," "not to harm...myself," and "if I persist in self-mutilating behaviors beyond the end of the next five sessions" I would be referred to another therapist. I was referred to Gary.

My contract with Gary was a little different. He had me write out my own contract, one I could live with. He asked me to write what I promised and what I would do when I was tempted.

> I, Rochelle Murray, promise that I will not kill myself or attempt to kill myself.
>
> I promise also that I will make every effort not to cut on my body when I am tempted to do so. This means that when I am tempted to cut I will first try other things - **calling someone in my support group**, playing with my dogs, reading my Bible, playing my keyboard, exercising, reading a book, or writing poetry.
>
> This contract is effective from today, July 28, 2003, until further notice—to be discussed with my therapist.

I clung to the statement "I will make every effort not to cut on my body." It didn't mean I was not allowed to cut, but it meant I would try not to. And I did try. It was nearly three months before the worst of it ceased, but I did try. During that time, all I could think about all day was cutting. And fear.

> I sit in trancelike state,
> slow movement,
> slow thoughts,
> repetitive movement,
> repetitive thoughts.
> Must end the masquerade.
> Fear.
> Confusion.
> FEAR.
> FEAR.
> FEAR!
> To zone out is to escape the fear.
> To cut, to let blood flow, is to release the fear.
> Fear.

I've experienced a lot of fear throughout this whole process. Ever since the first time I hurt myself. Ever since I was a kid. Fear of myself, my mother, my grandfather; fear of the cutting, of change, of my childhood and my memories; fear of trusting and being vulnerable.

> Scissors, knives, and razors.
> Could something be any crazier?
> First time.
> Shame, anger, disgust, fear!!
> Punishment.
> Why?

Once I discovered the razor, the scissors and knives held little allure for me. I wanted the razor, the keen, sharp edge to make the slice. Nice and neat. Easy for cutting words, too.

> Razor—
> the instrument
> the device
> the means;
> is slicing
> is cutting
> is gliding.
> Body—
> the destination
> the target
> the terminus;
> is waiting
> is accepting
> is bleeding.
> Me—
> the conductor
> the bearer
> the conduit;
> is staring
> is spacing
> is numbing.

Why?
for punishment
for relief
for coping;
is relieving
is expressing
is communicating.

One of the things the counselor before Gary had me do was keep a "Daily Mood Log." One of the logs I filled out dealt with the cutting. I was able to see some of my "stinkin' thinking." I was supposed to write what my automatic, negative thoughts were, identify the distortions in each thought, and substitute more realistic ones. Some of my negative thoughts were:

I deserve this, deserve to be punished.
It's easier to deal with the physical pain than the emotional pain.
It will help me not feel so bad.
I can't feel anything but all this crap and if I cut I'll feel a different pain.
I **have** to do this. I **need** to do this.
I hate you, Rochelle.
I wish I could do this to the people who have hurt me.
Why do you do this? You are so stupid!
Now you look the way you deserve to look.
I'm so confused about everything.
I wish the scars on the inside were as easy to deal with as the scars on the outside.
This pain I can control. I am in control of the pain when I cut.

I believe my thinking was so distorted because of all the junk in my background. I had all these hurts, all these holes in my life, so that I wasn't whole. I cut myself as part of that. All the junk in my life was like the bloody claws and fearsome fire of the scaly, red-eyed dragon I drew. When I drew *More of "The Junk,"* I painted the monster's hair with my own blood. There was so much I didn't understand, so much Gary was trying to help me understand.

CHAPTER 3: CUTTING

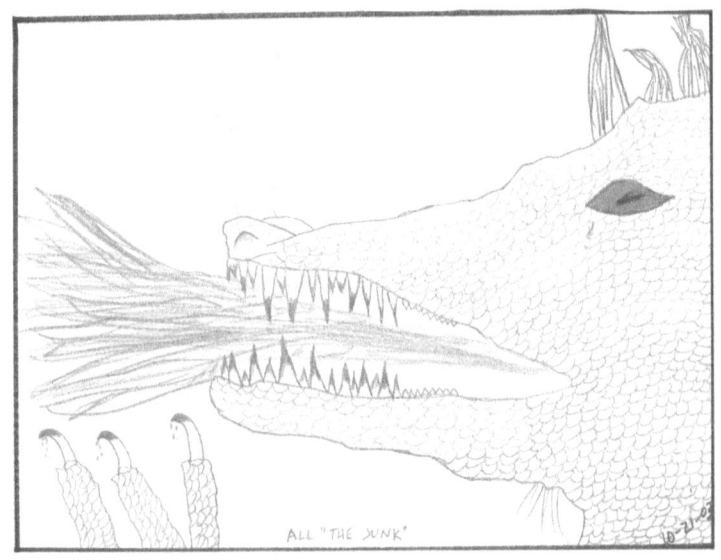

ALL "THE JUNK"

MORE OF "THE JUNK"

I don't understand the feelings I have about control. On one hand, I feel so out of control about the cutting, unable to control not just the cutting, but the urges to cut. On the other hand, when I cut I feel very in control. I'm in control of my feelings because I can numb them. I'm in control of the pain because I'm the one causing it.

One of the assignments Gary gave me addressed the issue of why I cut, the results, and what my next steps should be.

Why the Cutting?

- to punish myself for behaviors, thoughts, and emotions
- as a way of expressing visually what I am feeling in my heart and felt I couldn't adequately express through spoken words
- to feel pain, whether because I am feeling numb or because I feel I deserve to feel pain
- a way of letting out tension and stress
- a way of expressing self-hatred
- attempting to eradicate the emotions from my heart by cutting the name of the emotion into my skin
- a cry for help
- to numb myself so I would quit feeling so much emotional pain
- to give myself some physical pain to focus on instead of the emotional pain

Results of the Cutting

- When I cut, I feel guilt and shame over it, which leads me to want to cut more, which just perpetuates the problem.
- I have scars all over my body. These scars are:
    - ugly
    - unexplainable
    - an inconvenience
    - long-lasting, if not permanent
    - shameful

- anxiety-provoking
- I show that I have little or no respect for my body, my body that was created by God.
- When I cut words into my body I think I am attempting to say to the world, "This is what I'm feeling. This is how bad it hurts." But it doesn't say anything to the world because I keep the scars hidden. I may also be trying to eradicate the emotions from my heart by cutting the name of the emotion into my skin. But all that's done is increase the emotions because whenever I look at the words on my skin, I feel them all over again.
- Consequences
    - scars
    - shame
    - habit—became one of my first responses to stress, anxiety, fear, etc.
- One reason I cut is to give myself physical pain to focus on instead of emotional pain. But that doesn't work. Really what happens is that I have physical pain to focus on in addition to the emotional pain. And because the physical pain is often in the form of words carved into my skin, the physical pain just becomes a visual reminder of the emotional pain, which makes the emotional pain worse.

What Now?

- Learn healthy ways of responding to stress, anxiety, negative emotions, etc., so that the next time such a situation occurs, I will not react with cutting. I want to get to the point where I not only don't react with cutting, but where I don't even think about reacting with cutting.
- I have to quit keeping razors around. That way, when I do react with wanting to cut, I won't have a razor readily available. I'll have more time to react in healthy ways.
- I need to learn the difference between consequences and guilt. I'm having to live with the consequences of the cutting, but I don't have to live with the guilt, which just fuels more cutting.
- Get to the point where I don't feel so full of shame every time I see the scars, which occurs a number of times every day.

The Process

1. Think about it—sometimes there is a precipitating event/emotion, sometimes not
2. Try to determine why the compulsion at that time
3. Think who I can call—first line of defense
4. Call
5. Read (Bible or other positive book)
6. Play with dogs
7. Get out of the house if that is an option

Finally, the cutting began to taper off. I can't say *exactly* why. Maybe I had picked it apart, analyzed it, and found it lacking. Maybe I was finally opening up and dealing with all the hurt in my life. Maybe I was learning other ways to respond to intense emotions and deal with stressors. Maybe it was because Josh started pursuing me and we started dating. Maybe it was all of those reasons and more. But it was hard. It was so hard, even after five weeks.

Thinking, not doing—
it sometimes is good
when you're thinking of cutting,
when you easily could.

It has completely been gone now
for almost five weeks,
yet you still want to cut,
though your scars look like freaks.

What is the whole purpose
of wanting right now to cut?
I think it involves a release
of feelings that were pent up.

I've been so keyed up and on edge
and now I'm coming hard down,
the tears are easily flowing,
and instead of smiles there are frowns.

So I'm writing this poem
as part of my attempt
to not cry and not cut,
yet very strong is the tempt.

After a particularly hard fight against the temptation and not giving in, I wrote this poem about success:

Success

A home run,
no—a grand slam—
the feel when the bat connects,
the sound of the whack
and the wham.

Rounding the bases
with nary a care,
the shouts of the fans,
the wind whipping
through hair.

The difficult task,
a situation quite hard—
when you handle it right
you grow by miles and not yards.

After nine weeks of success I went to my mom's house for the Christmas holidays. Big mistake. Going to her house is always a mistake. The last four days I was there the cutting started again. When I called Gary, he advised me to "get back home, *now!*"

Right after Christmas, Josh and I started dating. At first there was still a little cutting, but not much, and since our wedding, there have been only a few times that I started cutting again. The last time I cut was September 6, 2005. With years of therapy, I've made tremendous progress. I've gone from over 530 fresh cuts in just a few months' time to not cutting. I've learned many better coping mechanisms and thinking patterns. I've talked about and grieved the incredible hurt in my life. I've worked on making peace with my past. Every so often I am still tempted to cut, but I don't give in. However, I still have the scars.

4
Scars

Scars,
like a strong-willed
slave,
back beaten
relentlessly,
viciously,
savagely,
until it remains only
in shreds,
later,
blemished and
disfigured
by the scars
left
behind;
or,
like a child,
hurt, abused, alone,
left to work out her
fears, terror, and shame
on her own,
bearing marks on her
soul,
spirit,
and heart
just as deep,
just as lasting,
just as painful
as those on the
strong-willed slave.
Scars.

My scars are an enigma to me. I hate them, but at the same time they fascinate me.

I look at my scars and at the same time am both repulsed and fascinated, hating and loving them, wishing they would disappear and desperately wanting them to stay and not fade. I don't understand the dichotomy, the paradox.

I don't understand the hatred of my scars that I feel at the exact same time as the desire to cut more and make more scars, or at least not let the present ones fade.

I don't understand the shame I feel about all the cuts and scars on my body that occurs at the same time as the pride I feel about all the cuts and scars on my body, as if they were war wounds or battle scars.

I don't understand.

I did not understand why I didn't want the scars to heal.

Scars.
Calluses on my body
reflecting
calluses on my
soul.
Scabs.
Signs of healing.
Pick them off.
Cannot heal.
Afraid to heal.
Don't deserve to
heal.

I did understand the reaction to my scars.

Scars.
    Noticed,
    Seen,
    Observed,
    Detected.

Reaction.
> Repulsion,
> Fear,
> Shock,
> Disgust,
> Anger,
> Troubled.

Me.
> Fear,
> Terror,
> Anxiety,
> Dread,
> Despair.

Scars.

The closest I have come to understanding my scars, both physical and emotional, was through a song I wrote about a month after the worst of the cutting stopped.

Scars

Verse 1:
>Scars, when I look at them dismay,
>scars, will they ever go away?
>Oh scars, I've got my scars and you have yours.
>
>Scars, when I look at them I cry,
>scars, and I always ask why,
>oh scars, they bring me pain deep in my soul.
>
>Scars, when I look at them I doubt,
>scars, and then I really want to shout,
>oh God, where were you when I got these scars?

Chorus 1:
>Scars, my child, He answered,
>are my specialty,
>for scars, my child, He told me,
>will bring you unto me.

Verse 2: Scars, how can they bring me to You?
Scars, do You really have a clue,
oh God, how much that they have hurt my soul?

Scars, on my body and my heart,
scars, they are bitter, they are tart,
oh scars, how can I live with all these scars?

God, how can You say what You just said?
Scars, their pain just echoes in my head.
Oh God, these scars of mine will never fade.

Chorus 2: Scars, my child, He answered,
yes, I have a clue,
for scars, my child, He told me,
are what my Son got dying for you.

Verse 3: God, please forgive my foolish words,
God, eyes now have seen what only heard,
oh God, please heal these scars upon my heart.

God, when I look into Your book,
God, and then I take a closer look
I see the scars of Jesus healed my own.

Scars, will they ever go away?
Scars, yes, I know they will one day,
oh God, when You come back to take me home.

Chorus 3: Scars, my child, He said now,
are marks of what you've been through,
and scars will help you remember
the scars my Son got dying for you,
the scars my Son got dying for you.

After writing this song I began to feel some hope. For years I had begged God to help me, and I finally sensed that help was coming. Despite all the scars on my body and my heart, I had a glimmer of hope that God could heal me, that He could work through the scars to change me. All my life I had believed in God, though there were many times I wondered where in the world He was. Now I was beginning to sense that He was right there with me in my sorrow, because His Son had scars, too. Scars *are* marks of what we have been through. A scar is the mark left after a wound has healed. Emotional scars leave lasting marks on our souls, but they are signs of *healing*! For me, the healing primarily came through therapy.

5
Therapy

Therapy,
like lancing
a boil
and draining out the pus;
or,
like scrubbing and scrubbing
with a scouring pad
and an abrasive cleaner
in an attempt
to get out
a permanent
stain;
or,
like an erupting volcano;
or,
sometimes like
watching an episode of M*A*S*H—
you laugh
and you cry
all at the same time;
or,
like a cave explorer,
trapped beneath
thousands of pounds
of rubble
that collapsed on him,
digging his way out,
one painful pebble
at a time.
Therapy.

S omewhere in my years of struggle someone told me that therapy is like tearing your heart out and laying it on the table. It's like tearing out the very essence of who you are and placing it under an electron microscope for the examination, scrutiny, analysis, investigation, and inspection of the scientist. Opening up to someone else for such a task, and beginning to trust, is a terrifying process.

> The patient lies silent on the table,
> numb, deadened, and anesthetized
> to any pain, any slicing, any removal.
> The surgeon stands confident,
> skillfully cutting through the layers
> and removing the hideous, cancerous growth.
>
> The client sits silent on the couch,
> wishing to be numb, deadened, and anesthetized
> to any pain, any slicing, any removal.
> The counselor sits confident,
> skillfully cutting through the defenses
> and removing the hideous, cancerous baggage.
>
> Patient and client, both willing participants,
> both submitting themselves to the
>   scrutiny of another;
> both trusting in the skill of another,
> both desiring relief from pain
>   and disease and turmoil.
> Both are fearful and timid,
> nervous about the outcome,
> but at the same time courageous
> for submitting to such vulnerability
>   in the first place.
> The patient has set his hope on
> the surgeon's skill to help him.
> The client has set his hope on
> the counselor's skill to help him.
>   And both are afraid.

Surgeon and counselor, both skillful and trained,
both offering themselves to another as one
> who can detect the problem;
Both trusting in their knowledge,
both desiring to help relieve the pain
> and disease and turmoil of another.
Both are confident and bold,
secure that whatever the outcome,
they will have done their absolute best
in accepting the vulnerability of another
and being faithful with it.
The surgeon has set his hope on
his skills to help his patient.
The counselor has set his hope on
his skills to help his client.
> And both are bold.

M. Scott Peck said in *People of the Lie* that therapy is "not the easy way out. It's a way of facing things, even if it's painful, even if it's very painful. It's the way of not running away. It's the right way, not the easy way."[2] The time I've spent in therapy working with Gary has been the hardest time in my life.

For me, therapy has consisted of:
> openness,
> honesty,
> vulnerability (all three of which are hard);
> some cover-ups,
> which eventually were uncovered,
> some half-truths,
> which eventually were whole;

Some digging,
> clearing,
> cleaning,
> fixing,
> repairing,
> and removing.

Sometimes I felt like an adult,
sometimes I felt like a little girl.
Sometimes I laughed,
      often I cried.
I dealt with memories and facts,
      feelings and thinking patterns,
most of which were quite warped
and in desperate need of an overhaul.
My thinking patterns, though,
      have changed.
My behavioral response patterns have changed.
My emotional response patterns have changed.

I am not the same person I was when I started.
I still have a long way to go.

Therapy.

6

Compulsion

Compulsion,
like the small,
brown moth
drawn strangely,
urgently
to the light,
obsessed
by the light,
addicted
to the light—
murdered
by the light.
Compulsion.

I started writing one of my journal entries as an attempt to not cut, but it turned into a dialogue between two parts of me, the part that wanted to cut and the part that did not.

I'm sitting here at my desk staring at a razor blade I found under some papers. I didn't know it was there when I threw out all my razors last Tuesday. I've already made two small cuts on my left forearm and I'm wanting very badly to cut some more. That's why I'm writing this, to try to figure out what is going on in my head right now and to try not to cut.

I started wanting to cut earlier today before I even found the razor. I was in the church kitchen helping to prepare for a luncheon tomorrow. At one point the conversation turned to children who are neglected and abused. That's when the urge to cut started. So I guess, once again, it is connected to my past. But is that all there is to it? I know that a large percentage of women who cut themselves were abused as children. So why do I want to cut **right now**?

There's a weird aspect to the cutting. It's as if I zone out and I'm in my own little world. I go sort of numb and I don't feel as if I have any say or any control over what I do. But, on the other hand, when I cut I **am** in control. I'm in control of the scars. I know where the scars come from. Same thing with the hurt and pain of cutting. When I cut, I am the one hurting myself. Not someone else, not someone besides me. Whether it's to punish myself, to feel because I am numb, to numb myself from overwhelming feelings, or to express physically the emotional pain I'm feeling, I'm still in control. And that is important, because there is less pain and less fear if I'm in control.

WHY ARE YOU TRYING TO CONTROL THINGS? YOU'VE NEVER BEEN ABLE TO CONTROL THINGS, SO WHY START TRYING NOW? YOU THINK YOU CAN CONTROL ALL THESE IMPULSES? FORGET IT! IF YOU GET CONTROL OF ONE IMPULSE, ONE OF THE OTHERS WILL GET OUT OF CONTROL. YOU CANNOT CONTROL ANYTHING! AS MUCH AS YOU WANT TO AND AS HARD AS YOU TRY!

But I need to control my impulses. I need to stop cutting. How else am I ever going to get well if I keep cutting?

HOW ELSE ARE YOU GOING TO DEAL WITH ALL THE EMOTIONS THAT ARE ALL BOTTLED UP INSIDE OF YOU IF YOU DON'T CUT? YOU CAN'T EAT LIKE A PIG OR YOU'LL LOOK LIKE YOUR MOM. YOU COULD NOT EAT AND EXERCISE AND TAKE LAXATIVES LIKE YOU'VE DONE BEFORE, BUT THAT'S NOT AS SATISFYING AS CUTTING.

But why do I have to do any of that? Why can't I just read or talk to someone on the phone or play with my dogs and take them for a walk?

OH SURE, YOU CAN DO THOSE THINGS, BUT YOU KNOW WHAT HAPPENS. YOU CAN'T CONCENTRATE TO READ. NO ONE IS HOME. AND IT'S TOO DARK TO WALK THE DOGS. REGARDLESS OF WHAT YOU DO, YOU'LL ALWAYS GO BACK TO THE CUTTING. AND BEFORE YOU ASK WHY, I'LL TELL YOU WHY—YOU HAVE TO. BECAUSE YOU'RE MESSED UP. YOU'RE DIFFERENT. YOU'RE NOT LIKE OTHER PEOPLE. YOU DON'T DO THINGS LIKE OTHER

PEOPLE. YOU DON'T SOLVE PROBLEMS LIKE OTHER PEOPLE. AND YOU DON'T DESERVE TO.

But that can't be true. Gary asked me to try not to cut and he said I **could** do this.

YEAH, RIGHT!! DOES HE REALIZE WHAT HE'S ASKING YOU? NOT CUT?! GET REAL. YOU HAVE TO CUT.

Okay, tell me why I have to.

BECAUSE YOU'RE A STUPID LITTLE JERK! YOU THINK ANYONE WHO WASN'T WOULD DO THE THINGS YOU DO?

But that's not a reason.

DUH! DO I HAVE TO SPELL IT OUT FOR YOU? YOU ARE TOTALLY SCREWED UP. EVEN THAT TEST YOU TOOK FOR GARY SAID SO!

But what does that have to do with me having to cut?

LOOK, YOU STUPID GIRL. GET IT THROUGH YOUR THICK HEAD. YOU DESERVE TO LIVE LIKE THIS. YOU DESERVE ALL OF THIS CRAP! YOU MIGHT AS WELL JUST GO AHEAD AND DO IT AND GET IT OVER WITH BECAUSE YOU KNOW YOU CAN'T BEAT THIS ANYWAY.

I can't do it.

CAN'T?! CAN'T?! IT ISN'T A MATTER OF WHETHER YOU CAN OR CAN'T. IT IS A MATTER OF WHETHER YOU WILL OR YOU WON'T. AND YOU **WILL** CUT. YOU KNOW YOU WILL.

Why?

WHY?! WHY?! BECAUSE YOU LIKE IT. YOU GET A RUSH FROM IT.

No, I hate it.

YEAH, YOU DO HATE IT. YOU HATE IT BECAUSE OF HOW YOU FEEL. BECAUSE YOU KNOW THE GUILT AND SHAME ARE GOING TO DIG IN EVEN DEEPER WHEN YOU CUT. BECAUSE YOU KNOW YOU DESERVE TO LIVE SUCH A HORRID EXISTENCE. YOU HATE IT BECAUSE AT THE SAME TIME YOU LOVE IT. SO GO ON AND CUT AND GET IT OVER WITH. QUIT TORTURING YOURSELF WITH YOUR FEEBLE EFFORTS TO NOT DO IT AND JUST CUT.

It's not going to happen. I don't want to be like that. I don't want to do that anymore.

LIAR! YOU ARE SITTING THERE RIGHT NOW WISHING YOU COULD CUT—CUT AND LET THE BLOOD FLOW. YOU KNOW I'M TELLING THE TRUTH. ADMIT IT!

No! I don't want to do that!

LIAR!

I'm not lying. I don't want to cut!

LIAR!
LIAR!
LIAR!
LIAR!

That night I gave in and I cut. The compulsion won. But it didn't always win. My next journal entry listed a number of things I did to fight the compulsion and I was successful. That time I called two friends, rode my bike, played with my dogs, ate, worked on an assignment for my class, and read some Scriptures I had written out on index cards. The compulsion may have still been there, but that time I won. I still didn't understand the compulsion, but I was learning ways to fight it. The fact that I sometimes won the battle proved to me that I could overcome the compulsion. I created a picture about this compulsion and how I felt the compulsion to cut and the compulsion to masturbate. I entitled it *Yes & No, No & Yes*.

CHAPTER 6: COMPULSION

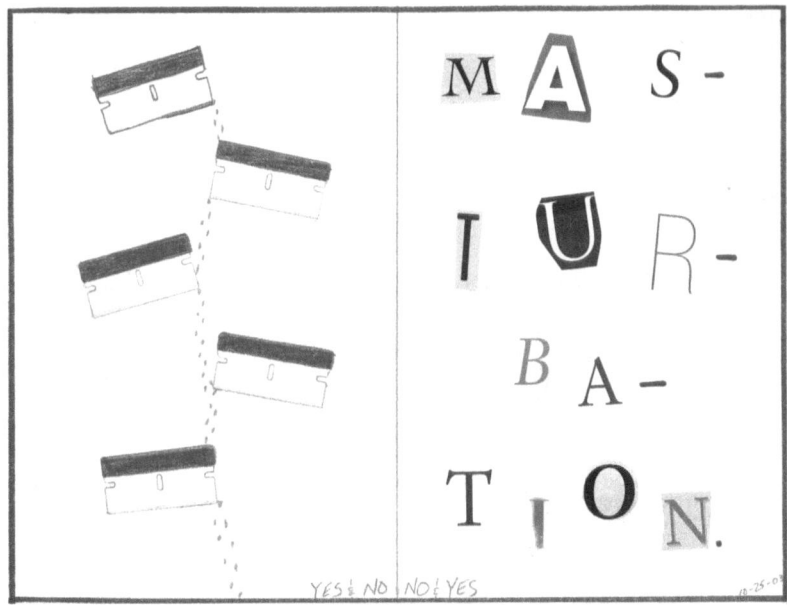

Compulsion

Slowly coming in,
the evening
tide
wraps its tentacles
around the
passive, waiting shore,
which is helpless
against the onslaught.
Slowly,
menacingly,
it curls tighter and tighter,
squeezing
the life
out of the helpless sand,
dragging it
under and outward
as it engulfs
and decimates

part
of the shore,
forever changing
the landscape,
forever changing
the shore.

The compulsion was part of why I asked Gary, "Am I crazy?"

7
Mental Illness

Mental Illness,
like a
cancer
eating away at flesh
and soul;
or,
like a
house of mirrors
at a local carnival -
confusion,
disorder,
chaos, and
fear;
or,
like an emaciated prisoner
held captive
by unbreakable chains
in a deep,
dark
dungeon
of depressing,
despondent
despair.
Mental Illness.

Mental illness. Those words frightened me. What did it mean that I had a mental illness? Did it mean I had less value than others or just that I was different from others? And if it meant that I was different, what did that differentness mean for me?

Voices.
Audible?
No.
Loud?
Yes.
Screaming.
Screaming what?
My shame, my guilt, my worthlessness.
My loneliness, my confusion, my
differentness.
Differentness?
Yes, differentness. I am so different
from others.
A strange combination of
differentness and
sameness.
I want to be like others,
to feel as they feel,
to think as they think.
My feelings are so
intense.
They frighten me.
Yet there is a need to
conform,
protect
the image.
Differentness.
Voices.
Screaming.
Screaming.
Screaming words of confusion and fear.
Screaming words of rage and shame.

I did not want to accept that I had a mental illness. Yes, I was depressed. Yes, I was hurting and in pain. Yes, I had a lot of pent up anger and rage. Yes, I was out of control in certain areas. Yes, I was seeing a psychiatrist and a psychologist. But mentally ill? Certainly all those things didn't make me mentally ill, did they? I was normal, wasn't I?

Chapter 7: Mental Illness

Normal?

I feel like a
fog.
I feel like a
storm.
I feel like a
turbulent airplane.
I feel like a
lunatic.
I feel like
Eeyore.
I feel like an
insect.
I feel like a
mystery.
I feel like a
hemidemisemiquaver.
I feel like a neophyte.
I don't want to feel like a
stone.
I don't want to feel like a
raging river.
I don't want to feel like an
earthquake.
I don't want to feel like a
maimed soul.
I just want to feel
normal,
whatever that is.
Is there such a thing?

Okay, maybe I wasn't normal, Maybe I was different. Maybe I was mentally ill. Does being mentally ill mean the same thing as crazy? Are they worlds apart, or is there a fine line between the two? And if there is a fine line, how do you stay far away from it? I did not want to walk the line.

Walking the Line

Time heals all wounds.
Sometimes time just creates
more wounds.
Over time some wounds
don't heal—
they fester.
So how much time is
required
to heal the wounds?
He says I am walking the line
between mentally ill
and psychotic.
How much time does it take
to get far enough away
from that line?
What does it mean to quit
walking the line?
Is it feeling better and
doing well in school?
Is it not cutting?
Is it looking good on the
outside?
Or is it more?
What does it take to
no longer
walk the line?
And even then,
how far away from the line
do I have to get to no longer
be mentally ill?
And what is to keep me
from going over the line
the wrong way?
He says I am
walking the line.
I don't want to fall.

Gary said that I was walking the line between mentally ill and psychotic for two reasons. First, during the worst of the cutting, I had started having auditory hallucinations. I heard music, always classical music. And there was never a source for it, even though sometimes I walked around the house with a flashlight at ten p.m. looking for one. I wasn't just humming classical music in my head. I was literally hearing the music, but it really wasn't there. This situation really frightened me. Dr. Patel put me on some medication that helped; but more importantly, I've been learning to better handle stressful situations and periods of time. It doesn't happen very often any more now that the cutting has stopped, but for a while it was happening several times a week. It seemed to be connected to the cutting. When the cutting was a problem, so was the music. It also seemed to be connected to stress. The higher my stress level, the more often I heard the music, whether I was cutting or not.

The second reason Gary said I was walking the line between mental illness and psychosis was that I had what in psychological terms is called a fugue. A fugue is a kind of psychological amnesia. A person can behave normally and rationally, but has no memory of the time or what he or she has done during it. It's a temporary escape from reality. One morning in January 2004, Miss Penny, the dean of women at the Bible school I was attending, came to see me at the Christian bookstore where I was working part-time. She took me aside and told me she was very concerned. She asked me to call my own house and listen to the message on my answering machine. Using her cell phone I did just that, and what I heard put me in a state of shock. The message was in my voice, but I was speaking in a very sexual, seductive tone. "Uh, yeah, Rochelle, yeah, I've been, I've been wanting to see you for a while. Oh yeah, oh yeah, yeah." I called and listened to it three times. I told Miss Penny, "I didn't put that on there," because I didn't have any recollection of recording that message. But it was my voice. I was very afraid.

I've had enough psychology courses and read enough books through the years to know what the implications are here. Gary asked me way back the first time I met with him if I "lose time," and I told him no because I don't have any of the things that would indicate to me that I lose time. When I am playing out scenarios, whether I am actually acting them out or just thinking or talking them out, I can lose time in the sense that three hours will have passed without me even realizing it. But I remember what I was doing during that time. The same thing happens when I'm cutting. But as far as I know, this is the first time that I've done something and had absolutely no recollection of doing it. Of course, if I were doing things I was unaware of, how would I know? But I guess there would be clues. Maybe that's what this thing with my answering machine is—a clue. But a clue to what? All I know is that I feel like I've been socked in the stomach and had my feet knocked out from under me. And I am very, very afraid right now. More than when I was having the auditory hallucinations. And I was scared out of my wits with that. But this is ten times scarier.

This whole crazy thing with the answering machine is constantly threatening to overwhelm me. I'm having to fight off the urge to cut. And I'm not sure I'm strong enough to fight it and win. Saturday morning in the shower I lost the battle over whether to masturbate. Sunday morning and this morning I did not give in. I find myself losing the battle to not think about it. I am so incredibly frightened by this. What happened? How did that message get there? What's going on with me? What does this mean? What's going to happen to me? I'm frightened because the desire to cut is back. I'm frightened because I'm afraid my mental health problems are going to destroy my life. I'm frightened because of the sexual nature of the message. I'm frightened because of the implications. I'm frightened because the message was there, it was my voice, and I have absolutely no clue whatsoever how it got there. That's one of the most frightening things of all. And I'm frightened because Gary leaves Tuesday for a three-week mission trip to India. All this is also affecting me physically because I have spent an inordinate amount of time in the bathroom since Friday morning. It's like I've taken a bunch of laxatives, only I haven't. I don't know what's going on or what's going to happen to me—in many areas. All I know right now is that I am very, very afraid.

As far as I know, that was the only time such an incident had occurred. As far as I know. But what about what I don't know? Were there other times that I lost touch with reality? Yes, I was definitely walking the line.

There were so many holes in my life, places where I wasn't whole. The day I learned of the fugue I drew a picture about how I felt. I felt incomplete in so many ways: the problems with my mother, the absence of my father, the huge chunk of my childhood missing because I couldn't remember it, the sexual abuse all the clues pointed to. How could I be

CHAPTER 7: MENTAL ILLNESS

whole with all that plaguing me? And all my problems—the depression, the hospitalizations, the cutting, the masturbation, the mental illness, the hallucinations, the fugue—how could I be whole with all of that plaguing me as well? I was walking the line, and I was afraid I was going to cross it and never be whole. I felt like my mind had turned on me.

Why Must This Thing Be?

Verse 1:   Why must this thing be? Mind has turned on me.
   And God, you promised hope. Now my hope seems gone.
   And God I cannot see where you are to me.
   And God where are you now? Don't give up on me.

Verse 2:   I know reason not why this pain has come.
   And fear has taken hold, fills my heart with dread.
   And now it's plain to see what becomes of me.
   I'll have to fight this pain all my whole life through.

Ending: And why must this thing be? Mind has turned on me.
   Why must this thing be?

I finally came to the point of acceptance of my mental illness. But I had a lot of questions. What did it mean? Was there a cure? Was it hopeless? Was it permanent or was mental health a possibility? If it were a possibility, how do I get there? The answers for me came through therapy: talking about the problems, the past, the pains; working through the chaos and the confusion, grieving the hurts, and healing the hates. It came through a lot of naval-gazing, by which I mean looking at myself honestly, being brutally honest and dealing with what I found there. As Scott Peck said, you cannot be "forever fleeing the light of self-exposure and the voice of . . . conscience."[3] Self-examination is tough. It's painful. But it's necessary. It was important for me to deal with the ugly parts, such as how I had treated people, including myself, and to deal with the terrifying parts, such as how I had been treated as a child. Mental health will remain elusive as the cancer of mental illness continues to eat away if these things are ignored.

Naval-Gazing

When you naval-gaze,
you can't see anyone else's hurt
but your own.
How can you encourage or minister
to another
when you are so caught up in
yourself?
Distractions—
what naval-gazing provides.
You don't have to work or study
or practice or go somewhere or
change
when you are naval-gazing.
When you have a
mental illness,
naval-gazing seems par for the course.
When you are in
therapy,
naval-gazing seems par for the course.
How do you go from
mental illness
to mental health

without naval-gazing?
And if you have a
mental illness,
whether you naval-gaze or not,
is there even such a thing as
mental health?

Mental illness is just that, an illness. It's like a cancer. But many times I found, to my frustration, that others did not react to it in the same way as a physical illness.

Mental Illness

I have a sickness, an illness,
that eats at me every day.
A silent killer it is not,
for it screams loudly when it gets not its way.

It's not cancer that I have in my body,
though it ravages my soul just as well,
nor is it heart disease, clogging my arteries,
yet it attacks and leaves me writhing in hell.

Name all the diseases you want to:
epilepsy, diabetes, asthma, and gout.
There are many legitimate ailments,
yet my disease leaves many in doubt.

My problem is not related to bleeding
from a wreck or accident of some awful kind.
Oh, that it were only that simple,
but no, my illness is found in my mind.

Say cancer, surgery, car wreck
and people want to know how they can help.
Say mental illness and the silence is deafening
and people shun you rather than help.

But just like diabetes or cancer,
it requires special treatment and care.
Sometimes it seems to go in remission.
Sometimes it takes years to repair.

I have a sickness, an illness,
it is one that is found in my mind.
Please don't expect quick fixes or cures,
please learn how to the mentally ill to be kind.

I have a sickness, an illness,
it is one that is found in my mind.
Please don't be afraid of my friendship,
please don't make your eyes ever blind.

I have a sickness, an illness,
it is one that is found in my mind.
Please don't expect me to always be happy,
please remember I am part of mankind.

I have a sickness, an illness,
it is one that is found in my mind.
Please don't ignore the fact of my pain,
please don't leave me lost, alone behind.

Though I had a mental illness, mental health was a possibility. I knew this because I was finding areas in my life that I needed to change, and I was striving with all my being to stop unhealthy behaviors and thought patterns. God was working in me to bring about change. Yet even knowing this was not enough to keep me from feeling lost and alone in my struggle.

A life sentence,
no thought of parole;
the depths of a cave,
black as coal.
A dungeon cell,
chained hand and foot;

a white wedding gown
all smeared with soot.
A child's anguished cries,
abandoned and lone;
a whimpering, lonely
and pitiful moan.
A gaping wound,
bleeding and sore;
a dying ember
crushed to the floor.
A starving soul,
hurt and abused;
these are all me
is what my heart mused.

This mental illness had done a number on me. I asked myself a lot of questions those first six months I was in therapy. Would it ever be possible

to break through all the crap, make it to the other side, and find my joy? I was still in the throes of the cutting and I felt so hopeless. Would I ever find mental health?

There are many different types and forms of mental illness. Through the years I had been diagnosed with major depression, generalized anxiety disorder, and post-traumatic stress disorder. During the first hospitalization, the doctors wondered if I had bipolar I and multiple personality disorder. They even sent me to another city to consult with a famous psychiatrist, but they finally ruled out both of those. Dr. Patel had diagnosed me with bipolar II disorder and borderline personality disorder. I have read books on all of them. Most of the diagnoses I have agreed with. To me, they are pieces of the puzzle of my life.

> There are pieces in the fog,
> pieces of my life,
> scattered amongst the mist.
>
> There are pieces in the fog,
> pieces of my life,
> here where I exist.
>
> Obscured from my sight
> in the cloudy haze,
> veiled and faint are the
> pieces of my life.
>
> Thick vapor keeps away
> the bright and clear.
> Oh, to put together
> the pieces of my life,
> the pieces in the fog.

The pieces were in the process of being put together. It was incredibly hard work, but I wasn't alone. Dr. Patel prescribed the appropriate medication. Gary guided me through therapy. Josh encouraged and supported me. Several others prayed for me. God strengthened and began healing me. The fog would eventually clear up. The pieces would eventually be put back together. The illness would eventually be health. I wasn't doomed to mental illness. But in the meantime I still had to deal with it.

8
Depression

Depression,
like a bleak, dark, stormy
night,
echoing with the
thunder
of the approaching
storm,
fog settling in,
casting a sense of
gloom and
shadow and
sullenness,
all at once
enveloping
the soul;
or,
like the despairing
widow,
cast suddenly
alone
after six decades,
weeping,
brokenhearted,
troubled,
forlorn,
forgotten,
left desolate
in her
mourning.
Depression.

Depression. Even the word is depressing, isn't it? Years ago I thought depression was my only problem, but I was wrong. It was enough, though. Even if nothing else was wrong, depression was enough. It's one thing to suffer with it for a few weeks or months or even a few years. But year after year after year? I first remember struggling with the depression when I was about eleven. On and off since then, more on than off, it's has been a part of my life. It never seemed to end. It never went away. I felt condemned to a life of depression.

> Who am I
> to think
> that I
> deserve to live,
> deserve to die.
> I cannot bear,
> I cannot share
> the weight that I'm
> condemned to wear.
> My heart is bruised,
> my soul is used,
> these all are things
> my spirit mused.

I felt the weight of the depression all throughout high school, particularly my senior year. I had started writing poetry a few years earlier and that year I wrote a slew of depressing poems.

> It is dark outside, inside, too.
> I find that I don't know what to do.
> The rain falls softly, outside—
> Inside—my thunderstorm and tide.
> The waves crash round about me,
> they trap me and I am no longer free.
> The foam stays as the waves reside,
> the scum on my feet dwells inside.

CHAPTER 8: DEPRESSION

All through the years since high school, the depression continued. Even when I got married and was so full of joy I could hardly contain it, the depression crept in and grabbed hold. Only one month after the wedding the depression was back.

> There is no reason
> why I should not be
> happy
> and yet it
> eludes me
> again and
> again.
> There is no reason
> why I should not have
> joy
> and yet I cannot
> grasp it,
> it slips
> away.
> There is no reason
> why I should not be
> content
> and yet contentment
> flies away,
> far, far
> away.
> There is no reason
> why I should be
> sad
> and
> depressed,
> and yet I am.

Sometimes the depression was related to the sin in my life. But there were times when I was shrouded in depression for reasons I couldn't understand at the time.

I Cannot Understand

Verse 1:
Who am I, O God?
Why are fears so strong?
Why is darkness here?
I cannot understand
why when I'm in Your hand
the darkness still comes.
O God, illumine me.

Verse 2:
Many years gone by,
darkness always nigh,
but it was from sin.
And here I am again
the darkness black within,
but it's not from sin.
So why, why all this fear?
Will darkness always be near?

Beyond My Grasp   8-13-04

CHAPTER 8: Depression

Joy is my favorite word and my deepest desire. I have pictures and plaques and jewelry with the word *joy* on them. Even my personalized license plate has *joy* on it. As I struggled with depression year after year, I clung to the hope that one day I would have joy that wasn't fleeting, but would stick around. Joy seemed beyond my grasp. The depression came around much more often than the joy. Sometimes the depression kind of sneaked up. Sometimes it came crashing down. Every time it was destructive and left ruin in its wake.

> At first it comes in slowly,
> like the evening tide—
> cautiously creeping up onto the sand,
> lapping calmly at the shore,
> taking bits of the shore out to sea
> as it curls its tentacles around the beach.
> But then...
> after a while...
> it is no longer a gentle tide,
> but a roaring wave,
> crashing,
> destroying,
> and changing the entire landscape
> into an ugly scar,
> wounded by the power of the water.
> Can the shore be rebuilt?
> Only the parts that are left,
> for with each crash of the wave,
> with each attack,
> each assault,
> part of the shore is decimated
> and devoured by the
> depths of the sea,
> never to resurface
> again.

Yes, depression leaves ruin and destruction. How does it ruin? How does it destroy?

Depression

Ad infinitum - it never ends
Battering - it beats and damages repeatedly
Callous - it is hardened, no softness
Depriving - it takes away, robs, strips away of joy and peace
Emptying - it leaves one hollow and void
Feral - it is savage and wild and attacks as such
Grasping - it seizes and takes hold
Homicidal - it kills, slowly, soul and spirit
Impenetrable - it cannot be broken into
Jading - it is exhausting
Killjoy - it spoils all joys and pleasures
Lavish - it is profuse and abundant
Merciless - it is without mercy and compassion
Nonchalant - it does not care about its victim
Obdurate - it is stubbornly resistant and unyielding
Parasitic - it leaches on to, feeds off of, and harms its host
Quadrupling - it multiplies and increases itself
Ravenous - it is greedy and voracious in its hunger for its victim
Stupefying - it makes one bewildered and numb
Trouncing - it thrashes and punishes severely and defeats decisively
Unfeeling - it is hardhearted and cruel
Vociferous - it clamors, shouts, and cries out; it can't be ignored
Wasting - it diminishes, wears away, and devastates
Xenophobic - it fears that which is foreign, such as joy and peace
Yoking - it puts its victims in servitude, bondage, slavery
Zealous - it is fervent, passionate and fanatical in its effort to consume

Almost exactly a year later I wrote another alphabet poem, also about depression and what it was doing to me.

Depression

Agony of soul
Blackness of mind
Cares weigh me down
Darkness so blind

Energy lacking
Fear greatly abounds
God seems so far
He seems naught to be found

Incredible sadness
Joy rarely around
Keyed up and on edge
Laughter's lost its sound

Mind is messed up
Need for true peace is there
Oppression of spirit
Peace of mind seems so rare

Quenched is my joy
Remarkably sad
Saddled with sorrow
Tailspin I'm in seems so bad

Understand my pain not
Vexed in my heart
Weary in body
Xerophytic, bitter and tart

Yearning for comfort
Zealous for hope
With this depression it seems
I can just barely cope.

    Sometimes depression requires medical attention and medication. Sometimes many trials are needed to find the right medication. That was the case for me. I started seeing Dr. Patel the first week in April 2003. He tried a number of different medications before he finally put me on the lithium at the end of July. Even then, he tried various medicines to complement the lithium. In January 2005, he finally added Risperdal, the combination that seemed to work best for me.

Even though I was on medication, ultimately I had to deal with the hurts in my life. That was the only way to overcome the depression. There are things in addition to medication that can be done day-to-day to help alleviate the depression. Finding a support group and leaning on them, eating a healthy diet, exercising regularly, keeping a journal of feelings and things to be grateful for, finding people to talk to instead of keeping things bottled up are all helpful strategies. All of these things helped me.

Turning to God and His Word was another helpful strategy. The first time I was hospitalized I spent hours going through the pages of the Bible, reading passages from the Psalms and other parts of Scripture that talked about God coming to the aid of His people. In many passages in the Bible the writer cries out to God for help. That's what I did. I wanted to break the chains of depression and addiction that bound me. I needed God's help to do it.

Break The Chains

Verse 1:
> My heart is torn, my flesh is weak,
> O my God, where is Your help?
> I am afraid, the pit is deep,
> I'm alone without Your help.
> O my God, please rescue me.

Verse 2:
> I cannot sleep, I cannot eat
> for my heart is all despair.
> I fear, I doubt, I'm full of guilt,
> I am haunted by my fears.
> O my God, please break the chains
> or I cannot live.

Depression was the bane of my existence. I cut because I was depressed. Or maybe I was depressed because I cut. It was a vicious cycle. And it left me in tears.

9
Tears

Tears,
like a trickle of
water
seeping out between the
cracks,
giving indication
that somewhere
there is a
leak,
somewhere,
something is
wrong;
or,
like a fresh spring,
cleansing,
refreshing,
and healing;
or,
like the torrent
of a flash flood,
gushing, roaring,
and consuming
with all force,
all violence,
and all terror,
sweeping away
everything in its path,
leaving destruction
and barrenness
that must be
rebuilt
with
Tears.

I recall tears streaming down my face and a razor blade in my hand. I recall being numb and unfeeling with a razor blade in my hand. Sometimes I could cry, sometimes I couldn't. Being unable to cry, being numb instead, was an occasional side-effect of some of the medications I took. Medicine or not, I hate it when I cannot cry. It's like a dam, holding back the water that's lapping at the edge of the spillway but not going over. Sometimes I also hate it when I can cry, when the water is pouring over the dam, when the tears won't stop. Sometimes it frightens me.

Tears

It is amazing what all is held in
one little drop,
one little tear.
H_2O and sodium chloride.
A little water,
a little salt,
a flood of emotion.
Fear, anger, sadness,
betrayal, shame, pain.
Is it possible,
feasible, or
attemptable
to begin,
to even start
to understand,
comprehend, and
fathom
the depth, the height, the breadth
of feeling
that is packed, compressed, and pressed
into one little tear?
I propose the answer
to that one simple question
is a loud, forceful, defiant, definitive,
resounding
NO!!
Numb, insanity, loneliness, terror,
rage, confusion, hurt, questions.
The list goes on and on and on.
Endless.
Tears.

10
Pain

Pain,
like a steel blade,
sharp,
deadly,
penetrating one's skin
and severing
body from body
as it glides
effortlessly
through sinew
and muscle
and bone.
Pain.

 person has to be in an incredible amount of pain to take a razor blade and deliberately cut their own skin.

So many types of pain:
- the pain of childbirth
- arthritic pain
- the pain of a toothache
- muscular pain
- the pain of a broken bone
- the pain of cancer
- and on and on and on and on

Cutting pain, burning pain, piercing pain -
all ways of describing our pain.
Throbbing pain, dull pain, sharp pain -
all ways to put words to our anguish.
And then there's my kind of pain -

emotional pain, psychic pain, mental pain.
The pain of:
- deception
- abandonment
- abuse
- legalism
- sin
- secrets
- family rules
- and on and on and on and on.

Gary once said to me, "It's like childbirth—a lot of pain, but the pain turns to joy when she holds her child." I'm not there yet. I'm still in pain.

I think there is a special kind of pain for those of us who cut. The kind of pain that begs to be numbed. The kind of pain that screams to be silenced by cutting. But how do I stop the pain? How do I get rid of, or at least lessen, the intense pain I've lived with for far too long? Sometimes I just tried to numb the pain.

Numb,
like an anesthetized limb,
feeling nothing,
responding to nothing,
sedate,
insensitive,
as the knife
slices open
and the blood
courses out,
yet the limb,
hypnotized,
lies still.
Numb.

Even when I tried to numb the pain, in reality it was still there. So I was back to my original question. How do I stop the pain? Early on in my therapy, I didn't think I could.

CHAPTER 10: PAIN

Pain

Supposedly pain is good for you.
It's been called the gift nobody wants.
Lepers don't experience physical pain.
As a result
they lose fingers and toes and hands and feet.
Physical pain—does it compare with
emotional pain?
I can be in physical pain.
I can hurt myself physically
and yet the emotional pain screams louder and
longer and harder
than any physical pain I can inflict on
myself.
What causes pain?
The list is endless.
What causes my pain?
The list is endless.
Does it ever go away?
No.
It hides itself in the shadows, lurking in the
background
waiting for the opportune time
to rear its ugly head
and seize me in its grips once again.
It devours.
Will it ever go away? Can I make it go away?
Punishing myself doesn't work.
Hurting myself doesn't work.
Crying only makes the pain go deeper in my heart.
Killing myself probably wouldn't even work.
Suicide.
Am I suicidal?
No, I don't think so.
I'm in pain, that I do know.
Enough pain to end the pain? Or would that really
end the pain?

My heart aches and hurts; is there no cure?
How many days?
How many weeks?
How many months?
How many years?
To contemplate the future with this pain
is fearful
and dreadful
and hopeless
and helpless.
Pain.
A gift?
No.
An endless curse, a fear, a cancer
eating away at my heart and soul.

I've found that the only way to stop the pain is to embrace it. I had to find safe people and a safe place to be able to work through the pain. Acknowledging I was in pain, discovering the source of the pain, talking about it, crying about it, and purging it were all parts of the process. It was incredibly painful, which is why a safe place and safe people were essential. Attempting to embrace pain without safety will only cause more pain, more depression, more tears, more cutting, more shame, and more anxiety. Don't be afraid to embrace the pain. It won't consume you. Embrace it, but do it in safety.

11
Hurt

Hurt,
like the young girl
crying out in
anguish
at the
violation
visited upon her
by one she loved;
or,
like the small dog,
unable to express
the pain and fear
he feels
from the stinging wounds
resulting from his
unknowing steps
into the fire ants'
domain;
or,
like the heart
once loved,
now betrayed
and abandoned
by the one
who once loved,
leaving her
desolate and despairing
in her pain,
all alone.
Hurt.

Obviously pain is a part of hurt. The dictionary describes pain and hurt as having many similarities, but they are different. Pain knows the source of the agony; hurt does not understand. Pain can explain what is happening; hurt cannot. Hurt goes much deeper. It involves elements of fear, aloneness, anger, broken trust, shame, sadness, and hatred. Pain is what I felt when I sliced open my skin. Hurt is what drove me to cut in the first place.

Plus More

Hurt,
like an open, gaping, and
bleeding sore.
Hurt,
like the feeling when someone says they
love you no more.
Hurt,
like feeling you are dirty and
never new.
Hurt,
when someone betrays and
abandons you.
Hurt,
when a promise is made but
never is kept.
Hurt,
when you feel you don't measure up,
that you are inept.
Hurt,
when feelings are invalidated and
you are ignored.
Hurt,
when because of your past you
feel like a whore.
Hurt,
when someone never says "I'm sorry"
to you.
Hurt,

when that same person deliberately
lies to you, too.
Hurt,
all of these things plus more.

Those words came after exactly three months in therapy with Gary. The hurt was staring me in the face. I couldn't stuff it, ignore it, or postpone it any longer. I had to deal with it. I wrote pages and pages in my journal describing ways I had been hurt by people I loved, people who claimed to love me, strangers, experiences, even myself.

What Is Hurt?

Anger-a secondary emotion. The primary emotion for anger is HURT.
What is hurt?
> It's the feeling you have inside when people reject something you have made or done or when they reject you, who you are, your very being.

What is hurt?
> It's the feeling you get in the pit of your stomach when you find out that people have betrayed your trust.

What is hurt?
> It's that horrible, empty feeling inside that comes when you realize that people you love—people who say they love you—show by their actions and their words that they really don't love you as much as they say they do.

What is hurt?
> It's that feeling you get when you let yourself down again and again and again. It's not being listened to and heard. It's having your feelings invalidated. It's being lied to. It's finding out that things are not the way you thought they were.

What is hurt?
> It's being laughed at or worse, ignored. It's not being believed when you are telling the truth.

What is hurt?
> It's comments that cut you down and make you feel less than you really are.

What is hurt?
> It's when people use you for their own pleasure or their own purpose or their own desire and don't really care about your feelings at all. It's

when you feel so bad inside that you simply want to lay down and die, or when the pain is so bad that the only thing you know is pain, so you cause yourself pain.

What is hurt?

It's having people you love always trying to change you to make you just like them, an extension of them. It's having your problems ignored or minimized by people you love. It's having to keep something from people you love because of how they will react.

What is hurt?

It's having people expect you to "get over it" when it is something that will take a long time. It's people who ask you to do something but then don't give you the opportunity to carry it out.

What is hurt?

It's looking at your body and seeing things that shouldn't be. It's looking at your life and seeing things that shouldn't be or shouldn't have been. It's feeling cheated out of your childhood. It's having a lot of problems and not knowing why. It's that feeling you get when you need to talk to someone and no one is at home.

What is hurt?

It's being put down, even subtly, for the way that you look, and not being accepted and loved the way that you are.

What is hurt?

It's the incredibly deep feeling that you have inside when you have lived with shame all your life. It's being so confused about something you can't even think.

What is hurt?

It's being so full of rage that you fear you will explode, killing everyone around you, including yourself.

What is hurt?

It's feeling so much pain and sadness that the bottle of pills or razor blade or rope is all you can think about.

What is hurt?

It's being terrified to cry out in the night for someone you love to come and take care of you. It's having no one listen to your cries for help. It's having to be perfect. It is having someone make fun of something that affects you deeply.

What is hurt?

It's not being able to sleep at night because of your fears. It's being left out. It's having someone treat you like a child when you are a grown adult. It's being expected to lie for people.

CHAPTER 11: HURT

What is hurt?

It's being so full of anxiety that your legs ache from trembling, but you cannot stop. It's being alone and lonely when all of your friends have mates. It's having your mother ask if all she is ever going to get is four-legged grandchildren, referring to your dogs.

What is hurt?

It's feeling like you are the reason for your parents' divorce. It's feeling and being afraid that you are crazy. It's hoping and having your hopes dashed.

What is hurt?

It's having others think you are fine when really you are crying and dying inside. It's not having memories of what you know happened.

What is hurt?

It's wrestling with the demons that plague you every day. It's feeling as if you will never be whole sexually. It's being afraid of your sexuality.

What is hurt?

It's looking at the scars on your body and realizing just how much you hurt. It's looking at the scars on your body and feeling the scars on your soul. It's having scars in the first place.

What is hurt?

It's being unable to laugh. Or cry. It's feeling numb. It's being expected to be able to handle everything.

What is hurt?

It's having been in counseling for years and years and still not having resolved the issues. It's knowing the Scriptures in your head but not in your heart.

What is hurt?

It's feeling like a hypocrite. It's questioning and doubting your salvation. It's wondering where God is. It's feeling rejected and abandoned by God. It's feeling as if you have lost all joy. It's not being able to reach your goals because your problems interfere time and again.

What is hurt?

It's knowing that if you weren't afraid of going to hell, that you would have killed yourself a long time ago. It's looking at yourself in the mirror and knowing that you hate yourself. It's having been in a psychiatric hospital three different times.

What is hurt?

It's writing this treatise. It's being so hard on yourself that you call yourself "stupid" hundreds of times every day. It's having your body violated. It's fearing that you are insane.

What is hurt?
> It's when you feel that people who are not family care more than those who are family. It's when you are crying and cannot stop. It's when you cannot cry.

What is hurt?
> It's having people take from you what is not theirs to take. It's that indescribable feeling that someone has murdered your soul. It's being afraid to confront people because of how they might react.

What is hurt?
> It's not having been allowed to experience certain emotions. It's that fear of failure that has come about as a result of failing so many people for so many years. It's being criticized. It's laughing to cover up the pain. It's being afraid of getting well when you are sick. It's being sick.

What is hurt?
> It's feeling as if you always have to please everybody. It's the loathing and self-hatred you feel for yourself, especially when you look in the mirror.

What is hurt?
> It's hearing of the pain in another's life and feeling guilty for having any pain of your own. It's living every day with a part of you missing. It's having an addiction and not being able to beat it. It's having someone not believe in you. It's feeling as if your dogs love you more than your own mom does.

What is hurt?
> It's feeling as if you will never get well. It's not having any hope. It's realizing that all of these things are written here because I have experienced them. I have experienced them all, and I hurt.

Hurt faced me everywhere and I began to process. As I talked through these things with Gary, I slowly began to heal from some of the hurt. For a while, the hurt was pervasive, nearly consuming my very existence.

Why Do I Hurt?

I hurt because I feel as if I can't quit masturbating and cutting.
I hurt because sometimes I don't want to quit
I hurt because I feel ugly and fat and unlovable and unwanted.

CHAPTER 11: Hurt

I hurt because I feel I am only useful to men as a sex object.
I hurt because I didn't have a normal childhood.
I hurt because I'm confused about so many things.
I hurt because I've wanted to die so many times in my life.
I hurt because I've actually tried to die.
I hurt because I've caused others to hurt.
I hurt because I feel like so many times I'm not accepted.
I hurt because it is very hard to trust.
I hurt because sometimes I trust too easily and then get hurt.
I hurt because I'm such a scaredy-cat.
I hurt because I seem to always want to cry, but I can't.
I hurt because of all my fears.
I hurt because the depression has interfered once again with my life.
I hurt because I have struggled with this awful depression for twenty-four years.
I hurt because I was taught things sexually that I was too young to know.
I hurt because it takes a razor blade to numb all the overwhelming feelings that are inside of me.
I hurt because when I was in high school I got called "Dolly Parton."
I hurt because I hate my breasts.
I hurt because of the things I do sexually.
I hurt because I'm so afraid that I won't get better. Every time I think I am, the depression comes back.
I hurt because I feel that no man will ever want me.
I hurt because I have to cut myself to numb the hurt.
I hurt because I want to marry and have children and yet at the same time am so terrified of that.
I hurt because I feel so far away from God and am so afraid He has left me for good.
I hurt because I feel like my life is so complicated and hopeless. I feel like I am beyond help.
I hurt because I am so sure I will be rejected when I disclose anything about myself to anyone.
I hurt because I was raised to view God as angry and punitive, yet that's not the picture I see of Him in the Bible.
I hurt because I'm so passive sometimes.
I hurt because I don't understand how God could love me.
I hurt because my faith is so pitiful.

I hurt because there are so many pages here that are filled with hurt.
I hurt.

Page after page of hurt filled my notebook. I wrote about it in first person and third person. I described it with metaphors. It still hurt.

Metaphors

Hurt is
a dam whose floodgates have burst open
and whose water is rushing furiously out, overpowering, destroying
and engulfing houses and towns as it goes.
Hurt is
the blackness of a cave
where no light is shining, preventing one from seeing even
his own hand held close to his face.
It is a thick, foreboding darkness with all of its terrors within.
Hurt is
a tall, formidable mountain
where there is no pass around either side
and no way to cross over it.
To get past it, one must tunnel through it.
Hurt is
a silent telephone,
or an empty mailbox.
Hurt is
a wound that is open and gaping
and has had salt poured into it.
Hurt is
the ache in the empty, starving stomach.
Hurt is
a glass that is deliberately dashed to the ground,
broken and shattered.
Hurt is
a fragile package that has been thrown around,
kicked, beaten, banged up, damaged and bruised.
Hurt is
the wild goose,

separated and lost from its flock and afraid of predators.
Hurt is
the young girl, crying silently in her bed
as she tries to remove all traces of him
from her body and her mind.
Hurt is
a dog that is neglected, abandoned and abused,
left chained up with no food or water or love.
Hurt is
a shipment that has been inspected and declared to be
damaged goods.
Hurt is
an old woman in a nursing home, left all alone
with no family, no friends—and no memory.
Hurt is
skin that has been sliced with a blade and is
bleeding and stinging with nothing to
stop the pain.
Hurt is
an antique doll, dusty, neglected and broken,
left in a dark, musty attic.
Hurt is
a flower,
broken off from its roots and tossed aside like garbage.
Hurt is
a student, confused and frustrated, asking questions
but never receiving any answers.
Hurt is
the woman, violated and desecrated by rape.
Hurt is
a desert, dry, dusty and desolate,
nothing growing, no moisture, no life.
Hurt is
a seabird, trapped, tangled, and choking from
a mass of discarded fishing line, rapidly losing life.
Hurt is
me.

I painted the hurt, bright red like the blood that flowed from my body when I cut. By acknowledging it, identifying it, talking through it with Gary, and then grieving it, I began to heal. The hurt was still there. It just didn't consume me anymore.

12

Anger

Anger,
like the raging madness of a
wounded bull,
pawing the ground,
smoke billowing from his
nostrils
as he charges his
fear-paralyzed victim,
thrusting sharpened
horn
again and again and again
as he gores the
once proud
matador
to death.
Anger.

Gary says that anger is a secondary emotion to hurt. It feels like a primary emotion to me. Sometimes I've felt so overwhelmed by the rage I felt boiling inside of me, I wanted to explode.

I am full of
Regret
Anger
Garbage
Exhaustion

I wrote it in my journal, and I cut it on my body. RAGE. I painted a picture about it, too. The picture actually represented three things. *Up and Down* referred to the state of my emotions. *Rage Slicing Through the*

Middle told what all the rage was doing to my insides, and the picture itself showed what I was doing to my skin. Sometimes I have dealt with the anger in unhealthy, potentially destructive ways:

- cutting myself
- hitting myself
- masturbating
- punching or kicking the furniture or wall or other things
- driving recklessly
- spending money recklessly
- stuffing it with food
- stuffing it with silence
- throwing things
- letting loose with a string of verbal expletives, slurs, or other verbal garbage

Sometimes I have dealt with it in healthy ways:

- hitting my punching bag
- going to the batting cages
- talking it out with someone

- crying
- playing or listening to music
- yelling in a safe place
- writing

Even when I have dealt with my anger in healthy ways, I have always been terrified of the volcano churning beneath the surface.

There are times I let a tiny glimpse
of all my anger show
and yet full force that lurks beneath
is for only me to know.

I try to keep it all in check,
against what I've come to fear—
the raging madness exploding out,
all the fury, straight and clear.

Seething and fermenting
and churning deep inside,
boiling hot with anger,
the rage just never dies.

What will happen when I blow,
when the eruptive anger thunders out?
Will the victim be just me
or will others feel its shrieking shout?

And what will happen when all the rage
and fury deep down inside
erupt its deadly blast at me?
Will I live or will I die?

Anger has been a part of my life for as long as I remember. I've either stuffed it or taken it out on myself, or I've vented it inappropriately. I was beginning to choose appropriate ways, but sometimes the anger was still so strong that it came out wrong before I even decided to think about how it could come out right.

I had dealt with some of the anger in therapy, but there was more underneath, boiling away, waiting for the eruption. I wasn't sure if it would it seep out little by little and get dealt with or just blow.

I have always been afraid of my anger. But I've always been even more afraid of someone else's anger, especially my mother's. Anger created anxiety.

13
Anxiety

Anxiety,
like the parent whose
child has
disappeared,
relentlessly searching,
anticipating
the phone call,
yet dreading it
at the same time,
full of
fear,
worry,
apprehension,
and panic;
or,
like the novice actor offstage,
knowing his cue is coming
yet, having forgotten his lines,
waits
in trepidation;
or,
like the agoraphobic who,
knowing the public appearance
is vital,
yea, demanded,
approaches the front door full of
dread,
fear,
and distress.
Anxiety.

Gary says that anxiety is a defense mechanism created by God. Problems come when it malfunctions. Most things that go awry are things that God intended for good; for example, food, drink, sex. Our fight-or-flight instinct is one of those things. Being safe enables us to enjoy life. Our fight-or-flight instinct kicks in when we are not safe. Anxiety is being stuck in a constant feeling of being unsafe, stuck in alarm mode. Vigilance is good, but with anxiety, the vigilance never shuts off. Anxiety can drive you. It can drive you to cut.

The anxiety and the tension inside me were so intense and the need to relieve them so urgent that cutting was often the only release that worked. Or at least the only one that seemed to work. As the anxiety built, the anxiety and the desire to cut fed off of each other, with the need to cut and release the tension getting stronger by the moment.

My anxiety was caused by a variety of things. Sometimes it was triggered by lots of noise or people. Sometimes by my emotions and thoughts. Sometimes by my scars. Sometimes by a phone call, especially with my mother. Stressful or new circumstances could cause it, as well as circumstances that weren't as smooth as I would have liked them to be. Being tired and not eating well also affected my anxiety. Because the anxiety could build so easily, it was vital for me to watch out for it and to do what I could to ward it off. Here is a list Gary gave me at one point:

1. Walk! At least once per day
2. No caffeine or stimulants such as chocolate :(
3. No sugars or simple carbohydrates like white, processed foods - wheat okay
4. No quick picker-uppers
5. Make one master list for each day
6. Drink milk 2 times a day
7. Eat proteins and veggies

I can't keep all anxiety from coming. It's a built-in, God-given mechanism. But I had to do what I could to keep from getting stuck in alarm mode. And one of the biggest things that got me stuck in alarm mode were my thoughts.

14
Thoughts

Thoughts,
like a school of fish
whirling in a
frenzied state,
creating the
illusion
of the perfect vortex,
all the while
driven
by the individual
fear
of the collective group
as each tries
desperately, wildly, frantically,
yet vainly,
to escape
being the
prey
for the school of sharks
waiting placidly
below
for the
crazed fish—
depleted of all ability
to fight
or flee—
to succumb
to the razor-edged jaws
of their predators.
Thoughts.

That is a pretty dark picture of my thoughts, whirling in a frenzy while waiting for the razor-edged jaws, but sometimes that's how it was.

> Thoughts—
> whirling, swirling, twirling,
> chaos all around.
> Thoughts—
> lift me up and slam me
> hard upon the ground.
> Thoughts—
> left and right confusion,
> scattered all about.
> Thoughts—
> serenity is fleeting,
> mind just screams and shouts.
> Thoughts—
> cannot stop the flowing
> of the thoughts within my brain.
> Thoughts—
> wearing hard upon me,
> they weaken and they drain.
> Thoughts.

Many times my thoughts were full of myself and usually those thoughts weren't positive. I called myself stupid, a freak, an idiot, and a jerk. I didn't talk very kindly to myself.

> I Am
>
> Alone–no one but myself to blame
> Bruised–and bloodied, scars remain
> Chained–I cannot break the bonds
> Despondent–hope seems far beyond
>
> Empty–filled seems far away
> Fractured–and broken day by day

CHAPTER 14: THOUGHTS

Gluttonous-I binge and binge and purge
Hurt-so deep I can't resurge

Ignored-and isolated I feel
Jaded-tired and worn, I reel
Keelhauled-and punished is my plight
Lonely-O, so alone am I

Marred-and scarred beyond repair
Nebulous-am I really here or there?
Oppressed-by evils all around
Perverted-like a female hound

Quenched-is any fire to fight
Ravaged-beaten, full of fright
Shamed-and shameful, that is I
Tormented-and tortured, "help" I cry

Unbalanced-crazy, sick in the head
Vacant-sometimes wishing to be dead
Wasted-feeling valuable is rare
Xeric-like a desert, dry and bare

Yellow-coward, full of fear
Zapped-of all and any cheer.
Am I all these listed here?
"Yes" is said with silent tear.

My thoughts were often obsessive. I would dwell on the same thing over and over, usually in more detail each time. Thinking about the cutting was this way. Sometimes my thoughts were racing. They would go from one thing to another in such rapid succession I could barely keep up. Even now, I always have a pencil and paper handy. I write everything down because when my thoughts start flying, I find it very difficult to focus and remember things. At times I fixate on questions. I may ask a myriad of questions or ask the same questions repeatedly. I may ask one or two questions, but in a number of different ways.

A question mark pops in my head;
Am I alive or am I dead?
How can I have a life that's full
when insanity has so strong a pull?

A question mark pops in my brain;
Will sunshine be or ever rain?
How can I share this life of mine
when it has really lost its shine?

A question mark pops in my skull;
Am I doomed to ever be emotionally dull?
How can my life be a work of art
when it is so messed up and torn apart?

I would rehash something I had already said to someone. I would also rehearse what I was going to say countless times. If I were practicing something I was going to say, I felt compelled to choose the exact words and say them with perfect intonation. So I would practice, again and again. This could be for something as simple as making a phone call to find out what hours a store was open. Over and over. Practice, practice, practice.

Often I would spend hours creating various scenarios in my head about an upcoming event or decision, something or someone I really liked, or something or someone I was really afraid of. The most disturbing scenarios I created involved my being raped.

I've been creating scenarios in my head again. For instance, this afternoon I spent an hour on the couch with a scenario of me getting raped. There have been many times since high school that I have created mental scenarios of being raped. What I just realized is that almost always the larger part of the scenario is not the rape itself, but being rescued and taken care of afterward. What's that all about? Is this some way of wishing I had been taken care of when I was a kid?

There are a number of ways a person's thinking can be distorted: all-or-nothing thinking, over-generalizations, discounting the positives, mind-reading/fortune-telling, magnification or minimization, emotional reasoning, "should" statements, and labeling. What I needed to do was

CHAPTER 14: THOUGHTS

substitute more realistic thoughts for the distorted thoughts; for example, instead of thinking "I never do anything right," substitute "There are many times I do things right." When I do this, it helps me to see things from a different perspective.

I wasn't always able to find a new perspective. One day, about a week after I started working with Gary, I drew a picture using the letters from the following words: illusions, dreams, thoughts, conversations, scenarios, rehearsals, imaginings, delusions. I entitled it *Thoughts In My Brain*.

Trusting, trusting,
belly up
as I trim her nails.
Don't deserve a
dog like this—
the storm within me rails.

Cutting, cutting,
hurting self,
it's punishment I need.
I deserve a
life like this—
my heart and skin to bleed.

Thinking, thinking
in my mind,
my thoughts disturb and lie—
thoughts of hatred
and of shame,
of how and when I'll die.

Trusting, trusting,
leads to pain,
an ache within the soul—
ripped up heart,
scattered thoughts,
broken, never whole.

Josh said that when my thoughts get out of control I need to change my focus as an act of my will. I said my will must be pretty weak. He countered with the idea that I probably just haven't exercised it. He said our will is like a muscle. They both will be weak unless they are exercised. He made the assertion that a lot of people think our minds just have a will of their own, but that isn't true. We control our minds. He said I need to not assume I am powerless over my thoughts, but to experiment with different ways to change or stop my thoughts. Exercise my will. Exercise the power to control my thoughts. I have a hunch that he might be right.

Chapter 14: Thoughts

The apostle Paul said in 2 Corinthians 10:5, "...we take captive every thought to make it obedient to Christ."

Walking by Faith with a Struggling Mind

At the
fairgrounds
walking,
wandering,
circling,
circling again,
and again,
and again,
passing the same thing
time and again.
Confusion.
Conclusion—
lost.
With a normal mind,
apprehension,
maybe some
uncertainty
or uneasiness.
With a struggling mind,
anxiety
and fear,
terror
and dread.
But by faith
I am still walking,
still trying,
still seeking
to be found.

My thoughts confused me, angered me, frightened me. That's part of why I hated being alone. My thoughts were the worst when I was alone.

15
Alone

Alone,
like a single human
on a deserted isle,
no hope for food
or shelter
or rescue,
surrounded only by the
relentlessly pounding surf
and the
viciously circling,
hungrily waiting
sharks.
Alone.

I *hate* being alone! I use every ploy I can think of to try to keep my husband home a few more minutes before he leaves for work. When he is gone and I am home alone, I engage in all sorts of things to keep from being alone:

- playing music very loudly
- calling friends or family on the telephone and talking for hours
- making and doing endless lists to keep myself busy
- getting lost in book after book
- continually playing with my two little dogs
- visiting with friends at their homes or workplace
- working extra hours at my own job
- and the list goes on.

I don't want to be alone. I don't want to be alone physically. I don't want to be alone in my thoughts. I don't even want Josh to go to sleep at night because then I am left alone until I finally fall asleep myself. So I stall. Alone isn't safe. I hate being alone. More accurately, I fear being alone! When I am alone, I feel unprotected. I feel—here is the dreaded word—vulnerable.

My dad wasn't in the picture
- he left me
- he didn't want me
- he abandoned me
- I wasn't good enough to keep him around
- alone means unwanted

My grandfather abused me
- I was alone when he came in my room
- alone means unsafe
- alone means getting hurt
- alone means fear
- alone means being betrayed
- alone means secrets
- alone means lies
- alone means losing yourself
- alone means being just like him
- alone means silence
- alone means hurt
- alone means pain
- alone means no hope
- alone means no end to the clamor inside my head
- alone means degradation of body and soul

Alone didn't feel safe. Plus, I was alone when I cut. And even though I was afraid of being alone, I felt very alone. I felt as if I were in one place and everybody else was in another. I felt all alone in my pain and my shame. I felt all alone in my cutting. No one else would do such awful things to their body. No one else could possibly feel the way I did, hurt the way I did. Early in my therapy with Gary, especially before I married Josh, I felt such isolation, with no one but my two little dogs. I even felt God had left me alone, yet I often cried out to God about how alone I felt.

CHAPTER 15: ALONE

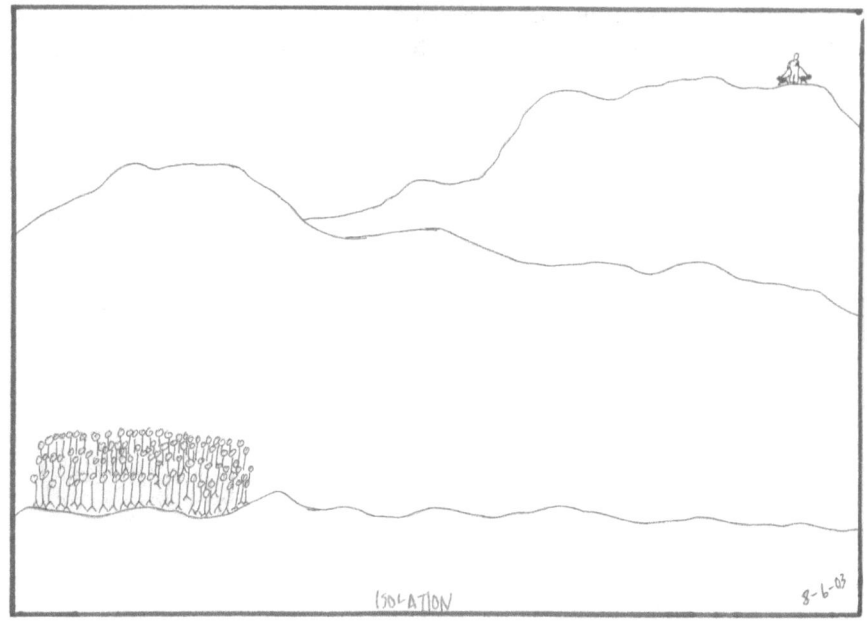

Alone

Verse 1:
My heart is torn with deep distress.
I cannot pray, I cannot rest.
Oh, tell me God, why must it be
that I'm alone on life's dark sea,
without a love I fear I'll drown.

Verse 2:
Abandoned here is what I feel,
alone without my God's appeal.
I beg You, God, desert me not,
for I'm afraid of sin's dark blot
upon my heart without You, Lord.

Ending:
But what if I am always here,
alone in soul, with no one near?
I fear my heart will break in two alone.
My heart is torn, God, hear my moan.
Please help me God, I'm so alone.

While I feared and hated being alone, sometimes I wanted to be alone. When I was alone I didn't have to be with people. When I was alone I didn't have to be with family.

16

Family

Family,
like a
safe haven
from the storms
of life;
or,
like the
storm
itself.
Family.

Family. I'm not even sure where to start. I've already shared some about my family and the unwritten, demanding rules. For now, I'll focus on my dad. The first time I met him I was sixteen. I still remember the first words he ever said to me—"Do you want to hit me or hug me or shake my hand?" I shook his hand, but I wanted to hit him. I wasn't impressed, though he tried to impress me. And he lied to me. He told me he'd been putting money in a college fund for me. I never saw it. It wasn't the money that upset me; it was the lying. I remember calculating the number of hours I'd lived compared to the number of hours he had given me. We talked for only two hours. Sixteen years of my life and he gave me only two hours of his. And the very first time he ever met his daughter, he lied to me. I felt pretty worthless.

After that two hour meeting, I had no other contact with him until I was twenty-three. I had been out of the psychiatric hospital for about four months when I tracked him down and met with him the day after Thanksgiving. This time I met his family as well. I also learned some information that I had always suspected, but had never known for sure. One of my half-sisters told me that the reason my mom and our dad got married was because my mom was pregnant. And her mom and our dad got divorced because of my mom. This from a half-sister I'd never met before! I confronted both my parents, who said it was true. At least my dad said it was true. My mother talked around it until I finally pinned her down with my questions. They both confirmed that they had promised each other never to tell me the truth about the circumstances of my birth. They had promised to lie to me.

A month later I met with my dad again. He wanted to do DNA testing. I'm not sure if he really wanted it or if his wife wanted it. He had remarried his first wife after he had divorced my mom. He excused the test by saying that my mother was sleeping around with lots of men when they were together and he didn't know for sure if he was my father. Whether that was true or not, I didn't know. They had both lied to me all my life. Here was a man I hardly knew, yet had been told was my father for twenty-three years, and he wanted DNA testing. So I did it. The results came back 99.999 percent certain that he was my father, verifying what we had known all along. But when the results came back, he said he and his wife "weren't ready to deal with it."

It was during this time, in early 1993, that I was hospitalized the second time for the depression. I received a very hurtful letter from him while I was in the hospital. I started creating scenarios in my mind of how I could kill my father and get away with it. I finally figured it wouldn't work, so I decided to kill myself instead. I was so messed up already, I thought, why should I bother sticking around? I felt so alone and rejected.

There aren't many things you can do to hurt yourself in a psychiatric hospital, but I managed. I took my shoelaces and the drawstrings out of the bottoms of my jackets. In the bathroom I strung them through the metal supports between the tiles in the ceiling. I climbed onto the counter and tied the cords tightly around my neck. I turned myself around, twisting the cords tighter. I was ready to jump off the counter when I got scared. I was supposedly a Christian, I supposedly believed in God. And I sure didn't want to go to hell. Maybe I didn't want to do this after all. But now I was up there and I was stuck. I prayed a desperate prayer that God would help me. I crouched there on the counter with the cords cutting into my neck and waited, praying that someone would come and check on me. Finally, after about fifteen minutes, one of the nurses found me. She immediately called for help and they cut me down. I started crying and couldn't stop. The depression finally stabilized and after four weeks

Chapter 16: Family

I was released from the hospital. About a week later I cut myself for the very first time.

Eventually, about three years later, my father and I reconciled. He apologized to me for not being there when I was growing up. His wife also apologized for keeping him from seeing me. Shortly after our reconciliation, I went to my father's family reunion. I met my father's mother for the first time and everyone was shocked at the resemblance between us. When I got my pictures developed, I was shocked, too. I looked just like her! And yet he had wanted to do DNA testing! Since that time my father and I have been getting to know each other. We have a distant relationship, but at least there is something of a relationship. Even so, I have a lot of hurt because of him.

I hurt because my dad left right before I was born and never wanted to have anything to do with me until I initiated the contact.
I hurt because of the feelings of abandonment I feel because of him.
I hurt because he didn't find me worthy enough to even tell me the truth the first time I met him.
I hurt because he never bothered to pay any child support, even though the amount he was supposed to pay each month was very small.
I hurt because I drew a picture of his prize longhorn for him and he's never bothered to put it anywhere, much less with all of his other longhorn stuff.
I hurt because I'll never have a dad in the emotional sense of the word.
I hurt because I'll never know what it is like to grow up with a dad.
I hurt because I feel so empty without one.
I hurt because he never remembers when my birthday is.
I hurt because my dad had me do DNA testing with him.
I hurt because he was upset with the positive results.
I hurt because I let him hurt me with that to the point that I tried to hang myself.
I hurt because I have wanted my dad to die, even plotting in my mind how I could kill him and get away with it.
I hurt because I once felt that way.
I hurt because I feel so awkward and out of place when I'm with my dad and his family.
I hurt because he never will talk about anything having to do with my mom or me as a baby and kid growing up without him.

I hurt because if he hadn't left shortly before I was born, I wouldn't have felt all my life that it was my fault he left—if I hadn't been born, he wouldn't have left.
I hurt because I have a relationship with him now and yet still feel so much anger and hurt.

The hurt I felt because of my family was strong. But it wasn't as strong as the shame.

17
Shame

Shame,
like a woman
dragged naked
from the
bed
that was shared
by the married man
for illicit sex,
his semen
still wetting her,
screaming
for all the world
to see
the perversion and
the shame
of her heart,
her body,
her soul;
or,
like the child
touched and fondled and
penetrated
by the very one who
gave her life,
now left alone
with her heart-rending
sobs
as she once again
must live with the
degradation of her
soul.
Shame.

At one point I had *shame* cut into my body in three different places. For years the shame ate at me, gnawing away at my soul. Shame. That was me. The shame I lived with painted blackness on my soul and its weight made my spirit groan.

How Can I Bear?

People,
people,
noises, crowds.
How can I bear
the noise so loud?
Inside my
mind
are shouts and screams.
How can I bear
what's in my dreams?
The cloud
above
my head is dark.
How can I bear
the devil's bark?
Blackness,
blackness,
shame in my soul.
How can I bear
to not be whole?
Silence,
silence,
I'm so alone.
How can I bear
my spirit's groan?

Even at age ten I was writing about shame in my autobiography. Every year the shame grew until it was a black beast gripping me in its deadly talons. I felt the shame like the devil's claws in my back, keeping me bound and tortured by the condemnation I felt in my soul. Every time I masturbated, every time I cut, every time I thought about my childhood and what I believed was done to me, the depression gripped me tightly and the shame grew.

> The devil's claws are around me,
> they have gripped my heart and my mind,
> entangling thoughts and emotions
> till it seems impossible to ever unwind.
>
> For twenty-three years I've been tortured
> by his sharp and poisonous claws
> as he's tried to bring my destruction
> with his strong and murderous jaws.
>
> His power is not near as awesome
> as that of my Savior and Lord,
> but I often call not for deliverance
> because I'm bound by such a tight cord.
>
> I know not how to surrender
> to the One who from shame can save—
> and I fear the devil's claws will still grip me
> from now till I go to my grave.

The shame I felt for the sexual behaviors ate at me every day. The biggest problem was the compulsive masturbation. It had begun when I was about ten and had become more than a problem. It was a compulsion. I couldn't stop. Through the years I had talked with several different people and counselors, trying to stop, but I never did. I scoured the Bible, looking for a verse that specifically said masturbation was a sin. And even though I never found one, I knew it wasn't right because I was engaging in sexual behavior outside the context of a marriage. It wasn't right because it was coming between me and God.

The shame of my compulsive sinful behavior kept me away from God. But that was only part of my shame. The other part was my grandfather. Shortly after I graduated from college, I went to a funeral for a man who a few years before had taken advantage of me one night when I'd had too much to drink. I wrote a poem about it.

> My heart was cold and bitter,
> the wind grew colder still
> as I stood beside the mourners
> atop a little hill.
>
> The man we mourned had hurt me,
> he had stripped and shamed my soul,
> yet drawn I felt to stand there,
> though why I did not know.

I felt much the same way about my grandfather, stripped and shamed by him and yet drawn to him. Or rather, drawn to memories and pictures of him since he was dead. At this point, I don't remember much about my grandfather. I remember being afraid of him. I remember watching him use the bathroom. I remember him in his boxer shorts. I remember his voice, his face, his eyes, and how frightening they were to me.

I don't know much about him. He died when I was barely nine and then he was never talked about. I do know what I think he did to me. I had the clues. At one point I thought I needed all my memories in order to get well, but I have enough memories to convince me. More memories may return in time, but for now, I know what I think was done to me, and I can work from there for healing to occur. Enough time has passed that I am removed from him and I have other, more pressing things I must deal with in order to heal. Things like fear and Mother.

I struggled with the thought that I could do all the things I had done sexually, especially in light of what I thought had been done to me. Instead of embracing sexual acts, I should have been repulsed by them. Yet the compulsive, destructive masturbation continued and dug the pit of shame deeper. I often cried out to God, asking Him to take away the shame, to help me wipe out the stain on my soul.

> O God
>
> I'm full of shame, O God.
> My heart is stained, O God.
> My sin is black, O God.
> A peace I lack, O God.

CHAPTER 17: SHAME

I beg You Lord,
give me help,
O God.

Over time the shame has faded to the point that I believe it to be gone, primarily because the compulsive masturbation has stopped. I finally had a strong enough motivation to stop, which came on April 8, 2004, when Josh asked me to marry him. It wasn't easy to stop. Many times I desperately wanted to continue. Gary had told me that if I continued, I was running the risk of messing up our sex life once we were married. One thing Josh and I did right was waiting to have sex until we were married. We were doing things, as Gary said, God's way. Once again, it was hard. It would have been much easier to give in. But we didn't; we waited. God has blessed us because of it. Despite my background, there is no shame in my marriage with my husband.

Shame had defined me most of my life. And it was finally gone. That gave me hope that others things that had defined me might be conquered as well. Things like fear.

18
Fear

Fear,
like a black night's fog rolling in
across the sea,
enveloping the wharf
in its deadly tentacles,
gripping the heart
and squeezing out life,
never showing light
or peace
or calm,
but only a
paralyzing,
stupefying,
mystifying
terror
within,
bringing only a
scream
that haunts
one's soul.
Fear.

I have avoided writing about fear because I don't like the subject. I have been putting it off. Some things you actually look forward to. That feeling is anticipation.

> Fear and anticipation
> Anticipation–to look forward to; expect
> Fear and anticipation are closely related.
> The difference is that fear has to do with

the unknown and anticipation has to do
with the known.
You anticipate a birthday, a party, an event,
a package in the mail, a phone call.
Usually when you are anticipating, it is
done with great eagerness and joy.
Not so with fear.
With fear, it is the unknown, the dread,
the worst possibility, the confusion, the
not understanding.
Me—anticipation or fear?
Fear

Fear–The feeling in the pit of your stomach
when the dogs start barking and there
is a knock on your window at 1 a.m.
Fear–What happens in your head when the
unknown quite possibly could be the
worst known.
Fear–It really is something that happens
in your head. It is an emotion,
an intangible. So how can I get
my head to quit letting the fear
happen?

Fear really does happen in the head. It happens when wild thoughts get out of control. It also happens in the body. The heart races, speeding up the pulse. Sweat glands secrete more. Muscles tense up as the body prepares to flee.

Sometimes fear is rational, it's reasonable, it makes sense. For example, if a huge dog is blocking the doorway, hackles up and growling through bared teeth, there is good reason to be afraid. But oftentimes fear is irrational. It is based on what might happen, like being afraid of automatic garage doors because they might come off their rollers and come crashing down on you. That's an irrational fear. An irrational fear may be rooted in a rational fear. I'm afraid when it is time to turn off the lights and go to sleep. That fear is rooted in the fact that as a child, bedtime was unsafe for me. When I was a child, being afraid at bedtime was a rational fear, but now it's irrational. No one is lurking in the darkness waiting to abuse me. My husband is there next to me and he will protect me, unlike my mother, who did not protect me when I was a child. The house is locked and secured. I have no reason to be afraid. But I still feel the fear.

Things That I Am Afraid Of

traffic
nighttime
noises at nighttime
anger
doing something wrong
being alone
being abandoned
scary music
scary movies
dealing with adults
dealing with children
authority figures
math
making mistakes in math
making someone angry
having a child
screwing up a child
loud noises
loud people
new situations
automatic garage doors
eye contact
what other people think
cussing
my anger
driving in snow and ice (actually, even rain)
the dark
my mother

my mother
my mother
my memories
losing control
people who are very different from me
pushy salesmen
making big purchases
embarrassing myself
confronting my mother
not measuring up (to whom or whatever)
confronting my past
losing the ones I love
my thoughts
God
thinking my little dogs might get hurt
thinking I might never get well
darkened hallways
shadows
the unknown
being afraid
death
all the possible situations and scenarios my mind can create
sticking out or drawing attention to myself
even thinking I might be sticking out or drawing attention to myself
offending someone or making someone mad
standing up for what I know is right
making phone calls
computer problems

Fear builds on itself. When I'm afraid, one frightening thought after another pops into my head. The fear grows and spins out of control until I'm so over-stimulated that I make myself sick. I spent a large portion of each day feeling very frightened. I was frightened by my mental illness, particularly the fugue experience, which I had found out about on the day that I drew this picture. I was frightened by people and things and situations and myself. I was frightened by how fractured I was. Fear defined me. Fear was going to be the last stronghold. I didn't want to be afraid all the time, but I was. I felt imprisoned by my fears.

CHAPTER 18: FEAR

My Fears

Verse 1:   God, where is Your help?
I cannot walk all by myself.
I feel alone, I need You near.
O God, save me from my fears.

Verse 2:   Why am I so weak,
So full of fear, I cannot speak?
I am alone with no one near.
I'm imprisoned by my fears.

My fear caused problems not only for me, but for Josh as well. It draws me into such self-focus that when I'm afraid I completely shut out the feelings and needs of others. I do this with Josh. I become so consumed by my fear that, in trying to eradicate it, I invalidate and minimize his feelings, which angers him and drives him away from me. His anger and withdrawal create more fear and the cycle starts all over again. I need to reach the point that I don't allow my fear to control and consume me.

But for now the fear is still a big part of my life, which may explain my procrastination in writing this chapter. I may be done with this chapter, but I'm not done with fear. Hopefully, I am getting better. With Josh and Gary's help, I'm starting to see the cycles of fear in my life and how pervasive it is. I am also starting to see that the foundation of my fear is my mother.

19
Mom

Mom,
like a
roller coaster,
twisting and turning,
rising and falling
through emotions,
and rules,
and actions;
or,
like a three year old
child,
demanding her own way,
self-centered,
self-focused,
selfish,
pouting and crying when
things don't go
her way;
or,
like a queen bee,
controlling the hive,
having the hive
revolve around her,
always on display,
always image-managing,
always dominating,
Mom.

On March 27, 2007, Gary told me that I was a success case. He and I both knew that I still had issues to work on and emotions to get a handle on. But in his view, I was a success case. I was no longer cutting.

I was no longer masturbating. I was no longer having hallucinations. I was a success case. Wow!

Now, four months later, I am sitting here at my computer trying to formulate into words what I am feeling. I just had an appointment with Gary and we talked, as usual, about my mother. I feel as if I am standing at the precipice of a vast canyon, with my toes just hanging over the edge. It is very high, and I am afraid of heights, but I glance down anyway. I have to descend the rock and I'm afraid. But for the first time I feel that I might actually have the courage to do this. Therapy has been like peeling away the layers of an onion. I have dealt with one issue after another, peeling away. Only one issue remains. Now I am ready. Now I have the courage to deal with my mother.

The more I learn about my mother, the less I like her. The less I like her, the less scary she is to me. I see how she acts and I realize that my mother is basically a little three-year-old child, scrambling to get her way. I see the irrationality of my fear of her more easily. I do fear her. It is diminishing. And it must, because seeing my mother for who she is and loving her for who she is is dependent upon my getting past the fear. As Gary said, she is at the heart of my struggles, and my many fears originate with her. I'm afraid of not pleasing her, of not having her approval. For a child, mommy's approval is vital. I've been that child. As a growing, learning, striving-to-be-healthy adult, I must put childish ways behind me.

Part of my fear of my mother is due to the fact that my mother is unstable. By unstable, I mean I cannot trust her. I never know how she is going to respond. She has various rules about different things. Some I can predict, but many are tricky and arbitrary. And, although she would deny it, her love for me is conditional. When I am doing things her way, not "rocking the boat," then she will show me her love. When I do rock the boat, when I am not pleasing her, she withholds her love and her approval.

As I have been working and struggling to grow past all of this, I have written many words about my mother. In our first session, Gary told me that he thought my mother was the biggest part of my problems. I didn't want to believe him and I didn't want to deal with her. I kept putting her off, but she kept coming back up. I asked Josh and Gary recently why she, not my father or my grandfather, was the foundation of all my dysfunction. Both of their answers pointed to the fact that she was there

CHAPTER 19: MOM

and they were not. My father was never there and my grandfather died when I was barely nine. But she was there. All my life she has been right there, smothering and controlling me, loving conditionally, modeling instability, and looming in my mind. Fear is the last emotion I have left to deal with in relation to my mother. Hurt was the first. Early in my therapy with Gary I wrote a lengthy treatise on hurt. Half of those pages were about my mom.

> I hurt
> because my mom lies to me
> and taught me to lie.
> I hurt
> because she's expected me to lie to others
> for her.
> I hurt
> because she'll believe me when I lie
> but sometimes won't believe me when I
> tell the truth.
> I hurt
> because my mom thinks I
> look like a boy.
> I hurt
> because she won't even try
> to understand what I'm going through.
> I hurt
> because she criticizes almost everything I do.
> I hurt
> because she expects me to keep secrets
> about things that need not be.
> I hurt
> because she ignores my feelings.
> I hurt
> because she's often told me I was a rotten kid.
> I hurt
> because her attitude toward me
> is scorn and contempt
> for getting help with my problems.
> I hurt

because I feel like I never measure up.
I hurt
because she didn't even think at all
about the consequences (me)
when she and my dad were having sex
and were not married (to each other).
I hurt
because they made a pledge to each other
never to tell me the truth.
I hurt
because all she cares about is
family image,
over and beyond what she cares for me.
I hurt
because she has no clue as to
what I'm going through
or who I am
(and at this point I don't want her to).
I hurt
because she thinks she knows me so well.
I hurt
because I feel that she's angry at me
for having a mental illness.
I hurt
because I feel as if I have to protect
my mother
when it should be the other way around.
I hurt
because Mom
has always tried to buy
my love.
I hurt
because she always wants to pretend that
everything is beautiful and wonderful and perfect
and that there are no problems,
no hurts
in our lives.
I hurt

CHAPTER 19: MOM

because she never says "I'm sorry" when
I have finally gotten up the courage
to tell her how I feel about her.
I hurt
because she's never said,
"I'm sorry you are hurting,"
but has only been concerned with
who knows,
what do they know,
why did she not know,
and don't let anyone else know.
I hurt
because she never sets boundaries
and does not respect them,
or puts them down,
or gets angry and offended
when I do.
I hurt
because she says people won't understand
about my problems
when she herself doesn't understand
or even try to.
I hurt
because she says people will think
I have a mental illness. Duh!
I hurt
because she's worried about the
"stigma"
and the image
and not about me.
I hurt
because she blames all of my problems
on my dad.
I hurt
because she interrupts me a lot.
I hurt
because she's disgusted by
the fact that I am seeing a

psychiatrist
and a psychologist.
I hurt
because she's still very, very angry
about me having accused Papa of abusing me
and she's never forgiven me for any of that.
I hurt
because she gets offended when
she asks me if I remember such and such
from my childhood
and I have to say no.
I hurt
because I know that I need to separate
from my mom
and yet I still feel so enmeshed and dependent on her.
I hurt
because Mom expects me to
fulfill all her dreams that she never fulfilled.
I hurt
because Mom thinks I don't
love her
if I don't do things for her,
when she wants them done,
the way she wants them done,
even wanting **my** things
done **her** way.
I hurt
because I've never heard her say
anything positive about me as a child.
I hurt
because Mom gives me a hard time
about not being married and
about her not having any grandchildren.
I hurt
because anger and confrontation were
allowed for my mom, but not for me.
I hurt
because my mom is manipulative with me.

Chapter 19: Mom

I hurt
because my mom always
invalidates my feelings.
I hurt
because I feel guilty about all the stuff
I'm saying about my mom since I love her
and there are times when we really get along
and have fun and laugh together.
I hurt
because I feel as if Mom loves my dogs
more than she loves me.

The hurt gradually lessened as I wrote about it, talked about it, and processed my feelings. It remains, but it isn't as intense. But hurt was not the only thing I had to deal with. My mother and grandmother were planning to visit for Thanksgiving that year. They were going to be in my house and I was going to have to set boundaries, like locking the bathroom door.

20

Boundaries & Image

Boundaries,
like the
lines in a
coloring book
of a four-year-old
child,
non-existent,
obscure
and blurred;
or,
like the
open barrier of
barbed wire—
a somewhat flimsy
barrier—
yet sharp,
cutting
and painful
for those who dare
to cross it;
or,
like the
thick,
towering walls
of the impenetrable
fortress,
forbidding,
prohibiting, and
preventing
anyone from
entering in.
Boundaries.

One of the family "rules" was that there were to be no boundaries between my mom and me. And there were none. Until 2003 or so, there was no physical privacy between my mom and me. Not when going to the bathroom, changing clothes, or taking a shower or bath. Even if I shut the door, which made her angry, she would walk right in. She felt she had a right to any part of my body, anytime she wanted. For example, she once said, "You need to let me see you with all your clothes off so I can see how much weight you've lost."

There were no boundaries regarding what she could talk about or comment on. My weight has always been a favorite topic of hers. Whether I have lost weight or gained weight, whether she thinks I am too thin or too fat, she freely made comments. And while she is extremely overweight, my weight was the topic of conversation, but her weight was off-limits. She didn't think there should be any boundaries related to my sex life with my husband. She made inappropriate comments and asked inappropriate questions, trying to gain intimate details. She didn't like the fact that Josh and I have set boundaries about what we will tell her regarding whether we will have children. She thinks she should know all.

I was in my early thirties when I finally started setting boundaries with my mother. I would either laugh off or not answer her invasive questions. I would shut and often lock the bathroom door. I made sure I changed clothes in as much privacy as possible. She didn't like my boundaries one bit. She would get upset and angry and I would hear about it. But I still set them. In the beginning, establishing boundaries with her proved difficult, because she was accustomed to violating them, but it got easier as I practiced.

One part of the "no boundaries" rule was that there should also be no secrets between my mom and me. This is one rule I'd been breaking for years. I kept many things from her because I knew that she either didn't want to or couldn't handle the information. Either that, or *I* couldn't handle her knowing. So I kept things from her, like the depression, the sexual stuff, the cutting, and any bad news about me.

This rule of no boundaries, no secrets was a double standard. There weren't supposed to be any boundaries between me and her, but she could put whatever boundaries she wanted between her and me. I wasn't supposed to have any secrets from her, but she could have secrets from me. She was entitled to know all about me, but not the other way around.

Chapter 20: Boundaries & Image

For this reason, Mom liked to believe that she and I were very close. That's what she told people. The reality is that I only let her see the little I wanted her to see. She liked to believe lots of things: I am perfect, she was a wonderful parent, the past (hers and mine) never happened. This poem shows the difference between what I showed Mom and reality, the part she didn't see. It shows what was on both sides of the boundary.

Outside....Inside

Slow moving,
silence around . . .
Mind careening,
no silence found.

Smile given,
innocence seen . . .
Smile vanquished,
heart is unclean.

Together with others,
never ignored . . .
Solitude only,
loneliness roars.

Awake and alert,
confusion no more . . .
Blurred and bewildered,
chaos at the fore.

Sanity noticed,
no scars or stains . . .
Forever branded,
insanity reigns.

At the beginning of therapy, the cutting was at the forefront because it was still an issue. Dealing with my mother was on the back burner. When I started dating Josh, my mother quickly moved to the front burner. Even though she had only met him briefly one time months before we began dating, and knew nothing about him, she did not like him and didn't want me dating him.

I was treated to a picture of how childish my mother could be. One of her friends, also a friend of mine and Josh's, tried on at least three occasions to talk to my mother about Josh, and my mother refused to talk to her! At spring break, my mother wanted me to visit, but when I told her I wanted to bring Josh, she said she didn't want him there. She wanted me to come, but by myself! When I called to tell her that I was going home with Josh to meet his family instead, she pitched a fit. One morning after Josh and I had been dating for several months, she called to tell me that she was "ready to meet him." I guess that was a good thing, because that very evening Josh asked me to marry him! Three weeks later she flew up to meet him.

The next three months were interesting as we prepared for the wedding. Josh had some issues in his past, before he became a Christian, and my mother was determined that nobody should find out about his past. All my life she had been trying to manage my image so that no one would know anything about my problems. Now she was trying to do the same thing with Josh!

21

Letters

Letters,
like telling stories, or
painting pictures, or
building bridges;
or,
like finally being able to
let out all of the
hurt and
fear and
anger and
dismay;
or,
like freedom to
speak my mind
without fear of
retribution.
Letters.

Once Josh and I were married she started to change in her attitude toward him. I continued to work with Gary, and the issue of my mother was increasingly the topic of conversation. During our first year of marriage I read a book about covert incest that affected me deeply. Covert incest, as defined by the author Kenneth Adams, "occurs when a child becomes the object of a parent's affection, love, passion and preoccupation. The parent, motivated by the loneliness and emptiness created by a chronically troubled marriage or relationship, makes the child a surrogate partner. The boundary between caring and incestuous love is crossed when the relationship with the child exists to meet the needs of the parent rather than those of the child."[4] As a result of reading the book, I wrote my mother a letter, one that she would never receive.

1-23-05

Dear Mom,

I've been reading a book lately and in it was the recommendation that I write you a letter, so I am. The book also recommended that I not give the letter to you, which frees me to be completely open and honest. And I think I shall do that very thing with this letter.

I guess I should tell you about this book I'm reading. It is called *Silently Seduced: When Parents Make Their Children Partners: Understanding Covert Incest*. The write-up on the back cover of the book asks two questions. First, "Did you have a parent whose love for you felt more confining than freeing, more demanding than giving, more intrusive than nurturing?" And, "Did you feel trapped in a 'psychological marriage' with this parent?" Then it says, "If so, you may be the victim of covert incest."[5] This book defines me—and you.

It says that in cases of covert incest, boundaries between parent and child do not exist where they should be present; rather these boundaries were violated, not physically as in overt incest, but covertly. Sexual? No, not really. But I **was** your surrogate husband. I did all the things your husband, if you had had one, would have done:

- yard work
- trash
- cleaning out
- lifting heavy stuff
- anything on the ladder
- going places with you where you didn't want to go by yourself (being your escort)
- you touching me all the time the way a wife would touch her husband (not sexually, but affectionately, and all the time; familiarly; intimately)

I think this all started around the time I was twelve.

I was a tomboy and you constantly made it clear that being a tomboy was not a good thing. You never felt like I did anything like a girl. You said I:

Chapter 21: Letters

- dressed like a boy
- walked like a boy
- laughed loudly like a boy
- sat and stood like a boy
- and every time I got my hair cut short you said I looked like a boy

I lost track of how many times you referred to me as being like or looking like a boy. Even when I got older and my breasts filled out—way out—you still said these things to me. I was a girl but it seemed as if you would have preferred that I had been a boy. You even did this with my dogs, saying Abbie should have been the boy dog and Patches the girl dog. And you use masculine terms to describe Abbie, the same ones you have always used to describe me. Why weren't you happy with me as a girl? You've never been pleased with me. I'm never good enough for you. Oh, you'll praise me plenty, but then you'll turn right around and criticize me. It just negates the praise.

Let's talk about boundaries:

1. When I was a kid until I was almost twenty-three years old, I called you "Mommie" and I called Grandma "Mom." I've never really thought about it before, but by making Grandma my "Mom," that gave you the freedom, so to speak, of having me in the husband role, even if it was completely unconscious.
2. Clothing–or maybe I should say lack thereof. I have always (at least until the last two years or so) walked around the house with little or nothing on, because that's what you did. And it has always been that way. Even when Papa was alive, he walked around in only his boxers. And remember the story you told me about you throwing cold water over the shower on Papa and him coming out of the shower and chasing you around the house with nothing on? Talk about not appropriate! And now that I'm careful about setting boundaries in this area, you make snide comments about my behavior. Or you want to see me with nothing on so you can see just how much weight I've lost. If I gain weight, are you going to want to see me with nothing on so you can see just how much weight I've gained?

3. Weight–my weight (not yours, only mine) has always been fair game for you. I'm too fat; I'm too thin; I've gained too much weight; I've lost too much weight; I'm going to gain too much if I eat that; I'm going to lose too much if I don't eat enough. There are no boundaries there.
4. My body. My body has never had any boundaries according to you. That's why I get so freaked out about keeping my scars hidden from you. I get comments from you all the time about my body: what I wear on it, how I hold myself, carry myself. You will comment freely on my makeup, my complexion, my hands, my weight, my hair, my clothes, my breasts, my feet.

Let's talk about secrets:

1. You and my dad planned together to always keep secret the circumstances of my conception and my birth. You both lied to me so many times, I never know whether to believe either of you.
2. Keeping my dad's identity secret, first from me, and later from anyone who might meet him.
3. Your frantic, almost desperate efforts to keep secret my struggles with depression, my hospitalizations (all three times), what I believe Papa did to me—even keeping things secret from Grandma.
4. Again, your frantic, almost desperate efforts to keep Josh's background hidden from anyone.
5. What other secrets are you keeping hidden? All this leads to the next subject.

Let's talk about image:

1. There is an unwritten rule in our family that says: Do nothing and say nothing to **ANYONE**, not even your best friend, that will in ANY FORM OR FASHION tarnish the PERFECT family image that we **MUST** maintain at **ALL COST!** At "ALL COST" includes the mental, emotional, and spiritual health of the youngest member of the family. That would be me. And you have worked diligently to keep the family image, and I have paid dearly.
2. Let's talk about how this family rule has been put into practice. When you took me to see the counselor when I was in middle school, you

told me not to tell anyone. I was in coun-se-ling. I was messed up. I had a prob-lem. And that problem better not get out to anyone!

3. At some point I learned that the rule not to talk about anything applied to discussing my dad. You never said anything bad about him while I was growing up, for which I am thankful. The problem is, you never said anything about him at all! You were keeping your own family rule, and I quickly learned that I was to keep it as well. I was not to talk about the fact that my parents were divorced. That has continued through the years to the point that before my wedding you wanted me to give you a picture of my dad from when he was younger and "still good-looking" so you could show your friends what he "used to look like." You didn't want anyone to meet him at my wedding and think, "Eeeough, yuck! She used to be married to that?!" "That," of course, referred to my dad and your opinion of his cowboy appearance. Once again, image. I happen to think his appearance is fine.

4. When Josh and I had just started dating, you said you couldn't stand the way he looked and that he had a cheesy grin. You said physical attraction is important, but he didn't have anything and you couldn't bear to look at him. That hurt me deeply. But frankly, I don't care what you think of my husband's looks. He's my husband, not yours, and I like what I see. I think my husband is a very handsome man. When he is being silly I think he looks very cute. There are tons of things I like about the way my husband looks, but I have absolutely no intention of telling you. Besides, your assessment of Josh was based on a two-minute meeting in a bookstore that had occurred months before we ever started dating. And about his "cheesy grin." I happen to love his grin. I find it very reassuring to know that my husband is basically a cheerful man. Let me be very clear on one thing. I'll put up with negative and critical comments from you about me, but Josh is off limits! You have NO right to say anything negative about him. That is one thing I will NOT TOLERATE! So...for the record, my husband is a very handsome man who has a very strong and beautiful body and whose really cute grin I really love. THAT is the truth about my Josh.

5. In early high school I was very shy and withdrawn, fearful, and self-conscious (not that I'm that much different now, just not as shy). I was very conscious of the image I was supposed to be projecting. By late high school I had come out of my shell, but I was still very much aware of the "image," especially my weight and how that played into it. I had

gained some weight and you made it clear how displeased you were about that. This has been an area of contention, an area of sensitivity, an area for "image" ever since.

6. In late high school I started going through a major depression again. When I contacted the same counselor, you got mad. You didn't want anyone knowing I was in counseling. And when I agreed to work at his ranch on Saturdays to pay for the counseling you wouldn't pay for, you got even angrier! You said if I told anyone I was working for the counseling, people might think we were poor or that my mom didn't manage her money well or something. You said I was to tell people (if I had to say anything at all) that I was working for a medical doctor friend (which he wasn't) and that I was getting paid (which I wasn't).

7. I learned that counseling and being in counseling were not good things for the image. I was in counseling the better part of my last three years in college. So I worked at doing what I had learned to do very well—hiding things. I learned how to lie to you very well.

8. After college I went away to grad school. I was also extremely depressed. I was still on your insurance, so I had to come home to go to a psychiatrist to get on an antidepressant. You were extremely concerned about anyone knowing. Then in May, I was hospitalized because I was so suicidal. You picked me up and we drove back home, where I admitted myself to a psychiatric hospital. I remember two things about this time. One, your demand that nobody know and two, the fact that what was happening to me was essentially ignored in all of our conversation. I was in the hospital for **six weeks** and not once did I feel any support or caring from you. I did feel your displeasure, disapproval, and anger at where I was and why. After I was released, I moved back in with you. That was probably a big mistake, but I didn't have anywhere else to go.

9. When I accused Papa of sexually abusing me, you said you found it hard to believe. You said you would only believe me because it was me, but you really didn't believe me at all. I never felt your support. All I ever felt was your anger. And once again, you focused on maintaining the image. You made it crystal clear who I was and was not allowed to tell, mostly "was not's," because it reflected on you! I don't understand how what he did reflects on you, but that was your attitude!

10. When I was hospitalized again in 1993, it was the "protect the family image" thing all over again. It felt like the family image was more

important to you than I was. You have no clue what all I went through, and you made it clear you did not want to know. As long as I kept my mouth shut, you were happy.

11. Here's something you don't know that I guarantee you would be horrified about if you did, because it strikes at your image big time. At Christmas break in 1992, I had just made contact again with my dad. I went with him that December to have DNA testing done to make sure he was my father. That has a whole world of emotions for me, in and of itself. I know it would create image problems for you if anyone knew (which some people do, so there!).

12. Between 1996 and 2000 I had what I would call a crisis of faith. I felt like I was running away from God. But really, I never gave up on God. During that time I was in counseling with three different people, trying to get better, to change, to heal. Finally, I knew that if the last lady I was counseling with couldn't help me, that was it. Killing myself would be it. On November 17, 2000, I realized that I could change, that I could trust God, that I was responsible for how I reacted to my problems. I couldn't just blame my parents anymore. I describe it as the day I came back to God. It was a very important day for me. A year later I wanted to have a celebration on the anniversary. I decided to let you in on what I was celebrating since the party was going to be at your house, where I was still living. I took you out to eat and I told you my story. The first words out of your mouth were, "Who knows about this?" You were horrified when I told you. You were concerned about why you weren't in the know, why were you just now finding out all this. You didn't know precisely because of your response. All you care about is your stupid image. Who cares that I experienced deep depression and wanted to die? Who cares that I nearly lost my faith? Who cares that I went through all that garbage? Who cares that I finally came back to God? Obviously, not you! And because of that I feel like dirt.

13. In 2002 I had a defining moment. I moved out of your house to go back to school. It was about time. I was thirty-two years old! I moved to a city eight hours away from you. Being away from you gave me the freedom to finally start dealing with you, and that fall I started going through another major depression. In July of 2003 I was hospitalized again. Because I was away from you, you didn't know about it at the time. When you came to visit me, I had been out of the hospital only

three days. I decided to tell you. Once again, the first words out of your mouth were, "Who knows about this?" Your obvious concern for your image obliterates any concern you might have for me. And knowing that hurts.

14. Because of how ugly you acted about Josh when we first started dating, I didn't tell you much of anything about him until after we were engaged and you came to meet him. We had a very emotional discussion in which one statement made your image mindset crystal clear. You said, "Grandma and I don't want anyone to know about this," referring to Josh's background. Never mind about grace, about a changed and transformed life, about the power of personal testimony. Only mind about your stupid family image, what people might think, how you look to others. You have absolutely NO CLUE what an incredible transformation God did in Josh's life. My husband is the most intelligent, funniest, gentlest, most honorable man I have ever met and you are clueless because of your stupid image complex! We will not hide!

15. One last thing. What makes me so angry about all of this image crap is that I have taken on some of that mindset myself. I'm not nearly as bad as you. But I absolutely HATE what is there. I HATE what you have done to me with all this.

Once again I have managed to get all worked up over you. I could probably go on forever in this letter, but I shall not. I've made my point. There are a thousand more things I feel I need to write, but not to you. I shall use my journal or other ways. I'm finished with this letter.

I have vented and dumped a whole bunch on you. None of this means that I don't love you. I love you anyway. I fear the loss of your love. I fear that your love is conditional. Indeed, I'm sure it is. Know that mine is not. I love you despite what you've done to me.

I'm having great difficulty closing this letter. But I'll never be giving this to you. You'll never be reading these words, so it doesn't really matter. Know that I love you.

Rochelle

P.S. I love you. I hate what your dysfunction has done to me. I have lots of scars because of you, emotional scars on my mind and heart and physical

CHAPTER 21: LETTERS

scars where I have cut my body with razors because of the emotional distress in my heart. Live with that.

I was an emotional wreck for about a month after writing that letter. I sealed it in a plain brown envelope and took a sealed copy of it to Gary. He read it but I didn't want to talk about it, so we didn't. Occasionally I would refer to it, but mostly I just ignored it. I did, however, feel that writing that letter was somewhat of a breakthrough, and in August of that year, after my mom came up to visit Josh and me for a week, I painted another picture. Shortly after I started therapy with Gary, I had painted a picture entitled *Is It Possible?* with a face and a solid brick wall with blue sky on the opposite side of the wall from the face. The new picture looked the same, except that there was a crack in the brick wall. I was finally breaking through the impenetrable, inescapable fortress. But I still had a long way to go. The crack was small and filled with tears, and as Gary pointed out, I still had no eyes on my face.

In June of 2006, after Josh and I graduated from Bible school, we moved to another city for his job. It was a good move professionally, but it had its drawbacks. I would now be continuing my therapy with

Gary over the telephone. And this move put us closer to my mother. Where before we were eight hours away from her, now we were only three. In the middle of all the craziness with moving, she begged and cajoled me to come home and take care of her so she could have hand surgery, despite the fact that my grandmother lived only eight blocks away from my mother and that my mother had a church full of friends to help her. No, she wanted me. She wanted me to drop everything and cater to her every need, just like she has wanted me to do my entire life. And instead of taking care of getting settled after a major move, I took care of her. I had only been in my new home for a few days when I found myself driving to hers.

Since the move she has done everything she could to get me there as often as possible. Sometimes I have given in and gone, sometimes I have stood firm. She has been here, too. Lots more than I've wanted. Having her this close has made my issues regarding her come to the forefront again. And there were new issues I had to deal with, things about men and marriage and babies. In September of 2006, I wrote her another letter. Again, a letter she would never see.

9-20-06
5:30 a.m.

Dear Mom,

I've been lying awake for over an hour thinking that I needed to write you a letter. You need to understand some things. First of all, I love being married and Josh is the perfect husband for me. You can't possibly understand since your own marriage lasted all of six months and since you went into your marriage with all the wrong reasons and circumstances. You were so concerned about the age difference between Josh and me. But Mom, the age difference between you as a 19-year-old kid and my dad as a 32-year-old **married** man is vastly different than the age difference between Josh and me, as two mature adults. Vastly different.

I act like a married woman because I want to. I am a married woman because I want to be, no thanks to you. When I got married I really didn't know how to cook. You didn't bother to teach me. I had to learn on my own. And I love cooking for my husband because it brings him so much pleasure. You can't understand that because, in your opinion, anything that isn't done

CHAPTER 21: LETTERS

for yourself isn't worth being done. Oh, I'm sorry, am I implying that you are selfish? Well, actually, yes, I am. But don't worry; other people won't think that about you because you do such a great job of image-managing.

You know, as long as I'm in the mode of sarcasm, how about this one. You did such a great job of preparing me for marriage, for being a wife. Frankly, I don't know how in the world I have managed to be a good wife (Josh and others tell me I am). You certainly didn't teach me. What did you teach me about men and marriage? You taught me that men were useful for fixing things and lifting things. Then you used me to fill that role in your life. You taught me that men were useful for providing you with an escort and driving. Then you used me to fill that role. You taught me that I didn't need a man, that women were better off without them. You taught me that men didn't play a necessary role in the family. You taught me that marriage was a selfish game to be played. You taught me that marriage was good because then you could have sex and babies without getting in trouble. You taught me tons about men and marriage, but nothing that was of any benefit. Why? Because my marriage is based on sacrificial love, something you know very little about.

Let's talk about babies. Unlike you and my dad, Josh and I are putting a lot of time and thought and prayer and conversation into the idea of having a child. Raging hormones, unprotected sex, "it can't happen to me," and "unplanned parenthood" are miles away from our situation. Josh and I have made the prayerful, well-thought-out decision that we do not want to have a child. And before you start slamming Josh, know this. Our decision was made largely because of how *I* feel about it, not Josh. It's a decision that I believe was made unselfishly. Your decision to have a child, if you can call it a decision, was made selfishly. You didn't wait until you got married to have sex. You didn't want to have protected sex. You didn't even want to wait until you found someone who was available to get married. You had a baby without thought to how her life would be affected by your immature, selfish actions. And now you want me to have a baby. And your desire for me to have a baby is rooted in the same selfish motives. All your friends are having grandchildren and you want one, too. Our decision is a little more mature, a little more thought out than that. I've always jumped through hoops for you, but I'm not going to jump through hoops for you on this. I don't have to explain myself to you. I'm under no obligation to explain to you all our reasons for not having a child. Because you can't understand. And I don't have to try and make you understand.

There are lots of things that Josh and I do wrong, lots of ways that we act selfishly. But like I said before, there is a vast difference between a 19-year-old and her married lover having a baby and a mature, married couple making the decision not to have a baby. A vast difference.

There's another vast difference between you and me, Mom. It's called image-managing. I said you didn't have to worry about people thinking you're selfish. You're able to convince people otherwise to the extent that only a few people see it. Are you selfish all the time? No, but for the most part you are. I see it particularly in the way you treat Grandma and it makes me mad. Most people don't see the selfishness. They don't see how critical you are of me. They don't see the childishness, because you put on a good image for them. You're so good at this that through the years you have managed to convince several of my closest friends that you are simply wonderful, despite what I'd told them to the contrary. I feel sorry for them because your image-managing has conned them into thinking you're someone you're not. Only Grandma, Josh, and I see the real you.

The worst part about all this image-managing crap is how you have tried to manage me all my life. You have always tried to manage my clothes, my hair, my makeup, my friends, my activities, and even my emotions, but it didn't always work. And when I bucked you, did I ever feel your displeasure! The worst was with my personal life. You image-managed my dad completely out of my life by never talking about him at all. And when I decided I wanted to meet him, you weren't happy at all. You've always been concerned about how it affected you, not me.

And let's talk about my depression and the hospitalizations. Yes, all three of them. Your image-managing took prominence over any concern you might otherwise have had for your daughter. "Don't tell anyone. Who knows about this? I don't want anyone to know about this." Never mind what I was going through. Just make sure to keep it quiet. Don't let the elders know. Don't tell anyone. You cared more about your stupid image than you did about me! Conclusion: I am not allowed to be sad because it interferes with your image. And what about on the other end of the spectrum? The most joyous time in my life was marred, once again because of your concern about image. Instead of sharing my joy about Josh and the wedding, you were worried about protecting your image by keeping us quiet about Josh's background and worried about what people would think about you when they met my dad at the wedding. Conclusion: I am not allowed to be happy because it interferes with your image.

Chapter 21: Letters

There is a lot of hurt when it comes to you. And there is a lot of anger. Maybe I will get past all this junk eventually. Well, Mom, I have said all I'm going to say at this point. Despite all the hurt and anger, I still love you.

Rochelle

P.S. I only thought I was done with this letter. Here's something else. I am no longer at your complete beck and call, no longer your puppet to manipulate or cater to your every whim. I have my own family now and that comes first. I say this and I do feel this way, so why do I always feel as if I am the one in the wrong when I stand up to you? Somehow I have got to convince myself that I have the right to be an individual, to have a life outside of you. On some level I have bought into your view that I am just an appendage of you. I'm not here for you to boss around or control anymore. I can write these things to you here, knowing I will never give you this letter, but I cannot say them to your face. I mentioned the hurt and the anger. There is also a lot of fear when it comes to you, always has been. I am afraid of standing up to you, afraid of your displeasure, your anger, your disapproval. And I don't know why. Josh says, "Why are you so afraid of that silly woman?"

And I wonder why in the world I want your approval so much. Why is it so important to me? Because it's never forthcoming. Instead I get the criticism, especially if I don't do things exactly the way you want them, exactly as you think they ought to be. I am so sick of your "oughts," literally. You make me sick. As Gary put it recently, you are "poison to me."

22
Revelation

Revelation,
like a
blind man
receiving his sight;
or,
like Saul on the
road to Damascus;
or,
like the unmasking of the
Phantom of the Opera;
or,
like a baby
learning to talk
and walk,
opening up a
whole new world.
Revelation.

In February 2007 my great-aunt died. She had no children and my mother and I were both very close to her. After spending six days with my mother dealing with cousins and funeral homes and nursing homes and my aunt's possessions, I was fit to be tied.

Ode to Mom

"I love you, too,"
but I can't stand you;
that's how I feel,
yes, I'm for real.

My mother you are—
I wish you were away very far.
Don't want to hear your voice,
sometimes I've got no choice.

Can't stand the sight of you,
you touch me and I go "eugh."
You literally make me sick,
you suck me dry like a tick.

I may be your girl,
but you make me want to hurl.
This poem is for you.
I think you're full of pooh.

I was having revelations about my mother and I realized that I really don't like her very much. I had been seeing things about her that I didn't like for several years, but this trip crystallized them for me. During those six days I made lots of little notes and wrote down as much as possible. The baby issue came up, even during this sad time. In fact, my mother brought it up the morning of my aunt's funeral. And of course she used the hit and run tactic. We were getting ready to go to the funeral, for crying out loud.

Her - So, have you and Josh just decided not to have kids?
Me - (being a coward) We don't know.
Her - What do you mean you don't know?
Me - (retreating down the hallway to the bathroom sanctuary, calling her names in my head) Just that, we just don't know yet.
Her - (speaking to the bathroom door) You can't just not know. Either you're going to have kids or you're not!
Me - (in hiding in the bathroom) We don't know yet!
Her - (silent treatment)
Me - (in my head) Of course we're not going to have kids! You think I want to have kids and do to them what you did to me?!

Chapter 22: Revelation

I actually did quite well on that trip, all things considered. There were a number of areas where I was able to set boundaries. Instead of trying to solve my mother's problems, as I usually did, I let her deal with things on her own. She was complaining about not having a camera and not being able to get pictures of the things she wanted to in the little town where the burial was held. Initially I thought maybe I could let her use my camera and then get it back from her sometime later or I could go up to the store and buy her a disposable one. But I quickly put those thoughts out of my head. Instead, I remembered that I don't have to solve her problems. It wasn't my problem and I didn't have to solve it. I set boundaries about who was going to ride with me on the four-hour trip to the cemetery. And she wanted me to stay overnight again instead of driving back to my home right after the burial, but I went home.

One thing has bugged me about my mom for a long time and really ate at me on this trip. She always wants to touch me. I want to slap her hands away. I feel repulsed and get angry when she touches me. I'm a very touchy-feely person with my husband. I am always touching him. I guess I get that from her. But I'm almost sickened by her touch. The longer I was there, the worse it got. She rubs on my back, when we are walking together she puts her hand through my arm. She always wants to hold my hand, touch my knee, scratch my back, hug me, kiss me, hold my arm. I don't want to be rude by pulling away, but I cannot stand it! I feel as if it is all an act, a phony act. Gary said he thinks that the way she touches me all the time is part of that covert incest.

That particular trip also confirmed for me, once again, that my problems do not matter to her. She found out I was not eating sugar and asked me why. I told her it was to help my anxiety. She said, "Anxiety? What anxiety? Since when do you have anxiety?" I was furious, but I calmly responded, "Mother, I've had anxiety for a long time. You know that." When we were driving to meet the preacher who was conducting the funeral, she talked to me about some things my aunt had written in her funeral preparations about having had lots of adversity in her life. My mother then said, "I don't know what adversity she's talking about. I guess she means her father abandoning them and her husband dying, but that's not adversity," she laughed. "That's just part of life." Not adversity? Well, my father abandoning me was certainly adversity to me! I would say that my great-aunt's father abandoning them and her husband dying young fit the definition of adversity. I would like to know what definition my mother was working from! That comment from my mother just showed again that she minimizes and negates people's problems. She has no empathy.

My great-aunt was quite elderly and had lots of anxiety. She saw a psychiatrist and took various medications. I have lots of anxiety. I see a psychiatrist and take various medications. She freely talked with other people about my aunt's problems. But my mother refuses to talk about my problems—with me, to me, with anyone else. And I am her daughter! What about *my* anxiety? What about *my* medications? Why is it that she cared so deeply about her aunt's mental health problems but she has never cared about mine?

That trip opened my eyes to my mother's behavior. I saw examples of how she has double standards, is completely self-absorbed, considers me her "grunt," puts on a good show for others, always tries to "orchestrate" things to her advantage, is a study in contrasts, bosses and manipulates my grandmother and me, constantly bombards me with "shoulds" and "oughts," bullies people, and basically suffocates me! And she is still up to her same old stuff.

After that trip, I asked Josh, "Where does she stop and I begin?" He said, "Your soul is your own." He talked about the enmeshment and that I now had to decide what were my beliefs and what were hers, what were my values and what were hers, what were my preferences and what were hers. Then he said, "You're on a great voyage of discovery as you create you." Discovery means I am seeing things. I ran to get the two pictures I had painted with the walls and no eyes. I explained to Josh the connection that I was seeing between my mother and the way I had painted the pictures with no eyes. I began crying; no, weeping, sobbing wracking sobs. I was having a catharsis.

I was finally seeing my mother with open eyes. I painted a third picture in the wall series the next day. My eyes were beginning to open. I was beginning to see. There were still a lot of tears, but the joy was beginning to seep into my life… Over the next six months in therapy with Gary I focused on my mother. Josh and I spent many hours talking about her and her impact on my life and what I needed to do to change. To change myself. I knew I couldn't change her. It was a revelation to me to understand that I don't have to be the kind of person my mother is. It

CHAPTER 22: REVELATION

was a revelation to me to recognize that I don't have to be chained down by her, that I can change myself and be a whole person in spite of her. Those revelations liberated me and that freedom brought joy!

23

Joy

Joy,
like an elusive
nocturnal animal,
hiding in the shadows,
creeping far away from
exposure;
or,
like the dawning of a
new day,
light slowly edging
over the horizon,
peeking over the treetops,
illuminating the darkness;
or,
like a thunderous trumpet section
in a glorious symphony,
regal and bold,
exploding with
beauty and
radiance and
Joy.

My mother visited us for a week in August 2007, and the weeks that followed were emotionally exhausting as I finally came to grips with my mother. My eyes were completely open in regard to her. I began to acknowledge that my mother lives in a fantasy world with respect to me and our relationship. She isn't psychotic in the way that psychiatrists use that term. She isn't seeing or hearing things that aren't there due to a malfunctioning brain. Rather, by an act of her own volition, she refuses to accept reality. She refuses to accept the reality of the circumstances of my conception or of her marriage and divorce. She desperately wants to believe that all is wonderful. She is a wonderful mother. I am a wonderful daughter. We are so close and very much alike. When my mental health problems rear their ugly heads, she doesn't appreciate the evidence that her world is a fantasy of her own creation. Instead of dealing with reality, she ignores it as best she can. She protects the fantasy at all costs, because reality is so ugly. Otherwise, she would be forced to face her own flaws, weaknesses, failings, poor decisions, and sinfulness, which she is totally unwilling to do.

I wrote a third never-to-be-shared letter to my mother. In it I discussed a memory that I had of my childhood that I had never been willing to talk about before.

8-18-2007

Dear Mom,

Once again I am sitting down to write you a letter. This is the third letter in three years. Hopefully this one will be much shorter than the others. I will only be addressing one issue.

You know, because you have been told, that I have very few memories from my childhood. When I was hospitalized that first time in 1992, one of the things that was at the forefront was my lack of memories. Now, whether or not you have chosen to remember that information is another story, since you conveniently forget what you don't want to remember. It's like when you said, "Anxiety? What anxiety? Since when do you have anxiety?" You knew perfectly well that anxiety was a problem for me; you just chose to forget. Anyway, the point is, I have very few memories from my childhood. Because of that, I pay a great deal of attention to the ones I do have. I want to talk to you about a memory I do have.

I must have been about seven or eight years old. We were in the den. Do you remember that brown and orange oval rug and that green ottoman? I don't remember what I'd done to make you so mad, but you were angry with me. No, you were furious. And you were yelling. I was terrified. I'm actually feeling a lot of fear right now just writing this. You were going to spank me. You were yelling at me and swinging your arm around, trying to hit me, I guess on the bottom. I don't remember if you were holding a paddle, a switch, a belt, or what. In my child's eye it seemed like it was a whip! But you were flailing around, yelling at me, hitting at me, and I was scrambling, trying frantically, vainly, to hide behind this big green stool we had. I felt like a tiny ant. You were so huge and so angry. I don't remember where all your blows fell, but I remember the yelling and my pathetic efforts to hide from you behind the green ottoman. I remember you lashing out at me wildly, again and again. Do you remember this? I do.

Last September I drew a picture of this memory. I entitled it, *Is There a Monster Side of Mom?* That day you were a monster. I've always remembered this incident, but I never spent much time thinking about it because I was always terrified of the implications. I never wanted to deal with it before. Even when I drew the picture for Gary last September, I didn't deal with it. But it is at the forefront now and I can't help but deal with it because I can't help but think about it, the incident specifically and your anger in general. And here's my question—was this an isolated incident or were there others? There are some other memories I have that seem related. I remember as a child that I was very frightened of your anger. And I can remember several times when I hid from you in my closets. Why did I hide from you? Why was I so afraid of you?

Is There A Monster Side of Mom?

Why am I still so afraid of you? Even now, as I gain more and more insights, I am still afraid of you. Why? Is it something that started way back with the green ottoman? There are some things I don't remember. Do you? Will you admit it?

Despite my fear of you, I love you.

Rochelle

My fear of her anger has always been prominent.. As I continued to think and write and pray and explore, I had a number of new insights about my mother, not just about her anger. Some were pretty simple, some were complex. I made a detailed list of them in my journal. One of my insights had to do with when I recanted my accusation that my grandfather had sexually abused me. I did that about three and a half years after I made the accusation in 1992.

New Insights
1. The idea that fear is a choice
2. Mom's anger
   a. third letter to Mom
   b. I have always been, and still am, deeply frightened by my mother's anger. Are these few memories I have simply clues to a much bigger problem?
   c. "You were a rotten kid." I've been told this many times through the years. She usually tempered her words by adding that I was a pretty good teenager. Maybe it was her way of justifying her behavior to herself. If it was my fault (I was so rotten) how could she not have responded as she did (lashing out in anger). She may have been a very angry young woman who deeply resented me (being stuck with a baby); she was young, immature, and has always been quite emotional. It's highly likely that she was very angry. Even so, why would a mother say that to her daughter? Talk about hurt! Her anger hurts and telling me I was a rotten kid hurts!
   d. I was so focused on my grandfather, I didn't think about the possibility that there might be more angles to consider. I either never thought about her anger being part of my problem or I refused to think about it.

3. Eye contact with Mom—Avoiding eye contact typically means either you are lying or you are not comfortable. My avoiding eye contact with her telegraphs my discomfort and if she knew anything at all about body language, she would pick up on it. Josh realized that he avoids eye contact with her, too, probably because he knows so much about her now, feels she is a phony, and isn't comfortable around her.
4. She thinks my primary loyalty should be to her and not to Josh. She refuses to recognize what the Bible says about leaving and cleaving.
5. Gary says that she won't abandon me. I'm all she has.
6. Therapy is a process. It's like a detective story. When I started my book I thought it was all about my grandfather, but as I've continued I've realized that he's only part of the story.
7. My mother targets my friends. Because of the enmeshment there is another family rule I hadn't thought of before—I am not allowed to have friends that aren't her friends, too. This really only became an issue after I graduated from high school She's done this particularly with Salli, Claire, and Melanie. She's tried with some of my other friends as well. She's even tried to do this with Miss Penny. I've had two friends through the years that she didn't like at all, and she didn't hesitate to express her displeasure that I was friends with them and try to drive a wedge between us. I've seen her trying to do the same thing with Josh and me. Once again, there are no boundaries with her. I'm not supposed to have a life apart from her. If she can't cut off my relationships, she inserts herself into them and co-opts my friends. She makes sure it's her relationship, too. The friendship is no longer uniquely mine.
8. My friend Salli—She was sexually abused when she was four by her mother's boyfriend. When she was five, she was taken out of the home and given to her adoptive parents, who then raised her in a stable, Christian home. She once asked me, "Why can't you just get over it? I was sexually abused and I've never had all these problems." Josh pointed out that Salli had been taken out of the situation she was in and was put in a stable one. I stayed in my unhealthy family system. I was never rescued. Salli got rescued, while I had to stay in the toxic swamp.

9. I wonder what my mother's home life was like when she was a child. Did he sexually abuse her, too? How could my grandfather have known how to have been a good father? His own father abandoned his family when Papa was only about four years old. That is an example of the generational thing you see in Scripture, the father's sins passed on to the third and fourth generations UNLESS someone very intentionally says enough is enough! That's what I am trying to do! That's what the picture *Generations* is all about. All this crazy dysfunction has run in the family and it's time for it to end. I can be different. I'm not just a reflection of my mom, mirroring her dysfunctions and flaws, passing the dysfunction down from generation to generation.

10. Josh said I didn't turn out like my mother because I wasn't allowed to be like her. I was there to serve her and from that I learned service. I'm also not like her because I am a truth-seeker.
11. A mother's love should be like a rock to a child. Josh never doubted his mother's love. He said it must be horrifying to doubt your mother's love.
12. Maybe she never wanted to think of herself as a parent. She would prefer to think of herself as my sister. She loved it when people would refer to us as sisters. I hated it!. In a sense, we were like sisters. I called Grandma "Mom" until I was twenty-two years old. So we were both calling the same woman "Mom." Apparently my grandma was the grown up in the family, the mother figure, whereas my mom was still acting like a child.
13. One sign of growing mental health will be when I don't feel the urge to call my mother. For example, when I made homemade cinnamon rolls I called her to tell her. I wanted her praise and approval.
14. Unless more memories come back, it seems I am very near the core of the onion, if not already there. What Gary said in the very first session is true. My mother is at the heart of my problems.
15. I grew up in an environment of deceit. When a child grows up in such an environment, it has far-reaching consequences on the child's mental health. Children who are told one thing but then see another begin to wonder if they are crazy. A child needs to know he can trust his parents and his own senses. My environment was one of deceit. I was lied to about certain things. I was told to lie about certain things. I was encouraged to lie about lots of little things. I learned how to lie—from her. And there were lots of secrets in our family. In short, truth wasn't valued.
16. In her case, the deception shows up with the fantasy. One way I've added to the deception was by "protecting" my mom by not telling her things. I allowed her to maintain the fantasy. But problems don't go away by pretending they're not there. This fantasy world she has created works for her, but I've been paying for it. She's paid some. She's completely lost the ability to have a healthy relationship with her daughter or with anyone, for that matter. She would rather sacrifice me than sacrifice her fantasy. That's where all my sadness is coming from.

17. Recanting–I keep thinking about this. I accused my grandfather of molesting me in 1992 when I was hospitalized for six weeks. I was hospitalized again in 1993 for four weeks. When I made the accusations, my mother was extremely upset and angry. She said she would believe me because it was me, but that she didn't really believe me because it couldn't possibly be true. All I felt was her anger and disapproval. Never once did I feel any concern or compassion or love. Only her anger. She was angry with me for what I'd done to her and the whole family, and she told me as much. Then in the summer of 1995 I read a book about false memories by a guy in one of those "anti-psychology" groups. I became convinced that, because I didn't really have any memories, I must have had false memories. So at Christmastime 1995, I recanted my accusation against Papa. I told Mom and Grandma and my great-aunt I'd had false memories. Okay, so it was done. The long saga was over. But something kept nagging at me. Several somethings. There were still all the symptoms, all the clues. There was still the depression, the sexual stuff, and the huge chunk of missing memories. I wondered who had abused me if he hadn't because I knew someone had. And I often wondered if I had been wrong in recanting, if he really had abused me. In 2002/2003, when the depression returned full force, when the masturbation and cutting came back with a vengeance and escalated to new heights, I knew I had screwed up by recanting. Josh asked why I fell so completely under the sway of that anti-psychology group. I was trying to live the fantasy. My mother was so furious at my original accusation and my grandma and great-aunt so upset, that I convinced myself my accusations were untrue. I was trying to live the fantasy; at least, I was trying to let my mother live the fantasy. I ignored my own experience, my own emotions, my own reality—for her fantasy. My father and grandfather betrayed me. Even my mother betrayed me by her fantasy world that ignored my mental illness. And in the recanting, I betrayed myself.
18. My mother has warped things for me, things like having children, watching mothers with their children, Mother's Day, trust (she wasn't alone on this one). She has also warped my concept of God (she wasn't alone on this one either) by not being what a

mother should be, not being a rock for me, not being trustworthy, not being someone I could go to, not showing unconditional love. She modeled a false god to me. She has also warped me when it comes to service, doing things for others. I often do things out of guilt. She has guilted me into so many things through the years and has put so many guilt trips on me that guilt is practically a permanent part of my life. She has also warped me in the sense that I feel like I have to explain myself for everything. Gary tells me I don't have to explain myself, but I feel like I do. This may be one aspect of the guilt thing.

19. Why is it I always want to share stuff with her? Oh, I need to tell Mom this. Mom would get a kick out of that. It's because my whole life revolves around her; habit. It's like an alcoholic making up excuses to drink. Keep going back to the poison, because you're addicted. Am I addicted to my mother? It's that enmeshment. I'm still struggling to cut the ties. I'm getting there. My relationship with her has never been healthy or normal. She views me as an appendage of her, with no independent existence. It's like she wants to be the god of my life. When she took me to counseling when I was twelve, I was a problem she wanted fixed. And besides, the school was urging her to take me. When I took myself to counseling in high school, she was angry. The fact that I had a problem didn't matter. I don't matter to my mother. Well, on some level I do, but mostly for what I can do for her. She is an extreme example of self-idolatry. We all struggle with it, wanting to be our own god, run our own lives. But she may have always been the queen bee.

As I dealt with all of these new insights, I found myself being incredibly sad, especially about my mother's anger and the recanting.

> What is going on with me?
> What am I feeling here?
> My heart is heavy laden
> and my spirit feels no cheer.
>
> I've lately gained new insights
> into my years gone by,

and what I've learned seems to tell me
that someone's been living a lie.

The wonderful mother she says she was
may not have been quite so –
I really have known that all along,
but my new insights have brought me so low.

Thinking about her anger
and what it has done to me
fills me up with great sorrow –
will my heart from sadness ever be free?

I lived as a child full of fear,
full of trepidation for my angry mom.
I've tried to avoid this subject,
but it crashes down on me like a bomb.

And now that I'm in my late thirties,
I have to deal with these memories so bad.
Oh, why must I contend with her anger?
It makes my heart so very sad.

After a week and a half of intense, obsessive thinking and writing, Gary told me that I had to shut it off. I was literally making myself sick. I wasn't sleeping. I had a visual hallucination. Gary told me to force myself to stop thinking and stop writing. So I did. I stopped writing. I forced myself to get busy doing other things. The result was an incredible sense of sadness, calm sadness. It took about three weeks of feeling weird to get to the point that I felt better. Gary said the fact that I was able to shut it off for several weeks showed that I can deal with my issues in a non-obsessive way. I still found the sadness very powerful, and Gary commented a number of times that the more we see reality, the more sadness there is. It's like what Solomon said in Ecclesiastes 1:18, "For with much wisdom comes much sorrow; the more knowledge, the more grief." Gary counseled me to try to find things each day that I found enjoyable. I had to be intentional about enjoying things. He said that I've learned to

CHAPTER 23: JOY

live on the edge of arousal so that normal life just doesn't feel normal to me. I fear the humdrum of life. But life doesn't have to be that way; thus, the need for me to be intentional about finding things to enjoy. Little by little the sadness lifted. It was still there, but it wasn't as heavy. Gary gave me permission to spend an hour a day writing, but only if I wanted to. I didn't have to spend time focusing on all the issues, but if I did, to work only for an hour.

I was amazed to feel that I might finally be able to say some of these things to my mom. Not sarcastically, of course, but the fear was beginning to subside. Gary said knowledge dispels fear. I was gaining knowledge about my mother, what she really is like, and the fear was beginning to be dispelled.

My fears started with my mother and they have grown and spread over the years to include many things. Therapy was like an onion, peeling back layers until now there was one layer left—my mother. There was also one emotion left—fear. Most of my fears are irrational fears, fears that don't need to be there, like the fear of my mother. That one fear included many facets: fear of her abandoning me, fear of not measuring up to her expectations, fear of not having her approval and not pleasing her, terror that she would find out certain things about me (my depression, the sexual issues, the cutting, etc.), fear that she would be unhappy with me or angry at me, fear of her anger. It almost paralyzed me at times. But as I continued to see her more clearly, the fear was fading.

Gary also told me that fear, particularly irrational fear, is a choice. I can choose to be afraid or I can say I don't want that anymore. Intrigued, I tested that idea. I was watching *Clash of the Titans* with my husband. In it are a number of scenes that I typically would consider frightening, including witches cooking people in their brew, two-headed wolves attacking, Medusa in her lair fighting with the heroes and ultimately getting her head cut off, a skeleton steering a boat, giant scorpions, and a sea creature attacking a city. Normally I would either not watch the movie at all or I'd leave the room or hide my eyes and plug my ears through much of the show. I would obsess about it for days, working myself up into a mass of fear. That night, I thought about fear being a choice. When I have irrational fears, I can choose to let the fear win, or I can choose not to be afraid of what reality says is not fearful in the first place. So during the movie, as a "scary" part approached, I reminded myself that my fear was irrational. This was only a movie. I did not have to be afraid. I kept at it throughout the movie and to my amazement, I watched the entire movie without hiding my eyes even once! I'd never done that before! I had chosen not to be afraid! When the movie ended I jumped up and down and hugged Josh, crying tears of joy because the implications of what I had discovered were far-reaching.

This applied to my mom and my fears of her. Now, when I found myself being afraid of her, I could tell myself the same thing. I don't have to be afraid. Fear is a choice. This is only my immature, selfish mother, not some monster from the deep, dead-set on eating me for lunch. This knowledge will help dispel the fear and keep me from giving in to her and being sucked into her dysfunction. Why? Because I'll have the courage to stand up to her. I'll have the strength to set boundaries with her. I'll have the will not to let the fear paralyze me.

Eyes Open, Walls Down, Fear Gone

One evening, talking with Josh, I said that by bringing things into the light, talking about things and processing things, my problems were losing their power. The twinges of sadness I had were healthy and different from all the depression that used to be so overwhelming. The depression and addictive behaviors were the results of not dealing with things. I was more and more able to work my way out of the sadness, anxiety, or weird mood. I was forcing myself to focus on something else. I was learning to master my emotions because I was learning to control my thoughts. I had a picture in my mind, a fourth picture in the wall series. I grabbed a sheet of paper and quickly sketched what I later painted, a picture with a face from the full front view, a slight smile and a few tears on her cheek, looking through the blue sky that had pierced a broken down wall. My eyes were open, the walls were down, and the fear was gone.

I had finally broken through the barrier to joy. The barrier was my fear of dealing with my mother and not viewing her realistically. I finally looked at everything, saw it for what it was, articulated it, talked about it, and in so doing, I dealt with it. I accepted it. A couple of nights later, we were sitting at the dinner table talking when I began crying tears of joy. I felt an incredible sense of joy, mingled with sadness, but joy nonetheless. My joy sneaked up on me. It wasn't what I'd expected. I had expected fireworks and bells and whistles, not quiet joy, not sad joy. It was a joy that wasn't just a feeling. It was an attitude, one that would require discipline to maintain. It would be easy for me to allow myself to fall back into the trap of living with an undisciplined mind. This joy, as Gary said, wasn't based on some energy high. It was a quiet, sustainable joy. He also reminded me that the joy of the Lord didn't mean the absence of tears. It's a peaceful, contented joy even in the presence of tears. And that joy has sustained itself despite my struggles.

My mother and grandmother came to our house for Thanksgiving. When my mother found out that I didn't recycle my plastic bags from the grocery store, her face contorted with disgust as she said to me, "You are a terrible person!" She was serious. I was very proud of my reaction to her. I responded very calmly, "No Mother, I'm not." I still had to contend with her, but I was healthier and stronger than I'd ever been.

When I first started therapy with Gary, he told me that he thought my mother was the biggest part of my problem. These years of therapy have proved him right. But the important thing I've learned during these years is that I am responsible for how I react to her. I'm not just a pawn, forced to feel and think and act as I have been programmed by her. I am responsible for myself. I can change. I still have a lot to learn. I still have issues to work through. But I have found my joy. And it is here to stay, even in the midst of trial.

Most important, I learned that God is faithful. He has never left me, even when I was in the depths of depression, even when I was cutting my body with razor blades, even when I was allowing the compulsive masturbation to keep me from Him. He has never left me. Even when I was a little girl, being abused and abandoned, God never left me. He was there with me, helping me to survive. Even through all these dysfunctional years with my mother, He has never left me.

My mother continued to drive me nuts and infuriate me. Right after Thanksgiving, Josh had surgery on his neck to remove a plum-sized mass. We didn't know if it was cancerous or not, and the six days we spent waiting for the biopsy report were very tense. Thankfully, it turned out to be only an infected lymph node. When I called my mother to tell her how his surgery went, she spent the first ten minutes telling me about her busy day. Only then did she ask about Josh. When we were at her house for Christmas and I asked if she wanted to see his scar, she responded sarcastically, "Well, I guess it depends on where the scar is." I said, "His neck!" She replied, "Oh . . . yeah," as if she had completely forgotten. She got a Christmas card from Josh's family. His mom had written, "We're glad Josh is fine . . . praying for Josh . . . praying just as hard for Rochelle." My mom called me and asked, "Why is Jan praying for you? What's wrong? Is there something I don't know about?" My mother is so self-absorbed! Gary said she exhibits narcissistic characteristics. Despite her narcissism, I continued to get healthier and experience joy.

When Gary told me that I was a success case, he told me there were five reasons for this. First, and foremost, was God - He never left me, I clung to Him, I repented of the sins I was responsible for, and He forgave me. He strengthened me as I struggled through my issues and dealt with the sins that had been committed against me. And He brought people into my life to help me. Second was the psychiatric component, meaning Dr. Patel and the medication. Third was the psychological component, the therapy. Fourth was Josh and how he loved me and supported me and showed me God's love by his actions. Finally, the fifth component was me. Gary told me that I was one tough kid. He said he had never before had a client who wanted to get well as badly as I did. I had an incredible desire for wellness. All five of these components worked together to bring about healing. And according to Gary, healing was happening. I was already a success case and I had found my joy. But I wasn't through with therapy. New chapters were just beginning.

CHAPTER 23: JOY

New chapters
in a book take you to
new levels
and new heights
you've never been before.
They open up more and more
of the story,
bringing
new elements,
new plot twists,
new events,
and new understandings.
They create,
like a chef creates a
gourmet meal,
like an artist creates a
beautiful painting,
like a sculptor creates
a lifelike statue,
like a poet creates
a poem.
They can fill you with
excitement,
apprehension,
anticipation,
and comprehension.
They can bring a whole new
part of the story
or they can bring
closure.

As the one year anniversary of being called a success case drew near, I began dealing with some new angles that involved lots of raw emotion.

24
Raw

Raw,
like a package of
spoiled, ground meat,
uncooked and inedible;
or,
like a gaping wound,
sore and
inflamed;
or,
like an open cut
that has had
alcohol
poured over it,
burning and
stinging;
or,
like your face
blasted by the
swirling snow of a
blizzard;
or,
like your back
blistered by the
blazing heat of the
sun;
all piercing,
all painful,
all
Raw.

It was one year ago, March 27, 2007, that Gary told me I was a success case. I always get reflective on anniversaries, and this one was no different. I thought a lot about myself and about my mother. And I wrote a lot about my mother, too. My words were raw because my emotions and thoughts were raw.

Mother. What a word. For some it brings thoughts of warmth and home and comfort. For others, like me, it brings . . . what does it bring? Nausea, revulsion, aversion, a feeling in the pit of my stomach so sickening I want to puke and explode and scream all at the same time. When someone talks about their mother in glowing terms, or even in neutral terms I want to tremble and cry with rage and envy and a yearning like nothing I've ever known. Mother, Mama, Mom, Mommie. It doesn't matter how you say it. It means the same thing to me: fear, conditions, controlling, criticism, anger, image, guilt trip, betrayal. My distaste for her, my disgust with her, is strong and raw and raging. It spills over into every mention, every word spoken of mothers—good mothers, bad mothers, so-so mothers, any mother. I'm full of gall, bitterness, and ire. I've a sour stomach. Bitterness. That's the word to describe my heart when it comes to her. How she looks to others is so important to her. But what about how she looks to me? To me she looks scary and frightening. To me she looks revolting and repulsive. To me she looks, well, like a giant, sticky, disgusting hairball coughed up by her stupid cat!

What was so raw was my facing up to how I really felt about my mother. I was admitting a sense of disgust and revulsion. I'd had issues with my mother for years, but this sense of revulsion was relatively new. I first noticed it when I was with her during the time of my great-aunt's funeral a year earlier and she was touching me all the time. That sense of revulsion was still very strong. I was seeing just how toxic she was to me. This toxic nature was something I wanted to explore further, so I picked up my pen.

Toxic

My mother is toxic to me. She gets the words right, but her actions don't fit her words. She says she loves me, but she has a funny way of showing it. And she's inconsistent. She's allowed to be angry, but I am not. She's allowed to cry, but I am not. She empathizes with other people, but not with me. Is she being a hypocrite and pretending when she empathizes with others or is she real with them? Either way, what about me? Why is she one way with the world and another with me? Her lack of empathy, her lack of concern, her lack of care for me make me stay guarded around her. Tears? Keep them hidden. Anger? Keep it hidden. Fear? Yep, it's got to stay hidden, too. I am angry with myself because I still want her love and approval. I want the blessing, but it never comes. That desire for her approval is original equipment. God designed us to want our parents' approval. But I have to face the facts. I'm not going to get it. Oh, she knows the right words, all right. She even writes them down in calligraphy and sends them to me: "Know that my love for you is totally unconditional." Unconditional. Yeah, right Mother. As long as I do what **you** want, as long as I am pleasing **you**, as long as I am not rocking the boat, as long as I am living up to **your** image. As long as—**then** I have your love. But do what *I* want, balk at your wishes, rock the boat, mar the image, then—oh, then there is no love. Only anger, icy disapproval, and total disregard for my feelings, my needs. Then there is only silence, criticism, and disparaging of my soul. Then your words cut me to the quick. "You are a terrible person. You were a rotten kid. How could you hurt me like this? Who knows about this?" Never empathy, never compassion, never support and encouragement, never helping me to reach my dreams and spread my wings and fly. Only control and enmeshment and smothering and criticism and disapproval. Then there is no love. "My love for you is totally unconditional." It sounds good, but it rings hollow.

I am also angry with myself for all the times I betrayed myself—for you. Especially the big time. I knew it had happened. I knew what he had done. I made the accusation. I needed you then. I needed your support, your help, and your comfort. I was dying inside and I needed your love, but all I got was your anger. "How could you say such things?" you cried! You were so angry with me. And all you seemed to care about was who knew. You didn't want to tarnish the image. You didn't care that life had tarnished my soul. So after three years of living with your anger and your image obsession, I recanted. I renounced what I'd originally claimed. "It was false memories. It didn't happen." But it did happen. And I was so confused, because I knew it had happened. I told myself, "Well, if he didn't, who did?" Because I knew it had happened. Yet I recanted. You were elated, and yet even after this, I have still felt your anger for having made the accusation in the first place. I betrayed myself for you, betrayed what I knew to be true, because of your anger and your image. But I know two things: it did happen and betraying myself for you didn't do any good because I still got your anger and your concern for image. All I did was hurt myself. I've been betrayed by people all my life: by my father, by you, my mother, by my grandfather—and by me. I didn't realize at first that my recanting was actually a betrayal of myself. I convinced myself it hadn't happened. At least, on the surface I did. Underneath, deep down, I knew it had happened. And I knew because of all the clues that it was **him**. It was wrong to recant. I did it for you. You were so angry and so upset. I had to do it for you. But I also did it for me. I recanted out of self-preservation. Bearing the brunt of your anger was wearing on my soul. And I was so intertwined with you that I had to please you. I had to gain your approval and love, so I recanted. Was I conscious of what I was doing? Not at first. I would have been terrified and horrified by what I had done. I wouldn't have believed I had betrayed myself in such a way. I'm horrified now. But over time, as I have gotten healthier and as I have gained a better understanding of who you really are, I see what I did. And I am saddened. So what do I do now, now that I see who you truly are? I'm not sure of everything, but I am sure that I've got to keep my distance from you because, Mother, you are toxic to me.

I continued to think and write about the way I betrayed myself when I recanted.

Fire

As a child, I was fascinated with fire. I wasn't a pyromaniac or anything. I just liked it. I liked to watch it and experiment with it. I would build little carefully-controlled fires in the dirt of the flower bed, sometimes even roasting a weenie or a marshmallow or two. I would do the same thing in the kitchen sink, lining the sink with aluminum foil first and always ready to turn on the water to douse the flames. My freshman year in college my social club was supposed to have a hayride and bonfire, but it got cancelled because of freezing rain. So my friends came to my room where we tried to roast marshmallows over the fire I had built in our dorm room sink. But the fire didn't burn very well and we ended up with a room full of smoke! We must have looked pretty suspect when the dorm mother came to my room to check on a report she'd received. It was thirty degrees outside and we had the windows wide open and two fans blowing! We nearly ran into her, literally, as we rushed to get rid of a trash can of "evidence." To our amazement, we never got in trouble!

What fascinates me the most about fire is how I used it to help betray myself on that cold New Year's night in 1996. The week after Christmas I had recanted. I had renounced my accusation against my grandfather. I claimed I'd had "false memories." How could I claim false memories when in reality it was mostly no memories? I had clues, tons of clues, and they all pointed to my claim that my grandfather had sexually abused me. And now I was recanting. But even then, I knew I'd been abused. What I ignored was the fact that all of the clues pointed to **him**. I ignored and I recanted. Three and a half years earlier, when I had been hospitalized for six weeks for severe depression, anxiety, and suicidal thoughts, was the first time that I accused my grandfather. It wasn't at my therapist's prompting or leading. It was my own conclusion, based on the innumerable clues in my life. Eight months later I was hospitalized again, this time for four weeks. I had lots of records from that period of my life—notes, journal writings, records of therapy sessions, details of dreams, letters I'd written, original poetry, music, and artwork from art therapy. I had pages and pages. And on the night of January 1, 1996, I stood in my mother's freezing backyard next to an old, battered, metal trash can and burned it all.

I thought I was doing the right thing at the time. But what I was really doing was burning up part of my life, part of me. In doing it, I betrayed myself. And I burned a hole right through my soul.

Postscript–I recently contacted the hospital to find out if I could get my hospital records. Maybe then I could get back at least part of that time of my life. They told me that they destroyed all records after seven years. It had been fifteen.

You may have wondered why I have written very little about those two hospitalizations. Now you know.

As I reflected on what I had done and written about how toxic my mother was to me, I found myself getting angrier and angrier. My raw emotions were churning and the rage was building, but I still had one more piece to write before the volcano exploded. I was finally recognizing what I was angriest about in regard to my mother.

"That Pole Thing"

I remember the first time it happened. I was a senior in high school, struggling with agonizing depression. I was also suicidal. I was carrying a razor blade around in my wallet and I can't tell you the number of times I held it to my wrist with tears streaming down my face. I wanted to die. I called the counselor I knew to try to get some help. You wouldn't call him for me. You were mad at me for calling him. You said you wouldn't pay for any counseling, either. That was the first time it happened. What was "it?" "It" was your total disregard for and lack of care about me and my mental health problems. As I was going to come to learn so clearly over the next twenty plus years, you refuse to acknowledge that my mental health problems exist. What I don't understand is why a mother, whose daughter was suicidal and wanted to die, would not get help for her? Why would a mother get angry at her daughter for trying to get help?

You also refused to accept or show any empathy when my spiritual health was in bad shape. There were several times during high school when I went forward during the invitation song at church to ask for prayers. That was a sure-fire way to make you angry. You were so concerned about what people would think about me, you, and our family, that you never bothered to show any concern for the spiritual struggles I was having.

At one point you went with me to a counseling session. You were angry and upset about attending. At the end of the session, the counselor suggested we go somewhere that we could sit and talk. The talk consisted of you telling me why I shouldn't be depressed, how it was all my father's fault because he wasn't around (never your fault, of course), and how you could never understand why anyone would want to kill themselves. I don't know what message you were trying to send to me, but what I heard was "I don't understand you and I don't want to and I'm not going to try."

When I was hospitalized for depression, never once did you tell me how sorry you were that this had happened to me, or how sorry you were that I was having to go through all this. Never once did I feel any support or empathy from you. All I got was your anger. As part of the hospital program we had family group therapy. You were extremely upset that you had to go to that with me. As a result of the hospitalization, I started setting boundaries and you were furious about that, too. Shutting the bathroom door? Unacceptable! Saying "no" to you? Unthinkable! In your view the worst boundary I set was about Grandma. I had always called her "Mom," but I started calling her

"Grandma" instead. She liked it, but you were angry about it! And you were angry because I wanted to tell people I was in the hospital so they could come visit me. It infuriated you that I called the preacher and one of the elders to ask them to be praying for me. That's kind of unbelievable - you didn't want me to ask people to be praying for me. Unbelievably sad.

Several months after I got out of the hospital I tracked down my father and met with him and his family. You hadn't seen or talked to him in years and yet you were giving me a litany of instructions as to what I was allowed to tell him about my mental health. You never called it "mental health" You didn't call my problems much of anything. If you did, that would be acknowledging them... You talked around them instead.

Once I was finished with the hospital, both in-patient and out-patient, and was off my medication, you assumed that I was fine. But I wasn't. I was still struggling with the crippling depression, anxiety, cutting, and other compulsive behaviors. But I had learned a lesson with you, so I kept things hidden. My close friends knew, but for you I painted a rosy picture. I kept the depression, my spiritual struggles, the cutting, and all the counseling hidden from you. Your words and tone of voice clearly indicated to me that my mental health problems were not acceptable to you. For eight years it was easier to hide my problems from you than it was to deal with your anger and guilt messages.

In November of 2000, I had what I have called a "coming back to God experience." Things seemed to get better for me overnight. On the anniversary of that experience, I told you about my experience of nearly losing my faith and returning to God, and you had a fit. The first words out of your mouth were, "Who knows about this?!" You were horrified and extremely angry when I told you who knew. And you angrily asked, "Why didn't I know?!" Never once did you say anything to me to the effect of "I'm so sorry you had to go through all that," or "I'm so glad you came back to God." It was all your anger over who knew and why didn't you know.

After I moved away to go back to school, once again I was struggling with the depression and anxiety. This time I had Dr. Patel, a psychiatrist who was really on top of things and worked at getting to the bottom of my problems. I also had a psychologist, Gary, whose work with me literally saved me. In July of 2003, Dr. Patel hospitalized me for a week. I was given several tests to determine what my problem was. Between the tests and the work that my psychiatrist had done with me for three months prior to that, I was diagnosed with bipolar II disorder and borderline personality disorder.

I didn't tell you that I was hospitalized. I did speak to you one time during that week, but I didn't tell you where I was when I called. I got out on a Friday afternoon. That evening you called me and told me that you were going to come visit me that Monday! I was a wreck. My very first session with Gary was that Monday morning and I asked him what to do about you. Should I tell you or not? Because he barely knew me at that point, he told me that he couldn't really advise me. I was going to have to make that decision. I hadn't told him yet about all your reactions to my mental health problems. I really hadn't made the connection yet between my mental health problems and your disregard for them. So I finally decided to tell you. I wrote you a letter. In it, I said I'd been hospitalized and what my diagnoses were. After you read the letter, the very first words out of your mouth were "Who knows about this?" Once again, image. And once again, anger. You were angry about who I had already told and you did not want me telling anyone else, especially the elders. You angrily asked me if this was going to be just like it was before with Papa, and me "telling God and everyone."

You were particularly concerned about the bipolar II diagnosis. In fact, you completely ignored the borderline diagnosis. You were fixated on the bipolar diagnosis, particularly because of your friend's daughter who is bipolar. She has bipolar I. Bipolar II is different. I tried to explain to you that with bipolar II the manic episodes are less severe but the depression episodes are much worse. But you weren't listening. You were totally convinced that my case was going to be exactly like hers, regardless. I gave you a pamphlet the hospital had given me about bipolar. I had underlined stuff that particularly pertained to me. You totally ignored the stuff I had underlined and instead obsessed over the comment about drugs and alcohol, asking me about it over and over again, when that wasn't a problem. I had not underlined that at all!. But it didn't matter. You weren't interested in what I had to say. You ignored what I said about the depression being so bad and got fixated on something that wasn't the problem at all.

Several months later, you commented about the fact that I was still seeing my psychiatrist and psychologist. Why was I still seeing them, you wondered, since I was doing better? If I was on medication and doing better, why did I need counseling? If this was just a chemical problem (as you viewed it), why did I need counseling?

That next summer, when Josh and I were getting married, you were awful. Josh and I had asked Gary to perform our wedding ceremony. You were angry about that. You didn't specifically say why you were angry, but I suspect it was because he was my therapist. He did perform our wedding and you talked with him like you were all buddy-buddy with him. Then several times over the next couple of years, when I would say something about Gary, you responded with, "Who's Gary?"

There have been some other things over the last few years that continue to show how you totally disregard my mental health issues. Josh gets angry too when he thinks about how you have treated me. I get angry, but I guess I'm used to it. Yet when he tells me that your behavior is outrageous and wicked, and that it turns his stomach and chills his blood, it gives me pause. And then I sit and think about it. And more than anything, I'm just weary. Your behavior, your treatment of me, wearies me. I am worn out, maybe with sorrow, when I think about you. Thank God I did not adopt your attitude toward myself and ignore my own cries for help. Thank God I listened to myself and got help. Obviously, if I had waited for your help I'd be in the loony bin by now. Or dead. The hard part for me is realizing just how much bitterness I have toward you. Bitterness is wrong and it will eat me alive if I let it. That's why I continue to talk about these things with Josh and Gary and Miss Penny and God. I'm trying to get over them, to get past them. I'm trying to heal and forgive.

The other day you were talking to me about your friend's daughter, the one who has bipolar. "You know, she has that, that problem, that, that pole thing." I wish I'd had the presence of mind to say, "Yeah, I know about that pole thing. I have it too, remember?" Maybe one of these days I'll be able to stand up to you and say what needs to be said about my mental health. You're such a jerk! That pole thing. What a stupid thing to say! Is Josh right? Is your behavior, your attitude toward me, your treatment of me wicked? Is that the truth about you? Can I handle the truth? I don't know. All I know is that your words and your behavior don't match. You say that I am the most important person in your life, but you don't care about me, not really. You don't care about my mental health or my spiritual health. You totally disregard my problems. You don't acknowledge the struggles in my life. What am I supposed to think about you? What am I supposed to feel? You say I'm your jewel, but you make me feel like dirt. I figure one day I'll get past all this. I just wish it didn't hurt so bad.

When I finished writing this essay, I read it out loud to Josh after dinner that evening. I hadn't read through it all at one time and I had written it in chunks, so I was not prepared for the full impact of reading it out loud all at once. I did okay reading it until the last few paragraphs, especially where I talked about the bitterness. I started getting choked up. When I finished it with the words, "I just wish it didn't hurt so bad," I sat there for a minute. Then I started crying quiet sobs. Josh came over and held me. I just cried more. I was trying to say, through the tears, that it wasn't fair. I was thinking about wanting to have a baby and how it was so unfair that what she had done to me made me afraid to have a child.

    I was still crying, but I was getting incredibly angry. The anger was escalating quickly and I told Josh that I needed to punch on my punching bag. I was crying and yelling and trying to get my jewelry off my hands and get to the exercise room. I started hitting the punching bag even before I got my gloves on. Josh helped me get my bag gloves on and I flailed away. He was holding the stand to keep it from moving while I hit the bag harder than I've ever hit anything in my life. I was punching and jumping and stomping and kicking. I was yelling and crying and sobbing. Josh said later that he could not even understand what I was screaming. I stopped a couple of times to try to breathe, and then I would just start pummeling the bag again. I even felt at one point that I was completely out of control. The fury had taken over. I was feeling rage, anguish, despair, grief, and other things I can't put my finger on. I finally stopped punching because I couldn't go on. I was spent, exhausted. We went inside and I drank some water. I cried some more, but I was much calmer. At that point, my overwhelming emotion was sorrow. That punching episode was April 1. Over the next two months I had seven or eight other punching episodes just as intense. My emotions were raw. I was volatile. The rage was spewing out.

    Now that all the anger was coming out, I feared that I would direct the fury at myself and that the results would be disastrous. The volcano had exploded, but I found that I was dealing with it in a healthy way. Instead of lashing out at myself with a razor, I was lashing out at the punching bag. And I was dealing with several issues all at once: the rage, my mother and the raw bitterness I felt toward her, my fears about having a baby, and feeling like a little girl. All the rage and fear I was experiencing made me feel so small, so unprotected, so vulnerable—like a little girl.

25

The Little Girl

The Little Girl,
like a scared
creature,
peeking out from
behind a tree,
hiding from life;
or,
like a dormant volcano,
boiling deep down
beneath the surface,
waiting for the right time
to erupt;
or,
like a china doll,
beautiful,
precious, and
exquisite,
yet incredibly fragile;
or,
like me.
The Little Girl.

In the very first session I had with Gary, he referred to the little girl. He told me that in talking and dealing with my mother, I needed to make sure my adult was in charge and not my little girl. We talked a number of times over the years about these two sides of my personality. He didn't mean multiple personalities, but that parts of my personality were controlled by the adult Rochelle and other parts were controlled by the little girl Rochelle. The little girl was the emotional part of me. Sometimes I'd make adult decisions, but sometimes I let the little girl part of me make the decisions. The little girl was very fearful and angry, just like I was when I was a child. She felt a lot of shame. The little girl Rochelle and the adult Rochelle were not integrated into one personality. Instead I felt fragile, fractured, empty, defenseless, helpless, unstable, broken, disconnected, disjointed, fragmented, and faulty. That was me. A whole Rochelle didn't seem possible. Having an integrated personality felt like something that would always be elusive to me.

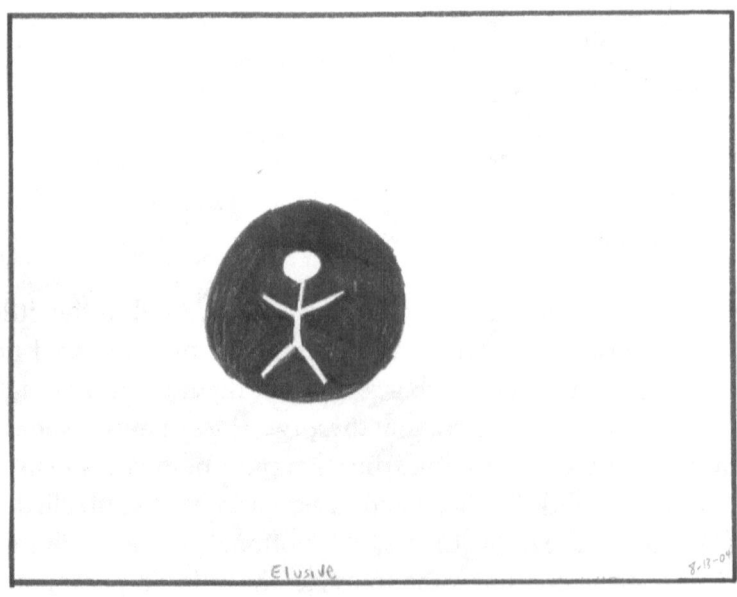

Chapter 25: The Little Girl

Many times I've felt like a child in an adult's body. In my interactions with other adults, I often felt like a little girl—fearful, shy, withdrawn. I felt others were in control, and I could only respond out of fear. My interactions were often influenced by how I learned to interact with adults as a child. For instance, I learned to give in to the other person, not to stand up for myself, and to be a people-pleaser. As a result, I had difficulty saying "no" and I constantly dumped buckets of guilt on my head for doing or not doing something.

Although Gary and I talked about the little girl on different occasions, the first time she really came to the forefront was in June 2005. I had started having dreams and flashbacks about my grandfather. I dreamed about crying out from my bedroom for my mom to come and help me, but she never came. I dreamed about my grandfather touching me inappropriately. I had many flashbacks of my grandfather. I saw him standing in the hallway, in the bathroom, and next to my bed. I had flashbacks of him when Josh and I were being intimate together. I had flashbacks of his face when I would look at Josh. It was a frightening time for me and I felt very much like a little girl.

One evening, as Josh and I were waiting to order some ice cream, I told Josh that when I was a little girl, my grandfather would take me to Baskin-Robbins where I always ordered two scoops, one each of chocolate chip and chocolate mint. Suddenly I felt little and afraid. I looked up at Josh, but I didn't see Josh standing there. I saw my grandfather. For a moment, I wasn't the adult Rochelle standing next to her husband. I was the little girl standing next to Papa. His image passed and we ordered our ice cream. I got two scoops, chocolate chip and chocolate mint, just like I always did when I was a little girl. Even though the image of my grandfather faded, the feeling of being so little didn't fade. Nor did the fear. As we ate our ice cream, my stomach started churning. Within twenty minutes, I had the worst case of diarrhea I've ever had. I'm certain it was connected to the flashback. My body was remembering something my mind had blocked out. Gary wondered if my grandfather used to take me to get ice cream as a bribe or reward. I don't remember why he took me to get ice cream, but he did it often. That same night I had vivid, fearful dreams about my mother and my grandfather. In the dreams, Gary and Josh both appeared to help me and comfort me. I awoke exhausted. The little girl was beginning to share her memories with me.

The little girl was the keeper of my memories. She knew what had happened to me as a child, even if she didn't allow the adult to remember very much. I gave her tremendous power. In October 2005 I wrote a poem about her and a hallway full of doors, but I never could decide how to end it. Was it the little girl's job to go through all those doors? Or was it my job to go through all those doors in order to reach my memories, in order to reach the little girl? So I wrote two different conclusions.

CHAPTER 25: THE LITTLE GIRL

There is a door at the end of my mind
that leads to a six-year-old girl;
she suspects what she will discover
when her memories begin to unfurl.

And that door is bolted and locked
like the steel door of an inner bank vault;
any effort to open it is thwarted,
the struggles to penetrate it are brought to a halt.

And this door is at the end of a hall,
long, dark, and foreboding this hall seems to be—
this door stands huge at the end
and it is locked with a one-of-a-kind key.

But between this door and where she stands now
there are countless other, yea, innumerable doors;
each one must be passed through,
none can be snubbed or ignored.

Some are wooden, some metal, some glass,
some are heavy, some flimsy and light,
some must first be unbolted,
some are unlocked and thus open quite right.

Door after door in the long, unknowing hall,
and the door at the end—where her memories are filed—
all of these doors must be traversed—
this is the task for the six-year-old child.
 or
this is the task to reach the six-year-old child.

After about six months, the dreams and flashbacks tapered off. I still felt like a little girl a lot of times, but I didn't dwell on it. About a year after I wrote that poem, I drew a picture. I couldn't decide on one title, so I gave it four: *Why is the Little Girl Hiding? Why is She So Afraid? Ask the Little Girl. All Her Life She's Been Afraid.*

More than two years passed before the little girl resurfaced in therapy in January 2008. I recognized that I reacted to Josh and others as a little girl would, rather than as an adult. For instance, when Josh would tease me, if he were getting the better of me and I didn't know how to tease back, I would strike out and hit him. Gary said that hitting was the little girl's response, and it was important to recognize when she was responding out of frustration or fear. We identified that when I'm caught off guard, I tend to revert to my childhood coping skills such as striking out, withdrawing, or fear. My child part was also still hanging on to the fantasy of a wonderful family. She was unwilling to give up hope that someday my mother would change and tell me she was sorry. Gary told me I needed to grieve the mother, the family, and the childhood I never had but so desperately wanted. I did feel like I was grieving. I still felt my joy, but the sadness and grief I felt over the family I never had were ever-present. The grief lessened as I wrote about it. I was glad, because the little girl's issues needed to be addressed.

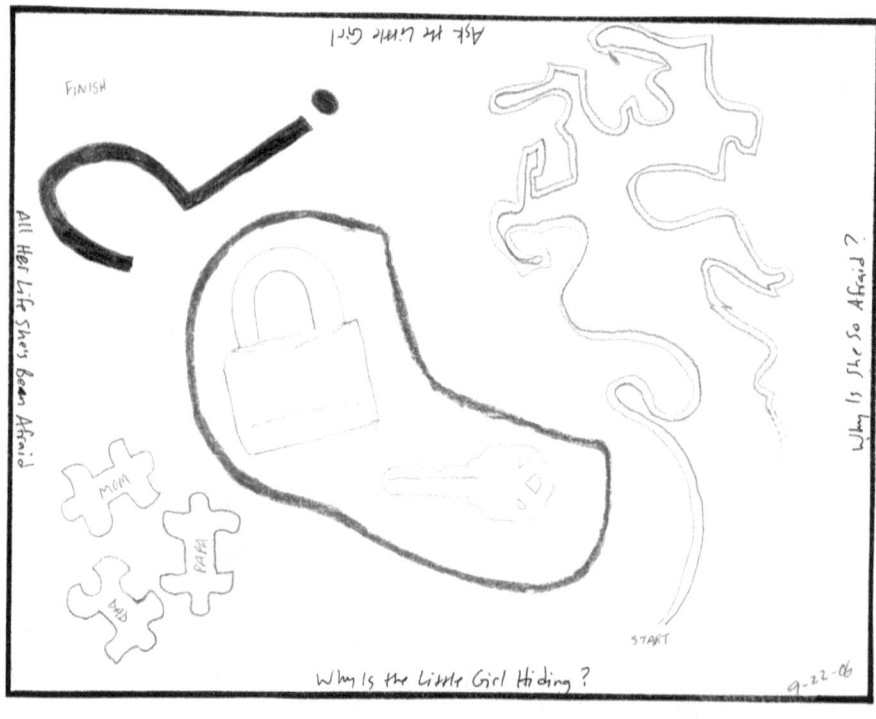

Chapter 25: The Little Girl

My Grief

I passed a funeral home today,
a family was grieving one passed away.
I thought of their sorrow,
I thought of their pain,
I thought of how grief leaves
such a raw stain.
But what do you do when your
grief's the result
of a family who caused you
so much heartache and tumult?
How do you grieve when there's
no physical loss,
but rather what you are grieving
is a life full of dross?
The sadness that fills up
my heart every day
is because life with my family
was so much dismay.
Abuse, betrayal, controlling and hurt—
because of their "love"
I felt like dirt.
I've been told I must grieve
the family I never had
in order for the heartache
to not be so bad.
I have to grieve the way
I wish it could be;
I have to let go of the mother
I wish were she;
I have to mourn
the dad I never knew;
I have to lament
what I know is so true.
I am vexed in my spirit

over things that were done
to me as a child—things that
should be done to no one.
I am sad in my soul
because of this mother of mine;
her love for me was like treating
my wounds with brine.
I could go on about
my grief and my pain,
and the resulting fear,
anxiety, disorders, and shame.
But for now I will cease
this written lament
and pray that I'll soon complete this process
and the grief will be spent.

Secrets lurked in my mind, but I had a guardian there. At first, I identified the guardian as my mind, but later I began to suspect the guardian was the little girl keeping secrets about my past, my mother and her anger, and my grandfather and his abuse.

The Secret

Somewhere in the corner of my mind is a secret, one carefully guarded and protected—from me. My mind knows the secret, my mind guards it, but my mind won't tell me the secret. The secret is about me, involves me, concerns me, but it isn't told to me. It's down in a deep, dark corner, surrounded by armed guards, chained all about, secured by padlocks, alarm systems, and sirens. All to protect it from me. But, as with many guarded secrets, there is a leak. Many clues provide evidence, give hints, of the nature, identity, and details of the secret.

It's odd that my mind keeps this secret from me since it involves me intimately. Indeed, it is a part of me, my soul, my life. Who guards the secret? My mind, I suppose. It has appointed itself defender and guardian of the secret. For some reason my mind doesn't believe me strong, capable, tough, sound, or safe enough to handle the secret, the truth. But I can. If the guardian of my mind is listening, I am here to say, to proclaim, "I can handle the truth!" I can handle the truth about him, about her. I can handle it because I already know it. It involves abuse, betrayal, abandonment, anger, fear, pain, shame, despair, and degradation. I know it all. I've experienced it all, felt it all, lived it all. And I've healed from it all. Or at least, I am healing. I've healed enough that I can handle it. So please listen, protector of my mind. I can handle the details and particulars. The big stuff's already known. The secret can be let out.

The Little Girl

A person's a person, no matter how small. That's what Horton said. But what do you do when the small person isn't reality, or at least, not anymore? She existed once, years ago when I was a little girl. Then I grew up. But now, as an adult, the little girl is still very much alive and active inside my mind. And she's in control of many things: thoughts, beliefs, emotions, reactions. How do I take control from the little girl? In her world, fear and being alone ruled. She still makes me afraid when I have no reason to be. The little girl is front and center when I face the worst, the dreaded, the mother. So many of my reactions and responses are those of the little girl. When will I learn that my world now isn't like my world then? When will I learn that I don't have to fear? Fear is the final frontier, the last bastion, the sole remaining dragon to be slain. The little girl and fear are inextricably linked. If I can slay one, I can slay both. But I do not want to slay the child. She is a part of me. Can I slay the fear without slaying the child? Maybe I need to get the little girl to grow up. Then I won't have to slay her. Maybe I need to integrate the little girl and the adult. Then they will no longer be at odds with each other, but work together, one. How do I deal with the dragon of fear without destroying the child? That is what I must do.

Integration became the focus of my therapy with Gary. I didn't want to slay the little girl. I just wanted to bring the two parts together, to unify my personality into one Rochelle. Instead of a little girl Rochelle and an adult Rochelle, one whole Rochelle. Just me.

Why Are You Crying?

I'm crying.
I'm crying for
the little girl.
She knows what
happened to me.
If I slay the
little girl,
I'll lose the
memories
forever.
I'm crying for the little girl.
She knows.
She knows what happened.
Oh!
What a terrible
burden
for a little girl
to bear.
If only she would tell me
she wouldn't have to
bear her burden
alone.

I decided to talk directly to the little girl part of me. I wanted her to know that she didn't have to bear the burden alone anymore. I wanted her to know that she didn't have to fear me. On the same day I wrote the piece about my mother being toxic, I asked the little girl . . .

Hey, Little Girl? Are You Listening?

It's me, Rochelle. I know you're there. You're a part of me. I want to tell you something important, so please listen. It's okay to grow up. It's okay for us to join, to integrate. It's okay. You can trust me. I know you don't think you can trust me, but you can. I know you shy away from trusting me with memories and emotions and thoughts because I haven't handled those things very well in the past. I've cut or cried or raged or, well, you know all I've done. But I want you to know I'm better. I might still cry or be afraid or be angry. But you have to know this: it is okay to cry and be afraid and be angry. I know that in your world those things aren't okay. They weren't okay, weren't safe, weren't allowed.

It's **not** okay to cut. Not for me. Not anymore. And **I PROMISE YOU, I WON'T CUT**. That's a solemn promise, Little Girl, one I will keep. You can trust me. It's not a promise made lightly, like other ones made to you by other people. It's a sacred promise. *I will not cut.*

You can trust me, Little Girl. You can tell me. You can share your burden with me. But the adult Rochelle, the integrated Rochelle, is allowed to cry, allowed to be angry, allowed to be afraid. Little Girl, I've learned ways to safely do those things. I've learned healthy ways to deal with tears and anger and fear. I can't stop those things from coming, but I can keep from being overwhelmed and overpowered by them. I've learned that I don't have to be afraid. I can make the choice to not be afraid. I've learned that I can be angry and not explode at someone else, or implode at myself or at you. And I can cry, Little Girl. **We** can cry. We can integrate and cry together. All those tears you've held back, it's okay to cry them now. No one is going to hurt you. You are safe with me. A couple of years ago I pictured many doors in my mind that needed to be unlocked and opened, including the one that holds the memories. I thought opening all those doors was the task of the six-year-old child. But Little Girl, you don't have to do it alone. I am here with you. I am here for you. We can open them together. Little Girl, are you listening? It's me, Rochelle. I'm here for you. You're safe with me. You can trust me. Trust me. Please.

I was finally beginning to communicate with the little girl, wanting her to trust me. Gary asked, "Why should she trust you?" I had been very hard on the child. In fact, he said, I'd been harder on her than my mother was. It was a sobering realization: I had cut her, carved her body, shamed her, ridiculed her, and divided her from me. I was going to have to learn to be nice to her before she would trust me. For example, I had to learn how to handle my anger instead of taking it out on her. I used to take it out on her by cutting. Now I punched the punching bag. But I still took out my anger on the little girl by cursing myself, calling myself names, piling guilt on myself, and stuffing the anger with food. So I wrote the little girl a letter.

April 9, 2008

Dear Little Girl,

I want to tell you, I need to tell you that I am sorry. I am so sorry for all the times I have hurt you. How can an apology of spoken and written words make up for all the damage I have done to you? It cannot. But I need to tell you, and you need to hear that I am sorry. I need to acknowledge how I have hurt you and you need to hear me say these things. Other people in your life have never acknowledged how they have hurt you. For years I didn't acknowledge how I hurt you. But I am acknowledging it now. I'm taking responsibility now. I'm asking your forgiveness now.

I've hurt you in so many ways. I hurt you for many years by shaming you with my sexual behavior. I shamed you with the masturbation and then, as if that weren't enough, I would hurt you physically while masturbating. But Little Girl, I don't do that anymore. I haven't masturbated in four years. In fact, yesterday was the four-year anniversary of when I stopped. I'm sorry for hurting you that way. I'm sorry for shaming you.

I've hurt you for years by taking out my anger on you. I've yelled at you, cursed you, hit you, and verbally abused you by calling you all sorts of names. I have been so angry that I was ready to kill you. I've held razor blades to your wrists, I've lined up pills to take, and I've tied cords tightly around your neck, ready to jump off a counter. Oh, Little Girl, I've hurt you so much. I am so terribly sorry.

And I've hurt your body. I've scraped you with scissors and knives and I've cut you with razors. I've cut lines and Xs and boxes and words into your body. Oh, I've cut the words. I've hurt you and shamed you and betrayed you with all the words I've cut into you. Little Girl, I'm so sorry. Can you ever forgive me? I don't do that anymore. It's been two and a half years since I last cut. It was so wrong of me to take out my anger against you like that. I'm sorry that I punished you like that. It wasn't your fault. Please try to forgive me.

I've hurt you by dividing you away from me. For so many years I was fragmented. Back in 1992, they even wondered if I had multiple personality disorder. But I didn't. I was just very, very fragmented. There was the adult, the little girl (you), the sick part (that masturbated and cut), and the image part (that I showed to others, including Mom). The sick part is basically gone. At least the self-destructive behaviors are gone. The image part and

CHAPTER 25: THE LITTLE GIRL

the adult are more closely related now (except with my mother). But at least with everyone else, I am not so tied to image. Then there is you. And me. We are communicating, Little Girl. We are beginning to integrate. We are slowly becoming one. Because we really are, you know. Even though I think of you as the Little Girl and me as the adult, we really are one. You're a part of me. I'm a part of you. I'm beginning to nurture you. You're beginning to trust me. I know trusting me is a frightening thing. I know it's hard. But I want you to keep trying to trust me. And I'll keep trying to prove to you that I'm trustworthy. I think acknowledging how I have hurt you is one step toward proving my trustworthiness. Unlike someone we know, I'm not pretending that I've done nothing wrong. I have done wrong, lots wrong. And I'm sorry.

And I need to apologize for something else, too. I think this is the hardest thing of all to admit, but I do admit it. Little Girl, I hurt you, I betrayed you when I recanted. You trusted me to make the accusation against the one who shamed your body and soul. I made the accusation. But then, after three years of living with her anger and her image obsession, I gave in. I recanted. I said it hadn't happened. I said it had been "false memories." And when I said those things, I betrayed you. You were counting on me and I let you down. Boy, did I let you down. I am so sorry, Little Girl. You were counting on me to tell the secret, but I gave in to the anger and the pressure I felt and I let you down. I caved in. I wimped out. Instead of helping you and protecting you, I betrayed you. Oh, Little Girl, I am so sorry.

I was even harder on you than Mother was. She didn't protect you from him. I didn't protect you from myself. And I didn't let you tell the truth. I hid it, masked it, disguised it, distorted it. A lot of the complaints I have about her I should have about myself, because I've done them, too. Little Girl, these last two weeks have been a sobering wake-up call for me. I see the truth of how I've acted toward you. I'm saddened. And I'm sorry. You have been afraid of me and afraid of my anger, just as I have been afraid of Mother and her anger. But Little Girl, there is a fundamental difference between her and me. I recognize my wrongs, I'm sorry for them, and I'm trying to change. And you know, Little Girl, that I have been changing. I've been in therapy for nearly five years now, trying to change. The masturbation is gone. The cutting is gone. I can get angry without taking it out on myself or on you. I'm dealing with my fears. All of the work I have done in therapy, Little Girl, has been done to try to get back with you. I want to connect with you, integrate with you. Little Girl, I want to help you. I want to protect you.

I know I haven't done a very good job before. Please give me a chance this time. I won't let you down.

And Little Girl, we're not alone. We've have people to help us who love us deeply, people we can trust. People like Josh and Gary and Miss Penny and Dr. Patel. And God. He will help us. He will protect us. He won't let us down.

Little Girl, I love you. I'm sorry for all the ways I've hurt you through the years. I'm working very hard to change so that I will never, ever hurt you again. Please know that. And please know that I love you.

Rochelle

I sincerely apologized to the little girl, and I was proving my repentance with my actions. About a week after I wrote this letter, I was cleaning out a bunch of old stuff. I found an old 11x17 frame with a picture of John Wayne in it. I put it in the giveaway pile. One of my friends went through my discards and when she found the picture, she wanted to keep the frame. She opened the back of the frame to remove the John Wayne picture and I received the surprise of my life. There behind it was a pencil drawing someone had made of me on September 4, 1976, when I was six years old. The portrait was yellowed with age around the edges, but otherwise in good condition. I had the portrait professionally framed and that picture has become my vision of the beautiful little girl that I was before I was so marred by sin (the sins of others and my own sins against myself). I find it ironic that I was trying so desperately to connect and integrate with the little girl, and I didn't even know that her picture was there. It was almost symbolic of how I had separated myself from her over the years. Now I was working to change that.

At the end of April, Josh and I traveled back to the city where Gary lived for a ministry renewal program we were involved in. It had been almost two years since we had moved away. Two years of therapy on the phone. Phone therapy is okay, but in-person is so much better. I was going to have the opportunity to sit down in person with Gary in his office for a change. I was thrilled! I met with him three times that week. It was a good week, but tough. We talked more about the separation between my adult and my child. He said when the two are separated, there is pathology (lack of memories, masturbation, cutting, etc.) The child and I were going to have to learn to work together.

Gary told me to explore the connection between the severity of my self-abuse (i.e., the masochistic masturbation, the cutting) and my need to convince myself that rejection or betrayal of the little girl was my only option. I had been on a mission to convince myself that my child was all the horrible things I carved into her. When I asked him why, he said I was trying to lose her because she was abused. In rejecting my little girl, I was rejecting the abuse, trying to lose it. It was a way of trying to be good again, of trying to make the past right. But, as Solomon pointed out, there is a way that seems right to man, but in the end it leads only to death (Proverbs 14:12).

Gary acknowledged that I was in a new chapter of therapy. It was a good phase but a very hurtful, volatile phase for me. I was beginning to come to grips with the *self*-betrayal that had happened. I first realized that I'd betrayed myself when I wrote about the recanting back in August 2007, but now, eight months later, it was sinking in. It was overwhelming to realize that I'd been harder on myself than my mother was. Gary said that a lot of my fears were linked to this hub of self-rejection. I was not only rejecting my own inner child, I was rejecting other children by being uncomfortable around them and by not wanting to have children of my own. We talked about my needing to nurture and love my little girl instead of beating up on her and betraying her as I'd done for so many years.

When Josh and I got home from that trip, I found myself wanting to nurture my inner child. I thought about the little girl all the time. I asked Josh to read me bedtime stories. I slept with a couple of stuffed animals that had been my childhood favorites. I made two copies of the portrait from 1976 and placed them in the family room and the bedroom. I had the original framed and hung on the wall of the study beside my computer.

I discovered an old cassette recording of myself from when I was little. I must have been about seven or eight. On one part of the tape I was reading a story from my bedtime story book. On another I was singing the theme song from a popular television show at the time and on a different part a classical music record played in the background while I sang along. I was surprised to hear myself singing along with the classical music. I was being silly and laughing. It made me feel good for the little girl. She did have some joy in her life back then. My hope was, as I continued to integrate my personality, that I would have more and more joy and laughter.

Gradually, my fixation on the little girl weakened. I still have her portrait hanging next to my computer, but I took the copies down. Occasionally I have Josh read me a bedtime story, but not often. At first I thought I was ignoring the little girl and I felt guilty. But then I realized what was really happening. I was beginning to integrate. I was no longer abusing and betraying my child. It was no longer the adult Rochelle versus the little girl Rochelle. I was starting to become just Rochelle. It felt peaceful. But the biggest difference was in my attitude toward babies. When we met in Gary's office and talked about my self-rejection, he warned me that, as I started to nurture my own inner little girl, something might change. He said that as I loved my little girl I might find some maternal stuff kicking around in me in ways it hadn't done before. Boy, was he right.

26
Babies

Having a baby,
like a terrifying prospect,
bringing fear
and panic
and anguish;
or,
like an old woman
stepping over
uneven, precarious ground,
tentative,
cautious,
hesitating;
or,
like someone
leaping around like a
jumping bean,
ecstatic because she
just won the
sweepstakes;
or,
like a wise man
making a decision
based on
facts,
research,
truth, and
reason,
having weighed the risks and
considered the cost;
or,

> like a kid before Christmas,
> joyful anticipation
> filling his eyes,
> full of eager expectation
> as to the wonderful things
> that await.
> Having a baby.

I wasn't sure what to think. I'd already been thinking about babies, and I was terrified! When I was in high school, I said I didn't want children. In my twenties I said I did want children, lots of children. As I got older, I just wasn't sure. For about two years, I had been saying no, but was that what I really wanted? When I'd had that first rage punching episode, I admitted that there was a part of me that did want a child, but I didn't feel I could because of all my issues. And yet all these maternal feelings were bubbling up. How was I supposed to process this? Was the age of thirty-eight and a half really the time to start thinking about having a baby? I made a list of questions and concerns about having a child.

I can't get pregnant while I am on the lithium.
Dr. Patel says he can substitute other things, but would they work as well?
Would I have the energy to have a new baby? Whether it's my age or my medicine or just my mental health condition, I never seem to have much energy.
What and when would we tell him/her about my problems?
I still can't seem to handle it when I even think someone is mad at me. That would send the wrong message to a child, that it wasn't okay to be angry (one of the many wrong messages I received as a child).
From what I've been told a baby changes everything in a marriage. I absolutely love the marriage that Josh and I have. I don't want to do anything to mess it up! Would having a baby mess up our marriage?
How in the world would I be able to handle nine months without my medication? If I simply lower it, I get all depressed and weird (weirder than normal, that is!). How could I handle being without it?
Having a baby would mean my mother would want to be around more—not good!
I'm almost thirty-nine and Josh is almost fifty-four. What role is our age going to play in us having the energy we need to raise a child? What will it

do to a child when he/she is a teenager to have a father who looks like his grandfather?

I am so fearful of everything. How would that affect a child? How would that affect the baby during pregnancy?

My Ob-Gyn was extremely concerned about my mental health history. He said that my risk for developing post-partum depression was very high and he was concerned about that if I became pregnant.

How would I raise a child so that he/she wouldn't have the same messed up beliefs, views, etc., that I have? Would I be able to have boundaries with my child and respect my child's boundaries?

Lots of noise, including crying babies, makes my anxiety skyrocket. What would having an infant do to my anxiety?

My doctor has told me that at age forty (only seventeen months away), the risk of birth defects goes up greatly. Would I spend nine months in fear, wondering if my child was okay? What would that do to the baby? And if I knew something was wrong, how would I handle it? I get freaked out when something is wrong with one of my dogs. What would I do if it were my child?

I read recently that parents with mental illnesses (particularly schizophrenia, depression, and personality disorders) have a higher incidence of having a baby with autism.

I would think that God was punishing me if I had a baby that had something wrong with it.

How in the world could the decision to have a child be wise? All of the factors seem to point toward not having a child.

I think, "Maybe God's punishing me. Having a child is something I may want very badly, but I can't have one, because it would be a very unwise decision." So, I am just filled with grief and sadness. I almost wish that all this maternal stuff hadn't started (and it started on April 1, three weeks before Gary mentioned it last Friday). If I could have kept the same I-don't-want-one attitude, then the hurt of wanting one and having to not have one wouldn't hurt so bad.

This world is so crazy and filled with so much evil and sorrow. Why in the world would I want to bring a child into it?

When I read this list to Gary, he asked, "Who are you trying to convince?" It was obvious that I was trying to convince someone.

Surprises

Gary says that for the last seven or eight weeks I've been in a new chapter of therapy. And what's in it? Lots of anger. Lots of sadness. And lots of surprises.

The first surprise happened pretty early. I realized that there was a part of me that really did want to have a child. When we met with Gary, we spent a lot of time talking about the little girl. Gary suggested that I needed to nurture her, and that some maternal stuff might surface as I did.

I spent a long time making a list of my concerns about having a baby. Most of them were reasons not to have a child. Gary wondered who I was trying to convince, and why. At first I said my mother. He didn't think so. I said maybe myself, and he asked me which part. As we talked about the little girl, he said maybe she's trusting me with something and I'm not hearing her. I told him I was definitely hearing all her anger. He said maybe there's something else she's trying to tell me that I'm not listening to, that I'm assuming that she's only telling me about the anger and hurt and frustration. But what about the deep longings of her heart? What has she always wanted?

That night after dinner, I was telling Josh about my session and as we talked, I began crying. Then I began sobbing. I sobbed deep, wrenching sobs. As Josh held me, I calmed down and we talked some more. Then I started sobbing again. This went on for over an hour. Here is what I discovered, concluded, admitted:

1. I really do want a child.
2. I'm afraid my baby might be damaged and that it would be because God is punishing me.
3. The little girl has always wanted to grow up, get married, stay married, and have a child who has a loving, devoted, protective, trustworthy daddy.
4. My mother always said she had given me the "Mother's Curse," that I would have kids just like me! Well, guess what? I hope I do have kids just like me because that means that they would be truth-seekers!
5. My mother has always talked about my having been strong-willed and how awful that was, but I think being strong-willed is a good thing. A strong-willed person won't just let herself be led; won't

always be victimized. A strong-willed kid will persevere, even when things get tough. The fact that I am strong-willed is what has kept me going through all these years of depression and therapy. That's where my will to get well is! And finally,

6. I was not a rotten kid!

In the days since that evening, I have felt extremely weird—in a really good way! How do I describe it? Josh and I made a list of reasons **to** have a child. And we've been talking about the possibility of getting pregnant and talking through some concerns. It's strange. I feel liberated. That's a surprise.

One of the things we put on our list had to do with my past. I said that having a child and being a good mommy would, in a way, be redeeming my past. Josh said it would be proof that my whole life isn't limited by or ruined by my past. By God's grace, I've overcome it. In a sense it's not my past that's redeemed, it's me! I don't have to spend the rest of my life being a victim. If I have a child, it would be redeeming the little girl. I've been on the defensive about babies and children for so long now, it's liberating to finally not be uncomfortable or fearful around them. The little girl and I are finally getting on the same page. For so long I had continued the self-betrayal by denying this maternal desire, like this area was the last bastion, and that's why I feel so liberated now.

Do I have questions? Absolutely. Do I have concerns? Oh, yes. But I'm not afraid to ask the questions and face the concerns. Josh and I spent his lunch hour today looking at a book of baby names. Gary's right. I am in a new chapter of therapy with lots of emotions and lots of surprises. I like surprises.

Over the next few days I felt liberated. I felt whole. Once again, I picked up my pen.

I feel so liberated, so light. I had a little anxiety yesterday, but it wasn't really anxiety. It was excitement, expectation, anticipation, rather than fear. What's going on? What is happening with me is that the grace of God is at work and truth is triumphing!

When we were in Gary's office, he told me that a hub of all my fears was this inner self-rejection, this self-betrayal. He said that connecting with the little girl and forgiving myself was key.

Tuesday night after my last session with Gary, I just sobbed. I told Josh I was so tired and weary of this process. But most importantly, that night I admitted some fundamental truths. I **do** want a child. I've always wanted to grow up, get married, stay married, and have a child who has a loving, faithful, protective daddy. And I've been different ever since.

I feel so liberated, so light. The very next day Josh and I were talking about some of our concerns about having a baby. We were focusing on how those fears might be resolved. The day after that I bought a baby names book and a pregnancy book and we talked about my getting pregnant and about questions we have for Gary, Dr. Patel and the ObGyn.

I know I am integrating. The question is: is the process now complete? Have I integrated? The battle within myself seemed to be over once there was no more self-deception. When I was little, I couldn't admit to myself that my mother was such a huge problem. I couldn't face the abandonment and the abuse that I had in my life. What little girl could face the fact that she had been betrayed by every person important in her life—her father, her grandfather, and her mother? Instead of facing the terrifying facts, I put the blame on myself. I had no frame of reference, no outside perspective to know that families weren't supposed to be that way, so the fault became mine. Thus, began the self-betrayal. And it continued for years. I am almost thirty-nine years old. It has taken that many years—years full of anger, fear, sorrow, and countless other emotions. And years full of courage. Courage, because at some level I knew that things weren't right with me, so I tried to get help from friends, ministers, and counselors. For years. And then, by the grace of God, I found His instruments. I found Dr. Patel and Gary and Josh. God has used these men to bring healing into my life. And now, five years after I began with them, I am finding myself in a new chapter of therapy. Could it be the final chapter?

Courage is one thing that has gotten me through this process. Another thing is the fact that I am a truth-seeker. I've been willing to look at the truth of my life and strive to change what was wrong. It's taken a lot of courage because the truth about my life was pretty ugly. What other people had done to me, and what I had done to myself, was ugly. My life was ugly. But now...

Now, I feel so liberated, so light. And so beautiful. I stood in the living room, with the stereo loudly playing Pachelbel's Canon in D Major with tears streaming down my face and my arms stretched toward heaven. I laughed with abandon the laughter of deep, pure, uninhibited joy! I once had a minister tell me, when I was so down on myself, that one day I would feel beautiful. He told me to let him know when that happened. It happened.

When I look at the portrait of the little girl, I am filled with wonder and joy. I was a beautiful little girl. And I am a beautiful woman. Have I integrated? Is that what this is all about? If I have truly integrated and am no longer at war with myself, then that would leave me stronger, more self-assured, and better able to deal with Mom and everybody else. Maybe I have integrated, because the ever-present fear in regard to my mom isn't there anymore. Oh, I realize that I can't get cocky. She may still be quite toxic to me. But if I'm dealing with her as a whole person, and not a fragmented one, then there's strength in that.

Josh and I decided that whether I get pregnant or not doesn't matter. I'd like to, but God is in control. He knows what is best for me, for us, and if He thinks it's a good idea for us to have a baby, then we will. I have to trust that God knows what is best. I have to trust that God has my best interests in mind. I have to trust. If I get pregnant, it'll be great, but if I don't get pregnant, it'll still be great. The important thing is that I admitted to myself that I do want a baby. I'm no longer deceiving myself, deluding myself, or betraying myself.

I feel so liberated, so light.

I bought a pregnancy book and started reading.

That book threw a pail of cold water on me. Just two days before, I was excited, full of life and laughter. But after reading a particular section in that book, boy, did my mood swing! I probably stripped my gears, I was so all over the place with my emotions. But Josh reminded me that Gary did say that this chapter of therapy would be a volatile time for me. No kidding.

I read the section on having a baby over the age of thirty-five. It was the risk of birth defects in that age group—one in 300— that sobered me. There's a higher risk for an older father, as well. I'm thirty-eight and a half. Josh will be fifty-four next month. I am sobered. I am fearful.

So, would getting pregnant at our ages be a risk or would it be trusting God? Josh says the answer to that question is "yes." Is God just saying, "trust me" on this? It feels so unfair. It took me thirty some-odd years to finally admit/realize that the little girl's deepest longing is my longing too, and now it may be too late. Is getting pregnant something that needs to happen for the little girl to trust me? Do I need to at least try to get pregnant in order for the little girl to trust me?

And I still fear that God would be punishing me if I had a child that was not healthy. It would be the ultimate irony for me to have gone through everything I've gone through and come out on the other side, only to have a damaged baby. I've prayed several times and Josh has prayed, too, that I will be able to get past this punishment mindset. Josh pointed out that Hebrews 12 talks about God disciplining, not punishing, those He loves. He suggested that maybe the painful work of therapy has been part of God's disciplining of me. I have to realize that God isn't going to punish me for something by giving me a damaged child. So, we really do have to bathe this in prayer.

Most importantly, is this really all about trusting God? If I don't trust Him in this, will I ever fully trust Him? From the very beginning, it's been about learning to trust Him. Proverbs 3:5-6 says, "Trust in the Lord with all your heart and lean not on your own understanding; in all your ways acknowledge him, and he will make your paths straight." I realize that I have both healthy and unhealthy fear in all this. The healthy fear is of birth defects. The unhealthy fear is that God is going to punish me with a defective baby. There is also unhealthy fear about trusting Him. And yet, trusting is key. The little girl needs to learn to trust me and I need to learn to trust God. I can't trust God if I don't love Him. And how can I love Him if I'm always afraid He's going to punish me? Indeed, I won't love Him unless I'm convinced that He loves me. I think the adult Rochelle knows that He loves me. But what about the little girl? She grew up frightened and unable to trust. Can I show her the truth?

Despite my fears, I was still excited. I recognized that part of what was going on with me had to do with the little girl and my mother. And God. I wrote a letter to the little girl and the next day I wrote a piece about my mother. It was Mother's Day.

Saturday, May 10, 2008

Dear Little Girl,

Boy, a lot sure has happened with us the last few weeks. You have been opening up and sharing a lot with me—emotions, fears, and deep longings, too. And, just like I promised, I've been faithful to you. I haven't cut you or hurt you or shamed you. I've handled the emotions, the mood swings, the volatile nature of my heart, all in wise, mature ways. I've punched on the punching bag, written in my journal, talked with Josh and Gary and God, and nurtured you.

Gary was right, wasn't he? He said when I started nurturing you that maternal stuff would start kicking around in me. That was no joke, was it? He got my attention when he told me that maybe you were trying to tell me something, but I wasn't listening. He said maybe you were trying to trust me with something, but I wasn't hearing you. So I started listening. And I started hearing.

I hear now what you were trying to tell me, and you're right. You have always wanted to grow up, get married, stay married, and have a child who had a daddy who loved her. A daddy who was there for her and wouldn't leave her. A daddy who would protect her and cherish her. That's what you've always wanted. It's what I've wanted, too.

I'm listening, Little Girl. I'm listening with ears wide open. I know your dream, and I'm beginning to share it. But I need you to listen to me, too. There are some things that I know as an adult that you don't and you need to. Some very important things. Some things I know as an adult in my head, but I don't know them in my heart. That's where you live. So Little Girl, I want you to listen, I want my heart to listen, as I tell you something very important.

God loves you. He cares for you. He adores you. He is a God who is faithful to you. He will protect you. He will not abandon you like your father did. He will not molest or mistreat you as your grandfather did. He will not guilt you, deceive you, beat you, or deny you as your mother did. And He will not shame you, reject you, abuse you, or betray you as I did. You were given a rotten picture of God, but that's not how He is. If you want a true picture of God, don't look to your father or your grandfather or your mother or even yourself. Look to the Bible. That's where the true picture of God is found.

Little Girl, you've been reading and memorizing the Bible since you were very young. It's true. What it says about God is true! He loves you! He loves you so much, He died for you to save you! And you can trust Him. You couldn't trust anybody else all those years, but you can trust Him. Oh, Little Girl, please listen! Please hear in my heart of hearts what I'm saying to you! Oh, dear God, please help the little girl. Please help us. Please soften my heart, open my heart to know Your love, to believe Your love, to trust Your love. To trust You. Please, dear God, help the little girl and me to integrate, to become one. One whole and healthy woman. Please undo all the damage that was done so many years ago. Help her to listen to me. Help me to listen to her. And help me—all of me—to listen to You.

Little Girl, for the first time, I'm thinking about getting pregnant with excitement rather than fear. This is something that I want, but there are concerns, mainly about our ages. The other things can be worked through. Little Girl, you have to understand that we'll do what we can, but ultimately God is the one who is in control. If He wants me to have a baby, I will. But if I can't get pregnant, I have to trust that God knows what is best. You have to try to trust that, too. Let's work together, Little Girl, on getting well, on undoing the damage, on trusting God. We are starting to integrate. Let's keep doing that. I love you, Little Girl. I love you.

Rochelle

Mother's Day

It's amazing the difference a week makes. Today is Mother's Day. If it had been last week, I would have had a very different outlook on the day.

Josh and I were at the Hallmark store yesterday and I saw a number of items about mothers. Instead of reacting with disgust and loathing, I thought maybe someday that'll be me. I thought of Mother's Day in the context of me possibly being a mother.

I don't know if the Lord has motherhood in mind for me or not. I hope He does. It'll be nice to have a different outlook on Mother's Day.

And all morning, I wasn't "weirded out" by comments about Mother's Day. Even knowing I didn't have a very good mother hasn't really upset me today, certainly not the way it has in the past. My outlook is different and I'm different.

At lunch today, three families went out to eat. One of them had two children, a four-year-old and an eight-month-old. I couldn't keep my eyes off of them. I watched them and watched their parents. I was particularly touched by watching the daddy interact with them. It made me think about Josh and the kind of father he would be. I was dying to ask the mom all sorts of questions about being pregnant and having a baby.

Three weeks ago I was buying Mother's Day cards with lots of angst. But now that Mother's Day is here, the angst is mostly gone.

CHAPTER 26: BABIES

I've talked to my mother three times in the last few days, three times since my change of heart. I guess it wasn't as much a change of heart as it was that I finally quit lying and started listening to my heart.

But anyway, I've talked to my mother three times. She's still my mother—selfish, obnoxious, and irritating—but the revulsion I felt toward her seems to be gone, or at least dissipated. I still have to be on my guard with her. I can tell from being on the phone with her this afternoon. She hasn't changed one bit. But I have.

The difference of a week is incredible. But it's really not the week that's made the difference. It's me. I'm different, because I'm honest now, with myself. And since I'm no longer deceiving myself, things seem so different, so clear.

And it's not just things about my mother and babies that are different. Things about God seem different, too, like I am hearing and seeing things for the first time. Josh said something in his sermon about worship being motivated by love and gratitude to God rather than by superstitious fear. My worship has been all wrong. I've had the right words, but my heart's been wrong. Now things are changing. When I was reading Scripture this afternoon, it was all so . . . different, like everything that I have in my head about God is slowly starting to make sense to my heart. I hope that continues.

As Josh said, my joy is jumping for joy. But I'm also sad. There's a sadness to all of this. It's what Gary pointed out from Ecclesiastes 1:18, "For with much wisdom comes much sorrow; the more knowledge, the more grief." So I'm full of sadness, but also full of joy. How does that compute?! It's strange, but that's the way it is.

So I'm approaching middle age and thinking about getting pregnant and having a baby. Okay, I'm a slow starter! If anyone asks why we waited so long, all we have to say is we weren't ready. My heart wasn't ready. Am I ready now? I'm certainly ready to think about it, because that's all I've been thinking about! If you had told me last Sunday that Josh and I would be talking about getting pregnant and having a baby, I'd have thought you were crazy. But it seems perfectly natural to be thinking about having a baby on Mother's Day. Still, a week ago, I would have never thought it.

And yet, I think Gary saw it. Now, I know he's not a prophet, but I still think he saw it or at least saw the potential.

And I just feel SO WEIRD!

I think what I feel is a little bit of normal!

And that feels weird to me.

I talked to Dr. Patel and he said I could go off the lithium and just take the Risperdal. He said that we could increase the dosage if necessary. He was confident, because of the progress that I had made in therapy, that I would be able to handle the switch. I was excited! I couldn't wait to talk to Gary and tell him what was going on in my head and my heart. But when I called him for my next session, his reaction wasn't what I expected. He talked to me about the risks. He said the decision to have a child was one that Josh and I needed to make as adults. It wasn't a decision that should be made by the excitement of my little girl. He said I needed to be fair with and acknowledge the risk factors and not view some kind of negative outcome as punishment. He talked about the importance of my adult making the decision, because if my adult makes the decision, I couldn't go wrong. My adult would deal with the risks and with anything that happens. He said I had to be honest with myself in facing the realities and risks of life.

I was quiet on the phone, and when he asked what I was thinking I told him I was angry. In the middle of my excitement all he could see were the "harsh realities." I had wanted him to share my joy and excitement, but he hadn't. That's not entirely true. He told me it had been a remarkable week for me and that my excitement was wonderful. He just didn't want me making the decision based on the excitement. He made it absolutely clear that he didn't want my little girl calling the shots. It must be my adult who says I'm willing to take the risks of getting pregnant at my age. The next day I wrote . . .

I'm angry. But I'm also too sad to be angry.
I've finally admitted my deep desire and now it may be too late.
I'm angry with Gary for throwing a bucket of cold water on my excitement.
I'm angry at my mother for everything she's done to mess me up to the point that it's taken me years of therapy to overcome and (1) admit my desire to have a child and (2) possibly be able, mentally and emotionally, to handle being a mother.
I'm angry at myself for all the years I hurt myself and betrayed myself to the point that I'm just now, at thirty-eight, beginning to get well, too late to have a child of my own.
I'm angry at God.
It's not fair that all my life has had so much sadness. But then, who says life is fair?
Do verses like Psalm 37:4 not mean anything?

I'm angry with God, but then He's probably angry with me. Why wouldn't He be? All I do is ask and complain and whine. Why can't I be content where I am?

Gary says to be fair with the risk factors, not to be afraid of them and not to view bad results as punishment, either. How in the world am I supposed to do that?

And where do faith and trust come into play with all this? If I pray for a healthy baby and trust that He will answer that prayer, what happens to trust if the baby is born with a birth defect?

Why am I so messed up in my understanding of God?

I'm angry, but I'm too sad to be angry. I tried to punch on the punching bag, but I was too sad. I'm hurting right now, but the pain is different from the kind I've experienced before. I'm not sure how to describe it. It is sharp, to be sure. I just know that my heart is hurting.

There is a longing in my heart, and I fear it will never be fulfilled. I fear that we're too old.

Oh, will I have to live with this ache for the rest of my life?

I was feeling incredible sadness, so much so that it seemed like I had given up all hope of ever having a baby.

Josh,

I don't know why I bother to get excited, to get my hopes up. You say I shouldn't give up hope, but I think I have. And it hurts so much now.

We're too old. I'll be thirty-nine in October. You're almost fifty-four. The risks are too high.

And if we did decide to try and I got pregnant and then gave birth to a baby with birth defects, I wouldn't want you to blame me and hate me for pushing the issue.

It's better to just give up now.

I'll get over it, just please try to be patient with me. I'm hurting right now.

Love,
Rochelle

P.S. I wish it would work. I wish we could have a child. I want to hope, but I'm afraid.

Dear Gary,

I'm hurt. And I am hurting. Two sessions ago you asked me who I was trying to convince about the baby issue. You told me to think about it, so I did. I realized it was the little girl's dream. I realized I really did want to have a baby. I was so excited, so full of life. But then when I told you everything, you totally poured cold water on me. You told me it was all exciting, but then you told me that just because I recognized the dream, doesn't mean I have to do it. And you reminded me of all the "harsh realities." I feel like you built me up only to let me down. Couldn't you have just shared my joy for a little while? You told me that the excitement was wonderful, but not to make the decision based on the excitement. I understand that, but now there's no excitement. Josh says I seem to have given up hope. I guess I have. I wish you had let me be in my self-delusion. At least then it wouldn't hurt so bad. And one of the hard things about this hurt is I want to talk with you and have you say wise things to help me feel better, but what you said is part of the hurt. I don't know how to get out of this pit I'm in. I'm sorry if I'm being stupid about this. I'm sorry if you're mad at me for what I've said here. I've always been honest with you. If what I'm thinking and feeling is off, maybe you can help me see straight. Even Josh says it seems like you built me up only to let me down. Please help me, Gary.

I love you,
Rochelle

When I talked to Gary several days later, he said he was sorry he had added to my distress, but he wanted to make sure I understood how important it was for my adult to make this decision. He said if the little girl makes the decision, she will always be disappointed when reality hits. I asked him about having a child with birth defects. He replied, "So?" I would need to love my child unconditionally, regardless. He told me not to worry about the excitement; he said the excitement would come when it was needed. But the excitement was unnecessary in the midst of weighing such an important decision. Having a baby, raising a child is something an adult does, not a little girl. The adult needs to weigh the cost.

Then he said how I do in the future with my mental health depends on now and whether I'm going to be swayed by unreasonable, faulty theological beliefs. It depends on the decision I make now about how I choose to view God. He said it is a choice, a decision. The adult deals with facts; the little girl deals with emotions. I had to decide to view God correctly by faith, although sometimes my insecure heart might waver. I asked him if it were really that simple and he said it was. Life is a lot simpler than we make it; I make life a lot more complicated than it really is. It is like obeying the gospel. You make the decision to be baptized and you accept by faith that God really has forgiven you. I had to make the decision to view God correctly, as the Bible presents Him. Gary said to put my decision in writing, date it, and sign my name to it. Then if my insecure heart wavers, I'll have it in writing and I can remind myself of the decisions I've made about how to view God. So that's what I did.

I am making the decision that if Josh and I have a child and it happens to have a birth defect, I will not blame God. I will not view the situation as God punishing me. The Gospel of John, chapter 9, makes it clear that birth defects are not God punishing the parents or the child. I am making the decision to have the right attitude about having a child. I will take what comes, for better or worse. I am making the decision that regardless of what kind of child we have (if we have one), I will love our child unconditionally, with adult agape love. And I am making the choice not to worry about the outcome. I am making the decision to give this to God and to do the best I can with whatever the outcome (no child, healthy child, unhealthy child).

I am making the choice to believe what the Bible says about God—that He loves me and forgives me. As long as I am walking in the light, trying to please God (however imperfectly), He continues to forgive me and keep me clean (1 John 1:7).

I am making the decision that I don't have to punish myself or keep trying to earn a place with God. I can't. I have a place with God solely by His grace. I am His child, His daughter.

I am making the decision to live my life with joy regardless of the circumstances. Happiness truly is a choice and I am in control of my own mind, my own decisions, my own emotions. I am not simply a victim of my childhood, my past, my family, or anybody else. I am responsible for how I live the rest of my life. Because I have courageously looked at and dealt with my life and my issues, I am integrating and I am no longer held back by my past.

I am making the decision to live life abundantly, as Jesus said in John 10:10.

Rochelle Murray
5-19-08

Josh and I spent quite a bit of time praying for wisdom in making the decision to try to have a child. We also asked nine families who were good friends to be praying for us. During the next week I had an appointment with my Ob-Gyn. Josh and I had typed a list of concerns and questions for him. He was very patient with us and very thorough. After talking with the doctor, Josh and I decided that yes, we did want to try to have a baby! We weighed the risks, counted the cost, and decided to try to have a child, even with my mental health issues, even at our ages. Later that day, I wrote a letter to God.

Dear God,

Thank you so much for everything You've done for me. You've helped me in so many ways and brought so much change into my life. Five years ago I was so depressed and hopeless. But You brought me through. You've been there with me the whole way. Thank You so much, God. You've brought healing into my life. At one time I despaired of ever having mental health, and yet I see that happening in me. And You brought this about through Your Word and through Your people. So many people have been praying for me all this time. So many people loved me. And Lord, there were three special people. You sent Dr. Patel into my life, and he has so much knowledge about how to help me. You used him and the medication to help me get back on track. Then you brought Gary into my life. Wow! How can I thank You enough for Gary and his wise, patient counsel? I'm not sure I'd have made it through without his help. Thank You, Lord. And most of all, God, thank You for Josh. For years I waited for him and cried to You and complained to You about wanting a husband. People used to tell me that when the time was right, he would come. They were correct. You brought Josh into my life at the perfect time. Thank You, thank You, thank You! I think a husband is supposed to give his wife a picture of God and a marriage is supposed to give us both a picture of Christ and His church. You have given me those pictures through Josh and our marriage. Thank You God.

And now, Lord, Josh and I are considering having a child. We would like to get pregnant and have a healthy baby. Please, Father, I ask You, to help bring that about. Lord, please help me be able to handle the switch in my medication. I'm nervous about that God, because the lithium has helped me for so long, but I can't get pregnant if I'm on it. Dr. Patel says he can increase the Risperdal and rely on it instead of the lithium. Please let that work, Lord. Please help my body adjust and please help the depression stay away and not get me. I pray, God, that I am healthy enough now to be able to handle this change. I'm nervous and anxious about this, God. Please guard my heart and my mind in this process.

Lord, I'm also concerned about being able to get pregnant. God, I pray that I am fertile and that we don't have problems conceiving. And Father, please give us a healthy baby. We know there are risks. Please bless us with a healthy child. I pray that the supplements the doctor has given me will help our child to be whole and healthy. Lord, please grant me the desire of my heart, a healthy child.

And Father, help Josh and me to be good parents. Help us to model You for our child. Help us to not make the same mistakes our parents made with us. Lord, I want to be a good mommy. I want to show my son or daughter unconditional, agape love. Help me to do that. Help Josh to do that. I know we won't be perfect, but help us to be loving and godly parents.

Dear God, it's surreal, me thinking and planning and dreaming about having a child. For so long I denied that part of me. Forgive me, please. Thank you for helping me grow and get healthier. Thank You for helping me to integrate with the little girl. I've still got more integrating to do, but every day my personality gets healthier and more whole. Please help me continue to heal and change and grow. Thank You, Lord, for everything. I love You. Help me love You more.

Rochelle

Gary was right about the excitement. It came. But it was genuine excitement for an adult decision that Josh and I had made, not the animation of a little girl. Gary was delighted for us and reminded us that in most of life the benefits are worth the risks. I told him I was nervous about going off the lithium, and he reminded me that the struggle I might have in going off my meds was one of the reasons I had to be sure I had the adult on board. This was not child's play. He was very pleased that I was more in charge of the little girl now. He said that it was not only an exciting time for me, but also a healthier time.

Dr. Patel gave me detailed instructions about how and when to reduce the lithium until I was completely off of it. To make sure it was entirely out of my system, I had to be off of the lithium for two months before Josh and I could start trying to get pregnant. If my mood started getting depressed or anxious, I could increase the dosage of the Risperdal. Over the next two weeks I lowered the dosage until I was no longer taking any lithium. For two more weeks I did quite well. But then something happened and my mood plummeted.

27

Violation

Violation,
like a house
broken into,
robbed and
stripped
of its contents;
or,
like a nation,
attacked and
trampled on by
one with whom
they had signed
a peace treaty;
or,
like a woman,
desecrated and
assaulted
by a stranger;
or,
like a person
whose confidence is
deceived and
betrayed
by her
friend.
Violation.

On Memorial Day weekend my mother came to visit. She arrived Friday evening and left Monday morning. On Saturday at noon, Josh and I went to a birthday party for one of the church members while my mother stayed at the house. We were gone for about two hours. My mother told me she was going to wash and fix her hair. I worried a little about her snooping in my stuff, but I had my journals hidden, so I didn't think about it too much. When we got home from the party, however, I could immediately tell something was wrong. Her face told me that she was upset and pouty and she remained that way the entire weekend. Strangely, for the first time in years, I didn't feel all that uncomfortable around her. But she was very uncomfortable, I could tell. I didn't ask her, though, what was wrong. A couple of days after she left, I wrote her a letter. Of course, I would never send it, but it felt good just writing it.

May 28, 2008

Dear Mom,

    I just wanted to take a few minutes to let you know something: I am not going to play your games! You were here visiting this past weekend and the whole time you were unhappy and pouty, but I didn't ask you what was wrong. I didn't ask if you were okay. I didn't ask if you were feeling all right. I know you wanted me to because that's what you always do, and that's the game I've played with you my entire life. You act upset until I ask what is wrong, then you unload on me. I've played your games my entire life, and I'm not going to do it anymore, because I'm not unhealthy anymore. I'm not ruled by the child in me anymore. I'm not under your control and domination anymore. I am independent from you. I have separated from you. I have left you and am cleaving to my husband. I have grown up. That is the truth. I'm sure you think I am totally insensitive and uncaring about your feelings, but the truth is that I am getting healthy. My behavior is mature behavior, something you wouldn't know much about.

    And I'm not afraid of you anymore, either. All my life I have been afraid of you because the little girl in me was in control. But she is not in control anymore. I am. And my adult Rochelle is not afraid of you. My adult has no reason to be afraid of you. Why should I be? You are pathetic. You act like a pouting, manipulative twelve-year-old. You act like a child, but you have no sense of play or silliness like a child would have. You are really pathetic.

    I am different, Mom. I am not the same little girl you controlled and manipulated when I was a child, when I was a teenager, or even when I was a young adult. For the last five years, I have been working diligently to

CHAPTER 27: VIOLATION

change, to grow, to get healthy. You will not be able to get away with the same garbage you've gotten away with for so many years. I will react to you differently now and you probably won't like it. Instead of looking for other ways to manipulate me and try to get your way, why don't you learn from me? Why don't you learn a few things about mental health and maturity? Am I perfect? Heavens, no. Will I always get it right? No. Am I the paragon of normalcy, mental health, and maturity? No. But I'm getting better and healthier all the time. Certainly more than you!

I love you. And since I love you, I am setting boundaries with you. I'm sorry if you don't like it, but that's what healthy adults do. I served you in a number of ways this past weekend, and you seemed extremely uncomfortable with it. I served you because I love you and I want what's best for you. I don't like you, but I love you. Maybe someday you'll know that.

Love,
Rochelle

A week later I was talking to my grandmother on the phone and she asked me if anything had happened between me and my mother during her visit. I braced myself for what was coming.

Violated

I was talking to Grandma today. She asked, "Did something happen between you and your mother when she was there?" I said, "No, why?" She said my mother had been upset since she got home over a week ago. I said I didn't know why she would be upset, that Mom seemed kind of pouty while she was here, but I didn't know what it was about. I said, "If she's upset with me, she can talk to me about it." Grandma kept asking why she was upset and finally she told Grandma, "Well, I found out what Rochelle really thinks about me." I told Grandma I didn't know what she was talking about and I left it at that.

I can't prove it, but I know that my mother snooped while she was here. And the only place she could have found anything was on my computer. I had my journal and all my notes about my book hidden safely away, but the computer was right there in the study. When Josh and I went to that birthday party, Mom stayed at the house. She took a shower and washed and fixed her hair, but there was still plenty of time for her to snoop. We weren't home more than thirty seconds before I could tell that she was pouting. She pouted on and off for the rest of the time she was here. She was very cold toward me and acted extremely uncomfortable around me. If she snooped on my computer, that would explain her behavior and her comments to Grandma.

I looked on my computer to see what she might have read. She easily could have been drawn to the folder that says "Rochelle's Stuff" and from there to the folder entitled "Therapy." In that folder there were any number of files she might have read, including ones named "Ode to Mom," "Mother," and "Mother's Day." If she read any of those, she would have gotten an eyeful, things like "she makes me sick, I am repulsed by her, can't stand her, she's so selfish," and so on. I can't prove it, but I know she did.

I am really pissed. Once again, she violated my boundaries. But this time, she is the one who got burned. I have no idea what, if anything, is going to come of this. I seriously doubt she would be willing to admit to snooping in my stuff. But who knows, she might surprise me. I guess if she comes to visit again, I need to put a lock on my computer! Wouldn't that surprise her, if she got on my computer one evening after we had gone to bed and found herself locked out!

Josh said maybe God can use this episode to answer our prayers. We have been praying for a number of months that God would work in my mother's life to bring her to repentance. If she's open to God, maybe that will happen as a result of this. She did wrong in violating my boundaries, but God is quite able to use our misdeeds to bring about good. Maybe that will happen here. We'll see. Josh also said that I need to look at this as Satan trying to get at me. He knows that I'm in the process of going off my meds right now, and he's trying to undermine how well I'm doing. I need to not let Satan get the upper hand and get me upset and all out of sorts about this. Josh is right. And just like I don't intend to let my mother win, I don't intend to let Satan win, either.

So what do I do? Nothing, really, unless Mom brings something up. Then I don't let her bait me or get me upset. I put it back on her and focus on where she got her information in the first place. In other words, I don't let her get away with violating my boundaries. Until then, I need to act normal when I talk to her. Of course, talking to her as little as possible is always a good idea.

I shouldn't be surprised that she violated my boundaries. She's been doing it all my life, but it still angers me. It pisses me off and fills me with

CHAPTER 27: VIOLATION

indignation. But there's something good from all this, something good I see about myself. Before, I would have been all upset and worried about how I could make it up to her, calm her down, and placate her. But I'm not thinking that way now. I'm angry. I'm trying to figure out how to set better boundaries with my computer in the future. I'm trying to figure out how to handle her if she does bring it up. But I'm not trying to figure out how to appease her. I didn't do anything wrong—she did. When she was here, Josh and I were nothing but nice to her. If she got her feelings hurt because she violated my boundaries and snooped where she shouldn't have, that's her own fault! The fact that I had stuff written about her on my computer is not wrong. She violated my boundaries by snooping in my stuff. And I am angry.

During the next two sessions Gary and I talked about the violation. I was concerned about what to do if she confronted me. Gary said that at some point she might confront me, but for now, just to let her sweat. If she confronted me, she would have to admit to snooping. Gary was very proud of how I was handling this turn of events. He said it was evidence that my adult was in charge rather than the little girl. We talked about how, in a way, there was a sense of satisfaction that my mother knew. I didn't like the way she went about it, but now she knew. I didn't have to keep hiding and being afraid of her anymore. Gary pointed out that if I am ever to have a healthy relationship with her, eventually my mother and I would have to deal with the truth. Now the first word of truth was known and the world hadn't come to an end. He said I was starting yet another new chapter of my healing.

I was doing fairly well without the lithium. I was having trouble sleeping, but my mood, despite what I suspected my mother had done, was remaining fairly stable. However, on June 20, I called my mother to ask her a question. And then it happened.

Confrontation

Well, it finally happened. My worst fear come true. My worst nightmare realized. And yet... I'm still here. I'm still alive. I'm still standing. I was right about my mother snooping in my stuff, violating my boundaries, reading stuff I had written about her that I had saved on my computer. She admitted reading it. Well, sort of. She admitted that she had been "impulsive." She said she was upset and it was **partially** her fault. She said that since it was entitled "Mother's Day," she thought it was for her anyway and it was something I was going to give to her. Never mind the fact that Mother's Day had been two weeks before. Never mind the fact that, even if it was for her, I hadn't given it to her, so she had no right to be reading it in the first place. Never mind the fact that she violated my boundaries once again! But she admitted reading it, and she confronted me about it! She knows I think she was an awful mother. She knows I think she's selfish, obnoxious, and irritating. She knows I can't stand her. And she confronted me about it. And I survived.

Oh, it's not over yet, not by a long shot.

It happened Friday morning. I called her to ask her a question. She told me she was out in the garage trying to clean and organize. Then she abruptly changed the subject and said, "I need to talk to you about something." I knew where it was going. She said that while she was visiting us, she wanted to use our computer while we were out of the house so she could type something. Once she opened the word processing program, she noticed a document named "Mother's Day." She claimed she thought I'd written something for her and wanted to read it. She thought it was sweet that I had written something for her for Mother's Day, but quickly realized that it wasn't written for her; it was written about her.

Then, she got all teary and blubbery, talking about reading things like "repulsive, obnoxious, irritating, and selfish." She said she wanted to leave our house right then, but didn't. But when she did go home, she told Grandma what I had written. Supposedly Grandma said she couldn't believe I had written such things about her. It's obvious she either memorized the thing or (more likely) printed a copy for herself, because she knew the content really well.

When I realized where the conversation was going, I grabbed my keys and literally ran a block to the church office where Josh was. I wanted to be with him where I'd feel some support and feel stronger. Fortunately, Grandma had at least mentioned that Mom had gotten upset about something while she was here. I suspected what she had done, and I'd had the opportunity to talk about it with Gary. While on the phone with Mom, I remembered what Gary had said and I did it. I kept the conversation on the real issue. She had read something that was never intended for her; she violated my boundaries. I said it again and again.

CHAPTER 27: VIOLATION

But it didn't matter how many times I repeated it, she always responded with "Yeah, I know, but . . ." She kept up her tearful tirade: "What have I done? How was I a bad mother?" I told her this was not the time to get into it; she was too emotional. She said, "Don't you think I should be emotional about this?" Then she started with the manipulation. "I guess I'll have to go through the rest of my life without knowing what I've done to my daughter!"

I think I handled myself pretty well. I didn't get emotional, and I didn't give in to her manipulation. I retained my composure. I didn't let her violate any more boundaries by getting into therapy issues. I didn't try to placate her or justify myself as I would have in the past. I did tell her that what she read was never intended to be seen by her; it wasn't intended for her. I wrote it as part of my therapy as I was working through some issues. She said, "What do you mean issues? What stuff are you working through? Why won't you tell me?" Again, I told her, "This is not the time to talk about it." She wailed, "The only reason you maintain contact with me is because I'm your mother." I told her, whether she believed me or not, that the reason I maintained contact with her is because I love her. Then, she said: "I guess I'll just go now. I love you. There's nothing else to say. You won't tell me anything." And she hung up on me.

The whole time she spoke in this desperate, pitiful, wounded tone, no doubt intending to make me feel guilty, as if this were my fault. But it wasn't. She was in the wrong 100 percent. She violated my boundaries. She snooped in my personal writings on my computer.

Once I got off the phone, I shouted, stomped, paced around, then finally cried. Thankfully, Josh and I were the only ones at the office. He told me how well I'd handled myself. I calmed down enough to come home and start pounding on the punching bag. I was really angry and I was punching really hard. After I calmed down, I left a message for Gary to call me and why. He called me back that afternoon (fortunately, he'd had a cancellation. He called it a "God thing").

Gary said he was pleased with how I'd done. He agreed with Josh on that. He told me that this was a positive thing. My worst fear had been realized and my mother hadn't left me. Instead, she's now suffering because her fantasy that we have a wonderful relationship has been destroyed. He advised me not to let her manipulate me into talking about any therapy issues with her. He said I'm not strong enough for her yet; she's too skilled at manipulation and control. He advised me to set a boundary with her: if she really wants to know about my issues, if she's really serious about working through this, she would have to meet with Gary and me. Gary said Mom and I will never have a healthy relationship unless and until she's willing to deal with the issues, mine and hers.

That night, after talking to Gary, I was feeling pretty good. Josh and I even went out to eat "to celebrate" the positive changes that were happening and how well I had handled myself with her. But on Saturday, I noticed I was feeling down. It eventually dawned on me that I was feeling guilty about causing my mother to suffer. I was doing what I've always done—excusing her and blaming myself. It was infuriating, because I know in my head that I've done absolutely nothing wrong. She did something wrong, but I still felt guilty as if it were my fault.

Saturday night I told Josh that I felt like my soul was being stretched on a torture rack because of the battle between what I know in my head to be right and what I was taught to believe as a child. I believed that everything was my fault, never my mother's fault. It was my job to make her feel better and help her maintain her fantasy. I sure wish I could stop this faulty belief system from getting me down.

I continued to struggle over the next few days and I spent a lot of time writing in my journal.

Placating and Excusing

I've been having a hard time since I talked to my mom on Friday. Here it is, Tuesday and I'm still upset. I'm handling her well by not trying to placate her or anything like that, but it is so uncomfortable. I am so programmed to placate, pacify, and appease her. It's been that way my entire life. I've always been expected to do that. And now that I'm not, it feels very uncomfortable. If Mom was upset, whether I had done anything to upset her or not, it was always my job to make things right. And if I didn't, she just got angrier. So I would placate. I would say or do something to win her over, to smooth over things, to calm her down. I'm not doing that this time. Well, at least not like before.

I guess, to an extent, I've still done that. Because I sent her an e-mail yesterday. She is leaving for a two-week trip overseas tomorrow and I just couldn't let her leave without saying something to her. I told her I hoped

Chapter 27: Violation

she had a good trip and that Josh and I would be praying that she would be safe. So once again, I guess I was placating. Will I ever learn? Josh said he didn't think I was placating. He thought I was simply doing what was right despite her misbehavior. Regardless, I sent it.

She sent an e-mail back.

"Thank you.

I love you.

You have always been the most important thing to me on this earth."

I was ready to cry when I read that. I wondered, if I'm the most important thing on this earth to her, why she doesn't show it? Why doesn't she treat me as if I'm important? If I'm so important, why has her image always been more important to her than my mental health? Why won't she stop violating my boundaries? Why does she always have to guilt me and manipulate me? Why won't she ever apologize to me or say she's sorry?"

Her e-mail felt like an attempt to guilt me, too. I'm sure in her mind she thinks I am most important to her, but she seemed to imply that while I'm important to her, she's not important to me. And, as always, there's never any admission of guilt on her part. She never says "I'm sorry. I'm sorry I hurt you." She only talks about how much I've hurt her. She did it before Josh and I got married. When she came to meet him after we were engaged, she got emotional and upset about how I had hurt her because I hadn't shared his background with her before. She never apologized for how she had treated me during our courtship or for how she had acted toward him or for the things she had said about him or for refusing to let me bring him to meet her at spring break. Instead she cried and carried on about how much I had hurt her and how it was all my fault.

It's always my fault. Even when I accused Papa of sexually abusing me, she made me feel as if it was my fault. **She** was going through hell because of what I had said; **she** was upset because of what I was claiming. What about the hell *I* was going through. What about what *he* had done? And what about the things she had done wrong? I may not have been the perfect child, but she wasn't the perfect mother either! She won't admit any culpability. The blame is always mine. And I always take it. On the phone Friday, I told her I was sorry, that I never meant to hurt her, but she never apologized to me. She never even said she was sorry for snooping on my computer. She excused herself by saying she was impulsive. Apparently she believes the old line that love means never having to say you're sorry. But I always beat myself up and heap the guilt on myself for everything, whether it is my fault or not. I excuse her and everyone else for everything that goes wrong and I blame myself. And sometimes I am to blame.

But not always. And not this time. I'm not the one who violated boundaries. I'm not the one who snooped in her adult daughter's private writings. Yet, I blame myself for what has happened between us. Gary says that I should look at these current developments as a positive thing. The Lord is providing an opportunity for me to unload stuff that has made me sick (literally) for years. Maybe now God can work in her life to help her face her own demons and work through her own issues. I know Gary's right, but I can't help but feel guilty and responsible for hurting her. And there I go, excusing her again and making it all my fault.

Josh says that it seems like the adult was in charge of the phone call, but the little girl has been in charge ever since. It's like I'm thinking that I have been a bad girl and gotten Mommie upset, so I'm beating up on myself trying to make up for it. I asked him how I was supposed to not think of myself as a bad girl in this situation, and he reminded me that I have to make a decision. It is my choice as to how I am going to feel about all this and how I am going to react. That's hard because I have been programmed to think that everything is always my fault. I've been programmed to excuse others. I've been programmed to blame myself and placate Mom when she is upset, whether with me or just in general. In fact, I do that with everyone. I do it with Josh. If he is upset, I think it is my fault, regardless of what he's upset about. And I try to make it all better. Trying to smooth things over with someone or for someone is not necessarily a bad thing, but it's not always my fault!

I feel like I am saying that I don't have any responsibility for any of my problems. Or that nothing is my fault, that I'm playing the blame game with the world. That's not what I am saying at all. I know that I am responsible for many of my problems. I've spent five years in therapy trying to undo some of the damage I've done to myself. I've abused and betrayed myself. There has been a lot of sin in my life, and I've brought much of it on myself. But sin is a two-way street. We sin against ourselves, but we also sin against others and we are sinned against. For me to take responsibility for something that is not my responsibility is wrong. Each person must take responsibility for their own sins, including my mother.

The adult in my head knows these things, but in my heart, I still feel like the little girl whose responsibility it was to make Mommie happy. I feel guilty and I feel like I've got to somehow make her all better. I need to put the adult back in control.

In my next session with Gary, we talked about conscience.

Conscience

I have an overactive conscience. That's why I take the blame for everything and always feel that whatever goes wrong is my fault. My conscience gives me the wrong messages because it was programmed incorrectly. I need to rewrite the program. The problem is that it feels wrong to rewrite my conscience. I need to do what's really right, even though it feels wrong, but it's really hard. It's the same process as searing one's conscience, but in the opposite direction. In this case, it isn't searing the conscience, but properly educating it. I have to rewrite my conscience with what I know to be true from reason, experience, and Scripture, not by what was programmed into it as a child.

I have wrong beliefs because of the way I was taught. I have believed that Mother is never wrong, it's always my fault, my job is to make Mom happy, I'm not allowed to get angry. I have to be perfect, and so on. To rewrite the program, I need to change my beliefs.

I need to believe true things. Mother can be wrong. I must take responsibility for my own sins, not the sins of others. It is not my job to make Mom or Josh or anyone else happy. That's their responsibility. It's my job to do what I can to be happy myself by controlling what I think and how I act. It's okay to get angry as long as I express it in healthy ways. I don't have to be perfect.

This overactive conscience thing is a real struggle for me. I feel guilty for so many things. If I think about something that would be nice to do for someone but don't do it, I feel guilty and beat myself up every time I think about it. The other day I thought I should call my neighbor and check on her. I didn't do it and now every time I see her house or think about her, I am filled with guilt and I beat myself up for not calling her. A twinge of regret would be okay, but not beating myself up. You know that old saying, "Step on a crack, break your mother's back"? Every time I walk on a sidewalk I think about it and purposely avoid the cracks. If I do happen to step on one, I feel guilty and berate myself mentally for thinking such thoughts.

Yesterday I was feeling a lot of anger toward my mother, and I found myself taking out my aggression on Josh. So I went and punched on my punching bag. At one point I cussed her and then I had an awful thought, wanting something bad to happen to her. I started punching the bag harder, this time in anger at myself and guilt for the thought I'd had. How could I think such an awful thing? Josh said it was a natural response to hurt and just an impulsive thought. But I had the thought, nonetheless. Then I started thinking about hate and feeling like I hate her. I hate her behavior, but there's a part of me that hates her as well. And that's wrong. More guilt. Then the magical thinking kicked in. What if the awful thought I had about her really happens?! It would be all my fault. Guilt, guilt, guilt!

How can I get to the point where I feel the emotions, but I am able to evaluate them from an adult perspective? The little girl is where the magical thinking comes from. Godly guilt is good when you have sinned. It leads you to repentance. Second Corinthians 7 makes that very clear. But what about all this guilt that I have about things I haven't done? What about all this guilt I have when it comes to my mom?

It's not just guilt when it comes to her. It is fear. I am still afraid of her. The little girl is still afraid Mom is going to turn into a monster. In a sense she does become a monster because she is acting like a child, but she is in an adult body. That is frightening to a little girl. But I have to keep the adult in control, not the little girl. My adult was in control of the phone call on Friday, but the little girl has been in control since. I need to put the adult back in control and realize that I don't need to be afraid of her.

I've wasted five days on her. For five days I've been down and upset and weird. If I learn something from these past five days, then they weren't wasted. I need to get to the point that I don't fear her—her disapproval, her tears, or even her anger. Sadness, outrage, and frustration are fine, but I've got to stop fearing her. The adult doesn't fear her. When I look at her through my adult eyes, I see a woman who is kind of pathetic. But when I look at her through my little girl eyes, I fear her. If I can keep the adult in control, it will help me not to fear her, and it will help me resist being guilted and manipulated by her.

I was really struggling. I was angry and depressed. I could up the dosage of the Risperdal if necessary. Dr. Patel had given me the okay. But I didn't know if that was what needed to be done. The day after my mother left on her overseas trip, I got an envelope from her in the mail.

CHAPTER 27: VIOLATION

Once again, she's succeeded in heaping on the guilt. I sent her that e-mail telling her I hoped she had a good trip and that Josh and I would be praying for her. I didn't call her. She e-mailed back telling me that I was the most important thing in the world to her. I still didn't call. Yesterday she left on her trip. Today I got a letter from her. It included her itinerary and instructions for what to do in case of an emergency, including financial instructions. And there was a note from her. "I love you more than you will ever know. Thanks for the e-mail, but I would rather hear my daughter's voice; especially since I'm leaving the country. I love you, Mom."

How do I deal with this? She says all the right things. And she succeeded in making me feel like the most worthless daughter ever to live. I won't even call my mother before she leaves the country. How cold and callous is that? But she doesn't understand! I'm trying to get well here. I'm trying to get past a lifetime of hurt. I'm trying to do what's right. So why do I feel so wrong?

My feelings are all jumbled up. I feel angry and hurt and sad and depressed and scared and confused. I go from one extreme to the other, from lying on the couch feeling so depressed I can't move, to punching my heart out on my punching bag, full of anger and rage. Is it because I'm off of the lithium or is it because of her? Or both? I just don't know how to deal with her and the feelings that she is stirring up.

I'm so confused and frustrated with myself because of what I wrote about her in that "Mother's Day" piece. I felt that way when I wrote it, but now I'm questioning and doubting what I said. Is it really true? Is she really that bad or is it just me? If I give in to these doubts I'll be betraying myself again and I don't want to do that. How do I deal with her? How do I get past the guilt? How do I stay true to myself? I reread one of the pieces I had written a couple of months ago ("That Pole Thing") to remind myself of why I have been so hurt by her all these years. I'm fighting with the little girl. She has been programmed to take all the blame on herself, and she has been programmed to never think that Mother is ever wrong. She's trying to get control here because my standing up to my mother is so uncomfortable for her. It's uncomfortable for me, too. Can I do this? Am I strong enough to win this battle of trying to be my own person with my mom? Am I strong enough to stand up to her or am I going to give in to her and betray myself all over again?

Gary said that going off the lithium was going to be hard. That's why he wanted to make sure that my adult was making the decision to have a baby, and not the little girl. He foresaw that it might be a struggle. He didn't foresee my mother snooping in my private writings and then confronting me about it. He didn't foresee me having to deal with that. That just adds to the difficulty of going off the lithium. How do I deal with her?

I think if I were still on the lithium I would be able to handle her better. But I'm not on it. I don't know what to do. Do I go up on the Risperdal? Dr. Patel said I could if I needed to. Is it time for that? I don't want to increase the dosage if I don't have to.

And now that she has thrown this curve ball, my emotions are all mixed up. I'm fine one minute, spitting fire the next, and zoning out the one after that. And I feel too depressed to do anything about it. I've been feeling depressed since the phone call last Friday. I've been able to fight it some. I'm not paralyzed with it, but I am depressed. Part of the problem is that I'm off the lithium, but it's complicated by her and her behavior. How do I balance the two, my mother and no lithium?

I finally made the decision to increase the Risperdal, and within twenty-four hours I was feeling much better. The depression lifted and I was able to be objective again. Two weeks later, when my mom was supposed to be returning from her trip, I found myself worrying all over again. Should I call her when she gets home? What if she calls me? Should I answer the phone? What do I do? Gary pointed out that, thanks to Caller ID, I didn't have to answer the phone. We decided that I wouldn't call her and I wouldn't answer the phone if she called. If she did call and left a message, I would only call her back when (1) I had prayed first; (2) I'd had time to think; (3) I chose the time to return the call; (4) Josh was with me; and (5) I had called Gary if I felt I needed to. Also, I would put her on the speaker phone if I needed to. I knew that she had gotten home safely from her trip because I talked to my grandma, but I didn't talk to my mom.

I had a dilemma, though. Her birthday was approaching. Should I call or not? I really felt like I needed to call her on her birthday, and Gary said that was a legitimate reason to call. I sent her a birthday present in the mail. On her birthday I called. Josh and I prayed first and then, when she answered, we both sang "Happy Birthday" to her over the phone. That is kind of a tradition of mine. It also let her know that Josh was right there with me. The phone call went fine. In fact, I could tell she was going out of her way to be on her best behavior.

CHAPTER 27: VIOLATION

Best Behavior?

I talked to my mother yesterday. It was her birthday. Josh and I sat down and prayed and then we made the call. When she answered, we sang "Happy Birthday." She was very excited and happy I had called. The whole phone call she was very cheerful and upbeat. I kept waiting for the other shoe to drop, for the hit and run. I asked her if she had gotten the package I mailed for her birthday. She had, but hadn't opened it yet. She told me some about her trip and we talked about her new television and our new digital camera. Wondering how to end the call, I finally told her I had to go. She said, "Thank you for calling me. It was good to hear your voice." I didn't say anything in response to that, like it was good to hear her voice too. I'm sure that's what she wanted to hear. Instead I told her I hoped she had a good birthday. Then we said we loved each other, and I told her goodbye.

When I got off the phone I had a mixture of emotions. I was elated that the call went okay, that she behaved herself, and I did well. But I was nervous. And wary. She said she would call me back after she opened her package. But I didn't worry or obsess about it. I just went on about my day.

That evening she called after she had opened her birthday gift. She went on and on about how wonderful her present was and how much she loved it. She was very cheerful and upbeat, almost to excess. No, definitely to excess. She gushed about how much she loved the gift. As usual, it was hard for me to get a word in edgewise. I was fine with her on the phone, but a little reserved. She talked more about her trip, again going on and on. As I was listening, I found myself getting angry. She was sharing her joy about her trip with me, but she never allowed any reciprocation. For instance, when I got married, was she sharing my joy, the most joyous time of my life? No. Am I able to share with her my joy about possibly getting pregnant? No.

It was a pleasant enough conversation, I guess. Quite different from what I had envisioned. That was good. But I'm still waiting for the other shoe to drop. She won't avoid the negative stuff forever. It was almost pitiful, listening to her. It was like she was desperately trying to be cheerful and get on my good side. I do feel that I have scored a minor victory with her. I refused to call her for a month and this time, when I finally did call her, she was on her best behavior. I guess you could call it that. But I'm still wary. And I hope she doesn't think I'm over being mad at her and I'm going to start calling again, because I'm not.

Gary said that she knows I'm getting stronger and she's more careful about engaging me. She's still feeling out these new boundaries I've set. But I have a good game plan—having Josh there with me if I talk to her and inviting her to meet with Gary and me. He said calling her for her birthday was good, and now I needed to leave well enough alone. The key, he said, was for me not to get into the compulsive calling that I've done in the past. Before, when I would feel fear, I would often call her in an attempt to feel safer. But that would be counter-productive here. Besides, Gary said he didn't want me calling her, so I didn't call. Another month went by and every day that I didn't talk to my mother, I felt stronger and weaker at the same time; stronger because I had gone another day without calling her, but weaker because every day I went without talking to her would make it that much harder when I did finally talk to her. And I didn't know how to interpret her silence. I thought not calling her would cause her to get angry and pouty with me, but she hadn't. Some days were hard for me, but most days I just went about my business and didn't worry about it much. I was living my life and continuing to heal.

I read a book about children of narcissistic parents, and I had my eyes opened to some things in my own behavior. I was seeing narcissistic characteristics in myself, and I didn't like what I saw.

I Don't Want to Be Like My Mother!

I've been reading a couple of books about toxic parents. One of them is *Children of the Self-Absorbed: A Grown-Up's Guide to Getting Over Narcissistic Parents.* In it the author describes four different types of self-absorbed parents. As I was reading some of the descriptions, I had somewhat of an epiphany—and I was horrified. Some of the descriptors, in fact many of them, described me! Some of the behaviors and attitudes I was aware of, but some I was seeing for the first time. I exhibit these behaviors and attitudes mostly with Josh. If I am this way now, what's going to happen if we are able to get pregnant and have a baby? Am I going to be this way with my child? How do I keep from behaving in these ways with my child? I don't want to be like my mother! I don't want my child to need to be in therapy and read books like this! I'm going to have to be on guard against acting in these ways if we have a baby. Actually, I need to work on them now, with Josh. I asked Josh if I ever smothered him and he said yes, sometimes I did.

CHAPTER 27: VIOLATION

I feel very sad today. I've been in therapy so long and I've had to change so many things. I've made a tremendous amount of progress, but I still have so far to go if I am going to be healthy. I am clingy with Josh and overly nurturing and overprotective with him. I complain a lot about just about everything. I am critical and criticizing—of myself, my house, other people, the way people do things, situations, you name it. I don't say anything critical to other people, but I say critical things about other people to Josh. I try not to be critical about Josh and I am **not** critical about Josh to other people. I try really hard not to be critical about him, either to myself or to him, but I still am at times. My feelings are easily hurt and I take offense easily. I am hypersensitive to perceived criticism, even when Josh and I are joking around and teasing each other. I want to know Josh's every thought and feeling. I constantly ask him what he's thinking. I use soothing behaviors to keep Josh from experiencing his feelings, especially if he is angry about something. He says I often minimize his feelings. I'm picky and think everything must be done my way. I've actually been working on not acting this way for the last couple of months. I remind myself that if we have a child and he or she does something Josh's way rather than mine, it will be all right. He can do it the way Daddy does it or the way Mommy does it or even his own way. It will be his preference.

It really was an epiphany seeing myself in these descriptions. I've got to change! I've got to get a handle on these things! I don't want to be like her!

Gary said it was good that I was seeing these things; it was encouraging. I wasn't looking just at my mother and feeling fear. I was looking at myself and making an appraisal of what my upbringing had done to me. I was seeing some of the residual damage, things I hadn't even been aware of before. And I was taking responsibility for myself. I started trying to be aware of when I would exhibit these behaviors and trying to change.

I was still not calling my mother. During the month after her birthday, there were a couple of times when she called me. I didn't answer and she didn't leave a message. In mid-August, I got an e-mail from her. It was, in my opinion, full of attempts to make me feel guilty. But it didn't work. And I didn't reply, either.

Judging

My mother sent me an e-mail today. It was a story and a video. She told me that since "I'm not as good with words as you are," for me to read the story and watch the video because they are "full of my wishes for you and Josh." The video had really pretty pictures, nice music, and some nice sentiments about wanting me to be blessed. But part of it was about not judging people. Coupled with the story she sent, I heard her message loud and clear—I shouldn't judge her. The story was about a lady who misjudged her new employer, but when the lady became ill, saw a different side of her, and the two became the best of friends through the years. The last five paragraphs were all about not judging and not hating. One part talked about hating people because we label them wrong and ourselves right. It stated that when we judge people in that way, we build a wall of separation that keeps us from ever really knowing them.

The problem is that the wall of separation between my mother and me wasn't erected because I am judging her. Her behavior has been erecting that wall, brick by brick, for years. Yes, the Bible says, "Do not judge, or you too will be judged" (Matthew 7:1). But the Bible also says that you recognize good and bad by the person's fruit, i.e., their behavior, their actions (Matthew 7:15-20). The Bible also states that we should "[p]roduce fruit in keeping with repentance" (Matthew 3:8). Knowing I am upset with her, instead of showing any sorrow or offering an apology for hurting me, my mother sends me an e-mail about not judging. In her view, because I am "judging her," I'm the one in the wrong. That's how it's always been. I'm wrong and she is right.

Am I never wrong in my relationship with her? No, not by any means. I've done many things through the years that have hurt our relationship, but I am working to change. I've been in therapy for almost five years now. I've made a lot of changes, but I have a long way to go. I see many ways in which I am very self-absorbed and need to change even still. I am working on changing.

But it's always the same with her. **I'm** the one in the wrong. There's never an admission of guilt on her part for hurting the relationship. Maybe I am judging her, but I'm judging her based on the fruit of her behavior that shows me that she is still in the business of handing down guilt and manipulation. That's what the story and video were all about. She sends these things under the guise of wishing blessings on us, but they are full of messages about not judging and not being critical.

Chapter 27: Violation

The author of the story talked about when she was a girl and would criticize someone in her grandmother's presence, the grandmother would remind her that unless she'd walked in that person's shoes, she had no right to judge. I'd like to see my mother take her own e-mail to heart. She has always been extremely critical of me, even to my face. The next time she tells me I was a rotten kid or that I am a terrible person I will remind her of this e-mail. Don't judge, don't criticize! She's critical of other people all the time, too. That's where I get it from. I struggle with being critical of others. But I recognize the problem and I'm trying to change it. Knowing I got that tendency from her doesn't excuse me for acting that way. I'm still responsible for how I behave. I just wish she would admit her guilt, too. And contrary to what she may think, I don't hate her. But I am sick of how she treats me. And as long as she is toxic to me, the best thing for me to do is stay away from her.

The longer I went without calling her, the easier it got. Some days were easier than others. Some days I felt fine; other days I felt quite sad. I had been off the lithium for two months, so Josh and I were able to start trying to conceive. The Risperdal was working pretty well, and Gary continually told me that I was doing remarkably well considering I was no longer on the lithium. I wondered how long it would be before I heard from her again. I didn't have to wait long. On Wednesday, August 27, I received a four-page letter from her.

28
Truth

Truth,
like a prisoner
in a deep, dark
dungeon,
escorted
slowly up the
winding steps,
and brought out into
the bright
light of day,
where he is
unchained,
unshackled, and
released,
free to go,
free to live
in peace,
free from
deceit and
shame and
fear,
full of relief
and joy—
ecstatic and
ready to
embrace life,
and live a life of
Truth.

When I checked the mailbox that morning and saw the envelope from her, I got a queasy feeling in the pit of my stomach. I didn't open it right away. Instead, I went to Josh's office before lunch and opened it there. We read the letter together. It was an apology. Sort of.

To my beloved daughter, Rochelle:

> First of all, I ask your forgiveness. I don't know what I did/have done/am presently doing that caused you to turn away from me and caused you to have to "work through" something. I am so appalled that I would have hurt you in any way. It is so heartbreaking to know that I have caused you any distress. My greatest desire in life has been for your salvation and happiness. This has been a constant prayer to God throughout your life. I have thanked God so often for blessing me with you and for the wonderful woman you grew up to be.
>
> I had thought we were close, and I was stunned to realize what you really thought of me. I don't even know what I did. I have not called you because I'm afraid to say anything for fear it will be "selfish, obnoxious, and irritating." I realize you must not want me in your life because of the person I am and because you feel I "was not a good mother." If you wanted to hurt me for whatever I do/did, you have succeeded greatly. I am so very sorry and greatly grieved that I hurt you.
>
> When I talked to you in June and told you I had read the document "Mother's Day," I asked for your forgiveness for opening and reading it. I honestly didn't think . . . I just momentarily thought you had written it for me. I am sorry. You had told me on the phone that you didn't want to talk about it right then because I was too upset and that we'd talk about it later. You've never called me since then, so I feel that you don't want a relationship with me. The birthday gift was very thoughtful because you are that kind of person. As I said, I'm afraid to call you because you haven't told me what I do or say that is "selfish, obnoxious, and irritating." I have soul-searched and prayed so about this and asked God to help me change, but I don't know what to work on.
>
> In your document, you stated how much you "dreaded Mother's Day;" "instead of reacting with disgust and loathing . . . calmer." I am so sorry for causing you anguish. You stated that you "didn't have a very good mother." "She's still my mother—selfish, obnoxious, and irritating, but the revulsion toward her seems to be gone—or at least dissipated." Nothing has ever broken my heart and spirit, knowing you felt that way and that I caused it. I was so blessed with you, but you were not blessed with me. I thank God

that you and Josh love each other so much and seem to be so perfect for each other, for I know you'll be happy from now on.

Something else in the document has me quite perplexed. It said, "I know I still have to be on my guard with her. I can tell from being on the phone with her this afternoon. She hasn't changed one bit." I don't know why or what I've done.

I beg your forgiveness. I love you more than anything on this earth, your mother.

She did not sign it "Mom," just "your mother." As I read the letter, the queasy feeling in the pit of my stomach got hard and I got angry. I spent the rest of the day thinking about it. The next morning, I woke up at 4:45 a.m. and couldn't go back to sleep, so I got up and started working on the computer, trying to analyze my mom's letter. I worked on it for about three hours, making lots of notes and typing out my conclusions. I was in a better frame of mind afterward.

The Letter

I knew the silence between my mother and me wouldn't go on forever. Yesterday I received a four-page letter from her. I'm still not sure what all my reactions to it are—anger over many of the things she said, sadness that this has all come about, sadness over her lack of insight, fear and confusion about how to respond. I've sort of analyzed the things she wrote.

First of all, she asked for forgiveness and said she was sorry five different times, but four times she states that she doesn't know what she has done. She used words like stunned, appalled, and perplexed. She said she had thought we were close, but she was stunned to realize what I really thought of her. She should take King Solomon's advice to heart to not pay attention to every word your servants say in private, because you may hear them cursing you. In other words, don't eavesdrop if you don't want to hear bad stuff about yourself. She eavesdropped on my writings when she violated my boundaries and read what I had written about her. She said that back in June when she told me she had read that "Mother's Day" piece she had asked for my forgiveness for opening and reading it, which isn't correct. She never said "I'm sorry" for doing that. She never asked for my forgiveness. She only admitted that she was impulsive and that it was only **partially** her fault. She never said she was sorry for violating my boundaries. She just kept excusing herself. If she really were sorry, why did she keep reading it when she realized what it was? And why didn't she leave it at that? No, she made a copy and took it with her. I know that because throughout this letter, she put in quotation marks the things I had said in the "Mother's Day" piece, exactly as I had written them.

She said that she is "heartbroken" and "grieved" that she caused me distress and anguish. She said I have broken her heart and her spirit. She said if I ever "wanted to hurt me for whatever I do/did, you have succeeded greatly." She is attributing motives to me that aren't there. She's forgetting what I said in June. I never intended to hurt her. That piece was never intended for her to read in the first place! She's hurt because of her own wrongdoing (snooping and violating my boundaries), not because I said something to her. I said nothing to her. She read my stuff on my own computer. That's the issue she keeps forgetting. And yes, **now** she has apologized for reading it, but she doesn't seem to realize that it was her misdeed that has caused her all this distress, not mine. I did nothing wrong.

She's also making assumptions and drawing conclusions. She said I've turned away from her. She said I must not want her in my life. She said I don't want a relationship with her. She bases this on the fact that I haven't called her and that I said I was having to "work through" some things. But I think the very fact that I am trying to work through things shows that I do want a relationship with her. I want things to work out. I haven't called because neither Gary nor Josh want me to call her right now and because I get so upset when I talk to her. I am simply setting a boundary here until I can call her without becoming so upset.

She seemed fixated on three words from my "document", as she called it: selfish, obnoxious, and irritating. She said that she is afraid to call me for fear that anything she says will be interpreted as "selfish, obnoxious, and irritating." She is afraid to call because I haven't told her what those words mean. She reminded me that in June I told her I didn't want to talk right then because she was upset and that we'd talk about it later. She concluded that because I've never called her since then to explain that I must not want a relationship with her. I have called her—on her birthday. But she's right, I haven't explained things. She's not going to like it when I do, because what I'm going to tell her is that she's going to have to sit down with me in Gary's office and talk there.

I think the biggest thing I was angry and sad about was what she said about soul-searching. She said, "I have soul-searched and prayed so about

CHAPTER 28: TRUTH

this and asked God to help me change, but I don't know what to work on." Have I really done that good of a job at hiding myself from her? I don't think so. We've had many times through the years that I have not pretended all was well and played along with her fantasy. We've had many times through the years that things have come to a head. Has she forgotten about those times? Has she forgotten how she treated Josh and me when we were dating? Has she forgotten the issues I had with her when I was hospitalized in '92 and '93? Has she forgotten her lack of support for me and my mental health problems? Has she forgotten how she treated me as a child? Has she forgotten all the times she has called me a rotten kid? Apparently! I don't see how she can honestly say that she has soul-searched and still be so clueless as to what she has ever done wrong! She doesn't admit to being aware of **anything** that she's done that would make me feel the way I did and write what I did. Saying she honestly didn't think and just momentarily thought I had written it for her does not excuse the fact that she still violated my boundaries and read it (and copied it)! She still snooped, whether it was preplanned or not. That's one thing right there! She said she was "so appalled" that she would have hurt me in any way. Well, I'm so appalled that she is so clueless!

And she played the guilt game and the poor me game, too. Right after she talked about me not calling her, she said that the birthday gift I gave her was very thoughtful but that's because I am "that kind of person." In other words, since I'm a thoughtful person I should call my mother and talk to her. At another point she said that "I was so blessed with you, but you were not blessed with me." And I can imagine the woeful and forlorn tone she said this in. Then she said that she thanked God that Josh and I loved each other so much and seemed so perfect together, "for I know you'll be happy from now on." I wonder if she was thinking, *But poor, pitiful me, all alone without even my daughter now. I'll never be happy.* She really is pitiful.

She said that her greatest desire in life has been for my salvation and happiness, that it has been a constant prayer to God throughout my life. She said that she has thanked God so often for blessing her with me and for the wonderful woman I grew up to be. I have no doubt these statements are true. I am glad that she prayed for my salvation and my happiness. What she needs to realize, though, is that part of my happiness is being healthy and I'm going to get healthy whether she cooperates or not. I'm still going to work through things.

She wants forgiveness. I forgive her. But forgiveness doesn't mean I'm going to open myself up to her toxicity unless I see true fruits of repentance and change that prove to me that I truly am her "beloved daughter" whom she loves "more than anything on this earth." I'm still going to guard my heart. Forgiveness is releasing someone from the debt they owe. It is a choice, a decision. I forgive my mother. I am releasing her from the debt she owes me, the debt of not being a good mother. But that doesn't necessarily mean reconciliation is going to happen, at least not automatically. Forgiveness takes one. I am making the decision to forgive her. Reconciliation takes two. She is going to have to show fruits of repentance and change that indicate she has truly owned her part of the problem. Actions and behaviors, not just the right words. She is good at saying the right words. Reconciliation will take her going to meet with Gary. Reconciliation will take her making an effort to do real soul-searching and make changes. It ain't gonna be easy! I'm not saying that I'm going to make it hard for her, because I'm not. I just know that the process of searching out your soul and finding what's wrong and sinful in your life and striving to correct it is incredibly difficult. I know, because I've been doing that for the past five years and it's been the hardest thing I've done in my entire life. I want reconciliation with her, but reconciliation is a two-way street. She's going to have to work, too.

I think this is a fairly accurate analysis of her letter. I just don't know how much of what I said should be said to her. I can't avoid her forever. Eventually I'm going to have to tell her I want her to meet with me and Gary. She's not going to like it, but that's the way it is. I just don't know how to best respond to her. Do I write her a letter? Do I call her? What? I think she needs to hear some of what I'm saying here. I'm just not sure exactly what.

The next day, I talked to Gary. He felt that my analysis of her letter was on target. I told him that maybe her snooping had forced me to make a major step in my therapy. He said "absolutely," and reminded me of Romans 8:28. "And we know that in all things God works for the good of those who love him, who have been called according to his purpose." God could and would work good out of this situation. Gary was proud of me because he said it was obvious that my adult was in charge with this, not my little girl. We decided that a letter would be the safest way for me to respond. I was intrigued as to how positive and how little fear I felt. He pointed out that there is always less fear when the dreaded thing happens. He told me to take my time in writing a response to her. I didn't

CHAPTER 28: TRUTH

have to be in a hurry. We scheduled another appointment for the following Friday. I was to work on a letter that week and we would talk about it then. I worked on my response on and off for two days. Since I was scheduled to talk to Gary on September 5, I dated the letter September 6. This letter was a letter she would receive.

September 6, 2008

Dear Mom,

I have no doubt that you love me and have prayed for me throughout my life. I very much appreciate your prayers. I believe that you have not intentionally tried to hurt me in any way. You said you don't know what you've done to hurt me and I believe you. You want to know and that's understandable. However, the things you want to know are private issues that I'm wrestling with in therapy. Let me remind you that a lot of your conclusions are based on a private document that you read on my computer that was never intended to be shared with you. Contrary to your conclusion, I did not intend to hurt you. The words that you read were never intended for you to read. But you did read it. And even if you didn't initially intend to snoop in my private writings, the fact remains that you did. You not only snooped, but you apparently printed out a copy of the document for yourself. What you read was obtained by violating my boundaries. I said none of those things to you nor did I intend to.

Now that you are aware of the fact that you have hurt me, we need to deal with some issues. Those issues, however, are therapy issues and need to be dealt with in a therapeutic context. If you really want to deal with them, then we will do so in a professional manner with professional help. I am inviting you to meet with me and Gary Walker. If you recall, he is the psychologist I have been in therapy with since I was hospitalized in 2003. The issues that you want to know about will only be opened between us in the proper context. I never said I didn't want a relationship with you. That's your own conclusion. But if you want reconciliation to occur, then we will deal with these things in therapy.

You may ask why I won't just talk to you about these issues. The fact is I'm not strong enough and not stable enough to go there alone. I've needed professional help and we need professional help. I love you. That's why I want us to get help. You asked me to forgive you and I do forgive you. But deciding to forgive you doesn't mean we don't still need to work through some things. I'm sorry that you are hurting. But keep in mind that the reason you are hurting is not because I said anything to you, but because you read something you were not supposed to read. You said that your greatest desire was for my salvation and my happiness. I want you to understand that part of my happiness is my being healthy—physically, mentally, emotionally, and spiritually. I've been working diligently toward that end for a number of years now in therapy. If you want our relationship to heal and be what it should be, then again, I invite you to come and deal with these issues with Gary and me.

I love you,
Rochelle

I felt really good about the letter, evidenced by the fact that I was not obsessing about it. Josh said that my letter was respectful, rational, objective, mature, not at all manipulative, not offensive, and quite powerful. He also said it would probably scare her half to death. He pointed out that if she had any sense at all, she would begin to see that the emperor had no clothes. In other words, she had lost her power over me. But even though I felt good about it, I found myself feeling quite sad.

> Sadness,
> like the tide
> creeping upon the sand,
> edging closer,
> slowly engulfing
> the shore;
> or,
> like a constant companion,
> ever present,
> never leaving
> your side,
> steady;
> or,
> like the endless view
> of water

CHAPTER 28: TRUTH

> when you're standing
> on the shore
> looking out—
> boundless,
> immeasurable,
> without limit.
> Sadness.

The sadness was strong, but I was also proud of how well I'd done, and the pride won out. When she got the letter, she was going to be blown away.

The Old Me

It's gonna blow her away. It's so unlike the old me.
The old me would have received her letter and immediately started falling all over myself in an effort to apologize.
The old me would have tried valiantly to explain myself, probably in vain.
The old me would have betrayed myself time and again as I took the blame for everything and excused her from any wrongdoing or culpability.
The old me would have opened myself up to more hurt and wounding as I allowed her to violate my boundaries all over the place. Actually, the old me would have never set any boundaries with her in the first place. Instead, I would have melded my soul with hers as a parasite sucks its host into itself.
The old me would have shriveled with fear at her anger and disapproval and allowed them to control me mercilessly.
The old me would have allowed myself to be manipulated into doing and saying exactly what she wanted because of her guilt-inducing messages and her tricky ploys.
The old me would never have stood up for myself or accused her of any wrongdoing or, heaven forbid, told her that she needed therapy.
She's been used to the old me for almost thirty-nine years.
But the old me is gone.
That's why my letter is gonna blow her away.

Once I wrote about the old me, it was like the light bulb suddenly clicked on and I saw that I'm different. The next day I sat at the computer and started working more on this book. I hadn't worked on it for about seven months. Every time I had tried, I'd gotten all obsessed about it and weird, but this time was different. I was able to work on it without getting overly focused on it. It felt so healthy. The next Friday morning before I called Gary, I wrote another piece.

Three Years

Tomorrow it's been three years.
Three years since I last cut.
Three years since I last carved up my body with a razor blade.
Three years.

September 6, 2005.
Three years ago.
So much has happened in those three years, but the biggest thing is I'm
    getting healthy.
Three years ago Gary suggested I try to write about my experience, taking
    all my poems and journal writings and compile them into a book.
He said it could help others.
He said it could help me.

When I started, I had no idea what it would turn into.
Three years later I'm working on chapter 28.
As I read through the book to edit it, I see so much change and so much
    growth and so much progress.
My book is a record of my healing.

I've been working on my book this week. A lot.
I've edited it once again and I've written four new chapters.
And what's amazing is that now, for the first time since I started the book
    three years ago,
I am able to work on it without
obsessing,
without getting
"weirded out."

CHAPTER 28: TRUTH

I'm changing.
I've grown.
I'm healing.
It's been over five years since I started therapy with Gary.
Five long years of
anguish and
toil and
labor.
And courage.
Five years of therapy;
three years since I cut.

Someday I will finish my book.
But not today.
Today I will celebrate.
It's been three years since I cut.

When I talked to Gary, he was thrilled when I reminded him that it had been three years since I had last cut. And he was thrilled with the letter I had written to my mom. He thought it was excellent and acknowledged that it took a lot of courage to write it. He told me it was a hard letter to argue with. I commented about how well I had been doing in working on my book and he asked, "That's because truth does what?" I replied, "Sets you free" (John 8:32). He said the truth had set me free from worrying about what will happen when the truth comes out. He reminded me of how much fear and terror I've felt for so long about my mother ever finding anything out. He said, "The minute you're not afraid, you can go about life." When you try to hide, you worry forever, but the minute you deal with truth, you are free. Once you deal with and are honest about your past, it takes away fodder for others to attack you. People understand about human failings and problems. It is our hiding that makes us sick. As long as I hide the truth and deny it, I am sick. But when I deal with truth, I get well. Then he talked about truth and my mother. He said the minute I am honest with her, she has no defense. She's afraid of truth. She's been hiding from it all her life: the truth about my birth, her marriage, my grandfather, our relationship, my mental health. Gary said I cannot heal her, but the serendipity of my dealing with truth is that I will help her. Truth is powerful! Over the course of therapy, I'd been making a paradigm shift—truth is good! But I had never really laid truth at my mother's feet. I started doing that in my letter. The truth makes me free. And Gary reminded me of something very important. If my mother never deals with truth, I will still get well because *I* am dealing with truth. Her response is not a condition for my happiness. It's not a condition for my getting well. This is my journey, not hers.

Over the last five years, truth had become more and more clear for me—the truth about myself, my childhood, my mother. Pieces were still missing, but missing pieces can't hide the truth.

CHAPTER 28: TRUTH

I mailed the letter on Saturday, September 6. I was anxious because I had no clue as to how or when she would respond, but I was proud of myself. I was getting well.

> The journey has been long and hard,
> winding roads,
> steep hills,
> rocky paths.
> I have stumbled and fallen
> along the way,
> but I always got back up.
> I always had help
> getting back up.
> God gave me strength
> and courage
> and determination.
> And I didn't walk alone.
> God gave me friends to
> walk beside me,
> friends to steady me,
> to encourage me,
> to guide me.
> He gave me wise and godly
> counsel.
> He gave me strong and joyful
> love.
> My journey is not over,
> I still have a long way to go.
> But I am not afraid
> of what lies ahead,
> because I know that
> what lies behind
> has made me
> stronger,
> healthier,
> happier.
> It's made me whole.

29
Grief

Grief,
like a
terrific wave,
crashing
mercilessly
over you,
knocking you
off your feet,
sucking you under
the dark, swirling water;
or,
like a
heavy weight,
pressing down on
your chest,
crushing your lungs
and making breathing
impossible;
or,
like a hot, humid day,
sweltering heat
sapping all
strength and
vitality and
life;
or,
like a
pervasive sadness,
creeping
over you,

overshadowing
everything,
allowing
nothing
to remain untouched
by its clutches,
gripping you
in the depths of
despair.
Grief.

I hadn't heard anything from my mother since I mailed my letter to her on September 6. So when she called on September 27, I was a little nervous as I answered the phone. But what she had to say had nothing to do with my letter. She was at the emergency room with my grandmother. I knew Grandma wasn't feeling well; I had talked with her that morning, as I did every day. Every day I called to check on her. She was eighty-seven years old and my mother was often so busy with her job and her friends, that Grandma sometimes got lost in the shuffle. Grandma had told me that morning that she thought she had a bladder infection and she was hurting a lot. I've never met anyone with a higher tolerance for pain than my grandma, so she must have really been hurting for my mother to have taken her to the emergency room. My mother said something about the pain being where the cancer was. A minute or two later, she said something else about the cancer. My mind was reeling. *Cancer? What cancer? Since when did my grandma have cancer?* I knew it was a possibility since she had had cancer several times in the past forty years. They had always been able to operate and remove it all. But cancer now? Grandma had been in the hospital in February with stomach pain, but they told me that it was because of scar tissue from previous surgeries. Was it cancer back then and they hadn't told me? I didn't say anything at that point to my mom. She said she'd call me back later that evening to let me know what was happening. I resolved to find out the truth when she called back.

That afternoon was rough. I was worried and scared and angry. Did Grandma have cancer again? And if so, why had neither she nor my mom told me? I talked to her on the phone every day. Why didn't I know something about this? That evening when Mom called, I confronted her, "What do you mean, cancer?" Mom told me that Grandma had been diagnosed with cancer in her abdomen in July. When I said, "Why didn't you tell me?" she responded with, "Well, you haven't been talking to me and I thought you knew. Grandma just told me a few minutes before I called that you didn't know, that she hadn't told you yet. She was going to wait until her next doctor's appointment in October to tell you anything. But I thought you knew." When I got off the phone, I fell into Josh's arms weeping. "Why didn't she tell me?" Waves of grief washed over me. I couldn't understand why my grandmother hadn't told me. I thought we were close. I told Josh, "I've got to go see her." So we made plans to leave on Monday morning.

The next day, after Josh preached, we came home instead of going out to lunch. We had just walked in the door when my cell phone rang. It was my mom. She was crying. They had moved my grandma to ICU during the night and she was still in a lot of pain despite the morphine they were giving her every two hours. Test results indicated that the mass was pressing against her stomach and causing a blockage. And it was fast growing. Mom said we needed to get there as soon as we could. Then she started crying harder and saying how scared she was because she was losing her mother and she didn't want to lose her daughter, too. I tried to calm her down and told her that she wasn't going to lose me. After I hung up, I began crying again. Josh held me as I sank to the floor, overcome by grief. When I finally calmed down, we rushed around getting ready to leave. Josh found someone to preach for him that evening and at 5:00 p.m., we drove out of town. Would my grandma even be alive by the time we got there? I didn't know what to expect.

It was about eight o'clock when we drove into the hospital parking lot. Grandma was awake and alert, although she was still in a lot of pain. She was glad that Josh and I were there and we were able to talk some. I wanted to ask her why she hadn't told me, but I didn't. That wasn't what she needed to hear. I told her how much I loved her and how glad we were that we were there. I wasn't looking forward to staying with my mother, but we didn't have to. She had been "cleaning out" a bunch of things and her guest room was full! There was, thankfully, no room for us. So Josh and I stayed at my grandma's house.

When Grandma finally went to sleep Sunday night, she slept a hard, labored sleep. The nurses even told us that there was the possibility that Grandma would never wake up. I was in shock. I think my mother was, too, but at least she'd had some time to think about things. She had known about the cancer. I hadn't. So it was with stunned disbelief that I listened as the doctor talked about hospice.

Monday evening they moved her to a hospice facility, which was the beginning of a harrowing routine. The three of us would spend the whole day there. In the evening, Mom would go home to shower and change. She would come back and spend the night on the couch in the room while Josh and I went back to Grandma's house to sleep. Grandma did wake up and Tuesday and Wednesday she was able to visit a little with a number of friends who came to see her. Were it not for the strength and support we received from visitors and phone calls, I don't know how I could have endured. I was also strengthened by Josh's presence and by the time I spent in prayer to God, which was often. And the hymns.

My grandma has always loved church songs and singing and so I spent some time every single day singing to her from the church song book. I think my singing was a comfort to her, but it was a comfort to me as well. "He Leadeth Me" was a song of particular comfort to me and I sang it to Grandma often. "He leadeth me: O blessed thought! O words with heavenly comfort fraught! Whate'er I do, where'er I be, still 'tis God's hand that leadeth me. He leadeth me, He leadeth me, by His own hand He leadeth me; His faithful follower I would be, for by His hand He leadeth me." God was leading me through this stressful time with my grandma, just as He had led me through all the hard times and struggles I'd had in my life. I hadn't always understood that God was leading me through my trials, but I was keenly aware of it as I sat by my grandma's hospice bed.

Thursday was different from the previous two days. Grandma woke up very little. When she was awake, she was barely responsive. Grandma knew that she was dying. While she was in ICU, she had asked my mother if she knew where the dress she wanted to be buried in was located. Grandma was at peace about her approaching death. She had lived a long, faithful life as a Christian, she knew she belonged to God, and she knew she was going to Him. She had always spoken freely about death and was never afraid of it. I was happy for the upcoming victory my grandma was going to receive. But it was still so hard.

> Life and death,
> reflections
> on a life
> lived well;

Chapter 29: Grief

laughter,
tears,
joy,
sorrow.
Sitting vigil,
time passing slowly
yet swiftly.
Weary bones,
aching heart,
yet joy
for her approaching
victory.
To live is
Christ
yet to die
is gain.
Joy for her,
sorrow for
me.

Grandma had made it known, both verbally and in her medical directive, that she didn't want chemotherapy, nor did she want any measures taken to prolong her life, such as a feeding tube or a respirator. When they transferred her from ICU to the hospice facility, they took her off of all IV fluids and medications other than pain medication. That was the way Grandma wanted it. But I didn't know what to expect, so on Wednesday I talked to the social worker. She told me that it could be two days or two weeks. I prayed that it wouldn't be long, that God would take her home soon. The hospice nurses told us it was important for us to talk to Grandma and tell her it was okay to go. On Friday, October 3, when my mom went home to shower and change, I did just that. Josh sat there and prayed while I sat next to Grandma's bed, held her hand, and talked to her. I don't know if she heard me, but I talked to her. I told her it was okay to go and be with God. God was waiting to receive her in his loving arms. I would be okay, Mom would be okay, and Mom and I would be okay. I'd do everything I could to work things out with Mom. I thanked her for the legacy of faith she had left me and I promised I'd see her again in heaven because I would remain faithful to God. I told her I was very proud of her for fighting the good fight and keeping the faith. And I told her how much I loved her and how much I'd miss her. I told her it was okay to go.

Mom did not. Mom kept grasping and hanging on like she always does with everything. "I can't let her go! I can't let her go!" And she hung all over Grandma, practically smothering her with her body and her tears.

On Saturday, October 4, Josh made the three-hour drive back to our home because he had to preach the next day. I didn't want him to go. It was hard watching him drive out of the parking lot, but I knew he had to go. It was hard, not because of my grandma, but because when he left, I would be alone with my mother. He told me before he left, "Don't telegraph weakness to her." Then he said I was stronger than I realized. He called often to check on me, and I had several friends who knew of my problems with my mom who called to check on me. One friend even came Sunday afternoon and stayed several hours with me.

My mother had been touching me all week and it just got worse when Josh left. Touching me, holding my hand, hugging me, and holding me tight in an embrace, again and again. The revulsion I experienced at her touch was strong, so all her touching strained my endurance.

It was also a strain watching her cry every time someone came in the room or her phone rang. She turned the waterworks on and off like a spigot. I got angry listening to her tell person after person, "I have no regrets." She had been so selfish and manipulative with Grandma, and yet my mom told people she had no regrets. I didn't say anything. I bit my tongue and held it in. It was an odd statement for my mother to make. I would expect such a statement from someone who was dying, but not from someone who was about to lose someone to death. Her focus was still on herself, not on Grandma.

Mom told people stories about Grandma and how she was so self-sufficient and didn't want anyone to do anything for her. Mom told them that Grandma wanted to do her own shopping. But oftentimes some of Grandma's heavier, non-perishable items would sit in her trunk for weeks until Mom finally got around to going over (they only lived eight blocks apart) and getting them out for her. My anger really started to rise when I heard Mom say five or six times, "A couple of years ago, Rochelle and I finally talked her into not changing her light bulbs anymore because we didn't want her getting up on a chair." What my mom failed to mention was that sometimes Grandma would go three or four weeks without a light in her bathroom because Mom kept promising to come change the bulb, but didn't do it! Listening to all this and watching my mom's histrionics, her distortions of reality, and her making herself the center of attention was just awful.

Josh returned on Monday and I was so glad to have him back! Grandma was worse. She slept almost all the time and was even less responsive than she'd been over the weekend. When she did wake up, I would kiss her and tell her that I loved her. My mom was still hanging all over her. I hadn't written in my journal much at all since we had gone there. I felt like I had completely turned off my emotions. I think I was still in shock. I did write a little bit after Josh returned.

> This is day eight.
> She's been in hospice for eight days.
> She's eighty-seven. She didn't want chemo or any other treatment. She was ready to go, ready to die and be with the Lord, ready for the ultimate healing.
> She's been so peaceful. Even the nurses have commented on how peaceful this process has been for her.
> But it's hard to watch. She's not in pain now, but it's hard to watch as she draws more and more into herself, shriveling up.
> I've prayed that God would take her home, wrap her in His loving arms, and usher her into eternity, into her victory. She's been a faithful Christian all her life and she's going to be with the Father. I just keep praying that He would let it be soon instead of drawn out. Maybe part of that prayer is selfish. I want this whole ordeal to be over. I am so incredibly weary, physically and emotionally. The social worker said it could be two days or two weeks. Today is day eight.
> The hardest part hasn't been watching my grandma die. She's ready and she's at peace. And I'm at peace about her passing. No, the hardest part has been being with my mother. And amazingly, I've done well. I have closed up and I'm keeping a tight rein on my emotions. I won't cry around her. That's not safe. I cried with Josh before we ever left home to come here. That's not exactly accurate. I didn't just cry. I sobbed. I wailed. I was on the floor, wracked with grief. And I will cry later. Alone. With Josh. When it's safe.

I talked with Gary on Wednesday. He said not to let my mother's dysfunction rob me of the preciousness of this moment. This was a precious, beautiful time when one of God's own was about to receive her victory. He encouraged me to read Scripture, pray, and sing, which I'd been doing. He encouraged me to look at pictures and remember and be grateful for my grandmother's life. I told him that I felt as if I had shut down emotionally around my mother and he said that was okay. I would grieve later when it was safe.

The doctor told us Wednesday morning that he thought she would pass that day. When evening came and my grandma was still with us, my mother begged me to stay with her at the hospice unit that night. At first I wasn't going to, but one of my friends offered to stay with us, so I did. My mom sat up all night in the recliner next to Grandma's bed, as she had been doing. I slept on the couch that was in her room. Josh went back to my grandma's house to sleep and returned in the morning. When the doctor came in Thursday morning, October 9, he was surprised that my grandma was still alive. Her breathing was really shallow and they told us that it probably wouldn't be long. I sang some more hymns to her and then Josh prayed. My mom was sitting on the edge of the bed, I was sitting right next to it, and Josh was standing between us. The whole time he was praying, I kept watching Grandma, thinking that each breath would be her last. About thirty seconds after Josh finished praying, she took her last breath. It was very peaceful. She was with the Lord now, and although I was very sad, I felt a joyful peace, knowing that she was home. I still kept my emotions in check, but a few tears slid down my cheek as I hugged Josh. We met with the funeral director that afternoon and scheduled the funeral for Monday, October 13.

That evening, once again, I marveled at my mother's behavior. Her mother had just died and she was worried about her nails! Her nail lady worked late that evening so my mom could have her nails done. But Saturday was the worst. In addition to my grief, I was concerned about being alone with my mother again, since Josh went home Saturday in order to preach Sunday morning, but I knew it was only for one day. Mom's cousin got there Friday morning, so I wasn't totally alone. And one of the elders was preaching for him on Sunday evening so that Josh could drive back in time for the visitation.

We planned to have congregational singing at the funeral, and we were also going to print a program that included a poem I had written.

CHAPTER 29: GRIEF

All day Friday I reminded my mother that we needed to go to the copy store to get the programs and song sheets made. She kept saying that it wouldn't take very long and we could go later. On Saturday we met with the funeral director at noon and then intended to meet her cousin for lunch. I thought we should eat a quick lunch near her house, which was also near the copy store, but she wanted to go to an Italian restaurant thirty minutes across town! The lunch took a long time and it was after three o'clock before we finished. I thought we would then go to the copy store, but again, no. She wanted to go to a shoe store that was going out of business! We spent more than two hours in the shoe store. She bought five pairs of shoes and three purses! She and Grandma had gone to this same shoe store only a few weeks before and she had bought five pairs of shoes then! She joked with her cousin about it being "retail therapy."

As the hours ticked off, getting later and later, and we still hadn't been to the copy store, I found myself getting angrier and angrier. We finally drove back across town to the copy store near her house. It was after five p.m. She kept saying it wouldn't take long. Wrong. That particular copy store informed us that they were no longer open twenty-four hours and couldn't have the order ready until noon on Monday. The funeral was scheduled for noon on Monday! Obviously that wouldn't work. So we drove *back* across town to a different copy store, one that was open twenty-four hours.

It didn't go smoothly. It took us more than two hours to get everything done for the programs. The staff told us they would be ready after eight p.m. on Sunday. We would have to pick them up after the visitation. While we were still at the copy store, Josh called. I walked to the other side of the store and said, "I don't have time to explain right now, but when we hang up, I need you to pray for me. I am livid at my mother!" And I just got angrier as we were leaving when she said in a syrupy voice, "You need to smile. See, things worked out, so you can be happy now."

One of the reasons I was so angry was because of the way she treated some of her friends from church. Two of them were scheduled to bring food over at four thirty that afternoon for our dinner that evening. When we got to the shoe store, Mom called one of them and told her she didn't think we would be back home by four-thirty and asked if she could bring it later? They agreed on six thirty. At six o'clock we were still at the copy store and it was obvious we were not going to be back at my mom's house by six thirty. So my mom called her friend back. "It's taking a little longer at the copy store than we thought. Can you just bring the food for lunch tomorrow?" I couldn't believe her audacity! Her friend wasn't able to bring it the next day, so my mother told her, "Well, we won't be much longer here. Why don't you just go ahead and bring it at six thirty and leave it on the porch? It'll be fine." When we finally got home after seven thirty that evening, the food was not fine. It was covered in ants!

Like I told Josh, I was livid. He calmed me down that night when I called him from my grandma's house. Thankfully, I was still staying there and not at my mom's. I was so ready for him to get back, for the visitation and the funeral to be over, and for us to go home. I had been there more than two weeks with my mother. I'd had about all I could stand of her and I was grieving the loss of my grandma. I needed to get home where I could cry and grieve safely.

Grandma's funeral was Monday. Her funeral was beautiful and comforting. As part of the service, Josh read the poem that I'd written in Grandma's honor. There were a lot of people there, giving their support and condolences. I shed a few tears during the funeral, but for the most part I kept myself in check.

By five-thirty that afternoon, Josh and I were on the road heading toward home. That evening it all caught up to me and as Josh drove, I wept. When we got home, I stayed extremely busy getting caught up with everything after having been gone so long. My mother called me every day, several times a day during the first week, but it tapered off after a while. I would still have to deal with her up close and personal when I went back to help her clean out Grandma's house. But, as Gary reminded me, I had my boundaries in place. The invitation for her to meet with Gary and me still stood.

The tears still flowed, but the shock wore off over time, replaced by sadness. I was happy for my grandma and her victory, but I was sad for me. Watching my grandma die had a profound effect on me. Someday it will be my time and I want to be at peace about dying the way she was. And I can be, because I know I belong to God.

> Death,
> for some a
> tragic event,
> fought and battled
> against

with every ounce of
strength;
or,
for others a
peaceful passing,
one moment
breathing,
the next
quiet and
still,
calmly accepting,
calmly receiving
the victory
promised
to those who are
faithful
unto
Death.

30
Time

Time,
like a grandfather clock,
methodically moving,
faithfully striking the
minutes and hours and days;
or,
like a day dreamer,
oblivious to the passing of time,
lost in thought and
memory,
caring not for what is,
but only for what has been
or what will be;
or,
like a thief,
stealing away from you
precious gems
never to be returned to you again,
bringing sorrow and regret;
or,
like a gentle hand,
cleansing and healing
the deep wound,
bringing health and
comfort and
hope.
Time.

The week of Thanksgiving my mom and I began cleaning out Grandma's house. Time went backwards for me as I remembered things about my grandma. It was a bittersweet time. Gary told me to look for the good memories of my grandmother and I found many, but it seemed like the good memories were blackened by the bad events of the week; namely, having to deal with my mother. I was continually having to set boundaries and continually having those boundaries pushed to the limit. My mother kept pressuring me to "sit on the couch with me so we can cry together." Sitting and crying with her was the last thing I wanted to do. Definitely not safe. One of my friends went with me to help for a few days. We drove down together the Saturday morning before Thanksgiving and she stayed until Monday afternoon. She drove back in our truck and then on Thanksgiving morning, Josh drove down. He and I drove back home together the day after Thanksgiving. Because my friend was with me when the week started, she and I stayed at my grandma's house, rather than at my mother's house, where there wasn't as much room. When my friend left on Monday, my mother started pressuring me to move my things to her house and stay with her until Josh arrived. Another boundary. I told her that I was going to stay at Grandma's house by myself. She was very unhappy about it. She pouted and complained every evening, but I held my ground.

On Tuesday, she and I went to the bank to take care of Grandma's financial affairs. Grandma had left her house to me and everything else she had divided equally between me and my mother. Mom wasn't happy about that. She started threatening to leave everything of hers when she dies to her best friend's kids rather than me because "you're not close to me like you used to be." My mother just doesn't get it. Money has always been very important to her and she uses it to control. She's done that with me since I was young. And it used to work. But threatening to cut me out of her will isn't going to bring reconciliation. It just pushes me further away. What would bring the two of us closer would be for her to quit living the fantasy that she was a wonderful mother and instead work to make some changes in her life. But looking honestly at herself and admitting fault and changing are things that she fears.

She was incredibly bossy and was constantly ordering me to do something. She had to have her nose in everything. If I cleaned out a drawer or a closet, she had to go back through what I'd done. She was manipulative. She ignored what I said. The toll of dealing with her was wearing on me. Even though I was sleeping at my grandma's house, I was still with my mother all day and all evening. I really wasn't sleeping much. Despite being on medication to help me sleep, I tossed and turned until

CHAPTER 30: TIME

two or three o'clock in the morning and then would only sleep a few hours. By four or five o'clock I'd be wide awake. It was all I could do to survive the week. By the time Josh got there on Thanksgiving morning, I was ready to go home. Friday afternoon couldn't come quickly enough.

I thought, once we got back home, that time away from her would help me calm down, but it didn't. My sleep patterns were still out of whack. I wasn't looking forward to Christmas because it wouldn't be the same without my grandma. My mother was coming to our house for Christmas and I'd have to be around her for another week. After she left on December 28, I counted up the days and determined that I had been around her more in the last three months than I had in the last six years.

As the New Year came and went, my problems continued. I was sleeping less and less and my mood got worse and worse. I was having frequent crying spells. I began having hallucinations again, both auditory and visual. So much anger and resentment toward my mother seethed inside of me that by the end of January my level of functioning was well below what it had been. I was so depressed that I feared I would have to go back on the lithium. Something had to change. The combination of being off the lithium, the death of my grandma, and dealing with my mother was finally catching up with me. I felt like I was falling apart. The last week in January, after talking with Dr. Patel, Josh, and Gary, I finally decided to go back on the lithium. Within forty-eight hours, I was sleeping through the night and my mood wasn't as black. But I was very sad, because going back on the lithium meant Josh and I couldn't try to get pregnant.

Time is supposed to heal all wounds, and as it passed time did its healing work on my grief over Grandma's death. But time was against me when it came to getting pregnant. Month after month I had not ovulated. My doctor had prescribed several medications, but to no avail. I still wasn't ovulating. He told me that at my age, the longer we went without being able to get pregnant, the less likely it was to happen. At the beginning of January, he told us that our next step was to see a fertility specialist. Josh and I weren't sure we wanted to go that route, and now it looked like it didn't really matter since I was back on the lithium.

I thought that the lithium would make things better for me, and it did to an extent. My mood wasn't as dark, I wasn't as volatile, and the hallucinations went away. But there was a problem. I kept getting sick. I was nauseated and shaking all the time. After almost a month of experimenting with the level of the lithium, Dr. Patel took me off of it again. It wasn't working for me as it had before. He tried a different medication, but that made me sick as well. Finally, Dr. Patel went back to relying solely on the Risperdal. He increased the dosage from what it had been before and it seemed to be working for the depression, but my anxiety was out of control. I was dealing with a lot of issues in therapy with Gary, and it was another two months before the anxiety leveled off.

As I look back on those first three months of 2009, that period of time is lost to me. Between the anger and resentment, the depression and anxiety, and being unable to get pregnant, it seemed like the time disappeared from September, when I got the call telling me that my grandma was in the hospital, until April. I was dealing with the grief of losing my grandma and the grief of being unable to get pregnant. It was a time of loss, confusion, frustration, sadness; a time of extremes. But it was also a time of healing, a time of becoming whole.

31

Becoming Whole

Becoming whole,
like a piece of china
glued back together;
or,
like a torn shirt,
sewn and mended;
or,
like a gash
that has been
stitched closed;
you can see the
patch,
the seam,
the scar,
but it has been
repaired,
fixed,
healed.
Becoming whole.

When I started thinking about getting pregnant, the little girl and I were finally beginning to communicate. I was listening to her. And during the first three months of 2009, the communication between us really picked up. I was dealing with a lot of fear about my mother. She had been giving me a lot of guilt messages over the phone. Gary and I began talking more about the covert incest that had occurred between my mother and me, and I wrote a letter to the little girl attempting to explain it to her.

January 10, 2009

Dear Little Girl,

    I'm writing you a letter because you have been struggling with a lot of fear lately, fear about Mother. I want to explain some things to you that I think will help you if you can understand. There is something called covert incest that I want to try to explain to you. Regular incest is what Papa did to you when he violated you sexually. It wasn't hidden from you. It happened clearly to you and your body.

    Covert incest isn't as clear. It's harder to see. Covert incest is what your mother did to you and still tries to do. She violated all kinds of boundaries, she smothered you, she invaded your world so completely that you were never sure where you stopped and she began. You were an extension of her. You existed for her. Boundaries were practically nonexistent between her and you. When a child is little, some of that is understandable. But as you grew older, the boundary violations continued. And she tried to control you. She still tries to control you. She uses guilt messages and manipulation to try to control you, to try to keep you solely for her use. Your mother also used money and anger to control you, for the same reason.

    This covert incest stuff goes a little deeper than just violating boundaries and smothering you. Mother put you in the role of her surrogate husband. That means that since she didn't have a husband, she put you in that role. She wanted you to meet needs that would normally be met by a husband. Am I talking about sexual needs? Not literally. She didn't do to you what Papa did. But by her placing you in the role of her husband, it was incest. She violated you and used you and abused you in ways a child should never have to experience. You were a child who had many needs; you were not there to meet her needs! She should have been meeting yours! And yet, she's always acted like your job was solely to meet her needs.

    She's not healthy. And I know that's frightening to you. To a little girl, seeing an adult acting like a child is scary. Any adult. But when it is your own mother who is acting like a child, and acting in covertly incestuous ways, it can be terrifying. That is why her guilting and manipulation this last week have gotten to you so much. You are still terrified of her. Her guilt messages and her manipulation have controlled you for a long time. Now that Grandma has died, she is also trying to make you her surrogate mother.

CHAPTER 31: BECOMING WHOLE

More covert incest! She is still trying to control you using the same tactics, she's just changed what your role should be. But it doesn't have to be that way any longer.

For years you have been tethered to her like a tetherball tied to a pole. And she has whacked you around and around that pole with every kind of guilt and manipulation and control that she knew how to use. She's still doing that. But, Little Girl, hear me on this: **YOU ARE NO LONGER TETHERED TO THAT POLE!** That chain has been broken. I have been breaking that chain through these years of therapy, and I broke it when I married Josh. You are not chained to her any longer! I know her guilt messages still frighten you, but they don't have to.

I've told you before, you can trust me. I'm here for you. I'm here to protect you from her. In the past I haven't protected you, but you've been watching me steadily get healthier over these last few years. And especially this last year, you have been able to trust me. I'm an adult and I'm acting in your best interest. I'm not an adult like Mother, an adult behaving like a child. No, I'm an adult who is working to protect you from her and her schemes. When she tries to guilt and manipulate you, you feel very tense and uncomfortable and unsafe. That's why I am not calling her or e-mailing her in an effort to placate and soothe her. I'm protecting you. You don't need to be exposed to any more of her awful incestuous behavior.

It is not your job to make Mother happy. I know it was always your job before. If Mother was unhappy or mad or upset, it was little Rochelle's job to make her happy. It was little Rochelle's job to soothe her and placate her until she was better. Even if it meant betraying yourself in the process, that was okay with her because her needs came first. Covert incest! That's ultimately what happened when I recanted. I was placating and soothing because she was so angry and upset with the accusations I had made. Little Girl, I let her win that time. I'm not going to let her win this round.

So, Little Girl, when she tries to guilt you, try not to be so afraid. I'm here to protect you. And when the tension feels too great, don't despair. Just go with the tension a little longer. You are tense because you are uncomfortable with not giving in to her. You are tense because you are uncomfortable standing up to her. Just trust me here. I'm the adult you can trust. I won't let her shame you any longer, though I know she'll try!

She has shamed you all your life whenever you didn't do exactly what she wanted. She tried to heap all kinds of dishonor and disgrace on you. And it worked, because you started shaming yourself. And then you grew up and I continued shaming you. We shamed our self by masturbating and cutting. Those two behaviors are intimately connected to Mother. Yes, they're connected to Grandfather, too. But the shaming that she did to you resulted in you shaming yourself and beating yourself up and punishing yourself with the cutting. It's all connected to her. That's why twice in the last two months, since I've had to spend so much time with her, the temptation to masturbate has been very strong. But you'll notice, Little Girl, that I didn't give in. I fought it and turned to Josh for help. I didn't shame you. I didn't hide it like we've always done in the past.

In the past, we have kept secrets and hidden the truth. You had to hide the truth of your awful situation from yourself in order to survive. What child can face the fact that her grandfather is violating her very body and soul? What child can face the fact that her mother is betraying her with every turn? That is not for a child to face. But I'm not a child. I'm an adult and truth, honesty, and exposure of secrecy are all healthy. And they are all needed to fight against the awful, cruel tether of covert incest. That's what I've been doing for five years of therapy. I'm fighting it, Little Girl. Please let me fight for you. You don't have to be afraid of her anymore. Little Girl, I love you!

Love,
Rochelle

During the time when my sleeping was so messed up, I spent many early morning hours at my computer. The letter that I wrote to the little girl on January 10 was written at Gary's suggestion in an attempt to reassure her. The next night, I was at my computer again, this time with a lot of questions.

Questions

It is 3:30 in the morning and, once again, I am sitting in front of my computer. I've already been awake for an hour, just lying in bed, trying to go back to sleep. I've quoted passages of Scripture, I've sung through songs. I've prayed, I've tried being still and quiet. And yet I was still awake. So I got up. Maybe if I type for a while, I'll get sleepy and can go back to bed. This is so frustrating. Is there just so much going on in my mind that I can't stay asleep? Since my mother left on Dec. 28, I think I have only had one or two

CHAPTER 31: BECOMING WHOLE

nights that I slept all night and didn't have bad dreams. That's been two weeks. I didn't have any bad dreams tonight. I don't remember any dreams tonight, but maybe I wasn't asleep long enough to start dreaming. I don't know how that works.

I'm not sure what I want to write about, maybe just stream of consciousness or something like that. I need to write something, because just sitting here with tears running down my face isn't accomplishing much. Am I crying because I am so tired or for some other reason? Okay, what's on my mind? Maybe if I can figure out what I've been thinking about since I went to bed, I'll know what to write about and I might figure out what my tears are all about.

I really want to know why I've been having such a hard time the last two weeks. Since September 27, actually. Is all of this sleep disruption part of the grief process or is it all about my mother or both? Or is it just because I'm off the lithium? I was doing so well when I first went off of it back in June. It seems the longer I go without it, the worse I get. Of course, dealing with Grandma's death and my mother hasn't helped. Why am I having so much trouble sleeping tonight? I wrote that letter to the little girl last night. Gary seemed to think that if I wrote her a letter and reassured her, I wouldn't be as fearful and tense. And I guess that's true. I felt better yesterday, just extremely tired. So why couldn't I sleep tonight? What's rolling around up there in my subconscious? Is it just more of the same? Am I thinking about some of the things I read in that covert incest book?

I feel very sad right now. I guess I've been thinking about my memories again. Or my lack of memories, to be precise. I've read some books that seem to say that if there is trauma in childhood, the memories actually may not have been encoded at all. But other books I've read say that if there was childhood trauma, the memories are just repressed somewhere in your mind. I tend to believe the second, maybe out of false hope. I don't know. It seems logical that if something traumatic happened to you, somewhere in your mind you would remember it. This covert incest book talks about persons who have been sexually abused and have repressed the memory of it. He says, "When amnesia of select or specific periods of childhood is not a consequence of organic brain injury, it can be a symptom of sexual trauma."[6] Well, I know I've never had an organic brain injury. That's why I think my lack of memories before age ten is such a significant clue as to what I believe was done to me when I was a little girl. I just wish I had more memories. Look how much insight I already have into my mother. I've practically written a book, for crying out loud! Just think how much more insight I could have if I had my memories. God, are you listening? I know that Gary says I don't have to have the memories in order to heal. We know what we think happened and that's enough. But I still just feel so incomplete. It's like I'm that tetherball chained to the pole, being whacked around, but the tetherball looks like Swiss cheese with all these holes in it.

Here's a question I was thinking about last night before bedtime. It shows a connection between my mother and her covert incest and the overt incest I believe happened. If my grandfather did sexually abuse me, how could my mother not have known? Or my grandmother? There were three adults and one child (and a dog) in that tiny little house. My mother's house is so small. How could she have been oblivious?

It's like that dream I had back in 2005. I was in my bed and my little dog Patches was in the room with me. A bat flew around trying to attack Patches. I kept yelling out for my mother to come help me, but she never came. She was in the other end of the house calmly eating a bowl of cereal, oblivious to my cries for help. Finally the bat flew into my hair and was attacking me; I was still yelling for help. Gary appears in the dream and he gets the bat out of my hair and then Josh appears and he comforts me. I can recall as a child lying in bed at night and **whispering** for my mom to come, whispering because I didn't want anyone else to hear me calling. My grandparent's bedroom, my mom's bedroom and my bedroom were all right next to each other with a tiny bathroom between two of the rooms. My door was across the small hall from the kitchen and on the other side of the kitchen was the den, where the television was. When I accused my grandfather back in 1992, one of the things my mom said was that Papa went to bed early and she and Grandma stayed up late watching TV and that's why they didn't hear anything. No, I wouldn't expect them to hear anything. I'm sure I was probably threatened or bribed into silence. But how could they not know?! I had stomachaches all the time, I wet the bed until I was a sophomore in high school, and I was an angry, angry little girl. How could they not even suspect something was wrong? I told Josh last night that one of the things I wonder about a lot, but don't really talk about is why she didn't protect me. She says I'm the most important thing in the world to her. So why didn't she protect me? And when I made the accusation, why didn't she believe me? Why did I receive only anger?

And it wasn't just initial anger. It was ongoing anger, enough to cause me to try to placate and appease three years later. That's when I recanted.

CHAPTER 31: BECOMING WHOLE

When I did it, I didn't consciously think I was recanting in order to placate Mother. But that is precisely what I did. I betrayed myself for her. And why? What had she done for me? Protected me? Loved me unconditionally? Kept me safe? Met my needs for emotional stability? Allowed me to have a life that wasn't an extension of her? I even went into the same profession that she was in. Granted, I think teaching is one of my gifts, but it just seems ironic. I am the fifth generation of teachers in my family. I wonder what else I was fifth generation of. Incest? Dysfunction? Abuse? Enmeshment? How many generations does it have to continue before it is stopped? That's what I am trying to do, break the chains. I'm just so incredibly weary.

Back to the recanting, the denial, the renouncing. I said it had never happened. I said I was wrong. I said it had been false memories. I denied the truth of what I'd claimed. I renounced the accusation against my grandfather. But how could it have been false memories, when really I had no memories? Maybe what I should have said was that I had had false clues, but that would be a lie. The clues were definitely not false. The clues were right there staring me in the face, slapping me into reality, daring me to deny them. And yet deny is exactly what I did. And why? I did it for her! I betrayed myself for her!! Would that I could have my memories. I don't think that regaining the actual memories of the details would be near as hard to deal with as what I've had to admit about what I have done to myself. She didn't protect me. Why did I feel so compelled to protect her? That's what I was doing. I was protecting her from the truth. She couldn't handle it. That's why all I got from her for three years afterward was anger and disapproval. So I recanted in order to protect Mother. In order to placate Mother. In order to appease Mother. In order to pacify Mother. That's been my job my whole life. When I recanted, I was just following the rules.

When I made the accusation, she didn't want to believe me. She was angry and upset with me. When I recanted, you would think she would have been ecstatic. And she was, eventually. But initially, it was almost like she thought I was lying when I told her it had been false memories. It seemed like I had to talk her into it, like I had to convince her that what I was saying was true. Of course, it wasn't true. I was trying to convince myself just as much as her. But what does her reaction say to me? It says I think she knew I was right when I made the accusation in the first place. Maybe that's why she's never given up her anger about it. Even now, fourteen years later, at times I still feel her anger about having made the accusation in the first place. Maybe that's because she knew I was right.

I am sitting here in stunned disbelief because the last paragraph is a new thought to me—that she knew I was right. If she knew I was right, why was she so angry at **me**? Why wasn't she angry at him? She took it out on me! She made me feel so worthless! She made me feel like dirt! She made me feel crazy! And yet, I think she knew I was right. Oh God, help me! I can't even see the computer screen for all my tears right now and my stomach aches from the heaving sobs that are coming from my body. Oh God, if she knew I was right, why was she so angry at **me**? Did she already know before I made the accusation? Did she know when I was a child? Then why didn't she protect me? Why did she make me feel like it was all my fault? Didn't she know that's the way my little girl already felt?

When I finished typing the last paragraph I was sobbing uncontrollably. I went into the bedroom where Josh was still asleep (at 5 a.m.) and I crawled up into the bed with him. Through my tears, I asked, "Josh? Can you hold me?" He woke up and gently held me as I cried.

I've asked so many questions in the last few pages. Will I ever get all the answers? After I read what I'd written to Josh, I asked him through my tears why was she so angry at me? He said it was probably because I had broken the rules. He's right. Some of the rules in my family were: don't talk about problems, pretend nothing is wrong, act and look like we are a perfectly happy family. When I accused Papa of sexually abusing me, I broke the rules. Apparently the rules were more important than I am. She says I'm the most important thing in the world to her. That's a lie. I see the truth now. And I'm filled with overwhelming weariness and sorrow and hurt.

By the end of January, when Dr. Patel put me back on the lithium, I was thinking and processing a lot about my mother and my grandfather. And about not being able to get pregnant. I felt like I had failed because I had to go back on the lithium. Gary tried to help me understand that I hadn't failed. He said that life isn't measured in what succeeds, but in what we try. I had tried. And he said for me not to give up hope. I told Gary that I felt like my efforts to get pregnant were a noble experiment that had failed.

Chapter 31: Becoming Whole

My heart aches,
not the ache of
depression,
but the ache, the
sadness,
of a dream
unable to be fulfilled.
I'm so sad.
There is sorrow in my heart.
Tears.
Reality is setting in.
I have no clue as to when I could
get to the point that I could try
going off the lithium again.
I'll be forty soon.
My body was not ovulating.
My doctor said that every month
I went without getting pregnant,
it would be that much harder.
But that doesn't matter anyway.
I had to go back on
the lithium.
Gary said I made a
great sacrifice
to try and get pregnant.
Josh said I was courageous.
He said it was indeed
a noble experiment.
I wish it had worked.
But it didn't.
And I am very sad.

Gary asked me if I had talked to the little girl about having to quit trying to get pregnant. He suggested I try to dialogue with her. He said that the adult Rochelle could handle the facts, but the child needed to make peace with this. I needed to explain things to her on a level that my emotional self could understand. He also told me not to let my foolish side get a hold of this and start blaming, blaming Mother or blaming self. When I talked with the little girl I needed to stick to the adult script, i.e. the physical reasons I couldn't get pregnant. The reason I needed to talk to the little girl about this was because Gary didn't want her pouting and angry. Sad was okay. So I sat down with my journal and had a conversation with the little girl.

It's hard to explain how this process worked, but I'll try. As I was talking to the little girl part of me, I just intuitively knew what her response was. I wasn't literally hearing her voice, but it was as if the little girl part of me were speaking to my heart. So I just wrote what she was saying. I wasn't just making up what I thought she would say. It really was the little girl part of me talking. It's difficult to explain and difficult to understand, but then, having different aspects to your personality is a complicated thing.

Little Girl, are you listening?

>Yeah.

I haven't been doing well. I'm sure you know that.

>Yeah, I know.

Little Girl, I've had to start taking my lithium again.

>Yeah, I know.

But do you know what that means? Do you really know?

>I don't know.

Little Girl, that means that Josh and I have to stop trying to get pregnant.

>How come?

Lithium is very bad for babies.

>How come you take it?

Chapter 31: Becoming Whole

Cause it's very good for me. It helps me not be depressed and volatile and messed up inside.

> But if lithium is bad for babies how can you have a baby and take it at the same time?

I can't, honey. But we tried. We tried for as long as we could.

> You didn't try hard enough!

Yes, Little Girl, we did. But there are some facts that you need to listen to.

> I don't want to listen!

Little Girl, I need you to listen. Please.

> Okay.

Little Girl, sometimes a woman's body doesn't work right and she isn't able to get pregnant, even though she tries. My body isn't working right. To get pregnant, a woman's body has to make eggs come out. But my body isn't doing that.

> Why not?

I don't know, honey. My body just isn't working right.

> Can't you fix your body?

Well, I took some medicine to try to fix it, but it didn't work.

> Maybe you didn't take the medicine long enough.

I took it as long as I could.

> What does that mean?

Well, honey, I already told you I had to go back on the lithium.

> So it's your fault!

No, honey, it's not my fault.

> It sounds like it's your fault. You weren't doing well so you had to start taking the stupid lithium again and now you can't have a baby!

Little Girl, we **tried** to have a baby, but my body isn't working right.

> It's your fault!

Honey, it's not my fault. Sometimes these things happen.

> It's not fair!

I never said life was fair. You know that. Life hasn't treated you fair from day one. But God can use whatever does happen for your good.

> It's God's fault! He could've made you get pregnant!

I suppose He could have, but that's not the way He usually works. He lets natural forces happen. And my body just wouldn't work to get pregnant.

> But you said we were gonna have a baby. You and Josh prayed about it all the time. I heard you!

Yes, we did. And the answer was no.

> Does that mean God doesn't love you anymore?

No, it does not mean God no longer loves me. God still loves me, but the answer was still no. But, Little Girl, God can and will work good out of this.

> I don't want Him to work good out of this! I want Him to let you have a baby!

Chapter 31: Becoming Whole

Little Girl, I've explained to you that certain things have to happen in order for me to get pregnant and they weren't happening.

> Then you didn't try long enough!

I tried as long as I could.

> It's your fault, I tell you! You did this on purpose! You were so worried about whether or not you would be a good mommy that you made yourself sick with worrying so that you had to go back on the lithium! And now you can't have a baby!

Little Girl, I am very sad that I can't have a baby.

> No, you're not! You didn't really want one. I heard what you said one time. You asked Gary if you needed to at least try to get pregnant so I would trust you!

Little Girl, I tried to get pregnant because I wanted to have a child. I know it was your dream, Little Girl, to grow up, get married, and have a child of your own who had a loving, faithful, protecting daddy. That was your dream, Little Girl, but remember—you are a part of me. It was my dream, too! You're angry and you're trying to find someone to blame, but it wasn't my fault. It wasn't God's fault. It wasn't Mother's fault. It wasn't anyone's fault. My body wouldn't work in such a way that I could have a baby. And sometimes that happens.

> You don't believe you!

What do you mean "I don't believe me?"

> You don't believe what you're saying about it not being anyone's fault. Gary told you today to not let your foolish side start looking for someone to blame. But that's what you're thinking. You're trying to explain stuff to me but you don't believe what you're saying!

How do I answer the little girl's accusation? She's right, I don't believe myself. I do think there is a culprit. A small part of me blames God. He could have opened my womb if He had been so inclined. Or He didn't have to let my grandma die when she did and maybe then I wouldn't have been under so much stress and my body would have cooperated. But more than blaming God, I'm blaming myself. If only I could have stood to be without the lithium a little longer, maybe then I would have ovulated and gotten pregnant. Lots of maybes, but none of them matter because I could go no longer without the lithium. I feel so weak, so defeated. And I blame Mother, too. I was doing fine off the lithium until she snooped in my stuff and confronted me about what she read. If she hadn't done that, I would have been fine. Gary told me not to let my foolish side get a hold of this and start blaming, but he didn't tell me **how** to not let that happen.

I started attacking myself mentally in this way several months ago. As the months went by and I didn't get pregnant, I started thinking maybe that was a good thing because maybe I wouldn't be a good mother because of all my issues. I started doubting and second-guessing everything about trying to have a baby. I got nervous that I might actually get pregnant. So much so that it was a relief to have to go back on the lithium. And of course, I blame Mother for the lithium. Gary said don't let my foolish side get a hold of this and start blaming, but how do I get my foolish side to shut up? How do I quit blaming? How do I accept the situation and come to peace about it? I can't help the little girl have peace if my foolish side is interfering with my adult understanding of things. The little girl's got questions I can't answer. What do I do?

After that dialogue with the little girl, Gary told me that my child doesn't know what to do with adult emotions, with the fact that I was relieved and sad at the same time. He said an adult can understand relief and disappointment together, but a child cannot. He told me to continue dialoguing with the little girl and to give her time. She wasn't happy with the situation. She was grieving too. He told me to try to comfort her. She is angry with me and doesn't trust me. A couple of days later, I had another conversation with her. This time she really opened up to me.

Little Girl, what are you thinking?

I'm thinking nobody's listening to me. Nobody's ever listened to me.

Chapter 31: Becoming Whole

I'm listening, Little Girl.

> No, you're not! You don't listen to me. You just beat me up!

Little Girl, I used to beat up on you and I am very sorry. I've told you how sorry I am. And I've been proving that I really am sorry by how I've been behaving. I haven't beat up on you in a long, long time. I haven't cut you in three and a half years.

> Yeah, well, that doesn't make up for a lifetime of hurt!

I know, honey. You're hurt. And I'm not the only one who has hurt you. You've been hurt by a lot of people in your lifetime.

> You could've made it up to me by having a baby.

Honey, I tried to have a baby. And I'm very sorry that I can't have a baby.

> No, you're not! You're just relieved you couldn't get pregnant. I'm not stupid. You think I don't know what you write in your journal? You think I don't know what you talk about with Josh and Gary?

Little Girl, I know you're not stupid. You're right, I am relieved, but I'm also very sad. It's very difficult to explain to a child how an adult can be very relieved about something and very sad about it at the very same time. But it's true.

> I'm not a child!

Yes, Little Girl, you are.

> I'm not a child! You think I don't understand about adult things, but I do! You think I don't know what it means to be relieved and sad at the same time? Why do you think I was crying so hard the day of Papa's funeral?

Little Girl, I am so sorry. I'm so sorry you have had to deal with adult situations and adult emotions all your life. I'm so sorry.

    Sorry doesn't make it any better.

Honey, I know that you are hurting. And I know that you're angry. About a lot of things. Can you tell me why you're hurt?

    I'm hurt because you don't like me. You're mean to me.

Little Girl, I'm trying to help you.

    Why should you? You've never helped me before.

Little Girl, I've been helping you for five and a half years. I've been in therapy, getting help for myself and getting better and healthier all the time.

    So?

So by helping me get better, I'm helping you.

    Yeah, but that doesn't mean anything.

Little Girl, I promise you, I'm getting well.

    Promises don't mean much!

I give you my word, Little Girl, I'm getting well.

    Prove it!

I've been proving it. I haven't masturbated in almost five years and I haven't cut you in three and a half years. And I'm setting boundaries and standing up to Mother, too.

    She's mean to me too.

I know, honey, and I'm sorry.

    And she doesn't listen to me either.

Chapter 31: Becoming Whole

I know, and I'm sorry.

> And she always makes me feel like everything's always my fault.

I know, honey.

> I always feel guilty every time you talk to her.

I know.

> And angry.

Tell me about your anger.

> I'm always angry but I can't ever let it out!

Why are you so angry, Little Girl?

> Everybody's mean to me. Nobody likes me. Everybody hurts me.

Who's hurt you, Little Girl?

> You've hurt me and Papa hurt me and Mommie hurts me. And I'm mad! And now you won't have a baby. It's not fair!

I know that life's not fair, honey, and I'm sorry.

> I'm sorry! I'm sorry! Can't you ever say anything except "I'm sorry?!"

I know you're angry, Little Girl. It's okay to be angry. You can tell me about your anger.

> Why do I wanna tell you about my anger? You don't listen to me. Nobody ever listens to me! Nobody likes me! They're always hurting me.

I'm sorry you are so hurt, Little Girl.

They're always hurting me.

I began having some very disturbing dreams with violent, sexual content. I began having flashbacks of my grandfather again. My mind was racing much of the time, and I couldn't seem to get control of it. Gary said it was as if my mind felt pressed to get stuff resolved, but he advised me to take it slow and not pressure myself. Then, in the last week in February, I had an experience and a memory that rocked my world.

Why Were You Crying Tonight?

On the wall of the church office there is a framed poster of a poem entitled "Hugs." I had the exact same poster on my bedroom wall when I was a kid. I loved that poster. In fact, I had the poem memorized. I can still recite parts of it. I was there today and saw it and kind of chuckled to myself. I said, "Little Girl, you love that poem, don't you?" The office was empty, so I read it out loud. When I reached the line that says "Hugs are good for fathers and mothers, sweet for sisters, swell for brothers," I hesitated. It was the word **fathers** that caused me to pause, not because of my own father, but because of my grandfather. I finished the poem, gave myself a hug, and then went about my business. But as I worked it struck me that Papa was like a daddy to me. At dinner tonight I was telling Josh about it, and all of a sudden I got choked up and I started crying, sobbing, "Papa was like a daddy to the little girl! He was like my daddy! In my baby book on the title page is a place for the father's name and in my child's print, I had written 'Papa!'" As the tears dripped onto the table, I told Josh, "It's not just me crying, it's the little girl." After I calmed down, I was just kind of sitting there when I had a flashback of Papa walking into my bedroom. It was very clear, but what was even clearer was the memory I had later that evening.

Later that evening, I sat at the computer and had a conversation with the little girl. I was listening to her. I was looking at her portrait as I talked to her. And by the end, I had tears streaming down my face. She is telling me things.

CHAPTER 31: BECOMING WHOLE

Honey, you were crying tonight.

> I know.

Why were you crying?

> 'Cause I'm sad.

Why are you sad?

> Don't you know?

I know, but I'd like you to tell me.

> He was my daddy. He did things with me. He picked me up from school. He played make-believe with me. I wrote his name in my baby book, but Mommie erased it. I didn't talk about my real daddy. I wasn't allowed to. But Papa was my daddy.

Why were you crying tonight?

> Because he hurt me. He wasn't supposed to. He was supposed to love me and play with me and sing with me and he did, but he hurt me, too.

You've cried about him before, haven't you?

> I cried when he died. At the funeral. At the hospital they wouldn't let me go in to see him. I wanted to tell him don't die. I was scared.

What else were you feeling?

> I was scared. They told me later he had already died, but I wanted to go see him and tell him to don't die. They told me later that the doctor told Mom that Papa had lived as long as he had because of me.

How did that make you feel?

> I felt guilty.

Why did you feel guilty?

> I thought I made him die.

Why would you think that, honey?

> I didn't tell!

Honey, what didn't you tell?

> I didn't tell! I thought he was mad at me.

Why would you think that?

> Because he died.

Little Girl, it wasn't your fault that he died. It was not your fault.

> Everything's my fault.

No, it's not, baby. Everything's not your fault.

> Yes it is. Everything's my fault. Mommie's divorce was my fault.

No. Mommie and Daddy had problems but those problems were not you.

> But he left right before I was born. And Papa left too. He died. And it was my fault. But I didn't tell!

Chapter 31: Becoming Whole

Honey, I believe you. I know you didn't tell. But it wasn't your fault. Little Girl, it's okay to tell. You can tell now. You don't have to keep a secret any longer.

> I'm afraid.

What are you afraid of?

> I don't want Mommie to die too.

Little Girl, someday she's going to die. We all die. You know that. But it's not your fault. It's not your fault. Do you believe me?

> I don't know.

I'm not going to hurt you anymore, Little Girl. I'm not going to hurt you anymore. Please believe me.

> I'll try.

That's good, honey. That's very good.

When I read the conversation to Josh later that evening, I started sobbing all over again. Josh said he was confused. Why would I think it was my fault that my grandfather had died? When he asked me that, the memory of what my grandfather had told me came back with force and with blinding pain. I cried out through my tears, "Because that's what he said! He said he would die if I told! He said he'd have a heart attack if I told!" The memory of what he'd said to threaten me, to keep me silent about the abuse, was clear and vivid. I cried uncontrollably.

Gary said it was understandable that the little girl would believe that it was her fault he had died and maybe that was why that memory was so buried. The little girl kept telling me, "I didn't tell." She wanted my adult to know that. By keeping the memory buried, she was keeping her supposed culpability for his death buried. For the little girl, this was a life threatening memory. She thought this information must be guarded at all cost. But she told me. And I didn't take a razor to her or shame her in any way. Gary said that was an important thing for the little girl. It was powerful. As much as I cried, as much as it hurt, it was very powerful.

After I had that memory breakthrough I began sleeping better and the disturbing dreams went away. Since I was experiencing lots of nausea and shaking, Dr. Patel had me stop the lithium and increase the Risperdal. It took about a month for the anxiety to level off and the connection with the little girl seemed to be a turning point. My anxiety, my sleeping, and my mood all improved. By May, I was feeling really well and in June, since the lithium was no longer an issue, Josh and I decided to start trying again to get pregnant. I still wasn't ovulating, but I felt at peace. Had the little girl and I completely integrated? I still had some work to do, especially in regard to my mother. But I felt different. I felt whole.

32

Forgiveness

Forgiveness,
like owing someone
twenty million dollars,
knowing that you can
never
pay it back
on your
minimum wage income,
and yet,
coming home one day
and opening a letter
that says
"Your debt is canceled.
You owe nothing;"
or,
like a slave,
shackled and chained,
groveling in the
filth and mire,
bleeding and scarred,
who one day
is released from his
chains,
cleaned up,
bandaged,
and freed to go;
Forgiveness.

I felt whole in the sense that the little girl and I were beginning to integrate and communicate. That was a good thing. In July, my mother came for a five-day visit (five days too many) and then later in the month,

Josh and I went there for four days to work more on cleaning out my grandma's house. When my mother left our house after her visit, she left me a note. In it was a poem she said she had read that "really struck a chord" in her and she wanted me to have it. The poem, "If Only I Knew," read, "If only I knew this was our last hug, I would hold you tight and hope to never let you go." I wrote in my journal:

> She thinks she's being sweet, but really her words only push me further away. She wants to hug me and hold me tight and never let me go? Yuck! That's the last thing I want her to do. I want to push her away from me. Every time I had to hug her, I felt sick. It was all I could do to touch her. She is so grasping and clinging. I just wish she would leave me alone.

When I talked to Gary, we discussed how her hugs feel like a chain, a prison to me. Rather than being something I enjoy, her hugs are entrapping and I am uncomfortable and afraid when I have to hug her. I doubt the sincerity of them because she has been so hurtful. You hug people you trust and I cannot trust her. Gary and I continued to talk about the fact that my mother is still toxic to me and about setting boundaries with her.

CHAPTER 32: FORGIVENESS

July 28 was the sixth anniversary of when I started therapy with Gary. Six years of therapy. I wondered again, for what seemed the hundredth time, how long it was going to be before therapy was finished. I realized I would likely deal with issues and negative emotions for many years, because healing is an ongoing process. Equally important, I recognized I would probably never trust my mother.

What Do I Really Want?

In my session with Gary today I was talking about how frustrated I am with the way things are going with my mother. She just goes on talking about this, that and the other as if there has never been a problem in the world between us. I feel like I'm just playing into her fantasy that nothing is wrong between us when I just say nothing. A few months ago she got weepy with me because I hadn't been calling her and she thought I was "mad at her again." I reminded her that if she wanted to talk about issues and problems, she was welcome to sit down in Gary's office and talk with me there. She totally blew me off and continued crying that I hadn't called her. Every time she calls me, she just goes on and on about her day and acts like there's nothing wrong. But I don't want to sit there and listen to her. I want her to acknowledge that there's a problem. Gary asked me what my objective was with her. Did I want to heal her? Because, he reminded me, that's not my job. My job is for me to get well. If she never talks with Gary, how is that relative to my mental health? My happiness and my well-being cannot be linked to any choices my mother makes or doesn't make. I shouldn't let her impede my growth. Gary said I'll never trust her the way a child should trust a parent. But if I'm waiting for her to make peace, and her making peace is a precursor to my peace, then she's still in charge; I'm being held hostage. My getting well does not depend on what she does!

What do I really want? That's the question Gary kept asking me. Do I want a civil relationship with her? Yes. I think I do. Do I want more? I don't know. What will change if I confront her? Will I feel better? Maybe, but it probably won't change her. Her old patterns aren't going to go away just because we talk about some things. What do I want to do? Gary said that there are different answers to that question and that's what makes it so complex. My wise adult wants reconciliation, but recognizes that having a civil relationship may be the best I can get. My wise adult recognizes that I will never trust my mother the way a child should be able to trust a parent. My foolish part wants to get even and hurt her the way she's hurt me. The more I think about it, the more I realize that this part is pretty strong. In her letter last August, she said she was "stunned, perplexed, appalled" that she had hurt me in any way. She said she had "soul-searched" and still didn't know what she had done wrong. I'd like nothing better than to tell her exactly what she's done and exactly how she's hurt me through the years. And I want to tell her this to hurt her. I want her to hurt for how she has hurt me.

And of course, there is the little girl part of me. Despite the fact that I think she and I are integrating, there is still some growing up that I need to do. My little girl says that it isn't right that I don't have a mother I can trust, who treats me properly. It's not fair. The little girl still has the dream that Mother and I can work it out and things can be peachy between us. But that isn't reality. I guess the question is how do I let the adult Rochelle prevail. How do I quit letting the foolish part be so loud, the part who wants to get even and hurt her? How do I get the little girl to quit holding on to the dream that things are going to be wonderful between us? Neither of those things is going to help me. My goal is to get well. My goal is to have good mental health. My goal is to grow up. But, as Gary said, if I'm waiting for her to change before I can be healthy, I'm being held hostage. And if I'm waiting to get even with her and hurt her, I'm being held hostage. And if I'm waiting for the little girl's dream of a wonderful mommy/daughter relationship to happen, I'm still being held hostage.

So the question comes back to me again. What do I want to do? Do I want to grow up or do I want to hang on to unreasonable dreams of childhood? Do I want to be free or do I want to be held hostage by dreams of retaliation? Do I want to get well or do I want to be held back by what she does or doesn't do? What do I want to do?

As I pondered these things, I began thinking a lot about forgiveness and what it meant.

What Does It Mean?

It seems I'm at a crossroads here,
a time I must decide:
do I forgive and move on with life
or do I let anger ever abide?

CHAPTER 32: FORGIVENESS

Is it really as simple as
making the choice,
and does forgiving her mean
I have no voice?

I have given voice to
my anger, hurt, and pain;
as I've written my book
I've been breaking the chain.

But does forgiving her mean
my voice is now still,
my scars no longer speak,
my cry has been killed?

What exactly does it mean
to forgive Mother dear,
does it mean I have to acquiesce
and keep her ever near?

Does it mean it doesn't matter,
the things she's said and done?
Does it mean the hurt is gone?
Does it mean that she has won?

Does it mean the lines are crossed
and boundaries are no more?
Does it mean I never think,
rather, all the hurt ignore?

What does it mean,
this forgiveness game?
Does it mean that it's mine—
the shame and the blame?

And is forgiveness just a game
that one plays at,

or is it serious business
and not just this or that?

Forgiving my mother—
what does it mean?
Will it ease the hurt
that cuts so keen?

My scars have spoken
so many a word;
will forgiving her mean
I am no longer heard?

Been thinking a lot about forgiveness lately. Been talking with Josh a lot about it. Been reading some books about it. Been writing some poetry about it. Asked a lot of questions. Wondered a lot of things. Pondered a lot of issues. Here are some of the answers I've come up with:

Forgiveness doesn't minimize what happened. It doesn't excuse the harm that was done. It doesn't justify the hurt that was caused. Forgiveness doesn't deny reality and pretend it didn't happen. It doesn't mean it doesn't hurt anymore. Forgiveness is deciding not to seek revenge. It is deciding not to seek pay back. Because, in reality, you can't be paid back for all the hurt. There is nothing that could be said or done that would make up for all the scars. So, forgiveness is deciding to release someone from the debt that they owe you (Matthew 18:21-35). But forgiveness is also an ongoing decision. It's not a feeling. It's a decision, and one that must be made over and over again.

I know all this intellectually. But my heart just wants to hang on to the bitterness and anger. Really, forgiveness brings freedom. It releases you from the bitterness that has shackled your heart. So why can't I seem to forgive? Or have I forgiven her, released her from the debt she owes me, the debt of not having been a good mother? Have I actually made the decision not to seek revenge, but it's just that my feelings of hurt and anger are still there? Will those feelings lessen over time? They aren't as intense as they used to be. Will those feelings continue to fade?

Gary said that as healing occurs with me, I will start to see her more through eyes of sadness rather than eyes of anger. I will start to see her less as a monster and more as someone to be pitied. I've had the benefit of someone helping me get out of my dysfunction. She hasn't. That's sad. She's tried to live her life with rules that don't work. They don't work in bringing about intimacy with her daughter or a man or her friends or her mother. That's sad. Gary said there is an element of compassion to viewing her through eyes of sadness. Rather than trying to get even with her and hurt her, or even trying to avoid her, I will have compassion on her. That doesn't mean I will let her violate my boundaries all over again. On the contrary, viewing her with eyes of sadness means I will see what is toxic and I will set good boundaries.

Do seeing her with eyes of sadness and forgiving her have anything to do with each other? It seems to me that having compassion on her and forgiving her mean I am excusing her behavior. If I say, "I feel sad for her because of the mess she has made of her life. I feel sad for her because of the boundaries she has broken and the lies she has listened to and the rules she lives by and the hurt she has caused herself," then that feels like excusing her. What about the hurt she has caused me? What about the mess she made of my life? And what about my grandfather? Can I look at him with eyes of sadness? I seem to have an easier time looking at him that way than I do my mother. His father abandoned his family when Papa was just a little boy. That doesn't excuse what he did to me at all. But I can feel empathy for him because I know what it was like to be abandoned by your father. But being abandoned by your father doesn't give you the right to abuse a child. So, feeling empathy for him does not excuse him of his sinful behavior toward me. It doesn't mean he is not responsible for what he did.

So why is it so hard to view her with eyes of sadness? Maybe, partly, because with her the hurt is ongoing. With my grandfather, the hurt he caused ended when he died. At least what he was doing ended. The results have continued for many years. But my mother continues to hurt me nearly every time I talk to her. At the very least, every time I talk to her I'm reminded of the hurt. I am so far removed by time from my grandfather (it's been almost thirty-one years since he died) that I seem to not be as affected by him as I am by my mother. I still have emotions I need to work through regarding him. I may have to deal with them for a long time, especially as more and more memories come back to me, like the memory I had of him telling me he would die if I told. But I've got to deal with my emotions about her on a regular basis. I guess that's part of forgiveness, working through the emotions as they come.

I said that having compassion on her and forgiving her felt like I would be excusing her. Excusing is something I was taught to do. In the past, I've tried to excuse her behavior just like she tries to excuse the behavior of herself and others. That's what she did when she violated my boundaries and snooped on my computer. "I was impulsive." That's what she did when I accused my grandfather of the sexual abuse. She said that his personality changed for the worse when he started having his heart attacks. That may be, but that is not an excuse for sexually abusing your granddaughter! And yet that was what she was doing. I took it a step further when I recanted. I excused him right out of having done it to begin with. And for what? For her. Maybe I'm afraid that the little girl is going to think I am recanting again if I have compassion on her and forgive her. Only this time, instead of recanting about what my grandfather did, I would be recanting about all my mother has done. How can I get my little girl, my emotional self, to understand that forgiving isn't the same as recanting and isn't the same as betraying myself? How can I get my little girl to understand that forgiving is actually freeing myself?

I had a good session with Gary dealing with the things I wrote regarding forgiveness. In fact, I took eight pages of notes in my journal. He talked about forgiveness not negating justice. He talked about the basic principle of reaping what you sow. We live in a cause-and-effect world. There are always consequences for what we do. We talked about some of the consequences that my mother is living with, a strained relationship with her daughter, for example. He said there are consequences she is living with because of her treatment of me that I cannot see. I cannot see what is going on inside her mind. My mother may be mentally unhealthy, but she is not stupid. She knows she has messed up and she's having to live with it. I told him that it didn't seem adequate given the hurt she has caused me. He pointed out that it's a faith issue. I'm going to have to trust that God knows how to punish unrighteousness.

But he also said that I have to be careful because I need forgiveness from God for my own sins, my own wrongdoing, but I'm unwilling to extend it to others. I said I wasn't unwilling; it was just very difficult. He said my making the decision to forgive her will release me. If I refuse to forgive, then I'm living in the shadow of her mistakes. Not forgiving her is only hurting me. But if I forgive, it sets me free from all the bitterness and anger I've felt toward her for so long. Forgiveness won't automatically make my feelings change, because forgiveness is not an emotion. It's the decision to not seek revenge or justice on my own. It's the decision to let God mete out justice. Gary said I can trust Him to do that. And forgiveness is not necessarily a one-time decision. With her, I will probably have to forgive again and again, or at least remind myself that I have forgiven her for something. After our discussion, I set about the task, the decision, of forgiving. I need to forgive in order to be forgiven. The Bible makes that clear. I went through the list of hurts she had caused me and typed out specifically the things for which I forgave my mother.

I Hurt – I Forgive

I forgive you for lying to me through the years, especially about my birth. I forgive you for teaching me how to lie. I forgive you for using me as your grunt. Even though I now have back and leg problems, I forgive you for all the times you expected me to do the heavy lifting.

I forgive you for all the critical comments you have made to me throughout my life. I forgive you for putting me down. I forgive you for always focusing on the negative. I forgive you for taking things that are in some ways positive (like being strong-willed) and always framing them in a negative way. I forgive you for criticizing me rather than helping me grow. I forgive you for the unreasonable expectations of perfection you put on me. I forgive you for making me feel as if I never measured up.

I forgive you for not respecting my boundaries. I forgive you for never setting any boundaries yourself. I forgive you for violating my boundaries over and over. I forgive you for violating my boundaries by reading stuff on my computer. I forgive you for violating my boundaries by never giving me any physical privacy when I lived with you. I forgive you for trying to buy my love. I forgive you for making me feel cheap and unloved.

I forgive you for always interrupting me. I forgive you for thinking that your way is the only right way to do things and for expecting me to be just an extension of you. I forgive you for your impatience with me. I forgive you for being so self-focused. I forgive you for using Grandma to justify and excuse your behavior. I forgive you for making Grandma your scapegoat.

I forgive you for not giving me wings to fly. I forgive you for always holding me back from separating from you and becoming my own adult. I forgive you for being so clingy. I forgive you for not teaching me independence. I forgive you for keeping me sucked into the estrogen ocean. I forgive you for expecting me to fulfill your dreams for you and not letting me be my own person.

I forgive you for your narcissism. I forgive you for your condemning attitude toward me whenever you weren't the center of attention. I forgive you for passing on some narcissistic characteristics to me. I forgive you for your insensitivity toward me in regard to getting married and having children. I forgive you for being self-centered instead of being supportive of me in this area. I forgive you for hurting me in this area rather than encouraging me.

I forgive you for your double standards. I forgive you for not allowing me to feel my feelings. I forgive you for not being a good parent by helping me deal with my feelings, but instead teaching me to stuff and ignore my feelings. I forgive you for invalidating my feelings. I forgive you for manipulating me and using guilt to try to control me. I forgive you for using guilt to get your way. I forgive you for using guilt to manipulate me into feeling as if I shouldn't have issues to deal with. I forgive you for your distorted love. I forgive you for not sharing my joy.

After having gone through that list of hurts and writing out how I forgive her, I feel good, but also sad. I also feel challenged. I feel sad because a daughter shouldn't have to forgive her mother for all these things. I feel challenged because even though I have specifically forgiven her for certain things, there are still things I need to forgive. Big things. What are those big things? Basically, I think there are six areas in which I have not forgiven her.

1. For always calling me a rotten kid.
2. For not protecting me when I was a little girl.
3. For the role I feel she has played in my fear of having a baby for all these years, and now it may be too late.
4. For the role I feel she played in my recanting.
5. For her total lack of concern for and refusal to acknowledge my mental health problems. This includes her obsession with image over and above her care and concern for me. It also includes her anger and lack of support when I was hospitalized and made the accusation against my grandfather.
6. For her refusal to admit her role in creating those mental health problems.

CHAPTER 32: FORGIVENESS

Six things. Six big things. And my grandfather. Have I forgiven him? How do I forgive all these hurts in my life? I think the reason these areas are so hard to forgive is that the hurt is still so strong.

As Gary and I continued to dialogue about forgiveness, he said he thought I had forgiven her because I am not seeking vengeance or pay back from her. Actually, I want good for her. I want her to heal. I want her to heal so that she won't hurt me any longer. I want her to heal because her life is pretty pathetic the way she is living it. Gary was right. I'm not seeking vengeance on her. If I were, I would publish my book in my real name. But I haven't. I've chosen a pseudonym because I am seeking healing. For myself and for others. And for her. But that healing may never come for her. She may choose to live with certain dysfunctions all her life. My mother and I have a ruptured relationship, not because I haven't forgiven, but because she cannot get honest. She practices a lie and tries to avoid responsibility for her own wrongdoing. That doesn't mean that I cannot heal. I am still healing.

I told Gary I felt stuck and he said it wasn't because I hadn't forgiven. It was because I didn't have closure on certain core issues, because I have unresolved pain. It was because I was still dealing with therapeutic issues that were central to my very being. He said I hadn't yet come to peace with certain things. I asked him how I was supposed to get closure if my mother never meets with me in his office. He said that closure actually had very little to do with Mother, or Grandfather for that matter. Closure and healing were going to come through therapy. And, he reminded me for the thousandth time, I was making lots of progress. He reminded me of how much I had changed in the last six years of therapy, how much I had healed and grown. After that session, I wrote Gary a note.

Gary,

So what's next?
You say you think I've forgiven. You say you think it's not a spiritual issue of forgiveness. You say it's not about forgiveness.
You say, instead, that I've still got unresolved pain, unresolved issues, therapeutic issues. You say I'm still traumatized. You say I still have issues that are core to the little girl, things I still have to come to peace with, areas I don't have closure.

I think you're right about the fact that I still have unresolved stuff to deal with. The hurt of all this is still very sharp. It doesn't consume me like it did before, but it still hurts. A lot.

So what's next?

How do I resolve the pain, the issues, the trauma? How do I come to peace? How do I gain closure?

You say that closure actually has very little to do with my mother or grandfather. Okay, so it has everything to do with me.

So what do *I* do?

What's next?

Love,
Rochelle

I spent a lot of time thinking about my conversation with Gary, and as a result I wrote a poem about the little girl, about the healing that had taken place for her and the healing that still needed to occur.

> Unresolved pain,
> a break in her heart,
> hurt deep and strong,
> soul torn apart.
>
> Issues so core
> to my little girl;
> abuse she has suffered
> as her life unfurled.
>
> Years and years
> of guilt and shame,
> betrayal so deep it
> left her heart maimed.
>
> Forgiveness is given
> vengeance left behind,
> but the hurt that's still there
> has her in a bind.

CHAPTER 32: FORGIVENESS

How does she release
the hurt and the pain,
how does she erase
her past's ugly stain?

Sinned against and abused
by those who were dear,
left her with hurt and with
pathology and fear.

But through years of courage
and healing her heart,
mental health has begun,
wholeness has a start.

But there's still the hurt,
will it ever remain?
Will the hurt always bind
like a strong iron chain?

She has joy in her life,
she has wellness, too,
but she still has marks on her soul
of what she's been through.

I guess that's the way
when you've come so far—
whenever wounds heal
there is always a scar.

I wrote to process my thoughts and emotions. And as I wrote I felt hurt and sadness, but also joy and peace. I've had so much hurt in my life, but I am healing.

How many more tears do I have to cry
to let the hurt out, to let the flood dry?
I'm not seeking vengeance, but the hurt is still strong,
how do I heal the ways I've been wronged?

I'm thinking a lot about protecting a child;
I wasn't protected. No, I was defiled.
Violated by one, betrayed by another,
hurts really bad to know it was my mother.

She didn't protect me from his awful ways;
as a result for years and years I have paid.
And she didn't have care or concern for my mind –
to my mental health problems she has been so blind.

She traumatized me by her refusal to care,
to heal from her hurts has been my constant prayer.
He traumatized me by shaming both my body and soul,
to heal from his shame has been my constant goal.

For six years now I've worked at healing the wounds—
sometimes I've felt as if my soul were marooned;
sometimes I've felt as if my heart was on fire;
sometimes I've felt as if I were trapped in the mire.

But healing has happened; I continue to get well;
I now live with joy instead of living through hell.
But the hurt still remains, though I have come so far;
though signs of healing, I will always have scars.

Today is September 6, 2009, a very important date. A very special, very significant date. Four years ago, on September 6, 2005, was the last time I cut. It was also the day I started my book. It is significant because one year ago, on September 6, 2008, I mailed the letter to my mother inviting her to meet with Gary and me in his office.

I have been rereading and editing my book over the last few weeks and every time I read through it, I am struck with wonder at how far I have come. When I look at the scars on my body, I am struck with awe at the progress I have made. Six years ago when I first started working with Gary, I was writing a book on my body with razor blades. I was cutting my body many times every day. I was trapped in the emotionally addictive behaviors of cutting and masturbation. Six years ago I was full of fear and rage and shame and despair. I was ensnared by enmeshment

CHAPTER 32: FORGIVENESS

with my mother. My behavioral and emotional response patterns were warped. Six years ago I was in the throes of mental illness.

Now, six years later, instead of writing a book on my body with razor blades, I am writing a book on paper with words speaking for me, speaking for my scars. Some of my physical scars have faded, some are still prominent, but I have healed from the physical wounds. It's the emotional wounds I'm still healing from, although great healing has already taken place. It's been four years since I last cut. It's been more than five years since I last masturbated. I am married to a wonderful man, and we have a strong and healthy marriage. I'm setting boundaries with my mother. I'm not as afraid of her as I used to be. I'm no longer living with all the toxic shame and rage and fear that once defined me. I have been forgiven by God for the horrible sins I committed against myself, and I'm forgiving those who hurt me so deeply by the horrible sins they committed against me. I am healing.

I still have healing to do. The pain of what my grandfather did to me and the hurt my mother has inflicted is still very sharp. But I am healing. As I continue to work with Gary, I continue to expose the infection, drain the wound, and heal from the hurt. As I continue to grow in my relationship with God and in my understanding of the Bible, I have a healthier outlook on my problems. God has used my problems and the hurts in my life to help me grow. It's been painful, but I have grown.

I still need to come to peace about certain things. Sometimes I complain that it's taking too long. I've been in therapy for six years. Shouldn't I be done by now? When I say these things to Gary and Josh, they gently remind me of how far I have come. I'm dealing with a lifetime of hurt and dysfunction, not something that can be fixed overnight. Healing is a process, one that I've been working at for six years now. It's a process that I'll continue to work at. I don't want to just get to a point in my healing and then stop. I want to keep healing and keep growing and keep becoming the person God wants me to be. I will turn forty years old next month. I don't want to say that forty was when I achieved mental health and that was it. I want to say that forty was the beginning of a second lifetime. Not a lifetime of hurt and dysfunction like the first forty years, but a lifetime of peace and joy and growth and healing.

33

Treachery

Treachery,
like a soldier
going over
to the other side,
giving up his
fellow soldiers
to the enemy,
causing the deaths
of those he once
enjoyed fellowship with;
or,
like a spy
spying on his own
people,
a double-agent
betraying his own
nation;
or,
like Benedict Arnold,
committing treason
against his own
country.
Treachery.

Mailing my letter to my mother a year ago was a defining moment for me. I set a boundary with my mother in a way I never had before. Whether she will ever meet with Gary and me, I don't know. Will she ever admit any culpability and wrongdoing? Will she change? Again, I don't know. I do know that my mental health is not dependent on her response. I am getting healthy regardless. I asked Gary in my note to him "What's next?" He said there were several aspects to consider.

First, he said I needed to continue helping my little girl trust my adult and not be so fearful around Mother. As I continue proving that I am a trustworthy adult by setting boundaries with her, I am reassuring the little girl that I don't have to be afraid of Mother. And as I continue to prove my trustworthiness to the little girl by not being self-destructive like I used to be, my little girl will trust my adult more and we will continue integrating.

Second, and related to the first aspect, he said that farther down the road, I may be able to distance myself from my mother's dysfunction and view her without so much fear. My adult isn't afraid of her, but my little girl still is. Over time, Gary said, that will lessen as I grow in trust of my adult. At some point I will be able to recognize both the dysfunction and the good in my mother. But in order for me to do this, I have to deal with the sense of outrage I have about her not protecting me as a child. He said I have to get to a point of not being afraid of truth. Right now I am afraid of truth, and the hurt and anger are ways I protect myself from Mother, because they keep her at arm's length. But eventually, as I continue to heal and the intensity of the hurt and anger decreases, I'll have a more balanced view of her.

Third, he said I needed to continue to grow in my ability to recognize and manage the chemical imbalance. I need to learn to take precautions during times of stress, illness, conflict, etc., so that things don't get out of perspective. Whether I'll ever be able to be off of all my medication, I don't know.

Fourth and finally, Gary said that I needed to keep increasing my ability to enjoy each day. Rather than living with fear about the past or the future, I need to drink deeply of today. Gary has been trying to get this across to me for a long time. I've gotten better at enjoying the moment. I just need to keep working on this area. One way I can do this is to remind myself of where I was. He said it is unbelievable what I have come through. I had one foot in psychosis. I was ready to break with reality because of all the dysfunction and self-destructiveness. Where I am today is amazing. And I need to look at today and relish it. As Psalm 118:24 says, "This is the day the Lord has made; let us rejoice and be glad in it."

I wrote in my journal on September 6:

> Josh and I were talking about Thanksgiving and Christmas last night and the possibility of me standing up to my mom about not going to visit her

CHAPTER 33: TREACHERY

then. I told Josh I was scared. The little girl is scared of standing up to her. It feels like my adult is, too. He makes it sound so easy, but it's not. I've been saying for five years now that Christmas is going to be different this year, but it never is. I have reasons, adult reasons, for not wanting to go there

1. We have a nice, roomy house with a guest bedroom and bath, but there we are cramped into her tiny little house with her single, claustrophobic bathroom.
2. She has a week off work at Thanksgiving and two weeks at Christmas. We don't. If we go for Thanksgiving, since Josh has to teach the Bible study on Wednesday night, we couldn't go until Thanksgiving morning anyway. And Christmas is on a Friday. We have already decided that if we do go there for Christmas, we would only go for one night because Josh can't afford to take much time off. If we do go there, she would have to do the lion's share of the cooking, which I can't see happening.
3. The fact is, I do most of the cooking. Why not use my spacious kitchen and dining area instead of being cramped into her tiny kitchen and closet of a dining room? Shouldn't the cook get to cook in her own kitchen where she knows where everything is?

It just seems silly and stupid to go there for all these reasons. But the biggest reason of all is I don't want to go. It's not safe.

I can't make my mind quit thinking about things. I've been thinking a lot about the cutting. I've been thinking a lot about my mother and the fact that I am obviously still so afraid of her. It should be an easy thing to just tell her we don't want to go there for the holidays, that we'd rather her come here instead. But it's not easy. It is so complicated. And so fearful.

I was angry with her yesterday. She called just to talk. That drives me nuts! In the course of the conversation she told me that she is now on Chandler's medical power of attorney. Chandler is a close friend of hers who had a massive stroke in June. He lives in the same city she does and has no family there, just lots of friends from church. Chandler's sister flew in and my mother went with her to check out various long-term care facilities since he hasn't gotten much better since his stroke. Since his sister lives three states away, Mom and another friend from church are now on his medical power of attorney. It just pisses me off! She is so involved and so interested in his care, just like she was with my Great-Aunt Madeline. And every time I hear her talking about Chandler this and Chandler that, I think about how ironic it is that she is so concerned about his physical health and yet she never cared about my mental health. And she's gotten in the habit of asking me in a concerned tone of voice, "Are y'all doing okay? Is everything going all right?" Like she really cares! It's a bunch of garbage! She is so phony with me. But what makes me mad is how everybody thinks she is just great. She is so concerned with other people and she is such a great image manager. It just ticks me off! Everyone loves my mother. I've heard garbage all my life about how wonderful she is, but I don't think so.

Thursday morning Jessica and I are going there to clean out Grandma's house some more. I am sick to death of having to deal with my mother and my grandma's house. I almost wish Grandma hadn't left her house to me because it just means more of having to deal with my mother. That's not really true, but dealing with my mother is so frustrating. I can't wait to get it finished and sold so maybe I won't have to deal with my mother as much. At least I'm not going by myself. I am so not looking forward to this trip.

Why am I in such a stinky, down mood today? It is supposed to be a great day. It's September 6. Four years ago today was the last time I cut. One year ago today was when I mailed my letter to my mother. I guess that is part of what is ticking me off. She has virtually ignored my letter. Granted, I'm not all that eager to sit down with her in Gary's office, but she has just ignored it and acts like nothing is wrong. I guess that shouldn't surprise me. She's been doing stuff like that all my life! But it ticks me off. And I guess the fact that this is the anniversary of when I last cut is why I have been thinking about the cutting so much the last two days. Not thinking about doing it. Just thinking about it. Usually on anniversary days I get real contemplative and melancholy. Maybe that's what I am today—contemplatively ticked.

The next day I was thinking more about Thanksgiving and Christmas and how the idea of telling her I did not want to go there for the holidays scared me to death. That made me think about the idea of treachery.

Treachery

I read a novel about a teenage girl who is a cutter called *The Luckiest Girl in the World*. The girl is a figure skater and when she keeps falling during a practice she wants to scream, "No more, no more! I quit!" Then it reads,

CHAPTER 33: TREACHERY

"For a moment she was afraid she had actually shouted the treacherous words out loud and she panicked."[7] I told Josh that's how I felt about standing up to my mother about the holidays—that it would be treachery. He said that made sense because I was raised to always do what she wants, to please her, to meet her needs.

I've been rolling the idea of treachery around in my mind for a couple of days now:

Standing up to her about Christmas and Thanksgiving—treacherous.
Breaking the chains of enmeshment—treacherous.
Seeking help for my problems—treacherous.
Accusing Papa of sexually abusing me—treacherous.
Seeking out and establishing a relationship with my father—treacherous.
Moving out of her house and going back to school—treacherous.
Marrying Josh—treacherous.
Setting boundaries with her—treacherous.
Going against her family image, her fantasy—treacherous.
Talking about her in therapy—treacherous.
Talking about her with Josh and others—treacherous.
Writing about her—treacherous.
Writing my book—treacherous.
Publishing my book—treacherous.
Getting healthy—treacherous.

All of those things are a violation of the allegiance owed to her. All of those things are a betrayal of faith to her sick system. Even though she violated my boundaries by reading what I had written about her, I was committing treachery.

But what about the treachery I've committed against myself? What about the faith, loyalty, and allegiance I owed to myself?

Masturbating compulsively and masochistically—treacherous.
Hating myself—treacherous.
Dividing myself from myself—treacherous.
Denying my childhood—treacherous.
Repressing my childhood—treacherous.
Blocking out my childhood—treacherous.

Recanting—treacherous.
Cutting myself—treacherous.
Shaming myself—treacherous.

I feel like a traitor. Either way, I'm a traitor. I'm a traitor to myself or I'm a traitor to Mother. How do I resolve this? How do I keep from feeling like I'm committing treachery when I stand up to her? How do I keep from feeling like I'm committing treason when I am getting healthier?

And as long as I'm on the subject of treachery, what about the treachery that has been committed against me? Let's start with my father. A father is supposed to be there for his child, love his child, protect his child. My father did none of those things for me. He left me, rejected me, abandoned me, deserted me. He was treacherous.

What about my grandfather? A grandfather is supposed to nurture his granddaughter. A grandfather is supposed to love and cherish and adore his grandchild. My grandfather did none of those things for me. He abused me, violated me, distorted sexuality for me, betrayed me, shamed me, confused me, heaped guilt on me, manipulated me, molested me. He was treacherous.

What about my mother? A mother is supposed to meet her child's needs. A mother is supposed to unconditionally love her child, protect her child, nurture her child. A mother is supposed to let her child become her own person. A mother is supposed to teach her child how to grow up. A mother is supposed to model God for her child. A mother is supposed to teach her child how to handle her emotions. A mother is supposed to support her child. A mother is supposed to be a stable rock for her child.

My mother didn't meet my needs, at least not my emotional ones. In fact, I've always been expected to meet her needs, even as a child. My mother's love has always been conditional. As long as I was meeting her needs, as long as I was doing what she wanted, as long as I was maintaining the family image, as long as I was not rocking the boat, then she loved me.

My mother didn't protect me. I was a little girl, vulnerable, innocent, powerless, and she did not protect me from him. We lived in a tiny house. I acted out and cried out for help in many ways, but she didn't protect me from him. And what if he abused her, too? If he did, how could she bring me into his house and think that it wouldn't happen to me? She didn't protect me.

CHAPTER 33: TREACHERY

She didn't nurture me. Instead she piled on the guilt and manipulated me. She still does. She smothered me and entrapped me. She didn't let me become my own person. She expected me to be an extension of her. She didn't teach me how to grow up because she is a model of immaturity. She's never grown up herself, so how could I expect her to teach me how to grow up? She gave me a warped view of God, one of punishing anger, guilting manipulation, terrorizing control. She didn't teach me how to handle my emotions. Instead she taught me to stuff my anger, live in fear, and deny reality.

My mother did not support me in my struggles. She supported me when I was living up to her fantasy, when I was reflecting well on her, when I was achieving. But she was critical of me and she did not, does not, support me in the important things like my mental health struggles. Instead of supporting me, she shamed me. Instead of supporting me, she ignored me. Instead of supporting me, she was angry with me. Instead of supporting me, she refuses to see the reality of my problems.

My mother has not been a stable rock for me. Rather than admit her failings, she has refused to take responsibility for herself. Rather than sincerely apologize for her wrongdoings, she has refused to admit any culpability for my problems. Rather than admit her woeful lack of good parenting skills, she hangs on to the fantasy that she was a wonderful mother.

She was treacherous.

I've lived with treachery all my life from everyone in my life, even from myself. Maybe that's why something as simple as standing up to Mother about Christmas seems so huge. I don't want to live with treachery anymore. I want to be faithful—to God, to Josh, to myself. I have to break the chains of treachery. How do I do that without feeling treacherous?

And how do I deal with the emotions I feel about all this treachery? I've faced all these emotions before. I've written and talked about it. But it's still so raw, so hurtful. And it's so unfair. I'm worried about being treacherous by standing up to my mother about Christmas and yet she obviously hasn't worried one bit about how treacherously she has acted toward me. Why am I so worried about this whole Christmas deal, so afraid of it? Am I afraid of being treacherous? I've been treacherous to her before, at least in her eyes. Everything I've done in an effort to heal and get well has been treacherous to her. Everything I've done to try to get out of the sick system I grew up in has been treacherous. So am I really all that fearful about being treacherous or am I still so fearful of her? Gary says that the little girl is still very fearful of Mother. How do I get her to not be so afraid? Is Christmas a matter of treachery or fear or both?

I felt as if standing up to her would be treachery, and just a week later that idea was played out.

My mother called me at 11:00 last night. Chandler died. She was upset and crying. When I talked to her again after dinner today, she was still crying. She didn't go to work today. My stomach was in knots listening to her. She was really emotional. Not safe for the little girl. I'm sure she was expecting me to be comforting, but I didn't say much of anything. I talked to two of my friends today who were also friends with Chandler and I feel like I am being pressured to go for the funeral. I don't even know when it is. I'm not sure it has even been scheduled yet. My mother didn't say anything about the funeral, but I know she's is going to pressure me to go. I'm feeling internal pressure as well. The part of me that has always been expected to appease and pacify Mother is screaming vehemently at me to go and "be there" for Mother. She said she has gotten all these phone calls today from people expressing their condolences and telling her things Chandler did for them. One lady said this was probably harder for my mother than for anyone else. People are treating her as if he were her husband! And I feel sick to my stomach. I'm angry and I don't know why I am so angry.

And my mother was talking about a young friend of ours from her church. Her preacher announced Sunday that Mary can't go home right now and she needs prayers. Mary has lots of issues from her family of origin and she has dealt with a lot of major depression through the years. The announcement at church was vague, and Mom started talking about Mary and that she must be all alone, that she has baggage and maybe she is in a place like that place I was in 1992. She couldn't even bring herself to say "psychiatric hospital." She called it "that place." And then she talked about how it is so horrible to be all alone and Mary must be all alone, and I need to call the preacher and find out what is going on so I can be there for Mary… And I am angry about that, too. When I got off the phone I punched on my punching bag for a while. Mom is so concerned about Mary.

And of course, she was and is all involved with Chandler. I'm sure she is sad. I'm sure she is grieving. The two friends that I talked to today asked me if I were okay because they knew how close my mom was to Chandler. Yeah, I'm okay. It's having to deal with my mother that is so awful. Chandler is at peace with the Lord now. I have no doubt about that. He's not suffering any longer. He is no longer trapped in that paralyzed body. Part of me feels like I am just a rotten daughter because I don't seem to have any compassion for my mother, but I just can't deal with her. She is so toxic to me and when she gets all upset and emotional it just makes it worse.

I just called myself a rotten daughter. That's what she has called me many times—a rotten kid. Anger. Anger. Anger!

Then, when I told her that next Friday Josh and I will be there to meet the truck from the children's home to pack up the rest of Grandma's furniture and the things we're giving away, she got emotional again and said that it all seems so final, like she's just throwing away Mom's stuff. And she was upset because it is going to be picked up when she is at work and she wanted to be there. I told her I thought it would be better if she weren't there.

And I'm worried about what others will think if I'm not at Chandler's funeral. I feel like everyone from Mom's care group at church will be mad at me if I'm not there for her. Josh says he thinks it would be a huge mistake to go for the funeral. He says this is my golden opportunity to thumb my nose at what everybody thinks. But that idea sounds terrifying to me. Of course, going sounds terrifying to me, too. I feel pulled from two different sides. Pulled is not the right word. I guess if you think of being pulled on a torture rack then it's the right word. I feel like the little girl will hate me if I go, but I also feel like the little girl is pressuring me to go and appease and pacify Mother. Maybe that part isn't coming from the little girl. Maybe that part is coming from my foolish part. I don't know. The pressure I am feeling is incredible, so much so that the thought of cutting to relieve the pressure has actually crossed my mind. I won't do that. I promised the little girl last year that I wouldn't cut anymore, but the thought has crossed my mind. That's how much pressure I am feeling about going and "being there" for Mother.

And I'm afraid Josh is going to be mad at me because I'm having such a hard time with this. He says he's not mad at me, just frustrated. I'm very tempted to lie to Mother and make up some elaborate excuse as to why I can't go. Gary will say that I don't have to explain myself to her, but I feel like I do. I don't want Gary or Josh to be disappointed in me. I don't want the little girl to be disappointed in me either. I want Josh and Gary and the little girl to be happy and pleased with me, but I feel so mixed up. Josh says this all seems like much ado about nothing. But it's not to me. It seems like a battle is going on inside of me. I'm afraid—which part, the little girl?—that Josh is going to be mad at me and disappointed in me. I want him to hold me and comfort me and help me to be strong. I'm really messed up right now. My emotions are in such turmoil. I can't even think straight enough to make this writing very cohesive. I'm angry, I'm confused, I'm feeling sick. I can't even say what I'm feeling right now. I talk to Gary tomorrow at 3:00. I can't wait.

The next evening I wrote some more in my journal.

I punched on my punching bag some more but I'm not sure it did any good. Now, instead of being angry and upset, I'm angry, upset, and tired. The pressure is mounting. The guilt and manipulation have started. I got an e-mail from my mother that she sent at 2 a.m. about all she has been doing to prepare for the funeral. She said that one of the guys from care group "started naming people who would come from out of town for Chandler's funeral. He looked at me and said, 'Rochelle and Josh will be coming...' He named several people. I figured you wouldn't want to come, but you are expected. The others in the room were all saying, 'Oh, yes, they'll all want to be there.'"

You figured I wouldn't want to come? Well, you're right about that, but it has nothing to do with Chandler. I don't want to come because I don't want to be around you. I can't be around you. You are toxic to me and I am not going to betray the little girl. Did you hear me? I am **not** going to betray the little girl! I did that once for you when I recanted. I'm not going to do that again!

Everyone is expecting me to come. I'm expected. Yeah, well, I know I'm expected. But I can't do it. That's what they don't understand. I can't be around you. You and your house are poison to me. And when you are emotional, as I know you will be for this, it is even less safe. It's not only not safe, it's incestuous.

You said the others were saying that yes, I'd want to be there? I'd want to be there if you weren't there. Don't you understand, Mother? I can't be around you. I might as well drink a cup full of arsenic. You are poison to me. I can't do this. And I can't get anyone else to understand because everyone else is so enamored with you. They all think you are wonderful. Can't they see it? It's not fair! It's not right! They can't understand why I won't be there. They're going to hate me for not being there for Mother. But

CHAPTER 33: TREACHERY

they don't understand. *I'll* hate me if I go. Gary said I had to be willing to take the risk that others would be mad at me and not understand. I have to take that risk for the little girl. I can't betray myself again. If I do, I'll never get well. She'll never trust me.

She was trusting me last night when Josh and I were making love. It was weird. I don't know if it was an actual memory, but I kept seeing myself as a little girl in my nightgown and panties. And I saw myself without my panties. Then I saw big fingers touching a little girl and little fingers touching a big man. I was intrigued. Is this a memory, Little Girl? Are you sharing a memory with me? I saw these things for quite some time, maybe twenty minutes. It didn't feel like I was just thinking it in my head. It was like I was seeing the pictures, like I was seeing a memory. I think the little girl was trusting me last night.

So don't you see? I can't betray her for Mother. I can't. **I can't !** I've got to be strong here. My wise adult has to be strong. But I feel so weak. So far, the guilt and the manipulation have only come through e-mail. It's going to come over the phone, too. How do I deal with her? How do I stand up to her? How do I let my adult take charge? How do I keep from caving in to the little girl's fear and guilt? How do I relieve all the pressure I am feeling in a healthy way? I don't want to cut. I don't want to hurt myself. I don't want to self-abuse. But the pressure is incredible—from myself, from Mother, from friends, from people in care group. I want to relieve the pressure, but I want to do it in a healthy way. How? The punching bag helps with the anger, but not the pressure of the guilt and fear.

Why am I so worried about what other people will think? I obsess about that. I know why. It's because that was the way I was raised. She always worries about what other people think. She's obsessed with image. I wouldn't be surprised if I don't hear something over the next couple of days about what other people are going to think if I don't come. And I'll probably get pressure and guilt from her to come by myself. The funeral is on Saturday. Good excuse for Josh. He'll be studying for Sunday. But she'll pressure me to come by myself. The temptation to lie and tell her I have the flu or something is so strong. It's the only way people will understand if I'm not there. But they can't understand. They don't know my mother. They haven't been poisoned by her like I've been.

And I'm hurt. She tells me all the things she has done for Chandler, and all the things she is doing to help with the funeral arrangements, and all the condolences she has received from others, like she is the grieving wife, and I'm hurt. She can do all this for Chandler, who is not family, but she can't— no, she won't— meet with Gary for me, her only daughter! She says I'm the most important thing in the world to her, but she sure doesn't show it. She said last year when Grandma was dying that she didn't want to lose me, too. I told her in my letter what she needed to do was meet with Gary. But she won't do that. She has totally ignored that. She just shows me how much she loves other people and how little she loves me!!!

I've got to be strong for the little girl, but I feel so weak. Dear God, please help me. I need Your help. I don't know what to do.

When I talked to Gary, he emphasized the importance of me not offering apologies, excuses, or explanations to Mother. He said that not going to the funeral wasn't about being right or wrong, it was about not betraying the little girl. It was about rescuing the child, not just from Mother, but from self-abuse. The urge to cut had gotten strong as I was dealing with the guilt and fear. The tension was incredible. I sent my mother an e-mail telling her that Josh and I were sorry that we weren't going to be able to be there for the funeral, but that we would be praying for her. I told her we had sent flowers to the funeral home. I didn't call her and she didn't call me. As the week progressed, the tension got worse. I was overwhelmed by feelings of fear and guilt. But not going to the funeral was the best thing. Gary told me to keep track of what my foolish part, what I called "the monster", was saying to me, and what the little girl was saying to me.

Her silence is frightening. And my monster is screaming loudly, telling me what a rotten daughter I am for not being there for my mother. And it's not just about not going to the funeral. It's not really about that. It's about not talking to her. I should be calling her. I should be letting her cry to me about her loss. I should, I should, I should. All these shoulds. I should be explaining to her why we can't come. I should give a good reason, a good excuse. Although, as Gary said, there's not a reason that would be good enough. But in my head are all these tapes playing—loudly—and I'm feeling guilty. Guilt, guilt, guilt. All this guilt. My mind is saying she's hurting right now. She's grieving. I'm awful for not calling to check on her. I'm awful for not going to be with her. I'm a rotten daughter.

My adult knows I'm not a rotten daughter. At least, I think my adult knows that. But my foolish part and my child are so loud right now that

CHAPTER 33: TREACHERY

the adult is being drowned out. Gary tells me not to let my monster get the upper hand. Okay – how do I not let my monster get the upper hand? That part is so loud right now. It's the guilt. That's what is causing my monster to be so loud. I've been programmed, brainwashed. I can't live my life without doing exactly what she wants me to do. I can't stand up to her without all the guilt kicking in. All my life I've been programmed to be there for her, appease her, pacify her. So much so that I recanted. That's how brainwashed I've been.

Not giving her a reason or an excuse for not coming is eating at me. I've been programmed to explain myself to her. That's why I learned to lie. How do I get my foolish part to be quiet? How do I get my monster to shut up? What do I do? How do I get un-programmed? Un-brainwashed? I've increased the Risperdal by half. It helped with the urge to cut. But my monster is still screaming. I don't want to just medicate the voice away, because then it is still there, not dealt with, just suppressed. And the extra Risperdal caused me to sleep a lot and be slow today. Good for the cutting. Bad for getting anything done. I exercised today, too. So, I've done what Gary suggested yesterday to help control the cutting urges. I increased the Risperdal, I exercised, I haven't called my mother. And it worked. I don't want to cut. But the guilt is eating away at me. My monster is so loud.

Then I had a conversation with the little girl.

Little Girl, I know you are scared right now. I know you are very worried and upset.

> I'm scared. You told her no. You aren't doing what she wants. I'm scared of her. I'm scared of her.

Why are you so afraid of her? I'm not going to let her hurt you. I'm protecting you from her.

> I don't trust you. She's too powerful. She's gonna hurt me.

How is she going to hurt you?

> She just is.

You can trust me, Little Girl. I'm protecting you from her by not going there.

> It's scary.

I know it's scary. Standing up to her is not something you have done very often.

> She's gonna be mad at me and upset with me.

So?

> So that's not safe.

Why is that not safe?

> Because when she gets mad at me she hurts me.

How does she hurt you?

> She says awful things to me. She hits me. She says things and does things that make me feel awful and rotten.

You're not rotten, Little Girl. You are not a rotten kid.

> She says I am.

She's wrong, honey. You are not a rotten kid. You are not a rotten daughter.

> I feel awful when she gets upset with me. She makes me feel awful.

How does she make you feel awful?

> When she says things that I should do or shouldn't do. I feel guilty. She makes me feel guilty. I feel guilty because she told me that I'm expected to be there for the funeral. I don't want to go to a funeral. Not with her there.

Chapter 33: Treachery

Why don't you want to go to a funeral with her there?

> She overwhelms me. She makes me can't breathe.

Honey, that's why I am protecting you by not going for the funeral.

> But I'm scared. I can't win. It doesn't matter what I do. If I go she takes control of me. If I don't go she makes me feel awful. And I'm scared.

Little Girl, I want you to try to be brave. I know standing up to her is scary, but the more you do it, the easier it gets. Be brave here, honey.

> You're not brave. You wanted to cut yesterday.

I wanted to, but I didn't. I did not cut, Little Girl, and I won't. I promised you that I won't cut you anymore. I'm protecting you now. Cutting was a way that I tried to cope with things, but it wasn't a good way.

> I don't want to cut. I don't want to be cut.

I know, honey. And I didn't cut you. I'm protecting you instead.

> I know. But I'm scared. I'm scared of her. She doesn't protect me. She gets mad at me.

What happens when she gets mad at you?

> I already told you, she doesn't protect me. And she says awful things to me that make me feel awful. And she hits me. She gets mad at me.

When does she get mad at you?

> When I mess up. When I don't do what she wants. When I tell secrets. When I make her look bad. When I'm sad.

Little Girl, I want you to know that when she gets mad, that is her problem. It doesn't mean something is wrong with you.

> Yes it does. I'm rotten. I'm supposed to be perfect. I'm supposed to make her happy. I'm supposed to do what she wants. I'm supposed to be there for her.

Honey, she was supposed to be there for you.

> But she wasn't. She didn't protect me. And she makes me feel awful for having problems. When I wet the bed she made me feel awful. When I'm sad she makes me feel awful. When I told the secret she made me feel awful. You made me feel awful, too. For telling the secret. Why'd you do that?

I was afraid. My adult wasn't very strong then. I was afraid of her anger. You were afraid of her anger. Telling the secret and standing up to her made us terrified. But my adult is stronger now. I can stand up to her now. I'm going to protect you now.

> I'm still afraid of her. I don't want you to cave in like you did before.

Honey, I'm going to protect you. I may not do it perfectly, but I am going to protect you. Please trust me on this. I know it's hard to trust me because in the past I haven't done a very good job of protecting you, but I will. I promise.

> Are you going to make me go back to that house?

I don't know, honey. But if we have to go back to that house, Josh will be there and my adult will be in control.

> I don't like being in that house. It's not safe.

I know, honey, but that house can't hurt you now. She may be in that house, she may say things that scare you and hurt you and make you feel guilty, but the house can't hurt you.

> I was hurt in that house. They all hurt me.

Chapter 33: Treachery

How did they hurt you?

> Papa hurt me and Mom and Mommie didn't protect me. They let him hurt me. And Mommie always got mad at me.

I won't get mad at you. I'll protect you, Little Girl. You're safe with me.

> Do I have to hug her again? That's not safe.

When I hug her, my adult will be in control.

> Do I have to see her again?

I will see her again, but my adult will be in control.

> How do I know that? How do I know she won't overwhelm me?

Honey, there will be times when you are still scared of her. But my adult is here. Josh is here. Gary is here. And God is here. We'll help you.

> I'm still scared.

I know. But the more we integrate, the less scared you're going to be. I love you, Little Girl, but I can't let you be in control of my emotions. My adult has to be in charge. That doesn't mean that I'm ignoring you or mad at you or anything like that. It doesn't mean I don't want you around. It means I'm protecting you. There comes a time when I have to grow up. That's what I'm doing, Little Girl. I'm growing up.

> It's scary.

I know. But the more I grow up, the less scary it will be.

> You promise?

Yes, I promise.

After I wrote out that conversation with the little girl, I felt better. I reread parts of a book about setting boundaries and I prayed a lot. I didn't call my mother until the evening after the funeral. Before I called her, I typed out a list of possible responses: I'm sorry we weren't able to be there, I'm sorry you were disappointed, I don't feel like I need to explain myself, I'm sorry you feel that way, I don't appreciate the guilt trip, I'm sorry you are hurting. I even role-played with Josh to practice how I could respond to things she might say. When I called her that evening, I was relieved but confused. She didn't seem upset that I hadn't been there. She didn't try to make me feel guilty for not being there or calling. She just gave me all the details of the funeral and her week, since she had taken the entire week off work to help Chandler's sister get ready for the funeral. Then she reminded me about the anniversary of Grandma's death coming up in three weeks. She wanted us to go to the cemetery together and do something together that Grandma would have enjoyed. I felt the same way I felt about Thanksgiving and Christmas, like it would be treachery to stand up to her by not going. That's how I'd felt about not going to Chandler's funeral, like I had committed treachery. Gary encouraged me to be honest with her about not wanting to go for the anniversary of Grandma's death. He said historically I make her think I want to be there when I really don't. I give her half-truths. He said I need to just tell her the truth, which is that I don't want to go. That's not how I want to grieve. He said I need to quit playing dodge ball with Mother. But dodge ball doesn't seem as treacherous.

34
Abuse

Abuse,
like a
caged animal,
poked and prodded,
starved and neglected,
beaten and bruised
till he becomes a
raging beast
full of fear
and anger
and despair;
or,
like a
small child,
trusting the
one she loves,
having her trust
shattered
by unwanted acts
of shame
and degradation;
or,
like a
tortured woman
inflicting pain on
herself,
harming herself
as she was
so harmed.
Abuse.

Once I stood up to my mother by not attending Chandler's funeral, the little girl really started opening up to me. I had lots of memory flashes about my grandfather, especially whenever Josh and I were being intimate. The memories came quickly and in great detail. Memories of the abuse I suffered at the hands of my grandfather weren't all that was opening up to me. I began remembering things about my mother, as well. One evening I told Josh about something my mother did and he said, "Rochelle, that was child abuse." I grew angry as I shared some more memories. The rage welled up inside of me as I admitted some things to myself. I had talked around this before, but I had never acknowledged that it was abuse. The next day, I wrote my mother a letter.

9-27-09

Dear Mom,

Once again, I am writing you a letter that I will never send. Maybe someday I can say some of these things to you in Gary's office, that is, if you'll ever go there and meet with him and me. But I am writing now because I need to deal with my thoughts and emotions. Last night I was full of smoldering rage and, rather than let it consume me, I punched it out on the punching bag. But I am still so angry.

It has to do with the green ottoman incident. You were out of control that day. You were a monster that day. I was desperately trying to hide behind the green ottoman while you were flailing at me. I don't remember if you had a switch, a belt, a paddle, or what. But I remember your rage. You were furious and you were lashing out at me wildly and with abandon. And the fact that I was trying to hide behind the green ottoman just made you angrier. You were huge in your anger. I was miniscule in my fear.

And that wasn't the only time. What about the time you broke the paddle on me? It was one of those paddle-ball paddles, the kind with the little rubber ball attached by a rubber band. It wasn't the regular-sized paddle. It was an extra-large one. You used it to spank me. And you broke it on me. I remember the paddle. I remember you using it on me. I don't remember the time you broke it on me, but I know it happened. Why? Because you bragged about breaking it on me for years. You thought it was funny. I've heard you tell that story many times. And you always laugh when you tell it, like it was funny. But it wasn't funny. How hard were you hitting me? The only way that paddle could have broken was from you hitting me too hard with it. And you thought it was funny!! How much fun is it to terrorize your child? Because that's what I was—terrorized.

So, there was the green ottoman incident and this incident where you broke the paddle on me. But there were many more times when your anger was out of control. I would hide from you in my closets and under the bed. I was terrified of you. I got spankings from you all the time. You've always laughed about that, but it's no laughing matter. How many of those spankings were given in a fit of anger? How many of those spankings were given when you were out of control? How many of those spankings terrorized me? And what about the other things you did in addition to all the spankings? You would pinch me really hard. If we were driving in the car and you got angry at me, you would backhand me. You would grab that nerve between my shoulder blades when you were angry at me, too. You did all those things.

Josh said that what you did constitutes child abuse. That term sounds so harsh, so brutal. But I was terrorized. I'm still afraid of you. Maybe I don't like that term because I'm trying to protect you. But what about me? Who protected me when I was a little girl? You didn't protect me from him. And who protected me from you? It's no wonder there is so much fear in my life. I got it from two different sides—sexual abuse from him and physical abuse from you. I try to rationalize it. You didn't beat me up. You didn't use me as your punching bag. You didn't come home after drinking and throw me around. I didn't live with that. So I rationalize. It wasn't that bad. You just spanked me. Hard. A lot. Out of rage.

I try to rationalize, but I can't. To do that would be betraying the little girl. You controlled me with your anger. You terrorized me. You hit me on many occasions out of rage. There is a difference between spanking a child as discipline and spanking a child out of anger. You crossed the line. You abused me. There, I said it. You abused me.

And what fills me with rage, what sent me to the punching bag last night, is that you blamed it on me! How many times have you told the story about breaking the paddle on me as if I had done something awful to cause the paddle to break? You never said you broke the paddle on me by hitting me too hard. But why else would a paddle break? And don't give me any garbage about the angle or something stupid like that. Force. That's what broke it. The force with which you hit me. It was your fault the paddle broke, not mine. But you always blame me! How many times have I heard you say that I was a rotten kid? More times than I can count. So that justifies you hitting me all the time? I don't think so! How many times have I heard you say that I was a strong-willed kid? So you thought you had to beat me into submission? Apparently. You beat me into submission and broke my will. If that's what you were trying to accomplish, it worked. You created a fearful, terrified person. But I'm getting my will back. My strong will is what has kept me fighting to get well all these years.

Do you remember that other paddle you had hanging in the kitchen, the brown one with the owl painted on it? Do you remember the saying painted on it? I know you do, you've laughed about it enough times. It said, "Insanity is hereditary, you get it from your kids." Well, guess what? It's not funny! It's wrong! You get insanity—*I* got insanity— from you! My mother! And you wonder why I think I didn't have a very good mother?

The letter you wrote last year amazes me. You said you were "stunned, perplexed, and appalled," that you had ever done anything to hurt me or upset me. You said that you had "soul-searched," but you had no idea what you had ever done that would cause me to feel the way I do about you. Soul-searched! That's a bunch of garbage. I shouldn't be surprised you wrote those things. You've always abdicated responsibility. It was always my fault. I was the rotten one, not you. Well, Mother – I was not a rotten kid! You were a rotten mother!

This is one area that I have ignored for too long. Another area has to do with you not protecting me from him. I'm not fully ready to deal with that yet. But this area I am dealing with. I'm not ignoring it any longer. I'm not betraying the little girl in this area any longer. I'm admitting it. You abused me. That's a strong word, but it's accurate. I looked up the word *abuse* in the dictionary. You misused me. You mistreated me. You inflicted physical and especially psychological harm on me. You abused me. And what makes it particularly vile to me is that you blamed me. I wasn't to blame, Mother. I was not a rotten kid. I was a beautiful, terrified little girl. Acting out because of the sexual abuse, yes. Strong willed, yes. But that calls for protection and compassion and loving discipline, not terrorizing, abusive anger. But that's what I got. I've ignored this for a long time. I'm not ignoring this any longer.

Gary said that recognizing the abuse was important for me. I was being totally honest with myself. He said it was very freeing for me to think about and write about it and healthy for me to verbalize it. And it explained my inordinate fear of her because, as a child, I feared for my safety in a very real way. Her emotional outbursts directed at me reinforced why I tried to hide things from her. Not only was I emotionally unsafe with her, I was physically unsafe too. And then he pointed out that when she stopped abusing me, I abused myself. She set in motion a mechanism of self-abuse, as did my grandfather. Gary said that you often see that phenomenon. People who are chronically abused keep abusing themselves. They feel they deserve to be punished. Mother released her own frustrations by whacking me and then I kept on whacking myself through the cutting. I told him I was abusing myself long before I started cutting. Every time I masturbated I was abusing myself. He agreed that that was a correct assessment. He said I had pain and pleasure in one package. In thinking about all the abuse I had suffered, from my grandfather, my mother, and myself, I felt as if my soul was crying out.

Her Soul's Yelp

Yelp–to cry out sharply, as in pain

She lies awake in her bed at night,
waiting for him to come in,
creeping and sneaking and
telling her lies
to keep her quiet about
his awful sin.
She feels the shame in her
body and soul,
gripping her heart with pain.
He's robbed her of her
innocence,
not once, but time and again.

Where is it safe? Where can she go?
Who can she turn to for help?
All alone in her shame and her fear,
her soul screams and yelps.

She waits again for the hitting blow,
coming from the one closest to her,

spanking and hitting
out of anger and rage,
it takes little for
her wrath to occur.
She feels the terror in her
body and soul,
gripping her heart with fear.
She's robbed her of her
security,
so afraid of
Mother dear.

Where is it safe? Where can she go?
Who can she turn to for help?
All alone in her shame and her fear,
her soul screams and yelps.

She marks time until the next cut on her skin,
until the next time she brings pleasure
and pain,
self-abuse, self-harm,
self-hurt,
has shackled her
with heavy chains.
She feels the shame and fear from
herself,
gripping her heart with grief.
She's robbed herself of
any hope;
can she ever turn over a new leaf?

Where is it safe? Where can she go?
Who can she turn to for help?
All alone in her shame and her fear,
her soul screams and yelps.

She hopes and prays for help to come,
wrestling in prayer to God,

watching for answers,
abiding for aid,
doesn't His silence seem odd?
She doubts His love of her
body and soul,
and it grips her heart with dread.
Robbed of faith and serenity,
she wonders if she ought to be dead.

Where is it safe? Where can she go?
Who can she turn to for help?
All alone in her shame and her fear,
her soul screams and yelps.

But through time and friends, help has
come to her,
God has answered her prayer for aid.
He took away the one
shaming her soul
and gave her strength to
resist the blade.
She feels His peace in her
body and soul
and it grips with solace her heart.
She may have been robbed of her
childhood,
but of strength and healing
she has a start.

Where is it safe? Where can she go?
Who can she turn to for help?
God and her husband and very dear friends –
and they have softened her yelp.

    The memory flashes about my grandfather were coming more often and in much greater detail. Josh was very patient with me during this time. Usually they came while Josh and I were being intimate. I was dealing with my thoughts about the sexual abuse at the same time as I was processing the understanding that I had been physically abused by my mother. It was an intense period. I spent quite a bit of time writing in my journal.

I remember when I first accused Papa of sexually abusing me back in 1992. Everything was colored by the fact that I was a victim of childhood sexual abuse. I'm feeling the same way now. Since I have admitted that my mother physically abused me, everything is colored by that. And it feels like a double whammy, sexual abuse and physical abuse. I feel tainted. And little. And everything makes me think about her. I read a magazine, I think about her. I see something on TV, I think about her. I'm involved in a conversation, I think about her. I get sad and feel little at the drop of a hat. I'll be fine and suddenly I'm overcome by sadness. It's bad enough that my grandfather abused me, but my mother?! I know what I'm about to say isn't right, but I have to say it anyway. What was it about me that was so awful? What did I do to deserve what I got? From both of them! Why didn't anyone protect me? Why did everyone hurt me? What was wrong with me? For so long I tried to punish the little girl for being so bad. Gary told me I tried to cut the little girl away from me, thinking I could cut the badness away. I don't want to do that anymore, and I won't, but I can't help wondering what was so defective about the little girl? I look at her pictures and I see a beautiful, frightened, angry little girl. And I just feel so little right now. When I think about everything, which is all the time, I feel sad and angry and little. I don't think I'm obsessing about it. It's just that it's always right there.

And I'm struggling with how to reconcile the good and the bad. Last February, in my conversation with the little girl, one of the things she didn't understand was how could he play with me and take me places and play make-believe with me and then turn around and abuse me sexually and emotionally. Same thing with my mother. How do I reconcile the times we had fun together and all the gifts she has given me with the emotional incest and the physical abuse?

Gary has talked about this before and one of the books I have about toxic parents addresses this very thing – a bewildering combination of abuse and love, a bizarre mixture of pleasure and pain. The author says that there is "an incredibly strong, perverse parent/child fusion...when a parent holds out a promise of love while at the same time mistreating that child."[8] This is really bewildering to me. How can she (him, too, but mostly her) say things like I'm the most important thing in the world to her and she loves me and she's proud of me and also say I was a rotten kid and I'm a terrible person?

CHAPTER 34: ABUSE

How can she give me such nice, expensive, abundant gifts and still treat me the way she did when I was a child and even now? Though there's no physical abuse anymore, there's still the emotional incest and verbal abuse, the guilt and manipulation. How do I reconcile these things? As for the gifts, even as a little girl I have always felt that my mother was trying to buy my love. She certainly wasn't trying to earn it with the way she treated me. She abused me and then blamed me. This perverse combination of abuse and love really confuses me. That's something I continued in my self-abuse through the masturbation, pleasure and pain in one package.

Maybe her gift-giving is why I have such confusing emotions about Christmas. Lavishing gifts on me seems to be the only way she knows to show me love. But Christmas is always uncomfortable for me precisely because of how many gifts she gives me. She'll give me twenty-five or thirty gifts. Something is wrong with that picture. And paired with her abuse through the years, I'm very confused. Does she love me or hate me? Sometimes it seems like there is a fine line between the two. She says she loves me. I say I love her. But I feel that it's expected. Every time we talk on the phone, it feels awkward at the end because I'm expected to say, "I love you." Shouldn't that be something you say because you want to, rather than because you're expected to say it?

And I still do the abuse/love combo to myself. Not with the masturbation anymore, where there was pleasure and pain combined, but through my relationship with food. I'll eat (pleasure), then I'll feel sick and I will loathe and berate myself for not having any self-control. That perverse combination of pleasure and pain, abuse and love, keeps living on in me. Wow. When does the cycle end? When can I ever break the chains of self-abuse that started with my mother and my grandfather so long ago when I was a little girl?

One evening after church, a group of us were at the burger joint and one of the guys started talking about how his mother used to pull off her shoe while driving and reach over the back seat and start spanking the kids with it, while she was still driving! As he was talking, I started seeing my mother leaning over the seat of the car waling at me with the paddle.

She would use one of those paddle-ball paddles. Her hand, too, if she didn't have a paddle. I don't know if she kept a paddle in the car or if she only took it on trips, but she would use that on me in the car. She'd be mad at me, probably because I was pushing her buttons, and she'd pull the car to the side of the road and start yelling and hitting. She'd be aiming at my bottom, but I'd be wiggling and squirming around trying to get away from her, so the blows would fall other places, too. We'd go on trips with another lady and her little girl and she and I would be in the backseat arguing or bugging each other and here'd come the paddle. As I was sitting there in the restaurant last night and Leonard was talking, I just sort of zoned out as I was seeing her in my mind's eye. He said his mom would be swinging at them with her shoe while she was driving and that the fear would be worse than the beating itself. Of course, Leonard's fear wasn't of his mother, it was the fear that they would have a wreck! But I had fear. Of my mother.

Later, when Josh and I were talking about it, I remembered how I would act as a little girl. For lack of a better word, I was obnoxious. I would irritate and annoy on purpose. I would keep at one thing over and over just to bug someone, usually my mother. Because of this, and because I was strong-willed, my mother's told me countless times, "You were a rotten kid." But I wasn't a rotten kid. I was a typical kid. Don't most kids act obnoxious? But rather than respond to me with patient discipline and loving training, she lashed out at me in anger. Don't most kids push their parents buttons? Does that make me a rotten kid? Does that make the hitting my fault? Because I provoked it?

Sometimes I'm obnoxious with Josh. I will bug him and pick on him just like I would do when I was a little girl. In fact, when I am being obnoxious with Josh, I feel very much like the little girl. And I think sometimes when the little girl is being obnoxious with Josh, she is doing it to test him to see if he is going to lash out at me like Mother would. But he never does. He is always very patient with me. Sometimes he'll tell me to quit and his voice will get firm, but he never loses his cool with me. In fact, sometimes he will turn it into a funny moment and he jokes with me. Why couldn't she have been more like him? Why did she always have to lash out at me in anger?

Gary told me a couple of weeks ago that her physical abuse of me explains a lot of my inordinate fear of her. I feel the fear especially when I'm talking to her, on the phone or in person, and she starts trying to make me feel guilty or talking about her problems or things that make me nervous. With her, I don't just get nervous, I become fearful. There's a guy at church that is a problem personality. I've told Josh that he is a male version of my mother. And because of the various encounters we've had with him, I am afraid of him. He gets angry at Josh sometimes because he doesn't like what Josh is preaching, so I am always nervous and fearful about what Josh is preaching if this guy is there, even though I know Josh is preaching truth. My fear of this guy stems from my fear of my mother and her anger. Anytime I experience someone's anger, there's a whole bunch of transference going on because of my mother's anger. And sometimes it is paralyzing. What's interesting is that during that memory flash of her hitting me over the front seat of the car, I zoned out. But I don't think I was feeling fear so much as I was remembering feeling fear. I felt little.

A book that I was reading on childhood sexual abuse suggested trying to write with your non-dominate hand. I thought that might help me be able to converse with the little girl, so I tried it. As I wrote in my journal, when the little girl was talking, I wrote with my left hand. Here, I have typed those sentences with a different font.

Little Girl, what was it like for you, growing up with so much abuse?

> I was scared. I tried to be good, but she was mad all the time. I wasn't good enough.

Honey, even if you weren't acting good, that didn't give her the right to hit you out of anger.

> But I was a rotten kid. She's told me that lots. She says I was a good teenager, but a rotten kid.

Honey, you were not a rotten kid! You were a beautiful, scared little girl. You were not rotten.

> Then why did she spank me and yell at me all the time?

She had problems controlling her anger and she took it out on you. It was her problem, not yours.

> But it was my problem. I made her mad. I wasn't any good.

Honey, people can get mad without hitting anyone. She was wrong. She was the one who wasn't any good. You were a beautiful, terrified little girl who was surviving as best as you could.

> She always said I was acting out.

You **were** acting out. You were acting out all your fear and anger and confusion about what was going on with Papa. But she didn't see it.

> She wasn't listening to me. Nobody ever listens to me!

Nobody?

> Nobody then.

Do people listen to you now?

> You do. And Josh listens and Gary and Miss Penny. But Mommie's never listened to me.

You're right, she's never listened to you. But I'm glad you have people who will listen now. I'm listening, Little Girl. Tell me what it was like.

> I can't.

Why not?

> I was hiding. I don't remember.

Where were you hiding, Little Girl?

> In the closet. Under the bed. Under the covers. On the ceiling.

What do you mean, "On the ceiling?"

> I spiraled up and floated on the ceiling.

When would you do this?

> When he was touching me.

Why would you hide?

> I was scared. I didn't understand. He told me he would die if I told.

Honey, it wasn't your fault that he died.

> I didn't tell!

I know honey, but even if you had told, it wouldn't have been your fault that he died. And it's okay to tell now. Whatever he told you to keep you quiet was a lie.

> Why did he lie to me? I thought he loved me. He took me to get ice cream. He played with me. Why did he scare me?

Honey, he was a bad man. What he did to you was wrong. It was wicked. It was not your fault, Little Girl. You did nothing wrong.

> I thought I was bad.

Honey, you were not bad. He was bad. You were not a bad girl. You were not a rotten little girl.

> If I wasn't bad then why did my father leave me? Why did Mommie hit me all the time 'cause she was angry at me? Why did Papa scare me? I'm bad.

No, Little Girl, you are not bad. Those things happened to you because they were bad. They were wrong. You were not bad. You were not a rotten kid.

> I'm scared.

Why are you scared, honey?

> I don't know.

I'm here, honey. I'm not going to hurt you. Josh's here. He's not going to hurt you. And we're not going to let you be hurt any more.

> Tell me something.

I love you, Little Girl. I love you and I'm going to protect you. You are a beautiful, precious little girl. I love you.

> I'm still scared.

I know, honey.

> And I'm mad!

Why are you mad?

> Because he lied to me! Because he scared me. Because he did those things to me. And I'm mad at Mommie too! And that scares me!

Why does it scare you to be mad at Mommie?

> 'Cause she just gets madder and she hurts me when she gets mad.

How does she hurt you?

> She hits me with the paddle and she yells at me and she says things that make me feel bad.

Is that why you're mad at her?

> Yes! I'm mad at her and I'm scared of her.

Little Girl, I am not going to let her hurt you.

> But she does hurt. She hurt me last week when she made me feel guilty.

Little Girl, I know that her words hurt, and I can't keep her from saying things that will make you feel bad. But I won't let her hit you anymore.

Chapter 34: Abuse

Her words hit.

I know, honey, I know. Listen honey, anytime she says something now that hurts your feelings, know that her words are directed to me as an adult, not to you, the little girl. And I will handle her words. I'm not going to let her guilt me or manipulate me anymore. I'm on my guard with her, honey. She can't hurt you anymore. I won't let her. Josh won't let her. Gary won't let her.

I know. But I'm still scared. I'm always getting hurt. Everybody hurts me.

Who all has hurt you, Little Girl?

Mommie. Papa. You.

I won't hurt you anymore, Little Girl. Papa can't hurt you anymore. And Mommie can't hurt you anymore.

I know, but it still hurts.

I know it does, honey. I know it does. We've had to live with hurt and pain for so long. We've had to live with the effects of abuse for many, many years. But we're getting well, we're working through things. You and I are coming together and you're sharing more and more with me. But the hurt is still there, I know, honey. Can you tell me what hurts right now?

I don't know.

What used to hurt the most?

It hurt when she would hit me.

Did it hurt when Papa would do things?

Yes. No. I don't know. I'm confused.

Why are you confused, honey?

> 'Cause when he would do things I liked it, but I didn't like it.

I know that's confusing, honey.

> It felt good, but it felt bad at the same time. And I didn't want to do things. But sometimes I did want to. I'm bad.

No, Little Girl, you are not bad. I want to try to explain something to you. Your body was made to enjoy certain kinds of touch. That's the way all our bodies operate. Just because you enjoyed certain things, doesn't mean you are bad. It's just the way you are made.

> Well I don't like it!

I know. But you're not bad.

> Do you promise?

Yes, Little Girl, I promise!

> The memories were coming with great clarity.

My memory,
like cobwebs in the trees,
seen only at a glance,
fleeting,
invisible, save in the
perfect light,
the right angle,
the exact reflection.

His violation,
her blows,
not glaring me in
the face
with all the fine details,
but lurking in the
shadows,

Chapter 34: Abuse

waiting for the light
to illuminate
the strands of silk,
or waiting for the dewdrops
of revelation
to grip the memory
and bring it into
light;
usually, though,
hiding amongst
the leaves and branches
of my life,
like cobwebs in the trees.
And yet,
when the right light
is cast,
it is crystal clear,
jumping out at me
through the boughs.
In fact,
then,
it is like the
awful horror
of walking into an
unseen cobweb
woven between the trees.

One Saturday afternoon, as Josh and I made love, I had an epiphany. I think the fact that it was light in the room made me realize something about the dissociative episodes I had as a child. All the times I would spiral up and float on the ceilings, I don't ever remember it being dark. It was always light. My grandfather picked me up from school in the afternoons.

Is that when it would happen? Or at least the worst of it? He wouldn't have to worry about getting caught since Mom and Grandma were at work. I don't have a clear memory of it happening in the afternoon, but I have a strong sense that that is when the worst of it occurred. Always before, I thought it had happened at night. But when I would spiral up and float on the ceiling, it was always light. I don't remember it ever being dark when I would do that. That experience is something I clearly remember. I did it many times when I was a kid. I liked being able to float on the ceiling. It was a powerful feeling. I remember, when I was in high school and college, wishing I could replicate that experience. Why was I able to float on the ceiling when I was a kid but no longer could? Remember the scene in the original *Willie Wonka and the Chocolate Factory* when the boy is floating up through the bubbles to the top of that room? That's what it was like. It's hard to explain. I wasn't wishing I could float or imagining that I was floating. I really was floating at the top of the room, looking down from the ceiling. I would spiral up from the floor or the bed and I would float at the top of the ceiling. And it was always light.

And I've been thinking about what constituted the abuse. I had a number of memory flashes in 2005 and I have had an incredible number of flashbacks this past year. At this point I've had flashbacks of my grandfather's face when Josh was touching me and during oral sex. I've had flashes of him when I smelled certain smells, especially Josh's genitals. I've had a number of images of my grandfather's fingers touching me as a little girl. I've had a number of images of little fingers touching a big penis. I've had flashbacks of my grandfather coming into my room and sitting on my bed in his boxers and tank undershirt and touching me. I've had flashbacks of myself as a little girl in my panties and nightgown, which makes me believe not all of the abuse occurred in the afternoons. I've had flashbacks of my grandfather coming down the dark hall and also of him standing by my bed. I've had flashbacks of me kissing his genitals. And of course, one of the strongest memories is the one I had last February of him telling me to keep quiet or he would die. That memory was so clear. Most of the flashbacks started out very general. But then they got more detailed to the point that it was obvious that it was my grandfather. So it seems to me, based on the flashbacks and memories I have had, that my grandfather would touch my genitals, make me touch his, and make me perform oral sex on him. This would happen sometimes at night after I had gone to bed, but also in the afternoons when he would pick me up from school. At least it seems that the dissociation, the floating on the ceiling, would occur when it was light and in the afternoons after school makes the most sense because that's when no one else was home.

Josh said maybe I had angelic help when I had my dissociative episodes. Jesus said in Matthew 18:10 that little children have angels in heaven. That's where the idea of guardian angels comes from. And in Hebrews 1:14, it says that angels are ministering spirits. The idea that as a little girl, I had an angel helping me gives me comfort. I don't know if that idea is exactly right, but I like the idea. My little girl likes the idea, too.

In my session with Gary that week, he said that dissociation is a common defense mechanism against abuse. That floating sensation actually occurs with a lot of abused children. He said it is obviously God's mechanism for defense, to be able to go to a safe place. And now my inner child was watching what was happening between my mother and me. She was seeing how I was standing up to her and setting boundaries with her and she was trusting me more. She saw that I didn't play Mother's games and that my adult was growing stronger. I was letting the little girl know that maybe I was safe because I didn't get a razor and torture her. There was integration and trust happening between my inner child and myself. That night I had a powerful experience. I wrote about it the next day. I hesitated to include this writing here because of the detail, but I think it is important.

I'm Beginning to Get Angry at Him

When Josh and I made love last night, I had a very powerful and strong experience. As Josh was getting close to climax, I began to get scared and feel really weird, like I was going to go somewhere. I couldn't really tell if I was about to dissociate or if a memory was breaking through, but it seemed like one of the two, or both, was happening. Then, as Josh was climaxing, the sensation got stronger and I felt very, very little and very, very afraid, almost terrified. As soon as he finished, I asked him, almost in desperation, to talk to me. I needed to hear his voice to ground me. He could tell something was wrong and started saying soothing things to me. As he talked, I felt calmer. Then I asked him to just hold me. I tried to explain what had happened and I told him that his orgasm was overwhelming to me. It was almost as if I was experiencing his orgasm as a little girl, like I was somehow remembering experiencing my grandfather having an orgasm when I was a little girl. And it scared me. Just how I experienced it, I don't remember yet. In other words, did I experience his orgasm because of oral sex I was forced to perform or because of me touching him or because he was masturbating in front of me or because he raped me or a combination of more than one of these? As Josh held me and I talked, I started crying. I wanted to be angry at my grandfather, but I was too sad. I was angry, but it was a sad, tragic anger, not exploding-on-the-punching-bag rage. I want to explode with rage at him, but I had a hard time doing so. He's just a picture, a memory in my mind. He's not flesh and blood any more that I can lash out at and beat to a pulp. But I am angry. He hurt me. He hurt me so bad! I cried that out to Josh as he was holding me. I want to explode with rage, but my anger is too sad right now. Josh said he thinks the explosive rage at him will come in time. I hope so, because I need to get angry at him. He nearly destroyed me sexually.

With Josh, sex is pure and beautiful, the way God intended it to be in marriage. Until Josh and I married, all I had ever known was distorted, perverted sexuality. My grandfather did that for me. Then I continued distorting and perverting it through the compulsive, masochistic masturbation and relationships with guys outside of marriage. Josh and I did it right. We did it God's way. We waited until we got married to have sex. That's why sex in our marriage is pure and beautiful. But there's a sense in which it isn't pure and beautiful because it is distorted by my past, by the abuse, the masturbation, and all the shame. I don't have shame with Josh, but our sex life is distorted by memories of my grandfather that keep flooding back.

CHAPTER 34: ABUSE

And it makes me sad. And angry. But in a sense, it's also exciting because it means that the little girl is trusting me more. She's giving me some of her buried memories.

I think I've entered a new phase of the healing process because I'm beginning to deal more directly with my grandfather and the memories of the abuse. I'm not afraid to remember. I was scared last night during the memory experience, but I think it was the little girl who was scared. My adult wasn't scared. My grandfather can't hurt me anymore and the memories can't hurt me. I've been wanting my memories and praying for them for many years now. There was a time when I thought I'd be overwhelmed by the memories and unable to handle them. But I don't think that's the case anymore. I think I can handle the memories. I think my adult is strong enough and I think my little girl is strong enough. She was strong enough to survive the original abuse. She and I can survive the memories of the abuse. And as she continues to share them with me and sees that I'm not going to hurt her by masturbating or cutting her, she is trusting me more. She likes seeing me stand up to Mother, hold my boundaries and not give in to her passive-aggressive games. And she continues to trust. The more I have stood up to Mother, the more the little girl has shared her memories of the abuse with me. And that's exciting. That's healing.

Gary gave me some things to think about when I told him I was having a hard time getting angry with my grandfather. His theory was that, as a little girl, my participation was not totally coerced. Indicting my grandfather meant indicting myself. I countered, "But the abuse wasn't my fault!" Gary agreed, it was not my fault. My adult knows that, but, he asked if the little girl knew it. I reminded him of the last time I had conversed with the little girl. She said sometimes she liked it and thought she was bad. Maybe she didn't know that it wasn't her fault.

Gary thought one reason my mind has resisted yielding up these memories is that there is guilt and shame and pain intertwined with pleasure. This was one reason I cut myself. He said that my little girl wasn't guilty, but she may not know that. She may not know that it was abuse; that it shouldn't have happened. I asked, "How do I get the little girl to understand that?" He thought she was already growing in that understanding and that was why the memories were emerging. Then he said, "There is no doubt in my mind that you were abused." And he said I didn't seem to have any doubts in my mind either. He was right, I don't.

I did after I recanted, but not now. I've had too many memories. Before, when I recanted, I had only had clues. But since 2005, I've had memories, clear and detailed memories. Lots of them. Especially this year. And they aren't false. Gary told me that my mind was yielding up information, to be patient with myself, that the details were coming.

I continued to have more and more detailed flashbacks. I drew about a dozen very graphic pictures of these memories. Gary pointed out the size differences in them. I was drawing huge hands and huge penises and little, tiny hands and little, tiny girls' bodies. The pictures I drew of my grandfather's face and body were huge, taking up most of the page, but the pictures of me were minute, almost hidden in the corner of the page. He said the size difference shows that as a little girl, I was exposed to sexual behavior and information way beyond my ability to understand.

Gary told me a long time ago that if the memories came, they would come when I was ready and could handle them. They were coming. And he said he had a hunch that my anger at my grandfather would come, too. I asked him how to handle the flashbacks I had when Josh and I were making love. He said to ask Josh for reassurance, to talk about it, to share with Josh what was happening. Certain things would trigger my mind and when that happened, to open my eyes. Seeing will help ground me. When there are things that trigger me it is probably an imbedded memory. And when it happened, Gary said to ask Josh for reassurance. He will not shame me. He will hold me and reassure me.

I wrote a poem about abused children, and then I wrote in my journal about the pleasure and guilt being intertwined.

How Many?

I hear the children laughing
in the schoolyard 'cross the street,
and I wonder for how many of them
is life a burning heat?
How many of those children
live in fear within their home?
How many of them struggle and
how many of them moan?
How many children endure the touch
that's a mix of terror and of love?

CHAPTER 34: ABUSE

How many of those children
float on the ceiling up above?
How many of them don't understand
the combination of pleasure and pain?
For how many of those children
is their hope dashed and daily drained?
How many of those children
are molested and abused?
I was one of them
is what my sad heart mused.

I've got all these thoughts running through my head. He told me he would die if I told. I remember that. How did that make me feel about what we were doing? If it was so awful that he would die if I told about it, how did that make me feel when I enjoyed it? How could I enjoy something that would make him die if I told it? How much guilt was I living with? It seems to me—and I'm thinking from the perspective of the little girl—that I would have been very conflicted by what he was telling me and how I was feeling physically. When he was touching me, it felt good. What if I liked it and what if there was a time or times when I initiated? Is that possible? And how did I feel about that? Could I even identify how I felt? Did I know what guilty feelings were or did I just feel awful but not have a name for why I felt so bad. I did feel like I was bad. The little girl said that several times in the last conversation we had, "I was bad." I said I was confused, and I said I was bad because sometimes I liked it, but sometimes I didn't like it and because it felt good and bad at the same time. I said that I didn't want to do things but that sometimes I did want to. Does that mean I initiated? And if I ever did initiate, does that matter? It was still wrong, it was still abuse. But if I initiated, does that make it ever my fault? My adult knows that it was never my fault, but how do I get the little girl to know that? And when he did die, I felt like it was my fault. I didn't tell, but I still felt like his death was my fault. So how do I get the little girl to quit feeling like things were her fault? I didn't make it any easier on her by cutting on myself and carving horrible words into her for so long. I was trying to punish myself. That was part of it. Was I trying to punish myself for the abuse? Oh, Little Girl, it was not your fault!

I told Gary I felt sick to my stomach thinking that I might have initiated. He said the little girl was in a state of terrible confusion—

Grandfather would die if she told, but it's something he does and she participates in and enjoys. Gary said I had to let the little girl know through my adult that it was not her fault. Ultimately my adult needs to take my inner child under her wing and reassure her that it was not her fault. I had the strong sense that it was a game that my grandfather and I played. Gary said that was probably right. Children like games. The situation put the little girl in tremendous confusion, which is probably why she would zone out and dissociate. She couldn't reconcile it in her mind so she repressed it. I put it in the category of things a child doesn't know how to deal with. I used God-given defense mechanisms to protect myself from the trauma. I dissociated and repressed the memories.

But, Gary pointed out, I didn't repress the guilt of it. "I'm bad" had been a dominant theme with me. It was why I cut. The cutting was directly related to the sexual abuse. It was a way to connect with the unrecovered feelings of how bad I was. Gary said when I cut, I was touching something in my very core. I was punishing myself. I felt like I deserved it. He told me that my anger at my grandfather was not coming yet because my inner child was concerned not just with what my grandfather did, but with what I did. She has questions. If I knew it was wrong, why didn't I stop it? Why did I enjoy it? Gary said that my adult understands that my grandfather betrayed me, but my child doesn't understand that yet. He urged me to continue talking about it because I am voicing the deep fears of the little girl and she's listening. She is wondering if we're going to come down on her. She is listening intently. She fears that we will come to her conclusion, that she is depraved. But that's not going to happen. She wasn't bad. She was abused. It wasn't her fault.

35

Holidays

Holidays,
like a
long-awaited party day,
full of excitement and
expectation,
all dressed up
and
decorated,
only to have the day
marred and
soiled
by an unwanted
visitor
who shows up
drunk and
violent,
throwing and
punching and
crashing and
raging and
totally destroying and
obliterating
the festive mood.
Holidays.

Holidays, birthdays, special days. They always seemed to be tainted by my mother's presence. When Josh and I got married, it was the most glorious day of my life and yet . . . and yet . . . my mother was there trying to orchestrate things her way, feeding off the drama of the day. Whatever special day it is, my mother's presence always ruins the festive mood for me. My birthday is in October, so every fall I start dreading the special days. Three months in a row of having to deal with Mother on special days. My birthday, Thanksgiving, Christmas. Amazingly, my mother agreed to come to our place for both Thanksgiving and Christmas. In fact, it was her idea, which was a great relief to me. I didn't have to worry about being "treacherous." She was coming here, so I would be on my own turf, but I was still going to have to deal with her. My birthday was first and it was a big birthday for me. I turned forty. The big four-o.

Forty Years

Verse 1: After forty years of living life, after forty years, I cry.
After forty years, my heart is sad, but now I have to try.

Chorus: I want my life to be a testament;
I want to heal from all the pain I've had,
for struggle has defined my life thus far, forty years for me.

Verse 2: I have worked so hard at getting well;
I have struggled and I've grown.
I've been honest and courageous as
I have tried to quench my moan.

Chorus: I want my life to be a testament;
I want to heal from all the pain I've had,
for struggle has defined my life thus far, forty years for me.

Verse 3: As I continue living life on earth, I know I'll keep getting well,
and to be a source of hope and help, my story I will tell.

Chorus: I want my life to be a testament;
I want to heal from all the pain I've had,
for struggle has defined my life thus far, forty years for me.

Chorus: I want my life to be a testament;
I know I'll heal from all the pain I've had,
for struggle will turn in to triumph, I'll have victory!
So on this special day I'll celebrate, forty years for me!

CHAPTER 35: HOLIDAYS

Miss Penny pointed out that forty was a significant number in the Bible. The Israelites wandered in the wilderness for forty years. Moses was being prepared for his ministry in the wilderness of Midian for forty years. Jesus was tempted in the desert for forty days. There is something about forty and the wilderness. I've been in the wilderness of my life for forty years. But the first forty are over. Those forty years were defined by struggle. The next forty years, however, will be defined by healing. Healing has already been happening and I have no doubt that it will continue. It hasn't been easy, and I don't expect it to get easy. And of course, dealing with my mother has never been easy. My birthday was no exception.

Last night on the phone my mother asked me over and over what I wanted for my birthday and wanted some ideas of what she could give me. I gave her two, but I told Josh later that I wished she wouldn't give me anything because her excessive gift-giving feels like she is trying to buy my love. And especially because of the physical abuse, her love seems so warped that I get angry and depressed when I think of her giving me gifts. She e-mailed Josh and told him she wanted to help throw me a big surprise party. Josh had already planned to have cake and ice cream for anyone in the congregation who wanted to join us, but now my mother is coming the weekend before my birthday to be here for the cake and ice cream. She wants to do something special for my birthday since it is a big one. If she wanted to do something special, why doesn't she leave me alone. I wanted my fortieth birthday to be special, yes, but without her! Now she's coming and I feel awful. Why couldn't I just have the guts to say, "No, Mom, I don't want you here." But noooo, I'm Miss Nice and Polite, and now she's coming. At least she'll be leaving on Sunday and won't be here on my actual birthday. Why does she have to make everything so complicated? When I got off the phone, I went out and punched on my punching bag. I'm still angry today, but mostly I'm depressed. I've been depressed most of the day. When I told her we weren't coming for the anniversary of Grandma's death because Josh has a funeral to preach, she was upset with me. "Why couldn't you come by yourself? I'd think Grandma's death was more important than some funeral up there." Then in the next sentence she talked about my birthday party. Why in the world would I want to spend my birthday with someone who sends me guilt messages all the time? I'm just so sick of her and sick of dealing with her! Why can't she just die and leave me alone?! There, I said it. I've thought it many times. But I said it. And I feel horrible for saying it. But that's how I feel. And of course, the magical thinking kicks in here. If she dies, it will have been my fault. My grandfather's death was my fault, at least that's what the little girl thought. I know that's really not true. But that's really how I feel about my mother. I wish she'd just die and leave me alone. How's that for a loving daughter? And I'm worried. My mother is coming for my birthday, and Gary's going to be in India for three weeks!

Gary said the little girl obviously doesn't want Mother there. He told me to make some agreements with the child and write out what my boundaries would be while she is here. It's important to anticipate and know what my boundaries are beforehand. He said it's key that I communicate with the little girl. In the past I haven't set good boundaries; I've just avoided. So I wrote out the boundaries that I wanted while she was here. I don't want to hold hands with her during the prayers or sit right next to her in church. I want a little space between us. I don't want to hug her more than two or three seconds. I don't want her orchestrating things at the birthday party. I was given the opportunity to enforce my boundaries sooner than I anticipated.

I did it! I stood up to my mother about something! I didn't avoid. I wasn't evasive. I told her no. Thank you, but no, thank you. I did exactly what Gary and I talked about in my session not three hours before she called. Gary discussed with me that before I have tried to be clever and avoid telling my mother what I am really thinking. The little girl is afraid of Mother and would rather find a clever way to say something, be evasive, instead of telling the truth. He said that part of my healing is for my adult not to play evasive games with Mother. He said the idea that my adult doesn't have to play games with Mother will be very healing for my child. The little girl knows that in the past I have wimped out with Mother. That's why my child doesn't totally trust my adult. And he said that for me to tell Mother I don't want something (like a hug or for her to hold my hand) is not just about me speaking truth to Mother, it's about my little girl trusting my adult. I told Gary that was very scary to me. He agreed. For the little girl, it is terrifying to stand up to Mother. When I stood up to her as a child, she would lash out at me in anger. As a little girl, there was a real reason to fear her physically. Her discipline impressed upon me that it wasn't safe for me to let her know what was going on inside of me. And as a result, I almost created a disassociated personality structure

CHAPTER 35: HOLIDAYS

as a method of survival. I would rather punish the little girl and cut myself than say something to her. But now, Gary reminded me, she can't hurt me physically. Her way of harming me now is through pouting, condemning looks and words, guilt-inducing messages that I'm not a good daughter and such. I told Gary I am afraid of her pouting. He said that's because I'm under the conviction, because I was schooled that way, that it is my job to keep Mother happy. Gary said it's time to change that. He said if I tell her I don't want a hug or don't want to hold her hand and she probes and starts wanting to know why, then that would be the perfect opportunity to remind her of my invitation to meet with me and Gary. He told me that when a situation arises for me to just be truthful. He said it's a character decision, not a courage decision. Speak truth rather than play games. And that's exactly what I did when she called last night.

She called to talk about my birthday. She's coming here for my birthday and for the cake and ice cream gathering we are having for the members of the congregation. I told her I didn't want a bunch of decorations or anything like that. Then she wanted to talk to Josh. She told him something she wants to do with pictures of me from when I was a little girl until I got married. Josh said he didn't think that would be a good idea, so she got me back on the phone and told me about it. I told her I didn't want that. Then she started with the guilt trip: "I've already spent a bunch of time on this. I've got pictures in frames and attached to scrapbook pages and everything!" I told her I appreciated the idea and the effort, but I really didn't want it. I just wanted cake and ice cream. She was upset and continued. "Why don't you want this all of a sudden? You wanted it when I gave you your thirtieth birthday party and you gave me my fiftieth. What's wrong now? Why do you all of a sudden not want it now?" I told her I just didn't want it. I just wanted cake and ice cream. She was upset with me and said in a wounded, pouting tone, "Well, I guess I'll just take the pictures out of the frames that I've already put them in." I said, "Thank you."

I told Josh afterward that I was glad she at least brought it up before she got here. It would have been that much harder to say no to her if she had shown up with all the pictures. I told Josh that I absolutely did not want a bunch of pictures of me as a little girl sitting around when my mother was here. I need to be completely in my adult when she is here. I don't need pictures of the little girl pulling me out of my adult. I love the little girl and I'm trying to protect her from Mother. That's why my adult needs to be totally in control.

I was nervous after the phone call, but I felt really good. I actually stood up to her! I stayed in control of the conversation and I didn't get emotional. I felt as if the little girl was very pleased with me. I'll have to be on my guard while my mother is here. But now that I've done it, as Gary said, it'll be easier the next time. I know she wasn't happy with me, but I've got to get past believing that her happiness is my responsibility.

When she came for my birthday, her behavior was much as I had expected, destroying and obliterating the festive mood. I was determined to have a good time at the party, regardless of her behavior, but it was difficult.

She Wants to Talk About Love

Well, my mother left about an hour ago. I survived! But I didn't escape unscathed. I had to endure more emotional blackmail. More guilt. And this time it was spiritual guilt. In church this morning, when we first sat down for Bible class, I put my Bible and purse on the pew so they would be between my mother and me when we sat down and I wouldn't have to sit right next to her. I wanted to avoid her trying to hold my hand during the prayers. She made some comment about me sitting so far away. Then I said something evasive about that being where I liked to sit and she got upset. She pulled out her Bible and a piece of paper and spent the entire Bible study time writing out Scriptures. She would set the paper down between us where I could see it clearly. She was using the Scriptures to guilt me. I know that's what it was about because one of the verses was "Honor your father and mother" (Ephesians 6:2). She was writing down verses about seeking the good of others, doing everything in love, loving with actions, forgiving, having the same attitude as Jesus, not paying back wrong, a foolish man despising his mother, etc. I found myself praying to God that He would help me keep my adult in charge. I wouldn't be surprised if I get these verses from her in the mail at some point. During Josh's sermon, she inched farther and farther down the pew until she was sitting a good three feet away from me. All I did was put my things on the seat between us. I found myself getting mad. She thinks love and forgiveness mean I have to sit **right** next to her. God never intended His Scriptures to be used as weapons, but that's what she was doing. She wants to talk about honoring your father and mother? What about the passages (in the same context!) that say for parents not to

CHAPTER 35: HOLIDAYS

exasperate or embitter or discourage their children?! Gary was right about my understanding of her having physically abused me bringing new levels of anger to me. As I watched her write out all these Scriptures, I thought about her lashing out and hitting me in anger. I was bitter. She wants to talk about love?! How dare she imply that I am not loving her because I wouldn't sit **right** next to her. What about yelling at a child in anger? What about hitting a child out of rage? Not just once, but over and over? What about smothering your child? What about using your child as your grunt and servant? What about emotional incest? What about emotional blackmail? What about manipulating and guilting your child into all kinds of things? What about not caring about your child's mental health? What about not protecting your child from being sexually molested? What about all that? She wants to talk about love? **HOW DARE SHE!** I am full of anger. I'm smoldering.

After church, we went back to the house and got ready for the party. Her pouting episode seemed to be over and she acted fine during the party. After the party she left to drive home, and I typed out on the computer what had happened and how I felt. My anger smoldered all afternoon. During church that evening I calmed down, and after church we went out to eat. But when we got home, my smoldering anger exploded into fury. I didn't have to wait for her to mail the page of Scriptures to me. When I went in the guest room that evening to check on things, it was glaring at me from the top of the chest of drawers. As I read through the verses she had written out I got madder and madder. At the bottom of the page she had written, "No pictures—eliminate from daily life? Touch? Real conversation?" I cried and yelled and punched on the punching bag. When I told Miss Penny what had happened, she said my mother was pouting like a stubborn, spoiled, little child who didn't get her way. She pointed out that although my mother was upset, she wouldn't talk to me, but acted like a child instead. I didn't know what to do with that page of Scriptures. Should I acknowledge it? Should I ignore it? What? I had to wait three weeks to talk to Gary about it because he was in India on a mission trip.

During those three weeks I was anxious about it, but I had other things to occupy my mind. I was having a lot of flashbacks about my grandfather. It was as if the little girl saw that I didn't cave in to Mother, and she started trusting me more. A week *after* my birthday I got a birthday card from my mother. It was very sappy. "Hope you know how much you've always meant. Hope you know how very much you're loved. Daughters and memories go hand in hand." I was sick to my stomach.

When Gary returned from India, he told me that he was proud of me for not playing her games. When I asked him how I should respond to the page she left, he said I should leave the sheet exactly where she left it. He said I didn't need to participate in these passive-aggressive games with her. As Thanksgiving got closer, I got more and more nervous about leaving the page of Scriptures in the guest room where I'd found it. Gary said I didn't have to, but it was a wonderful opportunity for me to not play the game with her. If she brought it up, I should remind her of my invitation for her to meet with Gary and talk about things there. I was very anxious about doing it, but I left it where I found it. And she didn't say a word about it! During her visit at Thanksgiving, she acted as if nothing had ever happened. As she was leaving, I helped her carry her bags out to her car. I noticed that the page was stuffed in a little bag of books she had brought. So she found it where she had left it and took it home with her. She even helped me decorate my house for Christmas the day after Thanksgiving. With the exception of one episode, her visit was relatively benign. But that one episode terrified me.

We had filled our plates with Thanksgiving dinner and had just started eating. Mom took a bite of a sweet pickle and started chewing. She started coughing. She started coughing harder, so she left the table and went into the guest room. After a few seconds I called out to her, "Are you okay?" I didn't get any response, so I went to check on her. I heard this strange sound coming from the room. As soon as I got to the door I realized that the strange sound was my mother trying to breathe—and she wasn't getting any air! She was half-sitting, half-lying on the bed and she wasn't able to get any air. She motioned for water and I yelled for Josh to get some water fast. Right before she took a drink, she gasped suddenly and got a breath. When she drank the water she recovered, but I was standing there terrified. She could have died. I reached out and took her hand and held it for a minute. This has happened before. She coughs really hard, her throat closes up, and she can't breathe. But she said it had never been this bad before. I was shaking inside and it was a long time before I calmed down even though we went back to the table and resumed eating and everything was fine.

I was acting fine on the outside, but internally I was very upset. What if she had died? Later that evening I went to my bedroom to lie down and

CHAPTER 35: HOLIDAYS

rest, and as I was lying there I kept talking to the little girl. I was saying over and over again – "It wasn't your fault, Little Girl. It wasn't your fault." I kept thinking that if she had died it would have been my fault. She's the one who wanted the pickles. She's the one who ate the pickles. But I bought them and put them on the table. What if I hadn't gone to check on her? It would have been my fault. I kept, almost obsessively, telling the little girl it was not her fault. Why would I think something like that was my fault? I started feeling guilty for all the times I have thought or wished that she would die and leave me alone. But when I was standing next to her by the bed, holding her hand, I was terrified that she would die. In the conversation I had with the little girl where I remembered that my grandfather said he would die if I told, the little girl told me, "I don't want Mommie to die too."

I was so upset. That night when Josh and I went to bed, I cried for a long time. It still upsets me. In fact, it's almost a week later and I'm just now able to write about it. I've avoided writing about it because I didn't want to think about it. Why would I think my mother's choking episode was my fault? Why would I think that if she had died it would have been my fault? Is that something Papa told me, too? That **she** would die if I told? I have always felt like everything was my fault, regardless of what happened. I'm programmed to think that way. But why? Is it because of my grandfather and what he said, or is it because of my mother? Or both? But to think it was my fault that my mother was choking on a pickle and couldn't breathe? Am I that warped? How messed up is that thinking? Why did I think it was my fault? I kept telling the little girl over and over – it wasn't your fault.

When I read what I had written to Gary, he said, "Wow. That's powerful. It's going to be interesting as you think about that." He pointed out that the little girl's role has always been the rescuer, the adult protector of Mother. Intellectually I have abrogated that role, but emotionally that is still a very powerful role that functions inside of me. He said I have fantasies of her not being in the picture, but in reality, the little girl has quite a need for her. He asserted that the little girl is afraid of losing her mother. There are some incestual responsibility issues with her, though. I was the little man of the house. I asked him how was I supposed to get past that. If the choking incident had not occurred, I would have thought that the caretaking issue was past, but this incident shows that it isn't. I still have an inordinate connection to Mother. He said that I'm making progress. It was good that I recognized and told myself that I didn't need to take responsibility for her choking. I told Gary that she called me a few days after she left to thank me for a nice visit and remarked that it seemed like old times. Her comment didn't sit well with me because fulfilling our old roles is not a nice thought. But, Gary noted, it is not like old times at all. She may have the illusion that we aren't going to have to resolve things, but I know better.

I made it past my birthday and Thanksgiving, and now it was Christmas. Three special days all with a mother focus. I wrote a piece a week before Christmas.

Why I Hate Christmas

"Heaven surely knows that packages and bows can never heal a hurting human soul."[9] These are lines from the Christmas song, "Grown-Up Christmas List." They are so true. I feel like my mother is trying to buy my love. She gives me packages and bows. Packages upon packages. For years now I have kept a list of what Christmas gifts I received. It helps me when I write my thank you notes. I looked at the lists of gifts my mother has given me for the past sixteen years. The average number of gifts my mother gives me each year is twenty-one. Twenty-one gifts!! That's the average! Some years it's been thirty! No wonder I feel like she is trying to buy my love. And many times she has told me, "I liked it so much, I bought one for myself!" I guess she thinks telling me she also bought one for herself makes it an extra-special gift. But to me, it cheapens it. That's like saying, "I bought you this really special gift, but I couldn't stand to be without one, so I bought myself one, too!" Maybe that would make the gift more special to someone else, but not to me. To me it just shows more of her greedy, acquisitive nature. She always wants more stuff. She doesn't have room for all the stuff she already has, much less more!

"Packages and bows can never heal a hurting human soul." My mother thinks all the packages and bows show her love. She thinks they make up for everything she's done wrong. But packages and bows can never heal a hurting human soul and that's what I have – a hurting soul. She has hurt me so deeply and no number of gifts can heal all the hurt I have. Underneath all the anger and fear, there is a hurting little girl. I honestly don't know what she could do to make up for all the hurt she has brought to me. I guess there isn't anything, really. It's called restitution. But there's nothing that can make up for all the years of hurt. She thinks there is. She thinks packages

CHAPTER 35: HOLIDAYS

and bows at Christmastime more than make up for anything she might have **possibly** done. She is unwilling to admit to having done anything to hurt me. And instead of all her packages and bows helping me to feel better, it just makes me feel worse.

Maybe that's one reason I hate Christmas. I get angry at myself because I play into her dysfunction. My guilting voice starts screaming at me before Christmas about how she always gives me so many gifts, and I feel like I have to somehow keep up with her. I don't give her near as many gifts as she gives me. It doesn't matter how many times I tell myself I am going to stick to a five-gift limit. I always do more and buy more and spend more than I want or even can afford. I think I have eleven gifts for her this year. I was "done" with her gifts and then my guilting voice started screaming at me. "You're giving Josh more gifts than you're giving her. She gives gifts to you **and** to Josh, but you only give her gifts from the both of you. That's not fair. You need to give her more so that it isn't so unbalanced when you and Josh are opening so many gifts and she doesn't have as many!" So I went out and bought her four more gifts. Then I had more for her than I did for Josh, so I bought Josh another gift. I am so stupid! I get so angry at myself!

If I feel like she is trying to buy my love, I feel more like I am trying to appease her. I feel like I am trying to make up to her for all the anger and hatred and bitterness I feel toward her. And that's another reason why I hate Christmas. I have such mixed emotions about Christmas. On one hand, I hate it, but the little girl (not the angry little girl or the fearful little girl – just the little girl) loves opening presents. But even more than opening presents, I love to watch people open the presents I give them! I can't wait for Josh to see what I got him. So on one hand I anticipate Christmas with excitement, but on the other hand I dread it. My conflicted emotions really make for a weird Christmas.

When I read that to Gary, he said, "What's the little girl up to with this gift thing?" He told me that my mother is desperately trying to show me that I am the love of her life, but he wanted to know why the little girl feels like she has to give her so many gifts. Why does she have to keep up that charade? Why does she play into her dysfunction? Gary said, "I'll give you a clue. A child has two or three things it wants—safety, approval, security. A child is not that complicated. Children are very concerned about maintaining equilibrium in the family. Even in abusive families."

He said the little girl would trade all those gifts she gives me for a caring mother. He's right. And the idea of maintaining equilibrium interested me. I filed it away to ponder. During and after my mother's Christmas visit, I wrote quite a few notes in my journal.

> I've got a stomachache. My mother called me earlier upset and in a panic because she had lost her keys as she was loading her car to come here for Christmas. She found them about ten minutes later. But my stomach still hurts. It was her being upset that got to me. Josh told me some very wise things. He said that her losing her keys was not my fault. It was not my responsibility to fix the problem. It was not my job to rescue Mother. Really, he said, the only thing I could do was pray. So I did. And Josh did. And she found her keys.
>
> But Josh hit the nail on the head. The little girl wanted to rescue Mother, and she felt scared and trapped because she couldn't. Josh said yesterday that the little girl wants to avoid upsetting Mother at all cost because the upset Mother is a monster. Now, Mom wasn't a monster when she lost her keys. She wasn't upset at me, but she was upset and that scares the little girl. When I was little and Mother would get upset or angry, she would lash out at me and spank me out of anger. So now, **any** strong emotion from her screams danger for the little girl, even her being upset because she's lost her keys. And as far as rescuing Mother goes, it's not so much that I want to rescue her for her sake. It's for my sake, for my safety.
>
> Before we opened gifts, she had her camera out. I wasn't even going to get mine out, but I saw she had hers, so I went ahead and got mine out. In a kind of sarcastic tone, she said, "I know you don't want a picture with me, but I want one with you." We stood in front of the Christmas tree together and I could tell she was upset. When she put her arm around me, she barely touched me. So what did I do? I rescued. I made a joke so she would laugh and not be upset. I put my fingers above her head like rabbit ears. She got better and we took the stupid picture.
>
> Today in the kitchen we were getting ready for lunch. I was standing next to the counter when she turned around and trapped me in a hug. Every time she hugs me I try to get out of it as soon as possible. And she keeps walking by me and reaching out and touching my arm or my back. And I want to shudder and scream, "Don't touch me!! Get away from me! Go home and leave me alone!" Gary said to try to do more than just survive her visit. Well, that's all I'm doing—barely surviving. My stomach has hurt most of the time

CHAPTER 35: HOLIDAYS

she's been here. If I have to hug and kiss her goodnight one more time I think I'll scream! Why can't I just say goodnight and leave it at that?

I am so ready for her to go home. I can only take so much of her. I hope and pray that I don't have a meltdown in January like I had last year. Last January, February and March were HORRIBLE! I don't want a repeat of that! But I worry about it. I just want her to leave me alone. She wants to hug me and touch me and kiss me and I am sickened by her touch. And I can't look at her. I avoid looking at her as much as possible. Eye contact is a definite NO! That feels unsafe, too.

Sunday morning stunk. Bible class wasn't so bad. Josh isn't teaching right now, so when it was time to sit down, I went to the bathroom and Josh sat next to my mother on the pew. When I came in late, I just sat next to Josh. Worship service was another matter. We moved up to a closer seat, and Josh and I put our Bibles and my purse on the pew where they would be between my mother and me, just like I did when she came for my birthday. Well, apparently she has gotten wise to that trick because when she sat down, she moved our stuff way down the pew and positioned herself so that there was barely any room for Josh and me to sit. When Josh and I went to sit down after we finished greeting people, we had to squeeze ourselves in to the pew, and she didn't move over one bit. In fact, she leaned toward me and said, "I can keep you warm on this side." Oh, I wanted to puke! Gary would say I had every right to ask her to move down, but I just couldn't do it. I asked her to hand me my purse. I put lotion on my hands and then set my purse on the floor in front of me. I asked her to hand me our Bibles and she did, but with a heavy sigh. I held our Bibles on my lap on top of my left thigh as some sort of barrier, I guess. When we stood to sing right before Josh's sermon, I put my Bible on the pew so that when we sat down it would be between us. Since Josh went up to preach, when I sat down I moved over a bit toward where he had been sitting. She started the heavy sighing again, in earnest.

I hate this! I hate going to church with her! I hate how I feel! I hate being around her! I just wish she would go away and leave me alone!

That sense of revulsion at her touch was so strong the last five days. Every time she would touch me, whether she was hugging me goodnight or just walking past me and reaching out and touching me, I felt sickened. Even when she would just get close to me, my whole body tensed. We worked a puzzle for a little while Sunday afternoon (which did not feel safe to me), and she kept getting up and coming over to my side of the table, leaning over me to look at the puzzle pieces. I felt smothered and trapped and sick to my stomach every time she did it. My stomach hurts right now just thinking about it. I am so repulsed by her. And now that she's gone, I've got this icky feeling like I wish I could scrub all traces of her off of me and my house. These last five days, I really noticed that my interactions with her (especially the ones that involved touch or physical closeness) felt incestuous. And it sickened me.

Christmas was over and I survived. But I had a lot to talk about with Gary. In fact, we started talking a few weeks before Christmas about my goals. What is my goal with Mother? That question loomed large in my mind.

36

Goals

Goals,
like a
confused
high school student
sitting in the
guidance counselor's office,
wading through
book after book
of colleges and
careers;
or,
like a
kid on a bike
that still has its
training wheels,
wondering when he'll
get up the nerve
to ask Dad to
take the training wheels
off,
worrying about
falling and
skinning his knees,
but wanting the
freedom
and joy
of flying
down the street
on his bike.
Goals.

I'd had several goals for 2009. One was to get my grandmother's house cleaned out and sold. At the end of September, we finally emptied it, and October was consumed with making repairs and renovations and getting it ready to sell. We listed it at the end of October and had a contract in three weeks. The fact that I had inherited the house made it necessary to deal closely with my mother on some things. That was frustrating, but we got it done. On December 18, we closed on the house, and when Josh and I got in the car after sending the final papers, I started crying. They were tears of relief. It was finally over. This year-long project of cleaning out Grandma's house and getting it sold was finally over. Dealing with my mother on this year-long project was finally over. I had reached that goal.

Another goal I'd had for 2009 that was not realized was to get pregnant. My doctor had tried two different medications over the last eighteen months to stimulate ovulation. Month after month, I took the medication, but never ovulated. Our next step was to see a fertility specialist in a city about two hours from us. Josh and I talked about it and prayed about it a lot. We also talked to Gary and Miss Penny about it. And then we made an appointment. On January 13, 2010, we will go for an appointment with the fertility doctor. I bemoaned to Gary that even if the fertility specialist said I wasn't too old and that I was a candidate for it, we probably couldn't afford it. He said, "Why not? Maybe that's why the Lord has given you your grandma's house right now." I told him we were going to invest the money for when I am old and Josh is gone (assuming he dies first). Gary suggested, "Maybe you'd rather have a baby." When I heard his words, hope sprang up in my heart. He was right. Josh and I talked about it and decided that we would use part of the money from the sale of Grandma's house to try to help us have a baby. So my goal for 2010 is the same as 2009. I want to get pregnant and have a baby.

Before Christmas, my mother called and said she thought I ought to call my friend Mary and encourage her since she was still having a hard time dealing with depression. Mom said Mary asked her how I had gotten happy. Then my mom said, "I don't know what all y'all had talked about—your dad, or what you thought your granddaddy did, or what you think I did." I started trembling when she said it. This is only the second time she has ever made a direct reference to my accusation against my grandfather in the fourteen years since I recanted. And she called him my granddaddy. She has never referred to him that way. He was always

Papa. And then there was her comment, "what you think I did." It wasn't an admission of any guilt on her part. It was what *I think* she did. She put it back on me again. Whatever is wrong is my fault. I just didn't know what to think about the comments that she made. She always manages to throw me into confusion.

When I told Gary about it, he said, "Don't think for a moment that she doesn't know what's what." He said she avoids things very successfully, but her comments give credence to the fact that she has put her finger on the big things in my life. She *does* know what the areas are. While she does not take responsibility, she knows what the issues are. Then he asked me some hard questions, ones I wasn't sure I had the answers for.

What Is My Goal? What Are the Different Voices Saying?

Yesterday's session with Gary was hard. He asked me one basic question in several different ways and I couldn't answer it: What is my goal with Mother? What is my long-term strategy? What do I want to accomplish? Is my goal just safety, hiding, protecting myself? Or is my goal relationship? Is the goal to **appear** that we have relationship, but not really have one? What is my goal a few years down the road? Why worry about offending her if I really don't want a relationship? If there's no goal of relationship, then why pretend, why not cut it off? But he said that there is something in me that doesn't want to do that.

I told him that there is a part of me that doesn't want a relationship with her. There is a part of me that does want to cut it off. But part of me doesn't. He said that is exactly why I can't answer his simple question, because the different parts of me aren't on the same page. He said I need to clarify what I am thinking. It may not be clear to me and there may be some resistance to clarifying because part of me is saying run, run, run! I asked him how I was supposed to clarify something that is so confusing. He told me to write about it and put it in different voices. There are different parts of me, different voices, all saying different things about Mother. And he said the voices have different weights. Some of the voices are overpowering and cause other voices to shut down and not be heard.

I asked him what voices were there and he suggested the following: angry girl, hurt girl, girl who wants a mother figure, wise person, foolish person. He said that's not an exhaustive list. I suggested there is also a guilting voice. He also said there's a quiet voice that isn't being heard. Josh thinks there are five basic voices. 1) the angry little girl who wants Mother to pay; 2) the fearful little girl who is scared of her and tries to appease her; 3) the little girl who is hanging on to the fantasy of someday having a good mother; 4) the foolish part that gives in to guilt and manipulation; and 5) the wise part that asserts herself, establishes and enforces boundaries, and isn't manipulated by fear or guilt.

Somewhere in there is the voice of the hurt little girl. But the angry little girl and the fearful little girl drown out her voice. Maybe that's the quiet voice Gary mentioned. I think there are several different aspects to each voice, like the fearful little girl who tries to appease Mother. She also wants to run, run, run! And hide. So the fearful little girl sometimes appeases and sometimes hides. The foolish part has more than one aspect, too. Josh said it's the foolish part that feels such guilt and gives in to the manipulation. I don't know if that is the foolish part or not. Certainly everything I am feeling when I feel guilt doesn't feel foolish. It feels powerful and overwhelming. Is that the foolish part? I don't know. But the foolish part also wants Mother to pay (that's the angry little girl, too). The foolish part wishes Mother would just die and leave me alone. Of course, I say this and then all the guilt kicks in and terrorizes me, so then the fearful little girl steps forward. All these parts are so intertwined. It's confusing!! No wonder it feels like I've got multiple personalities! I know I don't, but it sure feels confusing! They're all saying different things about Mother. That's what I've got to sort out and clarify.

<u>The Angry Little Girl</u>

"I hate her! I wish she would just die and leave me alone! I want her to pay! She hurt me so much. I want her to hurt too! She always hit me when she was mad. Well, I want to hit her. I don't want to have anything to do with her. I hate her! She didn't protect me! I don't want to go there and I don't want her coming here. I don't want her here for Christmas. I want to have Christmas without her. She ruins everything! She always hurts me and I want to hurt her! I can't stand her! I hate her! Why do you always keep talking to her and seeing her? I don't want to talk to her. I don't want to see her! I just want her to leave me alone! I hate her!"

The angry little girl has a very loud voice and she is yelling these things at me. But the fearful little girl's voice is even louder. But it is harder for the fearful little girl to articulate what she is thinking because the fear seems to short-circuit her brain.

The Fearful Little Girl

"I don't like her. She hurts me and she scares me. I always try to make things okay because it scares me when she is upset or angry. I don't like being scared. It scares me. She scares me. I wish I could just not have to be around her because she scares me. But I can't do that. I hid from her when I was little. In my closets. Under the bed. She would get so angry at me. It scared me. She would yell at me and hit me. I tried to get away from her and hide, but I couldn't. And I feel so bad when I don't make her happy. I always have to do things her way. And if I don't, I feel so bad. She is so big. I am so little. I try to always be good and make her happy, but I can't. And I can't think around her. My brain doesn't work. And that scares me. I want to be able to stand up to her but I can't. She's too big. I'm too little. I'm scared of her."

There's a lot there in the fearful little girl's mind, but it is hard for her to voice her fears. But even though it is hard for her to articulate her fears, and even though she wants to hide, her voice is still loud. So I've got two loud voices so far, the angry little girl and the fearful little girl. But there's even a louder voice, the guilting voice. But the guilting voice and the fearful voice are very closely connected.

The Guilting Voice

"You are so awful thinking that you don't want to have anything to do with her! Can you imagine what she would do to you if you told her you didn't want to have anything more to do with her?! She would come unglued! You can't make her feel bad! It is your job, your responsibility to take care of her and protect her and make her happy! You can't leave her alone! She doesn't have anybody else. Especially now that Grandma died, you **have** to be there for her. You're the only one. As Gary always tells you, you're the only one she has. And you want a motherless Christmas? What kind of awful person are you? What kind of daughter doesn't want to spend Christmas with her mother? You are so stupid! You are so thoughtless. You are such a jerk! You are a rotten daughter. You were a rotten kid! Everything is always your fault."

The guilting voice in many respects is her voice. She is the one who always told me I was a rotten kid. She is the one who always sends guilting messages to me. But I believe them. Is that the foolish part of me, the part that believes the guilt messages? Josh says it is. And how do I get **her** voice out of **my** head?! The guilting voice answers Gary's question by saying that

I must be a rotten person to think about not having a relationship with her, and I need to just suck up and get over it and be nice to her and be all gushy-gushy and lovey-dovey with her. The guilting voice tells me that the problems in our relationship are there because of me, not because of her. The guilting voice says. "You need to forgive. After all, that's what the Bible says. God's not going to forgive you if you don't forgive her!" The guilting voice tells me I need to love her and forgive her, and love and forgiveness mean that I can't act like there has ever been anything wrong or ever been any problems. I have to act like she is my best friend and I can't wait to talk to her and be with her. That's what the guilting voice says.

Of course, when I listen to the guilting voice, the fearful little girl comes to the forefront. But when I listen to the guilting voice, the angry little girl also comes out and she yells at me – "No! Don't do it! Yuck! Eugh, gross! Best friend? I don't think so! I hate her! She's hurt me so much! How can I stand to be around her? Yeah, maybe I'm rotten for not loving her the way she thinks I should, but then so what?"

And when the fearful little girl hears the angry little girl yelling, she gets scared all over again! And then the guilting voice starts yelling and it is all a big mess. No wonder I couldn't answer Gary's question yesterday! And isn't it interesting that the angry little girl and the fearful little girl both want the same thing—to not have to have anything to do with Mother. At least part of the fearful little girl wants that, to hide. The other part of the fearful little girl wants to appease and make Mother happy. I can't even get any agreement within the individual parts! It's so confusing in my head!

Other Voices

Somewhere in there are the voices of the wise adult and the hurt little girl who just wants a good mommy. But those voices are drowned out by the angry, fearful, and guilting voices.

What is the hurt little girl saying? What is her goal? "I just want Mommie to be happy. I don't want to be scared. I don't want to be mad. I just want things to be okay. I want Mommie to tell me she's sorry and make it up to me. I want Mommie to admit what she did to me. I want Mommie to be nice to me. I just want everything to be okay."

The hurt little girl is the part that is hanging on to the fantasy that things can be okay between us. I don't think it's the foolish part, as Josh suggested. The hurt little girl's voice is very quiet. The hurt little girl wants Mother to take responsibility for all her hurtful actions—the physical abuse, not protecting me from Papa, the guilting and manipulation, her disregard for my mental health problems. The hurt little girl wants reconciliation, but she wants it on her terms and that means Mother accepting responsibility and making amends and changing. Now is that ever going to happen?!

And where is the wise adult's voice in all of this? If the hurt little girl is quiet, the wise adult is mute. I don't know what her voice is saying at all. I really don't. The other voices are so loud, I can't hear anything the wise adult is saying. Maybe the wise adult doesn't even have a voice. Maybe the wise adult's voice is the voice of Josh and Gary. So how do I answer Gary's question? I feel very confused.

Gary said that what I wrote was excellent. It was exactly why I couldn't answer his simple question, because it wasn't a simple question. It was very conflicted for me. He thought it was interesting that I said the angry, fearful, and guilting parts were yelling at me. He said, "Who's me?" He said the "me" part was the hurt little girl part, and that part was made up of my past, present, and future. That part wants harmony and love and safety. That part has the core desires to be loved and safe and valued. But that part—me—was hurt and violated. My foolish part, which is out to sabotage me and rupture relationships (even my relationship with myself), tells me a lie. My foolish part tells me that I cannot tell anybody or they will die. It tells me I am shameful, and I deserve punishment, and I need to cut my body. My foolish part's objective is to screw up my life. Gary noted that I've never really identified these parts as different parts of my personality structure. And, he said, all these parts interplay when Mother sits down next to me at church. He quipped, "It's no wonder going to church with her is hard; there are too many people there!"

I told him I felt like I had multiple personality disorder. He said people with MPD typically don't know the various parts are there; the different parts aren't familiar with each other, the person just switches back and forth. He said I don't have MPD because my different parts are part of my personality structure and they are aware of each other. But, he said as a rule, with mentally healthy people, the various personality parts are not as split out as mine are; they work in closer harmony. With me, the various parts are more developed because my wise part is so underdeveloped. My wise part is still learning all the tools it needs to function in a healthy manner.

We started talking about forgiveness and vengeance. I know that forgiveness means that you are not seeking vengeance. And I told him I wasn't seeking vengeance on her. He asked, "If you were seeking vengeance, what kind of vengeance would you want to take on her?" I didn't hesitate. I said, "To make her hurt by telling her the truth about what she's done to me." Gary replied, "Sometimes the truth hurts, but that's not necessarily vengeance. It's interesting how you view telling her the truth of how she's hurt you as belonging to the angry, hateful little girl. You can still tell her the truth, but move it over to the wise part. You were told that your grandfather would die if you told the truth. You've been lied to." That session with Gary caused me to think deeply about some things.

There are several things I want to write about in response to my last session with Gary. One has to do with the idea that telling her the truth is not vengeance. Another is that I want to write a letter to my foolish part telling it to leave me alone! And the third is this idea or concept of **me**. Who is me? Who am I? That third thing is the one that I've been thinking about on and off for a couple of days now. Who am I? Gary said underneath the angry little girl and the fearful little girl and all the guilting and shaming that there is a hurt little girl. The me part is made up of my past, present, and future. My me part has been deeply wounded and violated and betrayed and shoved down in a corner and not allowed to grow as the other parts took center stage. So what is the me part? Who is me? Who am I? What is there at my core? I have tears running down my face as I write this because I'm thinking **I don't know!** I don't know who I am at my core!

I've been controlled for so long by the angry, fearful, shaming, foolish parts of me that me has nearly vanished! And that hurts so bad!! I started out as a beautiful little girl, and then he violated me and shamed me and betrayed me. And Mother hit me and emotionally manipulated and abused me and also betrayed me. So this beautiful little girl went into hiding. And because of it, my personality started splitting into all these parts. Not multiple personality disorder. The parts of me are fully aware of each other, and I don't just switch back and forth between them. They're all there, interacting all at the same time, so intertwined it is hard to distinguish one from the other at times, and yet so separate that they each have their own personality aspects. Not MPD, but awfully close. That's terribly frightening to me.

This assignment is hard, harder than writing about the different voices because that wasn't all that difficult. The angry, fearful and guilting voices are so loud it was easy to identify them. But somewhere in there is me. Who is me? Who am I? Am I a little girl or a grown woman, or both? What is there at my core? At my core, I'm extremely creative and I'm playful. At my core I am both a teacher and a learner. At my core, I love God and the Bible. And I know at my core I've been very, very hurt. At my core there is an extremely hurt and fragile little girl. But also at my core is a fighter. That's why I haven't given up. That's why I've kept fighting all these years to get well even though it's been the absolute hardest thing I've ever done.

So, at my core I am both fragile and a fighter. That seems contradictory. But I think it's true. I'm fragile because I've been so hurt and damaged. Picture a china doll that has been dropped and knocked over and thrown down many different times. And each time she is glued together again, piece by piece. She's still intact, but she's held together by glue. That's me. That's who I am. I'm not whole because I have been so hurt and damaged. My personality structure is like that china doll, pieced together. The angry little girl and the fearful little girl and the guilting/shaming voice and the foolish part are like the glue that is holding the china doll together. The glue is part of her, but the glue is not original equipment. They're necessary to hold me together and they've been doing that job for so long. And the glued pieces make her look fractured and fragmented. That's how it is for me. But at my core is a beautiful little girl that has been hurt and damaged. So who am I? I'm me. And I'm hurt. And I'm sad.

When Gary said that telling the truth is not vengeance, I had a strange feeling inside. I'm not sure how to describe it. Maybe it was hope: "You mean, I really can tell her how she has hurt me? I really can tell the truth? I don't have to hide any longer? The little girl can speak out? She can tell the truth? Her scars can speak?"

Last night Josh and I talked for a long time about the idea that telling her the truth is not vengeance. Gary says telling her the truth would be the wise part. Josh pointed out that vengeance would be something physical, like beating her up or shooting her or poisoning her. I definitely don't want to do those things. I asked him what my objective would be in telling her the truth, other than to hurt her with that knowledge. He said it would cause our relationship to be based on truth rather than lies or pretense, because any real relationship is based on truth. But he said I would be setting myself up if I am hoping that confronting her will make everything wonderful. I have to tell the truth knowing full well that her most likely response will be as the drama queen. She will change the focus from how much she has hurt me to how much I have hurt her by telling her. Josh doesn't think confronting her with the truth will be particularly helpful as far as changing her goes. He doesn't think she has the strength of character to accept responsibility. He suspects that any confrontation will just leave me frustrated and angry. He basically sees two options for me. Either I continue on with this counterfeit relationship, or I tell her the truth and force her to see reality and then see where the chips fall. I told him that telling her the truth is a terrifying prospect. I fear her wrath. I fear the drama queen in her. I guess I understand how telling her the truth is not vengeance. But it feels like I would be betraying her. And it's terrifying.

Gary said it was obvious that playing dodge ball with her was getting harder and harder. In the past, that was my way of survival, but now I had other options. I may be afraid of those options. They seem like complicated options. But there are options. He said I need to become true to myself and not fake what I truly am. So, Gary was getting me to think about goals. What is my goal with Mother? According to Gary, my goal should be truth. But it was truth that I was afraid of. However, over the next two weeks, I had a breakthrough.

37
Breakthrough

Breakthrough,
like Edison
trying 1,000 times
to make the
light bulb
work,
and all of a sudden,
after years of
labor,
the bulb
goes on;
or,
like Sir Edmund Hillary,
climbing,
struggling,
suffering,
to finally reach
the top
of Mount Everest;
or,
like Neil Armstrong,
setting the
first foot
on the moon,
taking
one small step
for man,
one giant leap
for mankind.
Breakthrough.

I thought about everything Gary had said to me the past few weeks. Could I really tell her the truth? I felt stuck. Telling her the truth was the healthy thing to do, but I felt like it would be such a betrayal. I was terrified to tell her the truth. Could I do it?

I Feel Stuck: Permission to Tell the Truth

My mother called late Monday afternoon. I didn't answer. She left a message to call her, said she had a couple of questions about what I had put in her Christmas stocking. I didn't call her back. She called Tuesday morning and I didn't answer. She called Tuesday afternoon. I didn't answer. She left another message to call her. Didn't say why, just that she needed me to call. I didn't call her back. Tuesday night after dinner she called again, this time on the house phone. Josh answered and she asked to speak to me. I said hello and she said, "Is your cell phone not working?" I said, "No, I mean, yes, it's working. What's up?" She said, "Well, I left you a message yesterday to call me and I've called a couple of times today and left you a message." I said, "What's up?" She said, "Well, if your cell phone is working . . ." I said, "What's up?" I didn't play into her game. She then proceeded to ask me her questions, albeit in a wounded tone of voice. Then she told me about two friends of hers whose husbands both have cancer. She was getting choked up telling me about them. When I got off the phone with her, I was angry. She gets so concerned and upset about her friends' health conditions, but what about her daughter's mental health? As Josh pointed out, this isn't a new issue with me. But every time I see her being so concerned about her friends, I get angry all over again. This doesn't feel like little girl anger. It feels like an adult anger. My mother shows great interest and concern for the health of her friends (mental and physical), but when it comes to her daughter's mental health, she shows disdain and disregard. That's enough to make any adult angry.

I feel stuck. Gary wants me to write about what the little girl wants from the adult and then write what the adult is willing to do. He said I have to be sufficiently miserable for progress to occur. I am miserable, but I'm stuck in the anger and hurt. And fear. Don't forget the fear. Gary said not to make excuses. Let my adult start speaking truth. But I can't hear my adult because the other voices are so loud. My scars (both physical and emotional) have spoken loudly of anger and hurt and pain and bitterness

Chapter 37: Breakthrough

and sorrow and fear, but can they speak truth? Can *I* speak truth, or is there still too much fear? That's the excuse—fear. Fear of her, of standing up to her, of upsetting her, of angering her. And fear of truth, because truth means I can't hide behind the anger and the hurt anymore. Truth means being true to myself and I'm not sure who I am. Truth means facing my fears. I've faced a lot of my fears. I've been facing my fears for six and a half years in therapy. Why am I still so fearful? That's an excuse. I get distracted by the whys. Why this and why that? Why, why, why? Even if I know all the whys, I am still left with the fear. I've still have to face the fear, whether or not I know why it is there.

Gary said that, for some reason, my adult is yielding to the little girl. He said Mother has more sway over me than just the belt. That's another why. Do I have to know the reason for the adult to quit yielding to the little girl? Do I have to know the why? I **want** to know why, but do I **have** to know why in order to change? Gary says it's time for my little girl to give my adult permission to be honest. He said to start with small, simple steps, small boundaries. I sent her that letter last year inviting her to meet with Gary and me. So why am I so afraid of small, simple boundaries like, "Mother, would you please give me a little space here." Or, "I'm not comfortable with a hug right now."

Session before last, Gary told me I was passive-aggressive with Mother. On one hand, I give her lots of gifts for Christmas, and on the other, I don't want her sitting right next to me in church. Confusing messages. He said I learned well because she is the master of passive-aggressive, confusing messages. I have to quit playing those games. Why can't I just send her another letter reminding her of the invitation? "Mother, you have been ignoring my invitation long enough. Either meet with Gary and me, or quit talking to me and seeing me. I'm tired of playing games with you." Why does that option seem less frightening than setting small boundaries?

What does the little girl want from the adult? Right now she wants a break from Mother. I don't want to see her or talk to her for a while. I need a break from her. That's one thing the little girl wants. Gary told me to let the little girl talk to me.

Okay. Little Girl, what do you want from me? What do you want me to do?

I don't want her coming here any time soon. I'm tired of her.

What else do you want?

> I don't want to go there. I don't want to have to go to that house. That house isn't safe.

What else do you want?

> I don't want you to make her mad or upset. She's not safe when she's upset.

What else?

> I don't want to hold her hand or have to hug her or have to sit close to her or have her touching me. That's not safe either. It feels icky.

Little Girl, you've been telling me what you don't want. What about what you do want? What do you want?

> I want you to tell her how she's hurt me. I want you to quit hiding. I want you to stand up to her. I want you to stand up for me. I want you to tell the truth about Papa. I want you to tell the truth about her. I want you to quit pretending that things are okay.

Little Girl, aren't you afraid for me to tell the truth?

> Yes. But I want you to protect me. Can you protect me?

Little Girl, I will protect you. That doesn't mean that Mother won't get upset or angry. When I tell her the truth, she's going to be very upset and angry. But I won't let her hit you. And I won't let her emotions overwhelm you.

> Can you do that? Can you really protect me from her?

Yes, Little Girl, I will do my best to protect you.

> Do you believe you?

CHAPTER 37: BREAKTHROUGH

My adult will protect you, but you have to let me. You have to let me be in charge. Will I be perfect? No. Will you be scared? Yes. Will I be scared? Yes.

I don't know if you can do it.

I'm not alone, Little Girl. I have Josh and Gary to help me. And my wise adult has been learning a lot over the last six and a half years. It's time for you to let me be in charge.

I'll try. But I'm scared.

I know you are, Little Girl. So am I. But we can do this.

It was New Year's Eve. There were only a few hours left in 2009. I always get very reflective on New Year's Eve and this year was no exception. I sat down at the computer and four pages later, I had written my review of 2009.

2009 in Review

There are only about eight hours left in 2009. It doesn't seem possible that it's going to be 2010. Last night Josh and I were talking and reviewing the last few years. There were two things I remember about February. One was the problem trying to get my medication regulated. The lithium made me sick and the other medicine he tried made me sick. And then after all that, it took a couple of months to get the Risperdal regulated. Once the depression stabilized, my anxiety went through the roof. February, March, and April were high anxiety months. I must have talked to Dr. Patel every week or two during that time. Finally my anxiety leveled off and we were able to reduce the Risperdal at the end of April.

The other thing I remember about February was the memory flashbacks I had. In particular was the memory I had about my grandfather telling me to keep quiet about the abuse or he would die. That was as strong a memory as I have ever had, quite shocking to me, but so clear. Also, I spent quite a bit of time thinking about and talking to Gary about sex and shame. With the resurgence of memory flashes, the feelings of shame returned with a vengeance. Even though I spent a number of weeks feeling the shame and thinking about it, once I finally talked with Gary about it, the shame seemed to lessen. It made for a couple of crazy months with our sex life though, because I was really weird about sex for a while. But once I finally talked about it with Gary, I got better.

By April, I was doing better overall and by the end of April things seemed to level off. The depression was better, the anxiety was better, the feelings of shame had gone away. Overall, I was functioning at a higher level than I had in months. I don't remember much about May and June. They were the calm after the storm. January, February, and March were kind of lost to me. In April, I leveled off. May and June were calm and peaceful. I remember asking Gary what happened the first part of the year. I didn't understand why I had such a major problem those months. The only thing I can figure is that I had a major meltdown after my grandmother's death and having to spend so much time with my mother from October to December of 2008. By the time January rolled around I was overloaded with my mother and grief and stress. And 2008 was stressful because I had been dealing with so much rage and volatility. And, I had gone off the lithium in order to try to get pregnant. 2008 was so incredibly emotionally taxing to me that once it was over, I literally fell apart. Also, that first third of the year, Josh and I had to take a hiatus from trying to get pregnant, but by the end of May, we were trying again. If the first third of 2009 was lost to me, I've more than made up for it in the last third.

The most important thing from the last third of 2009 was what happened therapeutically. In September, I finally admitted that the way my mother had dealt with me as a child was physically abusive. I first started thinking about that three years ago, in September 2006. This September, I finally wrote about the other things from my childhood that constituted physical abuse. She had abused me emotionally, but I finally admitted that she also physically abused me. It explains my inordinate fear of her. That realization was intense, but it was freeing for me as well. In admitting the truth of the physical abuse, I am continuing to speak truth to myself. And truth sets you free. I've still had a lot of issues and fear of my mother, but I have stood up to her more. I stood up to her about Chandler's funeral. I stood up to her about my birthday party. I set boundaries with her about sitting right next to her in church and I didn't let her guilting and manipulation from Scripture take root. I left her page of Scriptures right where she left it in the guest room. So, even though admitting that she physically abused me was hard, it has helped me grow in my dealings with her.

CHAPTER 37: BREAKTHROUGH

Also in September, I began dealing with more detailed issues concerning my grandfather. In the beginning of the month, one of my friends went with me to help work on my grandma's house for a couple of days. She knew I had issues with my mother, but during the trip, I told her that my grandfather had sexually abused me. That was freeing for me, too, because for the first time since I recanted in 1995, I talked about it openly with someone not in my most intimate circle. I opened up to a friend. For the first time since I recanted, I said out loud, "My grandfather sexually abused me." When my friend and I got back from our trip, she said, speaking about my mother's house, the house I grew up in, "How can you go back in that house?" She observed that when we were at my grandmother's house, I was okay. I was open and laughing and "myself." But when we were at my mother's house (where the sexual and physical abuse occurred), she said the change in me was incredible. She said I closed up, I transformed. And the change wasn't good. For the first time I realized just how much I hate that house. I have complained for years about how claustrophobic that house feels because it is so small, but it's not just the size that makes it feel claustrophobic. It's the memories of it and the trapped little girl that I was when I lived there. Since that trip, I haven't been back to my mother's house, and frankly, I don't want to. The longer I think about it, the more I really have no desire to ever go back to that house. I was physically abused in that house. I was sexually abused in that house. I was emotionally abused in that house. I hate that house.

From September to November, I had more memory flashbacks about my grandfather and the sexual abuse, vivid and detailed flashbacks. If I ever had any doubts about his abuse before, I don't now. In October and November I was dealing with abuse, physical abuse and sexual abuse. And the memory flashbacks about the sexual abuse were coming often. I started 2009 with flashbacks about my grandfather and ended 2009 with flashbacks about him. And Josh, through it all, has been wonderful, so gentle and loving and patient. Aside from salvation, Josh truly is the greatest gift God has ever given me. I am so incredibly blessed to have him.

This last third of 2009 has also been therapeutically important because of the insights I've gained into my own personality structure. I have, with Gary's direction, identified the different aspects of my personality. The fearful little girl, the angry little girl, the hurt little girl, the guilting voice, the foolish part. And the wise adult, the least developed part of me. But it is growing. With every day it grows. I have thought about the various aspects of my personality,. I have questioned who am I at my core. That question is one I struggle with.

As 2009 closes out, I am faced with another question, the one I've been dealing with in my sessions with Gary for the last several weeks. What is my goal with Mother? What do I want to accomplish? Do I want to be honest with her, or do I want to keep playing dodge ball? Gary said it is time for my little girl to give my adult permission to be honest. That's where I am today. As 2009 comes to a close, I am asking myself, "Are you ready to be honest?" I've thought that telling her the truth would be vengeance. Gary said it isn't. I've thought that telling her the truth would be betrayal. Gary said it isn't. Why would telling her the truth be betrayal? That question, the question of who am I at my core, and the question of what is my goal with her are facing me as I begin a new year. I hope to answer them soon. I hope to gain more clarity in my therapeutic journey. I hope to continue growing in my ability to set healthy boundaries with my mother. I hope to continue to heal as I continue to have memories of my childhood. And there's one other thing I hope for in 2010. I still hope to get pregnant and have a baby. Yes, I am forty years old now., but there is still hope. On January 13, Josh and I have an appointment with a fertility doctor. I don't know if anything will come of it, but I am still hopeful.

2009 has been a difficult year, but I think I have grown. As I grow in mental health I hope I'm also growing in Christlikeness, because that is God's goal for me. My prayer for 2010 is that I will continue to grow and be honest and change and heal. My prayer for 2010 is that it will be a year of truth.

On January 2, 2010, I wrote another piece. This one I had been thinking about for several weeks. As I was writing it, I knew that I was writing something very important. It felt like I had come to a deeper level of understanding.

Why Would Telling Her the Truth Be Betrayal?

Gary asked me the question, "Why would telling her the truth be betrayal?" Gary, Josh, and my adult all say it wouldn't be. But the rest of me doesn't know that. The rest of me says it would be betrayal. Why? Josh pointed out that telling her the truth would be betrayal in the sense that it would be betrayal of the sick family system I grew up in. And it's so sick that, even though deep down I knew the truth, the family system was upset

CHAPTER 37: BREAKTHROUGH

so I betrayed myself rather than further betray the sick family system. So telling her the truth would be betrayal because I would be upsetting the family system again, like I did when I made the accusation against my grandfather in 1992. In 1992, Mother's anger and disapproval were so disturbing that, though I didn't consciously realize it, I began looking for a way to reestablish equilibrium in the family and undo the damage I had done by making the accusation. Did you catch that? The damage *I* had done. It was my fault. The damage was caused by me, by my making the accusation, not by anyone else, not by my grandfather and certainly not by my mother. I didn't see the sickness in that. The sick family system I lived in had so warped me that I betrayed myself and what I knew to be true. I betrayed truth. I began living a lie.

Whether or not I was consciously aware of what I was doing, I began looking for a way to reestablish equilibrium in the family. At some point in 1994, I started distancing myself from everything that had to do with my hospitalizations in '92 and '93. I quit talking about things. I quit counseling. I quit taking my medication. I quit hanging around people I had met then. I even changed my career field. I'd been in the field of psychology. I had an undergraduate degree in it and was working on a master's in marriage and family therapy. I quit graduate school and went back to school to pursue a degree in teaching, the "family profession."

I began a campaign against psychology, reading books written from the viewpoint of people who don't think Christians can trust psychology. There is a school of thought promoting that end and I began reading and devouring everything I could on the subject. I talked with a lady in the church who was encouraging me to read these things. I even looked into getting a degree in "nouthetic" counseling, which strictly uses the Bible alone with no contribution from psychological theories or techniques. Finally, I read a book by one of these anti-psychology people about false memories. The author didn't think it was possible to repress memories and later remember them. He claimed they were false memories and viciously attacked anyone who claimed to have memories of childhood sexual abuse and anyone who worked with people making such claims. He said it was usually the therapist's fault for making suggestions of abuse to their clients.

I had never had a therapist, either before I made the accusation or after, who had made suggestions of abuse to me or who had tried to steer me in that direction, so I attacked myself. I actually read the book twice that year. During the months between the two readings, I began formulating my ideas. I became convinced that I'd had false memories. I reasoned that, since I actually had no memories, they had to be false. At that time I remembered very little of my childhood. I just had all the clues. I concluded that since I didn't have any memories, the accusation was false. I blatantly ignored the most obvious clue that was staring me in the face—I didn't have memories of my childhood, good or bad. Where had my childhood gone? I ignored all the other clues as well. I betrayed what I had known in my heart to be true and claimed I'd had false memories. How could I have had false memories when I really had no memories? Maybe what I should have said was that I had had false clues. But that would have been a lie. The clues were not false. They were real. They were true. What I was saying about false memories was the lie.

I came up with a little speech, a little spiel that I gave to everyone. I said that what I had claimed about my grandfather wasn't true, that I'd had false memories. I made myself out to be the bad guy by saying that I said those things about my grandfather in order to justify the sexual sin in my life. It was true that there was sexual sin in my life. But it was not true that I made the accusations against my grandfather to justify it. In the way I worded things, I actually indicted myself as having had wicked motives in making the accusation against him in the first place. But that wasn't true. I began living a lie. I didn't think it was a lie though. I had convinced myself it was true. That's the nature of deception. You deceive yourself to the point that you cannot recognize the truth. I totally rejected the truth of what all the clues were telling me. When I made the accusation, I was speaking truth. I may not have known the details then as I do now, but I knew it had happened. And I betrayed that knowledge, that truth, in favor of the sick family system.

And how did my sick family system respond? My friends thought it was confusing. They didn't understand my new claims, but my family loved it. My extended family said they were so glad I had gotten out of psychology, and they talked about how psychology had messed me up. My Great-Aunt Madeline (my grandfather's sister) cried and said she just knew that's what had happened. She said she'd never believed that her brother could have done something like that. She said that after I made the accusation, she had gone to a psychologist herself and had talked to him about me. He told her (without ever talking to me, but just basing his conclusions on what my great-aunt told him) that I'd had false memories, so my great-aunt had latched on to that. My grandmother just cried and told me how glad she was.

CHAPTER 37: Breakthrough

My mother's response was interesting. When I first made the accusation, she was so angry at me. She told me then that she couldn't believe it, but would only believe it because it was me telling her it had happened. But she really couldn't believe it. I figured she would be ecstatic when I recanted. And she was, eventually. At first, it was almost as if she didn't believe me when I said it had been false memories. She kept questioning me, asking if I were sure. So I worked at convincing her of the "new truth." And once I assured her that it had been false memories, she jumped on it, telling me we had to go right then and tell Grandma and Madeline. She couldn't wait for me to tell people the "truth." She was so happy that I had righted the wrong.

But how was I righting the wrong when the real wrong was being swept under the carpet? I wasn't righting a wrong. I was contributing to it. I thought I was righting a wrong because, according to the sick family system, the wrong occurred when I made the accusation. In reality, in truth, the wrong occurred when my grandfather began sexually abusing me. In reality, in truth, the wrong occurred when my mother began physically and emotionally abusing me. That's when the wrong occurred. But according to my mother and the rest of my family, I was the one who had done wrong when I upset the equilibrium of the family system and made the accusation. And because I was trapped in this sick system, I agreed and made myself out to be the bad guy, attributing wicked motives to myself. That's why I convinced myself that it had been false memories, why I recanted. And fourteen years ago yesterday, New Year's Day 1996, I stood in my mother's freezing backyard and burned everything from the hospitalizations, everything having to do with the accusation, everything from that period in my life. I burned it out of my life. I betrayed myself and the truth in order to maintain the sick family system.

But burning everything was a physical act. Emotionally I didn't burn everything. Emotionally I was still very sick, just like the family system in which I lived. For a period of time, maybe a year, I did well. But the sickness was still there in my soul and that's why the depression came back. That's why the masturbation continued and grew worse. That's why the cutting came back and got so incredibly out of control. That's why I still had no memories of my childhood. I knew in my soul that I had been sexually abused and I began questioning. I wondered who did it. Since I had recanted, I reasoned it wasn't my grandfather, but it had to have been someone because I knew it had happened. The clues were too strong and too numerous. Now, fourteen years after recanting, I've had so many clear memories come back to me. Now I have no doubt that it was my grandfather. But it took fourteen years to undo the damage that I did when I betrayed myself and the truth by recanting. I'm still trying to undo the damage.

So, why would telling her the truth be betrayal? It would be betraying the sick family system I grew up in. It would be betraying her fantasy of the perfect family. It would be betraying her vision of herself as a glorious mother. It would be betraying the equilibrium I have worked so hard to maintain the last fourteen years. But not telling her the truth would be a lie. It would be betrayal of me and betrayal of the truth. For the last six and a half years I have worked at trying to undo the damage that living in such a sick family system has done to me. And in undoing the damage, I am learning to speak truth. It is the only thing that will not betray me. I have to speak the truth. But I am terrified.

I had two sessions with Gary that first week in January. I told him I had written something I thought was important, but we wouldn't have time to deal with all three pieces in one hour, so I told him I would read the other piece when I talked to him in a couple of days. On January 5, I read him the piece "I Feel Stuck: Permission to Tell the Truth," and I read him the review I had written of 2009. After I read the first one, he noted what the little girl had said to me – "*Can* you protect me?" He said that the little girl obviously still had some trust issues with me and she raised an important question: Was I ready to call a spade a spade? He said I was coming to the point of confrontation. I've taken Mother on to some degree, but I haven't really taken her on with truth. I haven't leveled with her about the abuse. He said if I'm really going to get well, I'm going to have to deal with the hard stuff. Although I had invited her to meet with Gary, I really hadn't indicated what's wrong. He said my mother actually knows, but she isn't going to bring it up if I don't. She's the master of avoiding dealing with truth. I reiterated how I feel stuck. He replied, "You are stuck. It can't go anywhere unless at some point you are willing to deal with the very thing you're afraid of." I asked, "So, what do I do?" He replied, "You tell me." Something stirred deep within me and I cautiously said, "Maybe I should write her a letter that I actually send to her." Gary responded, "Why not?" From that moment on, things changed. I was no longer talking *around* the issue of telling truth. I was now talking *about* telling truth. It was no longer an intellectual idea to toss around in therapy. It was now something that was going to happen. It was becoming reality.

CHAPTER 37: BREAKTHROUGH

Two days later, on January 7, I talked to Gary again. This time I read him the piece, "Why Would Telling Her the Truth Be Betrayal?" Gary said, "Wow, I think you got it. And so, that's why we give so many gifts. Everything ties in with this. You've got to keep the facade of the perfect family." He said now I have some clarity and direction. I need to keep in mind something Josh noted. Although telling her the truth may be important to my healing, she may not accept it; it may not have the effect on her I want and I need to be okay with that. I'm not telling her the truth for her sake. I'm telling her the truth for my sake. Gary agreed and pointed out that she may employ all kinds of antics and may kick and scream! But, he said, if she wants to be free, she is going to have to deal with truth. My freedom is *my* dealing with and speaking truth.

Gary noted how interesting it was that on the outside I was maintaining equilibrium, but the inside, under my clothes, revealed a whole different picture. Through the years I've tried to be truthful with everybody except Mother. I am truthful with Gary, with Josh, with Miss Penny, with my close friends, but not with her. I've hidden truth from her. I was terrified of her finding out the truth. Gary said it was because my grandfather told me that people would die if I told. The little girl thinks she is keeping the family alive by continuing the lie. In her reality, I had to maintain the lie, hide from truth, or people die. I told him that when we first started talking about sending her a letter I got worried that she might have a heart attack after reading it. That was exactly what Gary was talking about. I have this deep fear that truth causes death. He said my adult knows that a heart attack wouldn't be my fault, but the little girl is still stuck in the sick family system that makes speaking truth a serious violation of the family code. That is why my telling her the truth is a betrayal. It is a betrayal of the family code. But not speaking truth is sick. Not speaking truth is a betrayal of God's code.

Gary said it was a really interesting defense I used when I got so involved with the anti-psychology movement. He said neutralizing any avenues that may have had the answers and discrediting the profession kept my alibi safe. In other words, attacking psychology made it is safe for me to recant.

He said he felt as if my path were more clear, that I had more direction. I had clarity in my goal with Mother. My goal with Mother is to not play this family dysfunction with her. I will speak truth.

Gary told me to write two letters. I didn't need to worry about who was writing the first letter, and I didn't need to worry about Mother reading it. Just give the child permission to write it. Let her vent. Let her say what needs to be said. He said she has a lot to say and she would do fine. That will not be the letter I will send. The second letter will be from my adult, not from the hurt child who has allegiance to the monster of the lie. He said just let the little girl talk. We would put it in adult words later. We would take the key concepts and figure out how to disseminate them to Mother.

I asked Gary what to do in the meantime if my mother called me. He said I should give her the first news of truth. Tell her I am having a rough time in my therapy and I need a little distance from her. Don't answer if she calls and if she leaves me a message to call her, send an e-mail telling her why I haven't called. I told him that scared me. He said I already have my defense if she starts pushing: meet me in Gary's office.

Gary said I'd made a lot of significant steps, but this step was a landmark one. Now I was actually taking on the monster and I wouldn't get well without it. The monster is the lie that I have to hide from truth.

The lie of the monster is that under no circumstances should truth be told. This distrust of truth is one way the monster has held my family in

CHAPTER 37: BREAKTHROUGH

bondage. The monster convinced my family that horrible things would happen if truth were told. The monster convinced me that horrible things would happen if I allowed my scars to speak. People would die. That's why I repressed the memories for so long. That's why my scars were silent and my voice wasn't heard. People would die. That's what the monster said. The monster lied.

The next day I sat down at my computer. I decided that I was going to do exactly what Gary had recommended, let the little girl talk. I addressed the letter to "Mommie," the same way I used to write my mother's name when I was a child. I told her the truth.

January 8, 2010

Mommie,

I've never written you a letter like this before. I'm scared to write it but I have to. I have to tell you the truth. You don't want to hear it. You never want to hear it. You always get mad at me when I tell the truth. You taught me to lie. But I'm so hurt by all the lies. I can't lie any more. I will die if I keep lying. But I'm afraid you will die if I tell truth. That's what he told me. He told me he would die if I told the truth. He told me he would die if I told what we were doing together. And he did die. And I always thought it was my fault. But I didn't tell. I couldn't tell because you might die, too. And then I finally did tell and all I got was your anger. It's true what I said Papa did to me. I didn't remember a lot of the details when I first told, but I knew it was true. I knew it had happened. I know a lot of the details now. Papa sexually abused me. He would touch me down there and do things to me and make me touch him and do things to him. He would get weird and scary when I would touch him. And I didn't want him to touch me, but I liked it at the same time. 'Cause it felt good. But I hated it. He was my daddy to me. And he hurt me. I didn't understand why I felt so confused and scared. But he told me he would die if I told. I couldn't tell anyone. Sometimes he would do it at night. Sometimes he would do it after I got home from school. I didn't remember all these details when I told the truth the first time, but I remember them now. And I remember how confused I was and how scared I was. I didn't want him to die. And I didn't want you to die too. But if I don't tell the truth then I will die. I've been dying inside for years. I always thought it was my fault what he did. I thought I deserved to die. So I punished myself. I would hurt myself when I would touch myself. And I cut myself. I still have scars where I would cut myself with razor blades. That's how hurt I was. But it wasn't just Papa. It was you, too. You hurt me, too. You used to lash out at me and hit me when you were so angry at me. You spanked me all the time when you were angry at me. I tried to hide from you. I tried to get away from you. You broke a paddle on me and you always laughed about that. But it wasn't funny. I was terrified of you. I tried to be good, I really did try. But I couldn't be good enough. I've never felt I was good enough for you. You always told me I was a rotten kid. Do you have any idea how much that hurt to hear you always say that? I was a rotten kid. That's what you always say about me. But I wasn't rotten. I was a beautiful, abused, terrified little girl. Maybe I was acting out but I was acting out because of what Papa was doing to me. And you didn't protect me. Instead you were always angry at me and I always had to do things perfect or you were upset. You scare me when you're upset. That's why I recanted. After I told what Papa did to me I never felt any support from you. All I felt from you was your anger. And your disapproval. And I wanted to please you. I wanted you to be happy with me. I didn't want to upset you. I wanted to protect you. But who was protecting me? You didn't protect me from Papa. You didn't even protect me from you. You always got mad at me and hit me. When I told what Papa did, you were so angry with me. I felt like you were blaming me for what Papa did. I felt like it was my fault for destroying the family. But Papa's the one who destroyed me. It wasn't my fault what he did. But I couldn't live with your anger. So I betrayed myself. I betrayed what I knew to be true and I convinced myself that it wasn't true. And I told you and everyone that I'd had false memories. But they weren't false. It happened Mommie. It happened. I remember. And you didn't care. All you were worried about was who knew. You didn't care what had happened to me. And I am so hurt and so angry because all it seemed like you cared about was your image. How many times have I heard you say to me, "Who knows about this?" It's no wonder I'm afraid of truth. Every time I have tried to tell you the truth about things you get mad at me and start worrying about who knows. I've got lots of problems, Mommie. I've had lots of problems for years. I'm getting better. But it has taken years and years to get to the point I'm at now. I'm not as afraid of truth as I used to be. I'm a truth-seeker and a truth-speaker. But I haven't told the truth to you because I'm so afraid of you. And you don't want to hear the truth. Every time I've told the truth, you've gotten angry. And your anger scares

CHAPTER 37: BREAKTHROUGH

me 'cause when I was little and you were angry I got hit. But you don't want to hear the truth. And that makes me feel like you don't care about me. You care more about your friends than you care about your daughter. You're always so concerned about your friends' physical health and your friends' mental health. But what about your daughter's mental health? If you really care about me like you say you do and if I really am the most important thing in the world to you like you say I am, then why have you ignored my invitation to go get help? You say you don't want to lose your daughter but you refuse to acknowledge that there are problems. You say you don't want to lose your daughter but you refuse to get help. You were losing your daughter because I was dying inside. I was dying inside and all you cared about was who knew! I didn't want Papa to die. That's why for years I never told the truth. And I didn't want you to die. That's why I recanted the truth. But I was dying! Don't you see? I was dying inside! And I wanted to die! I wanted to kill myself. I wanted to hurt myself. I did hurt myself. I have scars where I cut myself. And I hated myself. I cut horrible words into my body. I blamed myself for what happened. I tried to punish myself. I couldn't believe that it could have been Papa's fault or your fault. I thought it was my fault. I was a beautiful little girl and he nearly destroyed me. And you hurt me. And I hurt myself because I couldn't face the truth. But hiding from the truth has nearly killed me. That's why I have to write you this letter. I tried to get you to go with me to meet with Gary already, but you ignored me. You don't want to deal with truth. You're afraid of truth. But being afraid of truth kills you. It's not truth that kills. It's the lie that kills. It was killing me. I was dying inside. You think that if I tell you the truth you will die. I've thought that if I told the truth you would die. But Jesus said the truth makes you free. I've had chains on my heart for so long because I haven't told the truth. But I have to tell truth or I'll never get well. I'm afraid to send you this letter. I'm afraid of you. You always make me feel guilty and bad. You will hate me for telling the truth but I have to tell the truth or I will die. I will die inside. I want to deal with this but you ignored my invitation to meet with Gary. So I'm writing you this letter. I can't wait for you. If I wait for you I'll never tell truth. You'll keep avoiding and pretending and living the fantasy that nothing's wrong. But so much is wrong. I can't avoid it any longer. I can't pretend any longer. So I'm going to tell the truth whether you want me to or not. Truth is good. Truth is right. I can't live the lie any longer. The truth is that Papa sexually abused me. The truth is that you physically abused me. The truth is that you emotionally abused me. The truth is that I was dying inside no matter how good I tried to hide it. On the outside I looked good, but on the inside I was dying and shriveling up and bleeding and screaming. I was hurting myself by masturbating all the time so that it hurt. I was hurting myself by cutting myself with razor blades. I was hurting myself by carving awful words into my body. And you think you didn't do anything wrong. You wrote me a letter about a year and a half ago and you told me you were stunned and appalled and perplexed that you had ever done anything to hurt me. Either I'm a great actor or you're so dishonest that you can't see the truth. If that's true, then you won't accept what I'm telling you in this letter. If that is what happens, I'm sorry. I'm sorry for you because you're so enslaved by a lie. You aren't going to be free until you face truth and deal with truth. Even when the truth is ugly. Even when the truth hurts. The truth about my life's been very ugly. I've had to face a lot of truth about myself that's been very ugly and very hurtful. Not just the truth about what was done to me, but the truth about what I did to myself. I betrayed myself every time I masturbated. I betrayed myself every time I cut. I betrayed myself when I recanted. And I recanted for you. You were so angry at me for telling what Papa did. I lived with your anger for three years until I recanted. And even after I recanted I still got your anger. The last time I was hospitalized and I told you about it you said very angrily to me "Is this going to be like the last time with Papa where you told God and everyone?!" You worry about what everyone else thinks but you don't worry about me. I have a serious mental illness. And you worry about who knows and what will people think. Even when I was in high school and I was suicidal and wanted to go see the counselor, you were angry with me and didn't want me to see him and you didn't want me telling anyone. Why is it such a crime to tell someone I am having problems? Okay, admit it—I have problems! Your daughter has a mental illness. Your daughter was sexually abused by your father! Admit it! Admit it! Tell the truth! Quit hiding behind the lie! You're so worried about what people think. What about what your daughter thinks? She's dying inside and you don't care!

    I'm better now. I'm not dying inside anymore. But it has taken me years and years to start living inside. I've had a lot of help. God has helped me so much. If God hadn't given me Josh and Gary, I probably would have died. I would have died inside. And I would've died outside because I would've killed myself. But God protected me. And Josh protected me. And Gary protected me. But you didn't protect me. You didn't protect me from him and his hands and his body. He shamed me. He distorted sex for me.

CHAPTER 37: BREAKTHROUGH

He messed me up inside for years and years. And you didn't protect me. You want to know why I don't come to your house very often? I hate that house. I was abused in that house. I feel trapped in that house. And I feel trapped by you. When you hug me I feel trapped. When you touch me or get close to me I feel trapped. And I felt trapped when I lived with you. I was your little man. I did everything a daddy should've done. It wasn't right. It wasn't fair. I felt trapped by you. And I don't like you to touch me. It feels icky to me. And I can't ever set any boundaries with you because you plow over me and smother me. And I feel like you are always trying to buy my love because you always give me so many presents for Christmas. I've always felt like everyone in my family was trying to buy my love. I feel like I have to earn your love by being good enough. But I've never been good enough for you. You tell me you love me and you tell me that I am the most important thing in the world to you, but I don't feel that way. You make me feel guilty and you don't care about my mental health. I'm sure you think you love me. But your love is messed up. And I'm sure you think that I don't love you because I'm telling you these things. But I do love you. Love rejoices with the truth. That's what the Bible says. I am telling the truth. I have to tell the truth. If I don't tell the truth I will die inside. I do love you. I want you to be free. I want you to tell the truth. I want you to deal with the truth. Truth sets you free. I don't want you to die inside too. I love you. You're my Mommie. I don't want you to stay trapped by the lie. I want you to tell the truth. You have to tell the truth about things if you want to live inside. I love you. But I'm angry at you. And I've been hurt by you. I am not telling you all this to hurt you. But sometimes the truth hurts. I am not telling you all this to get back at you or take revenge on you. Forgiveness means not trying to get even. I'm not trying to get even with you. I forgive you. But I'm still going to tell the truth. God is a God of truth and He wants His children to be people of truth. I'm going to be a person of truth. I'm not going to hide behind the lie any longer. I will never get well if I don't tell the truth. I'm not telling you the truth for you. I'm telling you the truth for me. I've got to tell the truth. I can't betray myself any longer. If you don't want to deal with truth then I feel sorry for you because you'll die inside. But if you want to deal with truth then you can still meet me and talk with Gary. He's good at helping people learn to deal with truth. But even if you don't, I'm still telling the truth. Love rejoices with the truth. I love you.

Rochelle

When I read the letter to Gary, my voice choked with emotion. When I finished, he said this letter was long in the making and long needed. He asked me how I felt after I wrote it. "Tired," I answered. He asked what my adult said to the little girl after I wrote it. I said, "You did good." He told me that was important, affirming the child. Regardless of Mother's reaction, my adult needs to affirm the little girl. We talked about the vital nature of this letter. I wasn't saying these things to her out of malice, but out of necessity. I wasn't saying these things to hurt; I was saying them to set the record straight. I *have* to tell truth. Whether she likes it or not, I have to tell truth. He said this letter was the cry of a child that finally, with the insight of the adult, knows that it is okay to speak up and tell the truth. And speaking truth is incredibly liberating.

I asked him what the next step was. He said to let it sit for a while and let it season. In other words, wait. When I asked him how long, he told me that it will become obvious. At some point the little girl will ask my adult, "What are you going to do about it?" I told him I didn't want to lose momentum. He said, "Courage doesn't need momentum. Sobriety is needed. You're saying some very hard things and making some very hard decisions. You need to be clear-headed and steady." He advised me to tell the little girl not to worry and assure her that it would be dealt with. My adult is not going to behave as Mother did. My adult is not going to abandon this or ask the child to put it in false memory. My adult is going to love the child and help heal the child. My adult doesn't need to be rash. It will take some time to write the letter from the adult.

Gary told me to remind the little girl that she isn't in any present danger. He assured me that if she were, if this were a child protective issue and the abuse were ongoing, *his* adult would have acted a long time ago to remove me from the situation. Where was he when I was seven years old? I needed a Gary then. I needed an advocate. But I did have an advocate—God. Ultimately, God took care of my grandfather by allowing him to have a heart attack and die. That may sound cruel, but God gave my grandfather plenty of time to repent. He had one heart attack after another; God tried to get his attention, but he never repented. Finally, God said, "Enough." My grandfather's fifth heart attack killed him.

And God gave me the defense mechanisms of dissociation and repression. I used to think that repressing my memories was a form of treachery I committed against myself. Now I understand that it was protection against memories and emotions that I wasn't strong enough or

Chapter 37: Breakthrough

mature enough to handle at the time. So God allowed me to repress the memories until I was able to deal with them without falling apart. When I grew up and became an adult, God then gave me countless people to help me. There have been so many people in my life who have given me wise counsel and guidance and encouragement. He gave me Miss Penny and Dr. Patel. He gave me Gary. I don't think I would be alive today were it not for Gary. He gave me Josh, the greatest gift He has ever given me aside from the Bible and my salvation. And He gave me those things, too.

I've continued to have strong and vivid memories of my grandfather's sexual abuse and my mother's physical abuse. Gary and I discussed the fact that, as I have been speaking truth more, I have had more memories. He asked me a long time ago, "Why would the little girl trust your adult? Have you dealt any differently with truth than Mother has?" As I *have* dealt with truth differently and honestly, I have seen encouraging results. The evidence that I am getting healthier is that I am remembering more. He reminded me, "I've told you all along. It'll come to you." I asked him if he knew all along that truth-telling was what it would take. "Oh, sure," he said. "But you had to grow sufficiently before you were able to do this." He likened it to a dad waiting for his child to take her first steps. You have to have legs strong enough to hold you up if you are going to walk.

Gary said that, therapeutically, what I had written in the last two weeks was more significant than the actual telling her would be. He said that in order for the little girl to speak truth, I had to remove all the obstacles. Why couldn't I tell Mother the truth? He loved how eloquently I wrote about that in my piece, "Why Would Telling Her the Truth Be Betrayal?" And, he pointed out, that the piece was hard-coming. It took me weeks of thinking about that idea before I wrote the answer. The letter from the little girl to Mommie was easy, comparatively speaking. He told me as I was waiting, while I was giving myself time, to enjoy the lull. In other words, it will be difficult when I actually tell her. But I think what he was saying is that the hard part is over. Telling myself the truth and making the decision to speak truth to her was harder than it will be to finally speak truth to her. That will still be tough, but I've won the battle already. Regardless of Mother's reaction, regardless of her response, I've gained the victory. I am free. I am speaking truth. Truth sets you free.

After my session with Gary, I sat down at the piano. I wanted to write a song about truth. The words and the music came easily because I was speaking truth.

Speaking Truth

Chorus: I want to speak truth, I want to be true to myself and to my God.
There's joy to be found in speaking the truth,
it brings peace all around.
Life and joy will come to me when truth is my guide.
I want to speak truth, I want to speak truth,
from the truth I will not hide.

Verse 1: When a child is told a lie, it brings forth fruit of death,
but when truth comes to light, she will be so blest.

Chorus: I want to speak truth, I want to be true to myself and to my God.
There's joy to be found in speaking the truth,
it brings peace all around.
Life and joy will come to me when truth is my guide.
I want to speak truth, I want to speak truth,
from the truth I will not hide.

Verse 2: Our God's a God of truth – it is the only Way,
and when we speak the truth, Satan's lies are slain.

Chorus: I want to speak truth, I want to be true to myself and to my God.
There's joy to be found in speaking the truth,
it brings peace all around.
Life and joy will come to me when truth is my guide.
I want to speak truth, I want to speak truth,
from the truth I will not hide.

Verse 3: So speak the truth in love. You'll find rest for your soul,
and your life will shine so bright. You will be made whole!

Chorus: I want to speak truth, I want to be true to myself and to my God.
There's joy to be found in speaking the truth,
it brings peace all around.
Life and joy will come to me when truth is my guide.
I want to speak truth, I want to speak truth,
from the truth I will not hide,
from the truth I will not hide.

38
Blame

Blame,
like two kids
standing before
their mother,
shattered vase
at their feet,
each pointing
their finger
at the other,
proclaiming,
"He did it!
He did it!;
or,
like a terrified student
sitting outside
the dean's office,
having been
accused
of cheating
by his professor,
but knowing
he did not;
or,
like the horror
of the innocent man,
standing before the
judge,
flinching as
the gavel
slams down on
the bench,

hearing the judge
declare,
"Guilty as charged."
Blame.

My mother was calling with more frequency. I still wasn't answering the phone. Finally she left a message saying that she was worried because she hadn't heard from me in two weeks and to pleeeeeeeeease call her because she was upset. I didn't call. Instead, I sent her an e-mail telling her I needed some space. Two days later, Josh and I went to a workshop at the Bible school we graduated from. It was a very good trip. We got to see Gary at his office on Tuesday. We stayed with Miss Penny and her husband. And I was able to see and talk with a number of old friends who have been a part of my journey. I felt empowered after that week because I was continuing to speak truth.

My mother makes me sick!! I sent her an e-mail two weeks ago in response to all her phone calls and messages. I said, "Mom, I got your message. We are fine. I haven't been calling because I'm in a rough spot with my therapy and I need some space. Love, Rochelle." Two days after I sent that e-mail, Josh and I left for six days for the workshop. While we were gone, my mother sent me four e-mails and a card in the mail. In the week since we got back, I've gotten another e-mail and another card. Five e-mails and two cards in two weeks! She does not know what "I need some space" means! One e-mail was just something she forwarded to me. One told me what she had done over the three day weekend. Another told me what was going on with a friend of hers. And two were really obnoxious. One said, "Did I do anything when I was with you all at Christmas that negatively affected you?" Like I'm going to send her an e-mail telling her that! She's going to find out, all right. But it won't be in an e-mail and she won't like what I have to say! The e-mail I got today was a guilt message. "I'm glad you all made it back home safe. I didn't know until I read Josh's article in the bulletin I got today. Love, Mom." The two cards she sent really made me feel sick to my stomach. The first one said, "In case you need some help to cope....please find hug in envelope." Yuck!! A hug from her is the last thing I need to help me cope. The other card was just as sappy. "Thinking of you....Hope you can hear all my caring thoughts." Both of them she signed, "I love you, Mom." And in both of the cards, she included a Scripture reference. I looked up

CHAPTER 38: BLAME

the Scriptures she wrote down, and they were nice, but it is very difficult for me to accept those Scriptures from her as genuinely encouraging, because she has also used Scriptures to guilt me and manipulate me. And that page of guilting Scriptures she left for me to find at my birthday wasn't the first time she's tried using Scripture to make me feel guilty. I remember several times when I was living with her that she left notes in my bedroom that had Scriptures to try to guilt me. God never intended His Scriptures to be used as weapons, but that is what she has done. So when she writes Scriptures down on cards with the supposed intent of encouraging me, it's hard for me to take her seriously.

The longer I go without talking to her before I send the letter to her, the worse she may get. Josh thinks she's nervous and sending me these sappy cards is her way of sucking up to me. That may be, but it makes me sick. I wish she would just leave me alone. Gary said I would know when it was time to send the letter. Of course, I have to write it first. He said we would take the key concepts in the letter that the little girl wrote and formulate them into a letter to send to her. One thing I want to say is unless she's ready to look at her calendar and make an appointment with Gary, not to contact me. The fearful little girl and the guilting voice are saying that she's going to be upset, that I can't do this to her. But their voices are not as loud as they were. My adult isn't listening to their voices as much. Of course, I haven't sent the letter yet. Once I actually send the letter, their voices may be screaming at me.

While we were at the workshop, we stayed with Miss Penny. On Saturday evening, she and I stayed up talking for a long time. We talked about the meeting Josh and I had with my mother when she flew up to meet him after we got engaged. I was describing to Miss Penny how my mother's face was contorted with emotion as she twisted things around and was upset about how much *I* had hurt **her**. As I was trying to describe my mother's face to Miss Penny, I suddenly saw my mother's face contorted with anger and rage when I was a little girl. As I was seeing these images of my mother's face when I was little, I told Miss Penny how I would say, "I'm sorry, Mommie." And I remembered that I would say it over and over again, "I'm sorry, Mommie, I'm sorry, Mommie, I'm sorry, Mommie," when she would be angry with me and spanking me. I always felt like it was my fault and I would apologize over and over again, hoping she would calm down and not be mad at me and hit me anymore. I kind of zoned out as I was remembering it. Miss Penny patted my knee and it kind of jolted me back.

I felt so little as I was remembering. So little and helpless. I told Josh later that I find it interesting that I have continued to have flashbacks about my mother as well as my grandfather. As I continue to get healthier and stand up to my mother and protect the little girl, she shares more memories with me, about Papa and about mother.

At the workshop, one of the speakers for the ladies' classes was telling us about a fourteen-year-old girl she has been talking with and trying to help. She said the girl cuts on herself. When I heard her say that, instead of triggering guilt and shame and fear in me, I thought about the young girl and I decided that as soon as we had a break, I had to say something to the lady. I told her, "I want to encourage you to keep reaching out to that young girl. I used to be a cutter. And I want you to tell her that you met someone who used to be a cutter and tell her that she can overcome it. Don't give up on her. And encourage her to get some help, to start counseling with someone. Tell her she can make it." I asked the lady if she knew Gary. She said she did and I told her that he has worked with lots of cutters and could really help the girl. When I walked away from the lady, I felt strangely exhilarated. I had just admitted to someone that I had been a cutter. Someone who didn't already know. I said, "I used to be a cutter." That was powerful for me. It was liberating. I was speaking truth.

Later that afternoon, I had another opportunity to speak truth. I spent over an hour talking to Bethany, the new dean of women at the Bible school I attended. She has known me since I was in middle school. Her husband was my youth minister. I told her about my conversation with that lady. I told Bethany, "I don't know that you know this, but I used to be a cutter." She said, "I suspected that." I don't know what I had said to her in the past that might have clued her in, but I knew I hadn't told her before, so it kind of stunned me to hear her say that she suspected that I was a cutter. But what was powerful for me was that I told her. I said it again, "I used to be a cutter." Powerful. Liberating. It gave me freedom.

I spoke truth about my mother, as well. Bethany knows my mother and has for years, since I was a kid. She has known for several years that my mother and I have problems. I spoke freely to Bethany about her. Bethany said that when I was in high school, my body language always changed when I was around my mother. I would withdraw around her. She said it always seemed like I was playing the role of the dutiful daughter. And she said that looking back, she can see that I was afraid of her. Wow. Bethany saw it way back then. The fear that I've always had of my mother was being telegraphed way back then. Bethany said back then that she didn't know why my body language always changed when I was around my mother. She just thought maybe I was shy around her. But it wasn't that I was shy around her. I was afraid of her. Wow. Someone saw it years ago.

After I talked with Bethany, I spent over an hour talking with Jerry, a minister friend I had counseled with shortly before I started working with Gary. He already knew about the cutting and my mother, but it was good to just talk with him and fill him in on what has been happening with me. Even though he already knew, it was still liberating to talk about everything, just to say it all again. I was speaking truth. It was powerful. And then the next day, Emmett, another minister friend I had counseled with several times, asked me how things were going with my mother and I brought him up to speed. Again, I was speaking truth. As I was talking with these people, they all agreed that it was time to speak truth to my mother. They were confirming for me what Gary has been saying for so long. I knew Gary was right, but to hear so many other people confirm it was powerful.

It was especially powerful to hear it from Bethany and Emmett because they both know my mother. I wasn't trying to hurt my mother by speaking truth to someone who knows her. I was trying to hurt the image. My mother has maintained this glorious image for so long. It's an idol to her. And it's time for that idol to come down. Bethany said something nice. She said, "I love your mother and I'm not going to stop loving her. I'm going to pray for her. She has to be so miserable inside." She said she hoped my mother would come to meet with Gary because she needs a lot of help. And when Bethany prayed for me before I left her office, she also prayed for my mother. I know that if my mother knew that I had said all those things to Bethany, she would be horrified and enraged. She would say that I meant to hurt her by telling Bethany those things. But I did not tell Bethany those things to hurt my mother. I told her those things because they were true.

I was speaking truth. I have lived a lie for so long. I have lived the image for so long. I have lived the fantasy for so long. It is time to speak truth. I'm not speaking truth in an effort to hurt my mother. I'm speaking truth because truth needs to be said. I am a truth-seeker and I am going to be a truth-teller. I'm not going to let Satan lie to me any longer or deceive me into lying to myself or to others any longer. He's the monster Gary was referring to the other day. He has deceived me for so long. He has lied to me for so long. He has hurt me for so long. And I have hurt myself by listening to Satan's lies. No more. No more! Truth. I'm going to speak truth.

I'm not going to hide any longer. I'm going to speak truth. My scars are going to speak truth. No more lies! No more image! Truth!

Once we got back from our trip, I found out that I needed to have surgery to remove a uterine polyp before we could proceed with the fertility process. I was a little nervous, but other things occupied my thinking. I had started having nightmares. I have had bad dreams all along, especially dreams about my mother that often had weird sexual content. But usually with those dreams, even though I would wake up scared, I wouldn't be terrified. But I started having nightmares that left me terrified. One time I woke up screaming. In one nightmare, my mother made a surprise visit the day before my surgery. The back door to the garage was standing open and when I walked out, my mother was standing there. I screamed, and said over and over, "You scared me, you scared me." When I woke up abruptly, it took me a few minutes to realize that it wasn't real, she wasn't really there, and I didn't have to be scared.

Another nightmare went on for a long time and it was about being separated from Josh in a huge crowd of thousands. I was terrified and frantic because I couldn't find him. I was so alone in the dream, even though I was surrounded by hordes of people. I was lost and I couldn't find Josh. When I woke up from that nightmare, it took me a minute to realize that Josh was lying there in the bed right beside me. I woke up screaming from a nightmare about my grandfather. I have had a number of dreams about my grandfather before, but this one was so real. And so terrifying.

I was getting in an elevator and four or five little girls were with me. I was in charge of them. The elevator had trouble getting going, as if it weren't getting enough power. It felt like a rocket booster trying to get lift off. Finally the elevator door closed and started to rise. It went up in a spiral pattern and it felt really cool. I commented on how neat the upward spiral pattern was. When we finally reached the top, I gathered the little girls to me. The elevator had turned into a hotel room. We were at the top of a tall hotel. I went to open the door to see if we had reached the top yet. When I opened the door, sunlight streamed from behind the tall figure of a man standing there. I was terrified because I knew he was going to come in and rape the little girls. Then I looked again and realized it was my grandfather and I screamed. I don't know if I screamed out loud or just in my dream, because Josh was already up and in the shower, but I think it was both.

CHAPTER 38: BLAME

Then in the dream, and I think out loud, too, I started crying out in fear. Then I realized I was thrashing around in the bed and I opened my eyes. It was 6:23 a.m.

I went in the bathroom, and as soon as Josh stepped out of the shower, he could tell something was wrong. I told him I had had another nightmare. He held me as I told him about it. Then I realized that the elevator's upward spiral pattern was just like it was when I would dissociate as a little girl. I would spiral up off the floor and float at the top of the ceiling.

Several nights later when Josh and I were making love, I had a flashback that was different from any I had had before. I saw my grandfather and his fingers and me as a little girl, but this time instead of just seeing his fingers touching me, I saw his finger going inside of me. Josh told me that changes things under the law. The law makes a distinction. If he had just touched me, he would be considered a molester. It would be a second degree felony with a sentence of two to twenty years. But if penetration occurs, even with a finger and not a penis, he would be regarded as a rapist. It is considered Aggravated Sexual Assault, which is a first degree felony with a penalty of five to ninety-nine years or life. I thought about what he was saying to me and I got upset. I couldn't say out loud to Josh what I was thinking. I grabbed a notepad and wrote furiously for several minutes.

I keep thinking about all the times I acted out scenarios of being raped. How could I do that to myself? I was about thirteen the first time I did that. I'd act out a scenario where I was being a guy all tough and macho and aggressive and then I'd turn the tables and I'd be the girl and I'd use things to act out being raped. How could I do that to myself? What he did to me was rape according to what you say the law says. But he said it was a game and I liked the game that he played with me. How could I like something that you say is the most heinous crime someone can commit? You say even among inmates the crime of sexually assaulting a child is looked upon as the lowest of the low. I did that to myself and I enjoyed it when he did it to me. And sometimes I think I initiated the game. Am I the lowest of the low, too? Tell me it wasn't my fault. Tell me it wasn't my fault he died. I didn't tell. Tell me that it wouldn't have been my fault if I had told and he had gone to prison. I know it wasn't my fault, but I need to hear you say it. The little girl needs to hear it. I need to hear it. How do I reconcile what he did to me with what I did to myself? It's not like what I did was a one-time incident. I did it many times over the years, just like he hurt me many times. I was just like him. Tell me I'm not just like him. Tell me I'm not the lowest of the low. Tell me I didn't understand what I was doing. Tell me something because I'm hurting inside!

After I gave it to Josh to read, he told me no, it was not my fault. No, I am not the lowest of the low. And he said when I was hurting myself that I didn't understand what I was doing. I was acting out what was done to me. I sobbed and I kept repeating with a harsh cry that my mother always said I was a rotten kid and that made me think it was all my fault. I kept sobbing. My body was heaving and shaking. I have never cried that hard before. I was writhing in anguish on the bed. I don't know how long it was before I calmed down. Josh got me some water and that helped. I tried to slow my breathing down because I'd had an asthma attack from crying so hard. I told Josh that when I looked at him while I was crying, he looked mad. But he also looked compassionate. He said he was mad—at what my grandfather had done to me. And he felt compassion for the hurt and pain I was feeling. He said when I was crying, the depth of my emotional pain was powerful. He told me he could imagine that the only time someone might feel pain that intense was if they had lost a child. I said, "I did lose a child. I lost me." And I started crying again.

Later that evening, Josh was trying to get something across to me and I was not grasping all of what he was saying, so I asked him to write it down for me. He wrote:

You don't have a good grasp of how society views your grandfather's behavior. It is viewed as totally beyond the pale. Especially here in the South, people view a child rapist as someone who needs killin'. People have been lynched for such behavior. Had he been tried and convicted, I have no doubt he would have died in prison. This state would have never released him, and he easily could have been killed by his fellow inmates. I said all this to make the point as strongly as possible that no one would ever blame the child who had been victimized by such a predator.

At a quarter after five the next morning, I woke up from another nightmare. I got up, sat in my chair, and wrote in my journal while I wept.

CHAPTER 38: BLAME

In the nightmare, Josh and I had gone to the workshop. Jake and Allison were there with their new baby. They left the baby in my care for a couple of days and I forgot about him until the end of the second day. I didn't change his diaper, I didn't feed him, I didn't hold him—nothing! Two days! By the time I remembered to take care of him, he was filthy and sick. I fed him then, but he got sick all over me and everything else. The nightmare was so real that I could smell the baby's puke, even when I woke up. The baby was so filthy and sick. I couldn't find his car seat, nobody was helping me, Josh took off and left me, and I had to run all the way home in the dark terrified. Was the baby going to be okay? Could I get him cleaned up? What would I say to Jake and Allison? How would they ever trust me again? Two days I forgot about the baby. He was only a few weeks old. He was totally helpless. He was my responsibility and I forgot him! And I don't think this nightmare was really about me being afraid I won't be a good mother if we have a baby, although that may have been a small part of it. It was really about the little girl. I had a similar nightmare several years ago, only then it was someone's dog that I was supposed to be caring for. The dog almost died because I forgot about it and didn't give it any food or water for several days. The baby in tonight's nightmare could have died, too. I forgot about him. How could I have done such a thing? I am just really upset right now. He was so little and helpless and I forgot about him. I didn't take care of him. I neglected him. I abused him. And in the dream, he never cried. But I'm crying now out of deep sorrow and grief for that little baby in my dream. No, that's not right. I'm crying for me, for the little girl. I forgot about her. I forgot about me! I ignored me for so long! I am so weary of crying. I cried so hard and so long last night, I thought I would break from crying so hard. I thought I'd never stop crying. My stomach hurt from all the heaving sobs. I gave myself asthma last night I was crying so hard. Then I had this nightmare and start crying all over again. Why did Josh leave me all alone in my nightmare? He's never done that for real. He was right there last night when I was crying, holding me and comforting me. Why was I all alone in the nightmare? Because I was all alone as a child. I'm still crying now, but I'm crying about the little girl. She was all alone. She was all to blame. Just like in the nightmare. I was all alone and I was the only one to blame for not taking care of that little baby. But it's not true that I was the only one to blame in real life. I thought it was my fault. I thought I was to blame. My mother told me I was a rotten kid. She's told me that lots of times. I thought it was all my fault. I didn't take care of that baby in the nightmare. But no one took care of me when I was a little girl. Last night when I was crying, Josh said he had never seen that depth of emotional pain. He said he could only imagine that kind of grief in someone who had lost a child. I did lose a child. I lost me. And she blamed me!

When I finished writing, I climbed back in bed. I was still crying and Josh woke up. I told him I'd had another nightmare, and he gently held me while I cried. He said, "Honey, none of what happened to you was your fault." Eventually I fell asleep in his arms. Over the next several days, a number of times I said to Josh, "Tell me again." And he would tenderly say, "It wasn't your fault. You were not to blame."

In my session with Gary that week, I told him about the nightmares, about the crying episode, and how I felt like the abuse was all my fault because of what my mother always said to me about me being a "rotten kid." He told me that he had no doubt that my grandfather would have gone to prison had he been prosecuted. But, he said, on some level, my little girl felt very culpable about what happened. It seemed to him that once I began to answer the question of why I couldn't tell Mother the truth, I started to unravel all kinds of things. That's why I'd been having the nightmares. He said my crying episode was significant. The little girl doesn't completely trust my analysis that it wasn't my fault. She's harbored this idea of blame for so long because it was a game in which she found pleasure and because she reenacted it against herself.

I told Gary I just couldn't understand why I would act out rape against myself. How could I have done such a thing? Gary patiently explained to me that children often act out all kinds of things that have happened to them. It is actually a defense mechanism for a child. If a child doesn't understand what has happened to her, acting it out against herself actually gives her a feeling of control. In some sense, acting out what has happened to them empowers the child. It's their way of taking control, of gaining control of their environment. I didn't know what to do with my environment. I was confused as a child. By reenacting it against myself, the little girl felt like she wasn't just the victim. She felt like she was also the perpetrator. She didn't understand about defense mechanisms. She knew early on that something was wrong with what was happening. She had some sense of moral rightness, and she knew that the game Papa played with her was wrong. But she also liked it. And eventually she reenacted

CHAPTER 38: BLAME

it against herself. So, Gary said, the little girl feels like she violated and compromised herself.

I asked Gary how to get the little girl not to be confused, how to get her to understand that it wasn't her fault. He told me to do exactly what I'd been doing. Keep giving her reassurance. Every time I asked Josh to tell me again that it wasn't my fault, it was the little girl's way of seeking reassurance. Keep telling her. Keep encouraging her. Keep speaking truth to her. It wasn't her fault. She wasn't to blame.

After my session with Gary, I told Josh I wanted him to do me a favor. I wanted him to find for me where the law says what my grandfather was guilty of. I wanted to see it in print. I wanted some more reassurance.

Josh had told me that my grandfather would have been guilty of Aggravated Sexual Assault. Since Josh had been a lawyer years ago, I figured he knew what he was talking about, but I wanted to see it for myself. So Josh got on the internet for me last night and looked up the penal code for our state. He knew exactly what to look for. He was right. If my grandfather were tried and convicted today, he would be guilty of Aggravated Sexual Assault, a felony that is punishable by anywhere from five years to ninety-nine years, or even life in prison. Aggravated Sexual Assault happens when the victim is younger than fourteen. I was six and seven and eight years old. It said that a person commits that offense if he or she penetrated the child's sexual organ by any means, or penetrated the child's mouth by his or her own sexual organ, or caused the child's mouth to be in contact with anyone else's sexual organ, including the perpetrator's. If any one of those things happen, it is considered Aggravated Sexual Assault. There was more, but those are the things that pertained to me. All those things happened to me. I've had flashbacks of all those things. My grandfather did all those things to me. There was even a section where it said that the minimum term of imprisonment is increased to twenty-five years if the perpetrator puts the child in fear that death is going to be inflicted on someone. He told me he would die if I told. I was in fear that death would be inflicted on him. As I read the law, I felt empowered. The little girl felt empowered. She said, "You mean he was wrong? What he did to me was a crime? He should have gone to jail? You mean it wasn't my fault?" To see it in print and to hear Josh's legal mind talk about it was a powerful experience for me. And for the little girl. I was the victim of a crime. It was not my fault. Gary had told me that he suspected the little girl didn't totally trust my analysis that it wasn't her fault. But this was written in the law. This wasn't just my adult's analysis. This was the analysis of the State. This was the law. He was wrong. He was guilty. Not me. I told Josh I was going to use some of this information in my letter to my mother. At least the general part of it. I want to be able to say to her, "According to the penal code, Papa was guilty of Aggravated Sexual Assault . It happened, Mom. It's there in writing." Later that evening I told Josh I felt sad and angry and peaceful. It's an interesting combination of emotions. The peaceful part has to do with feeling relieved and vindicated. It wasn't my fault.

I think the experience of reading all that made a huge impression on the little girl, because last night I had a very powerful dream. I dreamed that I had driven to my mother's house for a visit without Josh. She needed help with something. Shortly after I got there, I took a shower and I was trying to slip from the bathroom to the bedroom in just my bra and panties so I could get dressed. My mother grabbed me from behind in a bear hug. I told her to let me go. She said no, she wouldn't let me go. I struggled with her, trying to break free. I kept telling her to let me go. She wouldn't let go, but I finally got away. I looked at her and I said, "I'm leaving Mother. I'm going back home." I picked up my cell phone to call Josh and tell him. She got upset. I told her, "You never respect any boundaries with me. I'm leaving now." I told her that she was acting the way she always does and that was why I didn't want to be there. Then she said, "Well, as long as nobody here knows about this, and as long as nobody there knows about this." I said, "Why are you always so concerned about image, Mother? It's always about image with you. It seems to me that you care more about your image than you do about me." Her face was contorted with anger, and I said, "It's all about you, isn't it?" and I left. In the next scene of the dream, I was with Josh excitedly telling him what I'd said to my mother. I was ecstatic, jumping up and down. I was jumping so high, I was actually reaching the ceiling and floating around. I told Josh, "Look, I can fly!" When I woke up and realized what my dream had been about, it seemed like there was an intensity to my dream that came because of reading through the penal code and seeing in print what my grandfather had done to me. The little girl was finally starting to believe that it wasn't her fault. She wasn't to blame.

That afternoon I wrote a first draft of the letter that I will send to my mother. I had some heavy things to think about, but none was as heavy as the weight I had borne for all these years. I recognized that once I sent the letter, things might get very ugly. I have to be prepared for that. But God will give me the strength to survive, just as He has given me the strength to survive all these years. And He will give me people to help me.

I was blown away by the realization that what my grandfather did is so incredibly hated by society. The reactions of my family to my accusation in 1992 were so out of line by comparison. I talked to a friend today who said my grandfather needed to have been killed. Hearing that makes me (and the little girl) realize how heinous a crime it really is and how vile it is to people. To me, it was always my fault. I couldn't see the vileness of it because of my family's reaction, especially my mother's. She should have been angry at him. But she wasn't. She was angry at me. There is something incredibly messed up about that. But my messed-up thinking was shifting. I was finally putting the blame where it needed to be—on my grandfather. I wasn't to blame for what happened to me as a little girl. It wasn't my fault.

39
Papa

Papa,
like a fuzzy dream
dreamt years ago
in a different place
and a different time;
or,
like Captain Kangaroo,
always playing with
the children,
making make-believe
believable;
or,
like a stand in
for the real thing,
making one wonder
who he really is;
or,
like a pathological liar,
always telling lies
and distorting reality
and making others think
they are responsible
for his detestable behavior,
bringing fear
and shame
and confusion
to an innocent
little girl.
Papa.

The more I thought about what my grandfather did, the angrier I got. For years I directed my anger at myself, hurting myself through the masturbation and the cutting. But now the anger was rightly placed. Now I was angry at him.

Smoldering

This afternoon I got angry at my grandfather. All morning I felt sad and depressed and underneath was some anger, but I thought I was too sad to get angry. But I was wrong. I thought about what the law said and that what my grandfather did to me was a crime. And I thought about the details it listed and that what it said described exactly what my grandfather did to me. I saw it in writing. All the flashbacks and memories I've had paint a very clear picture of what happened. And I thought about the fact that he framed it as a game. It was a game we played, an insidious game. It didn't seem dangerous, but it was a deadly game with deadly consequences. He would die if I told anyone about the game we played. The first time he told me that and every time after, he ensnared me in a lie so treacherous that it has taken more than thirty years to break through the deception. And it was deadly because when he started abusing me, he set in motion a mechanism for self-abuse that continued for thirty years. He said he would die if I told. What he didn't tell me was that if I didn't tell, I myself would die inside.

I also thought about all the sexual problems I've had, the dysfunction, the fantasies about rape, the masturbation, the mental scenarios, and the acting out. And all the shame. It all went back to him. He nearly destroyed me sexually. I am utterly amazed that Josh and I have a healthy sex life. And we do, despite the fact that flashbacks of my grandfather's abuse frequently invade our lovemaking. As I thought, my anger grew. It wasn't a flailing rage; it was a smoldering fury, very controlled. I punched on my punching bag. My punches were extremely hard, but very controlled. And the entire time, I was having flashbacks of my grandfather. I was seeing his face, his hands, his genitals. And I was smashing him. I was smashing his face, with those eyes that terrified me and that mouth that lied to me and deceived me. I was smashing his hands, those hands that touched me and fondled me and penetrated me and abused me. I was smashing his genitals, the ones that I had to kiss and put into my mouth. The ones that I had to touch and make grow hard. The ones that scared me and fascinated me at the same time.

Chapter 39: Papa

The smoldering anger and the flashbacks continued all afternoon and into the evening. My face was dark and disturbed. Every word was uttered through clenched teeth. Every thought was filtered through the lens of abuse. November marked the beginning of my anger at him. Now it is full-blown. But I am not blowing. I am smoldering. I am not yelling and wildly punching. I am burning with a deep-seated fury that has been building for forty years. For the first time, I can truly understand the desire to kill someone. That's how dark my thoughts have been today. He raped my body with his fingers and he raped my soul with his life. His wicked words and actions caused me to live in fear and shame. His wicked words and actions caused me to abuse myself and betray myself. Every time I masturbated I was doing to myself what he had done to me. Every time I cut I was trying to punish myself for what he had done to me, for what I thought was my fault. I blamed myself. All my life I have blamed myself. But I'm realizing it's not true. It wasn't my fault. And that is why I am smoldering.

As I pondered the amazing progress I had made over the last several months, I kept returning to thoughts of the little girl. I am forty years old. All those years I thought that I was to blame, that I was bad and vile and depraved because of what was done to me. I thought that I was a rotten kid, that I had to punish myself. But I wasn't bad or vile or depraved. I wasn't a rotten kid. I was a beautiful, precious, innocent little girl. It wasn't my fault. I was not to blame.

I continued to have flashbacks about my grandfather. After one particular evening of intense flashbacks while Josh and I were being intimate with each other, I wrote a poem.

> There was a ghost in our
>   bedroom tonight.
> He danced through the walls of
>   my mind.
> He haunted the room with his
>   presence,
> with flashbacks so cruel and unkind.
> It's not just tonight that it's
>   happened,
> for our house has been haunted
>   before.

> Every time I lie down with my
>   husband,
> this spirit shrieks up from
>   the floor.
> When my husband touches my
>   body,
> this ghost, he touches me, too.
> This ghost from my past, from
>   my childhood,
> does more than just jump out and
>   say boo.
> A haunting of flashbacks and
>   memories,
> what he said was a game was really a crime.
> It was abuse, and he lied and deceived me,
> and his actions still haunt
>   my mind.
> The ghost of my grandfather
>   comes out
> whenever my husband and I start
>   to make love.
> I see his face and his hands
>   and his body,
> and I cry out to God in heaven
>   above:
> Will this haunting go on
>   forever?
> Will my mind forever be oppressed by
>   his ghost?
> I want to be freed from his
>   haunting,
> that is what I desire most.

Gary said that's exactly how it seems to work. But, he reminded me, I'm not going to let the ghost run the show. I want to be well and if that means I must live through the flashbacks, so be it. But the flashbacks don't have to control me. I want to heal from all the lies, all the abuse, all the harm that was done to me when I was a little girl. My anger at my grandfather continued to grow and the next day I wrote a song with a very angry feel to it.

The Chains of Childhood

Verse 1: I was just a child, a little girl,
and my memory is now unfurled;
it was not my fault,
the blame belongs to him.

Verse 2: I am angry now, my fury builds,
he robbed my soul, she broke my will.
But I'm fighting back,
my anger spurs me on.

Bridge: I was little, I was lied to, I was abused,
he said it was a game.
But the outrage and the anger are growing in me,
no more taking his shame.

Verse 3: I was young and pure, I couldn't tell.
But I'm speaking now, I'm getting well.
I will not allow
the chains of childhood to win.
I will not allow
the chains of childhood to win.

Two nights later I had more bad dreams. I also had another flashback that gave me new insight.

Last night I had another dream that I couldn't find Josh. That's the fourth dream along those lines in the last two weeks. What's up with that? Sunday afternoon I took a nap and had another masturbation dream. It was so real that when I woke up, I wondered if I had masturbated. Then I realized it had been a dream. Last night at church, I was singing and suddenly, several flashes of my grandfather with no clothes on flashed in front of me. It was out of the blue and unexpected. Then when Josh and I were getting ready to go to sleep later that night, I was being a little playful and was just barely tickling him. He grabbed my hands and held them away from him when it hit me. I cried out, "Stop it! Stop it!" Josh let go and asked what was wrong. I was zoning out and breathing hard. He asked me again and I snapped out of it. I said, "He fought with me sometimes." I remembered that sometimes I didn't want my grandfather to touch me. I would try to push his hands away and he would restrain my hands. All my life, if I have been playing around with someone, wrestling or just teasing like Josh and I were doing, if I was restrained, I would panic and become violently angry. Now I know why.

Later that day, continuing to smolder in my anger, I decided to write a letter to my grandfather. I wrote the letter with a clenched jaw and a face dark with fury. Josh came into the study at one point and asked if I were okay. I turned and looked at him, but I couldn't answer. I was too angry. My fingers pounded out the letter on the keyboard, and then I stomped out to the exercise room where my fists pounded out my fury on the punching bag. I yelled and swung at the bag, this time wildly, with abandon.

2-15-10

Papa,

You were a wicked man. You hurt me in ways a child should never be hurt. The other day, I was so angry I wanted to kill you. But you are already dead.

And I thought that was my fault. You told me you would die if I told what you were doing to me, what we were doing together. You told me it was a game. If it was a game, then you made me culpable too. But it wasn't a game. It was something you did to me. Sometimes I wanted to play, but that doesn't make me culpable. I was a child. You were wicked. You lied to me. You abused me. You betrayed me. I was a child. You hurt me so deeply. I am forty years old and I still suffer from your abuse every day. I was just a little girl. Sometimes I didn't want to play. Sometimes I tried to push your hands away and you held my hands so I couldn't, so you could keep playing your game. If you hadn't died, how long would it have been before you raped me with your penis? You raped me with your fingers. I remember. And you said it was a game.

CHAPTER 39: PAPA

You said you would die if I told. I thought it was my fault when you died. You knew you were going to die. You had congestive heart failure. Yet you made me feel responsible for your death by telling me you would die if I told. When you did die, I was terrified. When the EMS guys were at the house I was petrified. And I wanted to tell you not to die, because I didn't tell. But you died anyway. And I thought it was my fault. And after you died, your doctor told Grandma that you had lived as long as you had because of me. They all told me that I was the one who kept you alive for so long, because you loved me so much. That just dug the guilt in deeper. Even now, when I think about what your doctor told Grandma, it makes the pit of my stomach hurt. You had lived as long as you did because of me. What was that comment supposed to make me feel? Even now, I don't know what it makes me feel. It upsets me, but I can't sort out my feelings about it. He didn't know what was going on. Nobody knew. How could they? I couldn't tell or you would die. But you died anyway. And it was my fault.

You ensnared me in a lie so heinous it nearly destroyed me. All the years I cut myself, I was trying to cut the bad little girl away. I thought I was bad because you died. I thought I was bad because of the game we played. I thought I was bad because of what you did to me. So I cut myself. And Mommie told me I was a rotten kid. I was horrible. That's why I cut myself. And I masturbated all the time and I hurt myself when I did that. I would use objects to rape myself, acting like I was the aggressive male and then being the female who got raped. And I would fantasize getting rescued. But no one rescued me from you. Mommie didn't. Grandma didn't. No one did. I had to rescue myself.

I can be mad at my mother and I am, but in the final analysis it goes back to you. You hurt me so badly. And you said it was a game. When I recanted I was rescuing the family. I didn't want to hurt anyone. But what about me? Who rescued me? What about how hurt I was? And you distorted God for me. You were my father to me. I wrote "Papa" in my baby book on the line for the father's name. Mommie erased it. But that's how I felt. You were the father in my life. All my life I thought I had trouble with the concept of God as father simply because of my real father not being there. And that's a big part of it. But the bigger part of it was you. You were like my father and you defiled me. You abused me. You debased and degraded me. You mistreated and injured me. You molested and damaged me almost beyond repair. And I thought it was my fault.

I thought I deserved to be punished. I punished myself. Just look at the scars on my body. No, don't. I don't want you looking at the scars on my body. I don't want you looking at me at all. Not that you can, cause you're dead, but just the idea of you looking at my body makes my skin crawl. You violated my body. You abused my body. You dishonored my body. You profaned my body. You defiled my body and invaded my body and molested my body.

And you distorted sex for me. That area of my life, my sexuality, has been so distorted and so perverted—all because of you! I shamed myself with guys before I was married. I allowed guys to shame me. I shamed myself with all the masturbation and fantasies. And all that shame started with you. I was full of shame for so long. Even in the autobiography I wrote in fifth grade, the year after you died, I wrote that I was shameful. You ingrained in me a deep sense of shame from early on. I was just a little girl, for God's sake! How could you do that to me? I was six years old! And seven! And eight! I was a child! I look at the little girls at church who are the age I was and I am full of deep sorrow and outrage. Innocent! Young! Pure! And you defiled me! You shamed me! You violated me! You robbed me of my innocence! You're a thief! A robber! A criminal! You should have gone to jail, to prison – for the rest of your miserable, worthless life! You wretched, wicked pervert. That's what you are! A wretched, wicked pervert!

I am full of fury and the thought of you makes me sick to my stomach. Every time I have a flashback of you, which is frequently these days, my stomach gets hard. I'm zoning a lot more as the memories of my childhood come back with clarity and force. For years I have prayed that I would get my memories back. That prayer is being answered and as the memories of you come back, I am finding that my anger builds and builds. You monstrous traitor! You stole my childhood!

I have a note that you wrote to me when I was a little girl. It says, "Dearest Rochelle, You are a very sweet girl. You are very, very precious. I love, love, love you. Papa." You hypocritical liar! How dare you say that you loved me! How dare you say that I was very precious to you! You abused me. You didn't love me—you hated me. Your vile, horrific behavior showed that you hated me. Precious? I was precious, but not to you. To you I was an object, something to be used and perverted and destroyed. Do you have to forgive someone if he is dead? I hate you Papa.

Rochelle

Gary said that the letter was quite intense and I needed to let it simmer for a while. Right now my emotions were staring me in the face. He clarified that forgiveness doesn't begin when the reality of hurt, lots of hurt and lots of betrayal, is so fresh. I told Gary that I felt overwhelmed with anger. I wasn't pushing it. It was just coming. Gary likened it to giving birth. At some point, you don't have to push any longer, the baby is coming. That's what was happening. He thought it was an interesting dynamic to see me finally focusing on my grandfather. Fully realizing that his behavior was criminal had given force to my anger. Gary said what was happening was exactly what needed to be happening.

I had one more major flashback before they began to taper off. It was as if I had finally remembered all of the major things about the sexual abuse that I needed to remember.

He Hurt Me So Bad

Last night when Josh and I were making love I had a number of flashbacks, some of things I've seen before and one that was new. The familiar flashbacks were of my grandfather having an orgasm and of me kissing his penis. The ones of me kissing him were especially vivid. As I kissed Josh, I was seeing me kissing my grandfather when I was a little girl. And I remembered that doing that was part of a game we were playing for me to try to make him hard by kissing him.

That flashback bothered me, but the flashback that upset me the most happened when Josh was touching me. I have had a number of flashbacks before of my grandfather touching me, but this one was different. My grandfather wasn't just touching me; he was stimulating me. He was masturbating me. I saw the little girl being masturbated. When Josh and I talked about the flashbacks I had seen, I started crying, then sobbing. I remembered what Gary had said about my grandfather having set in motion a mechanism of self-abuse that continued for many, many years. I thought about the thousands of times I had masturbated over twenty-five years and how badly I had hurt myself emotionally and spiritually by doing it. I even hurt myself physically at times. Scene after scene of times I had masturbated flashed through my head. And it all started with my grandfather. He is the one who first masturbated me. He is the one who taught me how to masturbate when he masturbated me. I cried out, "He hurt me so bad! He hurt me so bad!" Josh held me tenderly and said, "I know, honey. I know he did."

When I calmed down and quit crying, Josh gently reminded me of how far I have come. In another couple of weeks, it will have been six years since I last masturbated. I told Josh I was both sad and angry. I was sad for the little girl and what happened to her and how hurt and messed up I had been, but I was angry at my grandfather and what he did to me. He said, "Honey, you were the victim of a horrible crime. Repeatedly. You have a right to be angry." I am angry. I'm sad and I'm hurt and I'm angry.

I needed to allow the anger that was smoldering inside of me to serve as the impetus to keep fighting. My anger needed to be my incentive to continue speaking truth. My anger needed to spur me on to use my struggles to help others. My smoldering fury needed to stir up my strong will. The strong-willed little girl of yesterday needed to be the strong-willed adult of today. My strong will has kept me fighting to get well all these years. And my strong will is what I needed to muster the courage to keep fighting and keep speaking truth. Because it would take courage to speak the truth to my mother.

40

Courage

Courage,
like a young Masai boy
on his first
lion hunt,
fear filling his throat
as he stalks the
great beast,
spear held high,
ears full of the
roar
of the savage
animal,
terror building;
yet he still moves
closer and closer
until,
the moment of truth,
when he
hurls his spear
in a flurry of
teeth and
fur and
sweat and
blood;
breathless
he kneels beside
the fallen creature,
and marvels at the
Courage.

In the next session I had with Gary, we discussed when might be the right time to send the letter I had written to my mother. Should I send it now, before Josh and I started the process of in vitro fertilization? Should I wait until after I get pregnant, assuming I do? How would the stress of dealing with her affect a baby I would be carrying? And if we do get pregnant, was she going to want to be right in the middle of my pregnancy? I cannot have her falling all over me while I'm pregnant without me having said anything. She will make out as if nothing was ever wrong. So when do I send it?

Gary said we know that once I send it, I am going to worry. And we know that it will be a stressful time regardless of what happens and we have no clue how she will react. As my therapist, he was concerned primarily that I not lose my balance. I asked him point blank, "What is your recommendation? When do you think I should send it?" He replied, "My recommendation is to go ahead and tell her. Set the record straight. The minute the truth is out, Mother has to do something. She may deny, but she has to do something. It's going to be stressful for you, but I think the longer you wait, the more tension and anxiety are going to build. As a rule, it is best to face it and then we'll deal with the fall out. The waiting is hard and that adds its own stress. The little girl is saying, 'See, you're going to weasel out of it.' But I've seen it over and over with you, Rochelle. As you deal with truth, you get well. Truth is good for you." We discussed some details about the letter and when I got off the phone my stomach was tight and my palms were sweaty.

Later that day, Tuesday, February 23, I made some final changes to the letter. I postdated it for February 25 to give me a couple of days, printed it, signed it, and sealed it in an envelope addressed to my mother. I was trembling. Tuesday and Wednesday were long, hard days for me.

> Yesterday in my session with Gary, I decided it was time to send the letter. My initial reaction was that my stomach flip-flopped and I smiled at the same time. The little girl said, "It's about time." That's what the smile was about. But the little girl also said, "I'm scared." That's what the stomach flip-flop was about. Today I've vacillated between being ready to drive to the post office and being subdued and depressed. Gary suggested I send the letter certified mail so she would have to sign for it. That way she can't deny having received it. I'm just scared. I'm scared of what her reaction will be. My guilting voice has been quite loud since yesterday. Josh said that the

CHAPTER 40: COURAGE

guilting voice is Satan. He doesn't want me to speak truth. He is the father of lies and he does anything he can to further his agenda of keeping us away from God. He wants me to remain trapped in mental illness. He wants my mother to remain trapped. He doesn't want healing to take place. Josh is right. Satan is my ultimate enemy. Proverbs 12:22 says, "The Lord detests lying lips, but he delights in men who are truthful." I'm trying to be truthful. I'm speaking truth. I'm not hiding behind the lie any longer. It's time to speak truth. I'm trying to focus on Isaiah 41:10, which says, "So do not fear, for I am with you; do not be dismayed, for I am your God. I will strengthen you and help you; I will uphold you with my righteous right hand." God will help me get through whatever happens, however she reacts. And He has given me a strong support group to help me. I'm still scared, though.

Josh suggested I try to have a conversation with the little girl. Last night I had a mild panic attack. A memory seemed to be trying to break through. I don't have a definite memory, but I have an incredibly strong sense that, in order to keep me quiet, my grandfather told me not only would he die, but that Mommie would die, too. When I remembered him saying he would die, the little girl said, "I don't want Mommie to die too." I feel so responsible for her. I feel like sending her this letter is going to kill her. It's the right thing to do. It's time, but my little girl is so scared.

This morning I got an e-mail from my mother. "How are you? There is not a day that passes that I don't think of you. I pray for you daily. I miss you terribly. Are you still not ready to talk to me?" I don't miss her terribly. I don't miss her slightly. In fact, the last two months of not talking to her have been wonderful. I don't miss her at all.

The letter. I have to send the letter. But the little girl is scared. I know my adult doesn't have anything to be scared about. At least I think I know that. I haven't reread the letter since Tuesday. I don't want to think about her reaction. Am I scared that she is going to die or am I scared of her anger? Strong emotion from her is very frightening and unsafe for me. And I guarantee that this letter will evoke strong emotion from her. I'm worried that she will have a breakdown because of this letter. How do I stop feeling so responsible for her? I vacillate between "I'm ready to send it now!" and "I'm scared to send it!" Josh says to have a conversation between my adult and the little girl. But I can't hear my adult voice because the fearful voice is so strong.

I just reread the letter. I feel angry. I'm angry that I have to write such a letter to begin with. A child is supposed to be able to trust her mother. A child isn't supposed to be afraid of her mother. A child is supposed to be protected by her mother. She thinks sending an e-mail telling me she misses me terribly will make everything okay. She wants everything to be back to normal. But normal is sick in my family. Normal to her means me dutifully doing and saying what she wants. She doesn't want to deal with truth. But I **have** to speak truth or I'll never get well. I can't avoid this. I can't ignore it. I can't put it off any longer. I must have the courage to send this letter. Josh said courage means doing what is right even when you're afraid. It means not letting yourself be paralyzed by the fear. Okay, I'll admit it. I'm afraid. I'm afraid to send this letter. But it is the right thing to do. And I am going to do what is right despite the fear. I can deal with the fear. I betrayed myself before when I recanted. I won't betray myself again. I'm going to speak truth.

Little Girl, know this – I won't let you down. And I won't let you get hurt. You are safe now. No one can hurt you. My adult is going to deal with Mother. Josh won't let her hurt you. And Gary won't let her hurt you. You are safe. Whatever happens isn't your fault. Hear me, Little Girl, it is not your fault! However Mother responds is **her** choice. Her response is not your fault. You aren't responsible for her. I'm not responsible for her. I'm responsible for me and you. And I'm going to take care of you.

What Papa told you was a lie. It's okay to tell the truth. Truth is good. God delights in those who are truthful. Papa was wrong. He was a wicked man. It's okay to tell the truth. Little Girl, I love you and I'm going to protect you. I don't know how Mother will respond. I don't know what she will do, but I know what I will do. I'll take care of you. I will speak truth. I will do what pleases God. I will get well. I'm not going to live under Satan's control. Satan is the father of lies. I'm not going to live a lie any longer. Trust me, Little Girl. Telling her the truth is going to be hard. She's not going to like it. But it's the right thing to do. And we will survive.

God will get us through this. We are not alone. Josh is there and Gary is there. And you have a lot of other friends who are on your side, praying for you and supporting you. It's okay to be afraid. It's not okay to let that fear paralyze you. I'm not going to be mastered by the fear. I'm going to have courage, Little Girl. God is telling us the same thing that He told Joshua in Joshua 1:9, "Be strong and courageous. Do not be terrified; do not be discouraged, for the Lord your God will be with you wherever you go." And remember what James 1:25 says, that if you put God's Word into practice you will be blessed in what you do. God's Word says to speak truth. I am speaking truth. And He will bless us.

Thursday afternoon, after a lot of prayer (by me, Josh, and several others who knew I was sending the letter that week), I went to the post office. Sitting in my car outside the post office, I called Josh on my cell phone and he prayed for me once again, for the courage I needed to send the letter. Then I boldly walked into the post office.

February 25, 2010

Mom,

On September 6, 2008, I wrote you a letter inviting you to meet with Gary Walker and me in his office to discuss things. You have consistently ignored that request. I told you then that I have problems and that we have problems and we need professional help, but you have disregarded that letter. That's why I am writing this letter. You want to know what is wrong? It is time that I tell you. I'm not saying these things to you to hurt you. I'm saying these things to you because I **have** to speak truth. I have been afraid to speak truth to you because the first time I spoke the truth, you were so angry with me. But I have to speak truth. My mental health depends on it.

What is the truth? The truth is that Papa sexually abused me. When I made the accusation in 1992, I had a ton of clues, but very few clear memories. That isn't the case now. Over the last seven years I've had an overwhelming number of memories and flashbacks about what Papa did to me. It's true, Mom. He sexually abused me. According to the law, what he did was Aggravated Sexual Assault , and he should have gone to prison. I have the memories. I know the details.

I betrayed myself in 1995 when I said that I'd had false memories. I was afraid of your anger. I never felt any support from you when I was hospitalized in 1992 and 1993. All I felt was your anger and disapproval. I felt like I had destroyed the family by making the accusation. So I recanted. I convinced myself that it had been false memories. It was easier to live with the self-betrayal than to live with your anger and disapproval. It was easier to betray myself than to betray the sick family system I grew up in. But I was wrong to recant. It was not false memories. It happened. I remember. I did not destroy the family by making the accusation. Papa destroyed me when he started sexually abusing me.

Mom, I've had problems with mental illness for years and you have tried to ignore that fact. When I was in high school and I was suicidal, you got angry with me for calling [counselor] for counseling. And you didn't want me to tell anyone. Same thing with the hospitalizations. You didn't want anyone knowing and you were angry with me when I did tell people. You were so concerned with image. How many times have I heard you say, "Who knows about this?" You say that I am the most important thing in the world to you, but I feel that what is really most important to you is your image. I feel like you care more about your image than you care about me. If you really cared about me and my mental health, why have you ignored my invitation to meet with Gary?

I blamed myself for the abuse. I thought it was all my fault. You told me many times through the years, "You were a rotten kid." I internalized that and believed it was all my fault. And I thought the abuse was my fault because of how angry you got at me when I made the accusation. And when I was a little girl, you lashed out at me in anger. I was terrified of you, but I thought it was my fault that you would get so angry at me. How many times have I heard you laugh about breaking the paddle on me? You thought it was funny. But it wasn't funny. Lashing out at your child in rage is not funny. It is abuse.

I thought I had to punish myself for what had happened to me as a child. I thought I had to punish myself for what Papa did to me and for how you treated me. I did punish myself. For years I cut myself with razor blades. I still have scars on my body. It has taken years of therapy to get past everything. I'm still trying to heal. And part of my healing is speaking truth. I am not going to live a lie any longer. I am not going to live the fantasy that our family was just wonderful. It isn't true. What is true is what I have written to you in this letter. It was not my fault. I was a beautiful, terrified little girl. I was acting out because of what was being done to me. And I couldn't tell anyone what he was doing. He told me he would die if I told. So I lived with it. And *I* nearly died.

I have made so much progress and have had so much healing. But healing still has to occur. That's why I'm speaking truth. You don't want to

Chapter 40: Courage

hear the truth, but I must speak it. I have to tell the truth or I'll never get well. You may think I don't love you because I am telling you these things. But I do love you. Love rejoices with the truth. I do love you, but I've been hurt by you. And we need to deal with that. I don't know if you'll have the courage to deal with truth. I hope you do, because the truth is what sets you free. It's frightening to have to deal with truth. I know. I've lived it. But it's worth it. If you decide you want to deal with truth, Gary is waiting for us.

I'm sure reading this letter has been difficult for you. Dealing with my childhood has been very difficult for me. Once you've had the chance to read this, I would appreciate a note or e-mail acknowledging that you have received this and read it. However, please do not try to call me about this letter. I don't want to be subjected to an emotional or angry tirade from you. When you are ready to deal rationally with these issues, send me an e-mail letting me know when you can meet with Gary.

I signed it in my own hand, "Love, Rochelle." After I mailed it on Thursday and all day Friday, I felt scared and troubled and numb. And vulnerable. I felt so vulnerable. But I had done it. I'd had had the courage to mail the letter, to speak truth to my mother. My scars were speaking truth to the very person who had inflicted so many of the emotional scars. At 4:15 a.m. on Friday, when I couldn't sleep, I sent an e-mail to Miss Penny. Later that day she responded with some very encouraging words:

My dear, dear child,

I am praying for you right now and will be doing so throughout this day and the next and the next. It is okay to feel anxious, afraid, and worried. You feel that way but YOU ARE SAFE. YOU ARE OKAY and most importantly SPEAKING TRUTH SETS YOU FREE and YOU ARE FREE. I am so very, very, very, very proud of you and I pray that you are also very proud of yourself. What a JOY to know that TRUTH and TRUST in God radiates in your life and YOUR home. What a blessing it is for the little girl to have such a SAFE place to live and be loved in!

It takes much courage and support to be able to separate the dream world from reality and to feel true feelings. You have shown that courage and your precious Josh has given you the life support to LIVE FREE.

Perhaps you will find time today to sit at your piano and sing praises to God Almighty for power and strength to calm the storm and deliver you on the shores of peace.

I love you so very much.

Blessings and Hugs,
Miss Penny

On Saturday I was surprisingly calm all day. I stayed busy and tried not to think about the fact that at some point during that day, the postman would deliver my letter to my mother. That night I couldn't sleep. After lying there for two hours, I finally got out of bed and checked my e-mail. There was an e-mail from my mother.

Rochelle,

I received your letter today. I am *so sorry* that I hurt you. It was never my intention to hurt you. When I yelled at you, it was my frustration at my inability to be effective with you and at your disobedience. Mom yelled at me when I was growing up and I always deserved it. I'm not saying you deserved it, but I DID. I am quite amazed that you were terrified of me. I never dreamed you were afraid of me. Your actions did not even hint that you were terrified of me. I think of all the things we did together and had fun. Do you even remember those or only the bad things I did? Yes, I did get angry with you, but rage? My anger was when you wouldn't mind me and you would keep on and on doing something I had asked you to stop doing or when you completely ignored what I had told you and I was at my wit's end. Obviously, I didn't know what to do. I must have been a real monster. Because I was abusing you, I shouldn't be teaching children either.

I have spent so much time trying to think of what I had done. I've prayed so many times for God to forgive me for whatever I had done to you and for your complete healing and your forgiveness. I think I am dazed with what an awful person I am. I NEVER said you were a rotten kid. I would NOT have said "rotten." After you were grown, I did say you were a little terror. I then would proceed to tell how great you were as a teen-ager; and then the wonderful person you were as an adult. I am so sorry that hurt you. At church, lots of people referred to Ben Hamilton as a "little terror." I thought

CHAPTER 40: COURAGE

of it like that; you were strong-willed. I chose the wrong words. I thought you would think it was funny that you had been that way as a little child, but then did a complete turnaround. I did not for a second wish that to bring you pain. I shouldn't have said anything.

Regarding your invitation to meet with you and Gary Walker to discuss things: You said you weren't strong enough to talk to me about it. At that point I was greatly puzzled wondering what I had done, but I also had to think about that. I kept visualizing you, Josh, and Gary on one side and me by myself. I didn't think I was strong enough. Mom and I talked about it a lot. Mom was always so wise, but she didn't know what to think. Mom kept telling me that she thought I had been a good mother. It was less than three weeks till Mom went in the hospital. You acted okay when you were here when Mom was dying. I didn't know how deep the problem was. I thought you weren't angry with me anymore. I don't remember ever being angry with you over your accusation about Papa sexually abusing you. I was stunned, horrified, and extremely hurt to think my Dad could have done that and especially to my child, my daughter. When you told me about the abuse when you were in that hospital, I never told you I didn't believe you. You asked me if I believed you. I told you "yes, because you said so." What did I do or not do to make you think I didn't support you? I wanted you to get well. My anger and disapproval were my feelings toward my Dad for hurting you. Of course, you didn't destroy the family when you made the accusation. Mom and I desperately wanted you to get well. Mom and I discussed it a lot. We carried around a lot of pain believing he had done that. Mom thought her marriage must have been a sham and I was devastated that my Dad could have done that. I am so sorry that you felt like you had to say it was false memories.

"Image" Yes, image is important to me. While I was growing up, "reputation" and "image" were strongly emphasized. Mom was such a gentle person that ruining my reputation or image would have hurt her tremendously. Why would I WANT people to know what my Dad had done? I don't deserve any love from you. Being sorry and heartbroken will never be enough.

Yes, I'll go to meet with you and Gary. When?
Even though you don't believe it, I love you,
Mom
That's all I can write right now. I'm cried out.

When I first read her letter I felt a glimmer of hope. She got some things wrong, like saying she never said I was a rotten kid, but she was willing to meet with me and Gary. I was kind of amazed. I don't think Gary, Josh, or I knew what to expect from her. I expected anger, for sure. And defensiveness. And emotion. I didn't expect to hear from her that quickly. For the first time since Gary mentioned it last summer, I was able to see her through eyes of compassion. She is an unhealthy, sad, pathetic woman who desperately needs healing in her life. That is what I want for her. It was nearly four a.m. before I finally went to sleep, and the next day I was tired, but I felt peaceful. The healthier I get, the more I speak truth, the calmer I get. Gary was right. When I deal with truth, I get well.

Sunday night I talked to Gary. He was amazed and acknowledged that her response was far more than I had expected. I expected anger and denial, which I did get, but she actually showed a little self-insight in her response. Gary said it was as good an answer as I could have gotten at this point and it may set the stage for some real healing. That evening I e-mailed my mother back.

Mom,

Thank you for responding so quickly to my letter. I know you are hurting right now. Please lean on God, for He is "close to the brokenhearted and saves those who are crushed in spirit." (Psalm 34:18) You said you visualized Josh and me and Gary on one side and you on the other. I don't want you to think of this as an adversarial thing. I want us to work together to heal. You say you shouldn't be teaching children. That's not true. You are a good teacher, I've always said that. You made some mistakes with me, but that doesn't mean you can't be a good teacher. Yes, I do remember the good times and the fun. If there hadn't been any good times, why would I want reconciliation? But I do. I want us to heal. You said that you don't deserve any love from me. None of us deserves love from anybody. That's what is so beautiful about the gospel. We don't deserve God's love, yet He loves us anyway. I do love you. And I want you to heal. I want me to heal. And you are wrong. I do believe that you love me. And I forgive you. We just need to work on some things. I am so glad that you are willing to meet with me and Gary. Can you go at spring break? I know that's soon, but then you wouldn't have to take off work. Let me know.

> I love you,
> Rochelle

Monday morning my mother e-mailed me and told me she could not go at spring break because she already had a plane ticket to go visit her cousins. We e-mailed back and forth a couple of times, and as the day went by, I found myself getting angry. I reread her response to my letter several times and every time I read it I got angrier.

She Says She Never Called Me a Rotten Kid

I've been thinking a lot about my mother's e-mail response to my letter. And the more I think about the details, the angrier I get. The thing I'm most angry about is her vehement denial of ever having called me a rotten kid. She said, and I quote, "I NEVER said you were a rotten kid. I would NOT have said 'rotten.' After you were grown, I did say you were a little terror. I then would proceed to tell you how great you were as a teenager; and then the wonderful person you were as an adult... I thought you would think it was funny that you had been that way as a little child, but then did a complete turnaround." Josh says my mother scrubs her memory. Even he has heard her say I was a rotten kid. She's right about one thing. She would proceed to tell me how great I was as a teenager. I don't think I was all that great a teenager. Maybe the reason she thought I was a great teenager is because by then I was compliant with her. I was the dutiful daughter. So by saying I was a great teenager that makes it all right to call me a rotten kid? But she won't even admit to that! **I'm** not scrubbing my memory, remembering something wrong here. This is not a fuzzy memory from my childhood. This is something that she has said to me on many occasions after I became an adult. And she denies it!

Last September when I finally admitted to myself that the way she treated me as a child was physical abuse, one of the things that made me so angry was the fact that she had called me a rotten kid so many times, in essence blaming me for the abuse. And when I had that extreme crying episode a few weeks ago, finally understanding that what Papa did to me was actually Aggravated Sexual Assault , I kept crying out, "She told me I was a rotten kid! I thought it was my fault because she said I was a rotten kid!" The FACT that she has for at **least** twenty years told me I was a rotten kid is behind so much of my pain. And she denies it!

And I'm hacked off about something else, too. My mother said she couldn't go over spring break because, "I have a plane ticket to visit (her distant cousin) Stewart and family," and "I'll be able to talk to him about Mom, and I frequently hear from Anne, and really enjoyed staying with Cindy when Mom and I went for Stewart and Elizabeth's big anniversary party. It's a little more family, which I desperately need. I'm sorry, but the ticket is non-transferable and no money back." Josh said if resolving things with me was really important to her, she'd cancel her trip. Gary and Miss Penny both agreed with him. Gary said that if she really wanted to do this, she'd say, "Forget my trip to see my cousin. My daughter is more important." And Miss Penny said, "So what if she'd lose the fare? We aren't talking about life savings here and you are worth more than anyone's life savings." They are all right. If I really am the most important thing in the world to her as she says, then she'd be canceling her trip and getting herself to Gary's office in a heartbeat. But she's not. And her little spiel about her cousins just reinforces where I rank with her. She frequently hears from Anne, she really enjoyed staying with Cindy, it's more family, which she desperately needs. She needs her third cousins? What about her daughter? I thought I was the most important thing in the world to her? That's what she says, but all this explaining and excusing just shows me that I'm really not the most important thing in the world to her. And that hurts and it makes me very angry! I'm sick to death of being lied to!

So I see where I stand with her. I suggested another couple of weeks that might work and she replied with a list of things she had going on with her job that would prevent her from going during any of them. She said she had a holiday on a certain Friday in April, asked if that would work, and if Josh be at the meeting. She seems to think that this is going to be a one-time, quick fix. When we go to meet with her and Gary, I'm not driving eight hours just to meet with her for one. It'll be like it was during the ministry renewal Josh and I did—a number of sessions over several days' time. We're talking therapy here. She and I need therapy. She doesn't understand what therapy means! Therapy means she has to work at this, too! I've worked my butt off the last seven years trying to heal. This is not a quick fix. I've got forty years of hurt built up and issues that need to be worked through

CHAPTER 40: COURAGE

and resolved, and she thinks a one-time meeting is going to take care of the problem?! And she had the audacity to ask whether Josh will be in the meeting? Of course he'll be in the meeting. He's my rock and my strength and my support!

And I'm mad at myself for sending that reply to her big e-mail. I was appeasing. Gary said he thinks the little girl sent that e-mail. He said my mother doesn't need to have her guilt assuaged. She needs to feel godly sorrow for what she has done and how she has acted. But I sent her that stupid e-mail telling her not to feel so bad. My adult definitely wasn't in charge when I sent that. But, Gary told me not to let that get me down. I have still done very well and he is still very proud of me.

Something else that ticks me off is that she said she doesn't remember ever being angry with me over my accusation about Papa sexually abusing me. Again, she has scrubbed her memory. And she asks, "What did I do or not do to make you think I didn't support you?" It's not that she did or didn't do any one thing. It was her whole way of being. Her body language, her tone of voice, her unwillingness and anger about having to go to family group when I was in the hospital, little comments she's made through the years, her anger at me for wanting to talk to people about what was going on with me, including asking people to pray for me, and more. And it goes further back than that. It started in middle school, the first time I was in counseling. She didn't want me letting anyone know. And she refused to pay for counseling for me when I wanted to go when I was suicidal as a senior in high school. And she always angrily asks, "Who knows about this?" when I tell her anything bad about me..

She says that she and Grandma desperately wanted me to get well. I never felt that from her. What she desperately wanted was for me to get over it quickly, not tell anyone, and quit creating emotional turmoil for her. She said she was in pain thinking that her dad had done such a thing, and was devastated that her dad could have done that, and didn't want people to know what her dad had done. But what about her daughter? It's all about image for her. The way she said things in her e-mail, it is obvious that her image is tied up in what her dad did. But there's no concern for me. I thought before that she would be devastated if she knew how deeply I was affected by everything. That's wrong. She is devastated because of how **she** feels about everything. She says she is heartbroken. Is she heartbroken because of how hurt *I* have been, or because of how hurt **she** feels?

Since her big e-mail letter to me, we have e-mailed back and forth a couple of times. She said she couldn't go at spring break. I offered some alternate dates and she replied with a litany of things about her job that would preclude her from coming on a bunch of different dates—school functions, testing, meetings, etc. So I see where I rank in importance. In one of her e-mails, she told me about a friend of hers who she is busy helping to pack and move. So, she can find the time to help her friend pack and move, but she can't find time or make time to try to heal her relationship with her daughter. That just reminds me of all the other times she has done things for her friends, but hasn't cared about me and my mental health. More of the same with her. Of one of the things that would prevent her from going she said "I would have to be in the hospital to miss that." More of the same. And then after the one date she suggested, a three day weekend at the end of April, she said, "It just seems so long." No, Mom. What seems so long is the number of years I've had to deal with your crap! She wants to sound eager to go, but when you compare that comment to all her excuses, it sounds so hollow and so pathetic!

Every time I read my appeasing reply to her big e-mail, I get a sick feeling in the pit of my stomach. Gary's right. She needs to stew in her guilt for a while. Godly sorrow is what leads to repentance. And Gary's right about the fact that the little girl is the one who sent that e-mail. I'm angry. I'm not angry at the little girl. I'm angry at my adult. Gary says that the little girl is the one who is angry at my adult. Regardless, I'm not going to let that throw me off track. I'm just going to be more careful. Gary suggested that I suspend communications with her for now. Let her sit and think on things. Obviously, she had a moment of sorrow when she sent her big e-mail response, but her narcissism is still quite strong. I just hope that my slip-up won't cause the little girl to quit trusting me right now. Hopefully, she will know that my adult is still going to take care of things. Hopefully, what I did by speaking truth and sending the letter in the first place will outweigh my mistake. I asked Gary and Miss Penny if they thought Josh and I should go ahead with our plans for in vitro fertilization. Gary said absolutely, do not wait on her. Miss Penny agreed and said, "Pursue the in vitro with the assurance of knowing you cannot be denied the opportunity of being parents just because your mother will not do the right thing. That is her choice. You choose life and abundant life. Praise God!" I'm still trying to sort out my emotions about everything that has transpired in the last week. I'm glad I have Josh and Gary and Miss Penny, and I'm glad I have God, because I sure couldn't handle all this on my own.

Even though I was angry, I was still doing well. I vented to Josh, wrote about it, thought about it, reread what I had written, then went on with my day. Gary said it was good that I could suspend it and go on with things. I was able to do this because I had spoken truth and truth was on the table. Gary said that her response was more than either one of us had expected, but it didn't mean that she had now aligned herself with truth. As Josh said, she has scrubbed her memory. And she was obviously avoiding going to meet with Gary, even though she said she would. Gary said that ideally I should have kept the pressure on rather than sending her that e-mail, but we can reassert pressure. He suggested that I wait until I hear from her again, and then we would formulate a reply. I may want to say to her something to the effect of, "You don't seem to understand the importance of this, the gravity of the situation, and until you do, I'm suspending communication."

Gary reminded me that my mother has a lifelong pattern of denying the truth and lying to herself. Just because she has been confronted with the truth doesn't mean that she is now truthful. That was clearly seen by her denial of things, especially her denial of ever having called me a rotten kid. But that will be dealt with. We will have to confront her on some details. And Gary would work with me on preparing for the face to face confrontation. I asked Gary if he thought my mother had the strength of character to face things. He said "I don't know. But an interesting piece of the puzzle is that you are all she has. Once the confrontation begins line by line, it will be interesting. But your adult is strong enough to do this." He said that in the whole scheme of things, the biggest hurdle was over. We would help her understand some of the details, but the great fear of confrontation is gone. I told him I disagreed; the face-to-face, eye-to-eye part is most frightening to me. Gary stated, "I understand, but you have to remember that the truth is still out. Josh is here. I'm here. You're not doing this solo. You're not going to recant. There are no big secrets yet to be divulged. The big secrets are out." He quipped, "I'd rather be in your position than hers right now." I agreed with that! She is going to have to evaluate a lot of things, big things.

After a couple of weeks of suspended communication, I e-mailed my mother once more.

Mom,

    Apparently I need to clarify the parameters. When we go to meet with Gary, the idea is to spend a week there, not a weekend, meeting with him in therapy on a daily basis, both individually and with all of us. Then there may be subsequent meetings later. I'm not sure you understand the gravity of the situation. The problems that exist weren't created overnight and they won't be fixed with a quick one-hour meeting. Therapy requires time and commitment. Until you are willing to commit to therapy, I want limited contact with you. I'm not going to rush this just for the sake of having a meeting. I want this done right.

                                                                                               Rochelle

There were several e-mails back and forth over the next couple of days and we finally scheduled a week in mid-June. During the two and a half months until mid-June, Josh and I planned to proceed with the in vitro fertilization. I was concerned that the in vitro process might conflict with the meeting. Gary assured me that if I needed to reschedule, I had every right to do so. He told me that the baby process should take precedent. As he pointed out, the problems with my mother weren't created quickly and they wouldn't be resolved quickly. I planned to have limited contact with my mother until we met with Gary. He told me to wait and see what happened in her heart. In the meantime, I had things to do. I had life to live. I had things to pursue. Like getting pregnant. But I'd had the courage to confront her, and I'll have the courage to meet her face-to-face in Gary's office.

41
Trust

Trust,
like rappelling off
a cliff
into the darkness
below,
banking on the
ropes
to hold and secure;
or,
like jumping out of
an airplane,
free-falling
through air and space,
earth rapidly approaching,
reaching for the rip cord
and hoping the chute
will open;
or,
like exploring an
underwater cave,
tunnels and
passages
twisting and winding,
intricate labyrinth,
air tank getting low,
praying that
the map
is right.
Trust.

On April 7, I had an ultrasound and Josh and I both had lab work done, thus officially beginning the in vitro fertilization process. The next three weeks, I took birth control pills to suppress my ovaries. Then on April 29, we traveled to the fertility clinic for a baseline ultrasound, blood work, and our teaching appointment for the fertility nurse to show Josh how to give me the shots that I would be taking in my stomach over the next two weeks to stimulate my ovaries. It was all very exciting and a little anxiety producing, particularly all the travel. Josh gave me the shots and he did a great job. During those two weeks, I had four ultrasounds and lab work, each time showing that my ovaries were responding very well to the medication.

During the whole process I did a lot of journal writing, including writing many prayers to God. I also wrote a letter to the little girl. And with everything that was going on, Gary marveled, "God has brought you a long way. When I think back to the day I met you, it's amazing how far you have come."

5-4-10

Little Girl,

I want to tell you something very important. Mother's Day is this Sunday. I mailed a Mother's Day card to her today, but I am not going to call her and I am not sending flowers. I've talked with Gary about this and I've talked with Josh about this and I think this is the best thing to do, the right thing. I want you to try and not be nervous about not calling her. Will she be upset? Yes, but not at you. She'll be upset at my adult, but my adult can handle it. She may send me a guilting e-mail or she may do nothing. But you don't have to worry, Little Girl. My adult is in control. My not calling her is not cause for alarm or anxiety or fear. Not calling her is part of speaking truth. If I called or sent flowers, it would be wrong because I would be sending a false message. So only sending a card is the right thing to do. You haven't seemed all that anxious about it, but I'm writing this letter to you to help you be calm on the actual day. I know if you are going to get all anxious about it, that it will be on the actual day of Mother's Day. But, like I said, you haven't seemed all that anxious. Maybe just a little worried.

I'm proud of you, Little Girl. You've been doing so well. I haven't felt as if you have been all full of fear, even about the prospect of actually meeting

CHAPTER 41: TRUST

with Mother in June at Gary's office. I know that I have made incredible progress, but so have you, Little Girl. And I think our progress is connected. As I have been speaking truth and getting healthier, you have been getting less fearful. And that's wonderful.

Little Girl, there's something else I want to talk to you about and that has to do with Josh and me trying to get pregnant. This whole in vitro process is complicated and a little stressful, but it is also exciting. But I want you to know, Little Girl, that it may not work. The doctor told us that at my age there is only a twenty-five to thirty percent success rate. But Josh and I are hopeful, and we are praying that God will work through this process to enable us to get pregnant. However, there's no guarantee. And I want you to understand that if it doesn't work that it will be okay. I know your dream was to grow up, get married, stay married and have a child who had a loving, protective, faithful daddy. Josh will be that kind of daddy if we are able to have a child, but it may not happen. I want you to try and not be angry with God if it doesn't work. I want your faith in God to stay strong, even if it doesn't work. I think I'm talking to both you and me here. I know I have worried about how I will react if it doesn't work and we are not able to get pregnant. But Little Girl, I want us to understand that even if I don't get pregnant and even if we don't understand why, know this – God still loves us and He is still in control. He knows what is best and I have to trust that His will is what is best. But I am praying that having a child is His will for us.

Little Girl, a lot is going on in our life. A lot of really wonderful, exciting things. Even if I don't get pregnant, there are still a lot of wonderful things going on. I'll tell you Little Girl, what Gary always tells me – live in the moment! Don't get trapped by fears and worries about the future, don't get trapped by grief over the past – live in the moment! God's Word says in Psalm 118:24, "This is the day the Lord has made; let us rejoice and be glad in it." Remember that Little Girl, regardless of what happens, and remember that God can and will work good out of every situation – baby or no baby, dealing with Mother – whatever, God is there! I love you, Little Girl, and I'm proud of you!

Love,
Rochelle

Gary and I talked a lot during the in vitro process about faith and trust in God. I was concerned about how I would react if it didn't work, that it would affect my faith in God. He told me he wasn't worried. "You've done too much walking with Him to lose your faith." He said the nice thing was that I could make the decision that day as to how I would respond. We talked about the difference between asking for a miracle and asking God to work through natural processes. God has not promised a miracle, but He has promised to work through things (Romans 8:28). On Friday, May 6, in the middle of the two weeks of shots, I wrote a prayer to God.

5-6-10

Dear God,

    It's been a long time since I've written a prayer to You, but I am going to try and start doing that again. I want to be pleasing to You, Lord. Yes, I want You to give me the desires of my heart, but that's not the only reason I want to be pleasing to You. Gary said yesterday that I've walked with You too long to lose my faith if we can't get pregnant. Lord, I've made so much progress and growth over the last seven years. Mental health, which I once thought was an impossibility, is possible. It's here. I know I still have growing and healing and changing to do, but Lord, look at how far I've come. And spiritually I've grown by leaps and bounds. The idea of considering it pure joy when I face trials that James talks about in James 1:2-4 is something that I can now wrap my mind around. But Lord, I don't want to have to count it pure joy if the IVF process doesn't work. I will, but I don't want to. You have brought so much growth and healing to me, it's incredible, phenomenal. Seven years ago I couldn't imagine how my life could ever heal. And yet I have. And it's all because of You and Your Word and Your people. You have brought such incredible healing to my life. And I thank you Lord.

    Father, I need You to please help me. If the IVF process doesn't work, I don't want my faith to waver. I want to have an unwavering faith like Abraham. Paul says that Abraham didn't weaken in his faith, that he didn't waver through unbelief, but that he was strengthened in his faith. I want a faith like that, Lord. Regardless of what happens, if we can't get pregnant, if the IVF process doesn't work, Lord, I want my faith to stay strong. Please God, please help my faith to stay strong—yea, be even stronger. But Lord, even though I am praying for a stronger faith if the IVF process doesn't work,

CHAPTER 41: TRUST

what I am continuing to pray for is that it **will** work. Please God, please work through the process to enable me to become pregnant. I know that nothing is impossible with You. I know You haven't promised me a miracle in this, but I know you work through things. Your Word does promise that. So, I am asking You to work through the IVF process to enable me to get pregnant. And Lord, if I do get pregnant, please guard me so that I won't miscarry.

Lord, like Hannah in the Bible, I am pouring out my soul to You, asking You to open my womb and give me a child. Please Father, don't forget me. Lord, I promise that if Josh and I are so blessed to have a child, we will raise our child to know You and love You and obey You. We will commit ourselves to raising our child in the training and instruction of the Lord. Father, You know how committed I am to my marriage and how committed I've been to my healing. Lord, I will be just as committed to my child. Lord, remember me. Lord, the Bible says that Isaac prayed to the Lord on behalf of his wife because she was barren and You answered his prayer. I pray that You will answer Josh's prayers that he prays on my behalf, that I can become pregnant and have a child. Father, You know the desires of my heart. Please grant me the desires of my heart.

Lord, Gary told me that I could make the decision now as to how I will respond if the IVF process doesn't work. So, Lord, today I am deciding that if the IVF process doesn't work, (1) I will be sad and I will grieve, but I will honor You as God, as the God who is in control. I will honor You as my Lord. I will accept Your will. (2) I will try my best not to be angry at You and blame You, although I know You are big enough to handle my anger. But (3) I trust You, Lord, to be in control of my life. I promise, Lord, that I will trust You. I will try my best (4) to not go into a depression, but instead to rejoice in my suffering because I know that You will work through my suffering to grow me and mature me. And (5) I will pray to You for wisdom to understand what You are trying to teach me through my suffering. Father, I do trust You. Help me to trust You more. Especially help me if we are unable to get pregnant. Help my faith, Lord.

God, help me to be persistent in prayer. Father, please, I ask You, I petition You for a child. I know You want me to pray and not give up, so I am praying just that, Lord, that You will bless us with a child.

And God, I need to talk to You about when we go in June to meet with my mother. I need You to be with me that week, especially if it comes right on the heels of finding out that the IVF process didn't work. If we have to go into that meeting with my mother under those circumstances, oh Lord,

I ask You for strength. Please God, give me strength. But regardless of the IVF process, please Father, help me when we meet with my mother. Help me to be calm and in control of my thoughts and emotions. Help me to be wise in my dealings with her. Help Gary and Josh to be wise. Be with Gary that week and give him the strength and the wisdom he needs to help us. And please, Father, help me to continue to speak truth to my mother. Help my anxiety to be under control and for me to not obsess and worry over things that week or even afterwards. Help me to trust You for the strength and help I need to get through that week. Help me be honest and firm. Help me to conduct myself in a mentally healthy manner with her. And Lord, please help her. She will need a lot of help that week and beyond if she is going to really look at the truth of her life and change. Thank You, Lord, that I know You are going to help me. Father, I lay my requests before You this morning and wait in expectation. Thank You, Lord. for listening. Thank You for hearing me. And Lord, once again, I ask You to please bless us with a healthy child. I love You, Lord. Help me to love You more.

Gary told me that my prayer to God was a very fair request. My cries were going out to the Lord; now we had to wait and see what happened. We were doing our part; in fact, we were doing everything we could do that is known to mankind to try to get pregnant. Now we wait. And Gary reminded me that God is always faithful. Baby or no baby, God is faithful.

5-14-10

Dear God,

Well, it's almost here, the retrieval date for my eggs. Lord, thank You that You have helped my body respond so positively to the medication. I'm encouraged by that. Please Father, please grant me my heart's desire for a healthy child. Lord, it seems like my body is willing. Please Lord, work through the medication and the process to allow us to become pregnant. Lord, I know that this whole process is an exercise in trust, whether it works or not. If it works, I have trusted You. If it doesn't work, I still have trusted You. And either way, I will need to continue to trust You. Dear God, please work through this process to bring us a healthy child. Lord, help me to trust You more. Please Lord, open my womb.

CHAPTER 41: TRUST

I had several follicles ready from which my eggs would be retrieved. May 16 was the big retrieval day, the day they retrieved my eggs and Josh's sperm. The doctor was able to retrieve several eggs and of those eggs, a few were mature and fertilized normally! On May 21, we went back for the transfer. My doctor decided that, because of my age, he wanted to transfer three embryos to my uterus. He teased us and assured us that in all his years of doing this, he'd never had a woman my age, into whom he had transferred three embryos, have more than twins. I laughed and told him there was always a first time! After the transfer, we had to wait eleven days before I would have my blood pregnancy test. Those eleven days were faith-building. Indeed, this whole process has been faith-building, an exercise in trust. I chronicled my thoughts and emotions in my journal through prayers to God. I prayed for a child. I prayed for help if we weren't able to get pregnant. I prayed that my focus would be on God and not on my desires. I prayed that my desire would be for God. I prayed for help in surrendering my will to God. And as I prayed, I felt my trust in God growing. Before Christmas, I had written a song about my unfilled desire to have a child, but I hadn't finished it. I completed it during the waiting period.

Trust

Verse 1: Dear Lord, I'm sad, my desire unfulfilled, oh, to have a child. My heart is full of love for my man, but I still want a child.

Verse 2: But Lord, I trust Your hand in this. I know Your will is right and good, dear Lord, I trust.

Verse 3: Dear God, don't know if You'll ever fulfill my desire, my prayer, my longing for a child.

Verse 4: But Lord, I know You'll work good for my life, with or without a child.

The next few pages are prayers I wrote to God during the waiting period before the blood pregnancy test. I think they show several things: my trust in God, my desire for a positive result, my desire to be pleasing to God, and how far I have come.

5-22-10

Dear God,

    Well God, they're in there. Three embryos. Please Father, please let one of them become a baby. I have three chances. Please Lord, at least one. Lord, please help me over the next ten days not to worry and obsess. I know it's going to be hard. Help me to stay busy and help me to stay focused on You. Lord, Your Word says for me not to be anxious about anything, but to present my requests to You—with thanksgiving. Lord, I am so thankful to You for everything You have done to make this IVF process possible for us. Thank You, God, that everything has gone well thus far. Lord, I look at the pictures they gave us of the embryos and I am utterly amazed. To think that they are actually in my body, in my uterus, and that they might grow into a healthy baby is just mind-boggling. Father, please. Remember me. Open my womb, Lord, to receive these embryos. Lord, I'm asking You, I'm begging You and pleading with You. Please Father, we want a child. Lord, please knit a child together in my womb. Weave a child in Your fearful and wonderful way. Open my womb, Lord, please.

5-23-10

Dear Lord,

    I'm struggling, Lord. I want to lay down my will to You, but at the same time I desperately want to grasp hold of my will and keep what *I* want in first place. When Josh was preaching this morning he talked about how we need to get to the point where we want **Your** will to be done, even if it means not getting what *we* want. Lord, there is a part of me that does want Your will to be done, but there's another part of me that wants what I want. And You know what that is Lord—a baby, a healthy child. But Lord, a child may not be Your will for Josh and me and I have to get to the point where I accept that. Lord, help me! Help me surrender my will to Yours. Help me lay down at Your feet my deepest longings and help me to do so, Lord, because You are my Lord and because I want to please You, not for any other reason. Help me give up the notion that by "surrendering" my will to

Yours, that You will then give me what I desire. Help me surrender because that's what You desire, not because I think I might get something out of it. Putting You first above my desire to have a child is not a guarantee that You will then allow us to have a child. But Lord, regardless of whether or not You allow us to have a child, I want to put You first.

How can I not put You first? I've seen the incredible way You've taken care of me and protected me and guided me and helped me. How can I not put You first? I am overwhelmed with wonder and gratitude at how majestically You have worked in my life. You have brought such incredible healing to me where once was such sickness and sin. How can I not surrender everything to You? You surrendered everything for me! I look back over my life and I am blown away by how You have worked in my life to bring healing. You have blessed me above and beyond. When I see all that, I have no choice, no other option. Lord, I surrender. I surrender to You my desire to have a child and I put my trust in You and Your will. I want Your will to be done in my life. I want You to be first. I am still asking You to allow me to get pregnant and have a healthy child. Indeed, You want me to present my requests to You. But Lord, whatever happens, I accept. Help me to accept it. Lord, I know You want me to be persistent in prayer. I have been and I'll continue to be. But Lord, I recognize that in asking You for a child, I am asking knowing that Your will will be done and trusting You for that. Help me, Lord, to always put You first. Help me to be consumed, not by my desire for a child, but by my desire for You.

5-26-10

Dear Father,

Trust. That's what You want me to do. Trust You. I do trust You, Lord, and I want to trust You more. Please help me to trust You. You have brought me so far, how can I not trust You? Lord, we want to have a child. Please Father, I implore You, let us have a child. Your Word says that children are a gift from the Lord. Please Father, give us such a gift. If there is any way that my body will work to sustain a life, please Lord, allow me to carry a child.

5-28-10

Dear Lord,

It's getting close to Tuesday. I'm excited, Lord. Will it be positive? Will it be yes? Will it have worked? I pray so, Lord. Please Father, work through this IVF process to enable me to become pregnant. Lord, You are faithful—even if I don't get pregnant—You are faithful. Like that song says, "I will declare it to my heart. . . .You are faithful!"[10] Help me on Tuesday if it is negative. Help me not be devastated, but help me be hopeful for another try. Help me to trust in You. Lord, I want to trust in You. I want to be strong in my faith. Help me be strong in my faith, Lord. Lord, You know my desire, to have a child. Please Father, if there is any way, please give us the gift of a child. Lord, You are faithful. I trust You, Lord, that You know what is right and You will be with us whatever happens.

May 30, I was calm in my spirit and spent a lot of time that day reading my Bible and praying. May 31, I started getting nervous. I had some symptoms that made me think maybe I was pregnant, but I didn't know. Those symptoms could have just been caused by all the hormones I was taking. I prayed a lot that day that God would help me to be comforted the next day if the test was negative. That night I didn't sleep very well at all. And then it was June 1.

My appointment for the blood pregnancy test was at eight a.m. I was able to have the test done at my Ob-Gyn's office in our hometown, rather than having to travel to the fertility clinic two hours away. That was a blessing. We got there early, and they drew my blood at seven forty-five. The nurse told me that it would be forty-five minutes to two hours before they would get the results, but that they would call me right away. Josh told me that he wouldn't go into the office until I got the call, so we went out to breakfast and then ran a couple of errands. At nine fifteen, we were driving away from the bank when my cell phone rang. It was the doctor's office. This is how the conversation went:

> Me: Hello?
> Nurse: Rochelle?
> Me: Yes…(said expectantly)
> Nurse: This is Crystal from Dr. Davis's office.

Me: Yes…(said even more expectantly)
Nurse: How are you today?
Me: Fine (thinking to myself, *would you just tell me?!*)
Nurse: I have your results.
Me: Yes…(*come on, hurry up!*)
Nurse: Your hCG was 538.
Me: And that means…?
Nurse: It means that you're definitely pregnant!

Pregnant! I was pregnant! I started crying tears of joy and Josh was grinning from ear to ear! As soon as I got off the phone, Josh prayed a prayer of thanksgiving to God, thanking Him for the incredible blessing He had given us! We were ecstatic! About an hour later, after she had received my results by fax, the fertility nurse called me. She told me that the hCG level of 538 was very high, which often times indicates that the woman is carrying multiples. Wow! We are scheduled to go back to the fertility clinic on June 21 for my first ultrasound. We will find out then how many babies I am carrying!

The first person I called was Gary and then I called Miss Penny. The rest of the day Josh and I made phone calls and just smiled at each other. I don't know how many times I said to him that day, "I'm pregnant! We're going to have a baby!" And, of course, I had to thank God.

Dear Lord,

I am so humbled and so thankful to You for Your love to Josh and me. Lord, I'm pregnant! That is so incredible! After two years of trying, I'm actually pregnant. Oh, Father, You are so incredible. I can't believe it is actually true! You helped me get pregnant! Lord, thank You, thank You. It seems so simple to just say thank You, but that's what I have to say. I am so grateful to You for Your care and Your love. I know that You love me, even if I hadn't been able to get pregnant, You still would have been faithful to me. But what You have done by helping me get pregnant is immeasurably more than all I asked or imagined. That is so like You. I am just so full of gratitude to You, Lord. Thank You, Father. Oh, thank You!!

Lord, I pray that You will be with me and my baby (or babies) and protect us. Keep me from miscarrying. Protect us Lord, please. God, I ask You to guard us.

I wrote another song two days before the pregnancy test and after we found out that we were pregnant, I added a bridge to the song.

I Want You, Lord

Verse 1: Psalm thirty-seven, four: "Delight yourself in the Lord, and He'll give you the desires of your heart."
And what desires do I have? I want a child of my own, and a long life together with my man.

Chorus: But the one desire of all that I want is You.
I want You, Lord, more than anything, for nothing I desire compares with You.
I want You, Lord, how my heart does sing,
above all other wants and other desires, I want You.

Verse 2: I may not get all that I want, for life, it sometimes is not fair,
but You promise You will meet all of my needs.
And what need do I have that's greater than
my need of God?
Well I can't think of a thing greater than that.

Chorus: So I say, the one desire of all that I want is You.
I want You, Lord, more than anything, for nothing I desire compares with You.
I want You, Lord, how my heart does sing,
above all other wants and other desires, I want You.

Bridge: Well, Lord, You're amazing and Your love is immeasurably
more than I could imagine or even think
and I thank You for my child.

Chorus: And still the one desire of all that I want is You.
I want You, Lord, more than anything, for nothing I desire compares with You.
I want You, Lord, how my heart does sing,
above all other wants and other desires, I want You.

CHAPTER 41: TRUST

Over the next couple of weeks our friends were teasing us, telling us that we were going to have triplets. We wouldn't know until June 21 how many babies I was carrying, but they were teasing us, nonetheless. Josh's family came to visit us the weekend after we found out and brought us our first baby gift. Or should I say gifts – plural. His mom had hand-crocheted three baby blankets, one for each potential baby! We are both looking forward to my doctor's appointment on June 21 so that we will know what to expect, how many to expect! But in the meanwhile, we had a trip to make. It was time to meet with my mother at Gary's office.

Josh and I decided after talking with Gary, that if the week went well, at the end of the week, we would tell my mother that I am pregnant. *If* the week went well. It was a good thing I was so excited about the baby (or babies!) because that kept me from obsessing about the upcoming week with my mother. In fact, amazingly, I was extremely calm about it. I was calm because I was trusting in God and in Gary to get me through the week.

42
Face-To-Face

Face to face,
like Dorothy and the
lion,
the scarecrow, and
tin man,
standing before the
great
Wizard of Oz,
trembling,
shaking,
full of fear and
trepidation,
terrified by his
great power
and awe;
or,
like the next scene
where the Wizard
is revealed
for who he
truly is,
a little old man
behind a curtain,
speaking into a microphone,
frantically
turning knobs and
pushing buttons,
inspiring
laughter
and relief
and pity.
Face to face.

On Monday, June 14, Josh and I arrived for our big week of meetings with my mother and Gary. At five p.m., Josh and I met with Gary and planned out the week. My mother was supposed to arrive at six. I had been pretty calm and hadn't worried during the eight-hour drive, but when we walked into Gary's office, the anxiety hit. I was more tense than anxious. While we were planning, Gary devised a signal. If he saw that I was responding to my mother as the little girl rather than as my wise adult, he would click his pen. During the whole week, I only got clicked once!

It was a little awkward when my mother first arrived, but we got through the preliminaries and Gary had Josh start the first session with a prayer, as he did all week. Gary did a marvelous job of facilitating the meetings. In the first session, Gary had me begin by reading aloud the letter I had sent in February. Then Gary had my mother read aloud her e-mail response. Gary asked me to elaborate on my story. I began with middle school, when the depression started, and I told my story. I elaborated on the depression, the suicidal feelings, the cutting. I talked about my hospitalizations in 1992 and 1993 and how I felt my mother had responded. I talked about the clues and the memories that had come back. I gave details about the sexual abuse and my grandfather. I was a little frightened saying these things to her, but at the same time, I was empowered because I was saying them. The fear was not winning. And the whole time, I felt like my adult was in charge. My mother expressed her sorrow over not knowing the signs of child sexual abuse. She also admitted that she had idolized her father, which made it harder for her to deal with my accusation. We only had one hour that evening, and reading the letters and telling my story took most of the time. But the next day we planned to meet with her for two hours. Gary and I decided that I should proceed topically, and he asked Josh and me to think about what topics we wanted to cover on Tuesday.

The next morning I was still tense. We had decided to cover four topics: her anger at me about the accusation, her lack of regard for my mental health problems, her calling me a rotten kid, and the physical abuse.

We first addressed her anger about my accusation of my grandfather's sexual abuse when I was hospitalized in 1992. She admitted that she wasn't happy with me telling any details to anyone because she felt that the family problems should stay private. She didn't want people to know what her dad had done. Then she said that from her youth on, she had internalized that people had to handle their problems on their own or they were weak. From that point on, I relaxed. I realized that I had nothing to fear in her. She was the one who was weak. After a lifetime of reaching out and seeking help for my problems, I know for a fact that it takes incredible strength and courage to admit you need help. It's not a sign of weakness, but a sign of strength and courage and intelligence. And humility. Pride often keeps people from asking for help. And so with that comment, I realized something very fundamental about my mother—she is a very weak and prideful person. I was sitting across from her in a position of strength, while she was in a position of weakness. I had nothing to be afraid of. That comment was a turning point for me.

She told me that she was angry that I wanted to tell people, but she was also angry at her dad and what he had done to me. She said hearing my accusation destroyed her faith in her father and what she thought was a wonderful childhood, both hers and mine. Gary stated that her "seeking help is a sign of weakness" philosophy was part of her personality structure, and that she had a tremendous amount of hurt in dealing with her disappointment with her father. Gary said, "The truth is, you were terribly hurt and very angry. Your anger was about what had happened and about the fact that it was being made public. Can you see how Rochelle felt you were angry at her?" My mother said she could. She said she didn't respect my reaching out and Gary pointed out that, to me, that seemed like abandonment. Gary told her that I needed a sincere apology, which she proceeded to give me.

The issue of her anger at my accusation and her lack of concern for my mental health problems sort of melded together at times. My mother didn't want me telling people and yet, as Gary said to her, it was the not telling, the hiding and internalizing, that made me so sick, so much so that I was almost two people. He told her that I was trying to live up to her image, and yet her philosophy prevented the very intimacy that we both wanted. Gary emphasized how much fear I've had of her, especially of writing and sending my letter. He said to my mother, "You didn't want that, but it's come to that because of your philosophy."

We talked about the lack of boundaries and privacy and how they masqueraded as intimacy. She thought we were emotionally close, but that just wasn't the case. At one point, she said to Gary, "Rochelle was an extension of me." I agreed that that was how it had seemed. My mother said she was realizing that I'd had more emotional distress and hurt than she'd ever had and more than she'd ever imagined. She admitted that she had built a fantasy, and said she had tried to make everything great for me since I didn't have a dad. She said this has all been devastating to her. Gary said, "Devastation is a good concept. When you build something crooked, you have to tear down and start over. That's what this week is about—rebuilding."

My mother admitted that she was very controlling, and she said she felt threatened when I moved out to go back to school. She feared losing me when I got married. She wanted me to have my own life with Josh, but she still wanted to have me as hers. Gary acknowledged that it was probably extra hard for her to let go because she didn't have a husband. I had become her life. Mom said, "I wanted Rochelle to be her own person, but I feared losing her." That's why she was so controlling. Throughout all of this, Gary brought her to the point of sincere apology several times. My mother would genuinely apologize and ask for my forgiveness, which I extended.

After I felt like we had sufficiently dealt with the issues of her anger at the accusation and her lack of concern for my mental health problems, we moved on to the next issue—her calling me a rotten kid. This one was hard for me because it connected to everything about the abuse. Because she had called me a rotten kid so many times, in my mind, that meant that the abuse was my fault. When I heard her say I was a rotten kid, I heard an indictment. I got what I deserved. I told her that she had obviously blocked out using the word *rotten*, but *rotten* was the exact word she had used on many occasions. Gary noted that Josh had witnessed her calling me a rotten kid. She agreed that she had blocked out using that word. She said I was a very strong-willed child, and a very difficult child, but she'd always been proud of how I had turned out. She confessed that she was overwhelmed by my behavior as a child, because when she was a child, she never gave her mom any problems in public.

Gary pointed out, "In Rochelle's mind, *rotten kid* felt like she deserved the abuse." Mom replied, "No one deserves abuse. I'm the one who was confused. I didn't see it as putting her down. Now I'm afraid to say anything, afraid of how it might be construed." Gary said, "You now know abuse was taking place in those years. Something in that statement made her think she was a bad kid. She had a secret to keep. She didn't want your dad to die, so she had to keep the secret. And when you told her that she was a rotten kid, she felt that she wasn't validated as a good

Chapter 42: Face-to-Face

child." Once again, Gary brought my mother to the point of apology. She stated, "I said it in humor, but you didn't take it that way and I'm sorry. You were not a bad kid or a rotten kid. You were a fun little kid. I didn't view you as a bad, corrupted kid that deserved to be abused. I see now that there was a real reason for it. You weren't a rotten kid, you were acting out. I'm so sorry."

With about thirty minutes left in the two-hour session, the issue of the physical abuse at her hands remained to be tackled. This was the hardest issue to deal with for me. Even though I knew she was weak, I was still afraid of her reaction. Gary helped me start by telling her that I felt as if she had disciplined me very angrily. My mother responded by saying that she felt very confused, shocked, and horrified to think that I thought she was abusing me. She never dreamed I was scared of her. She said that when she spanked me she would give me one swat with the paddle and that she only used the belt one time. She said she tried to discipline me correctly, but got very frustrated. I told her the memory I had of the green ottoman incident, in which I tried to hide behind the green ottoman while she was swinging at me and lashing out at me in anger. She voiced her shock at my use of the word *swinging*, but said she was sorry that she didn't know how to do it right. She said, "I loved you, but I had such a hard time with your actions. I tried to tell you 'I love you' a lot. I'm sorry I wasn't adequate at handling discipline in a better way."

Gary tried to bring some clarity to the conversation by pointing out that it is hard to separate what was happening to me with the sexual abuse from the acting out I was doing as a child. Mom couldn't understand why I wouldn't mind her, but it was easy to see now. Gary said it was a complicated thing. Abuse was taking place and I felt misunderstood. My acting out was a call for help, but instead of help, I got punished. Gary told my mother that he knew this discussion hurt her deeply, but these things needed to be said. He acknowledged that it hurt her to realize that my acting out was really a cry for help, and that it hurt her even more to realize that instead of helping, she had actually made it worse. But, he noted, she was validating me now and helping me now by her candor in admitting her mistakes and sincerely apologizing for them.

As the session wound down, my mother asked Gary, "What happens to a man to make him change like that? He wasn't like that when I was a child. He was honorable and kind and loving and gentle. What would make him do that? How does that happen to a person? I'm having an extremely hard time bringing this all together. I hate what he did to my daughter, but I loved him all my life. What do I do with that? I don't know how to make them coexist." Gary acknowledged her hurt and confusion and said she obviously had some grieving to do. She would have to work through some of her own issues.

After that two-hour session, I was exhausted, but feeling good. I thought things had gone very well. When we met with Gary afterward, without my mother, he said he was very proud of me and also of my mother. He said that we were further down the road than he thought we'd be by this point and he was encouraged. Josh thought her apologies had been genuine, and he was surprised of how aware she was of her own philosophy that "seeking help is a sign of weakness." Gary said that even though she is aware of her philosophy, she admits that she doesn't know why she feels that way. But, he remarked, the same man who told me not to tell anyone also raised her. Although I had tried to keep that same philosophy in relation to her, I was now challenging it with the most feared person of my life. And I was surviving. He wanted to make it clear to me that forgiving her doesn't mean that I could now trust her. He said, "I don't want your little girl thinking, 'Oh, now I can tell her everything.'" He stressed that I needed to be careful my child doesn't take over, thinking she's found her long lost mother. My mother would still be controlling without even realizing it, and her perception of a mother/daughter relationship was still enmeshed. Obviously, she has her own therapy issues.

After we left Gary's office that day, Josh and I spent a wonderful afternoon sharing our pregnancy news with our friends. We went out to eat that night at our favorite restaurant. The next morning I had an appointment with Dr. Patel, who was very encouraged by the many positive things that were happening. I told him that I'd like to try to start going off of the Risperdal so that I would be able to breastfeed the baby. I could safely take the Risperdal while pregnant, but not while breastfeeding. He was concerned about mood swings if I stopped taking it, but he was willing to try. He told me to cut back by a quarter of a tablet for two weeks and then another quarter every two weeks. He suggested I try this and see how far I was able to go, using sleep as a gauge. He just wanted me to be aware that the number one thing to avoid was depression and psychosis.

CHAPTER 42: FACE-TO-FACE

On Wednesday we arrived at Gary's office before my mother. I told Gary I'd like to tell her about the pregnancy. He advised me to wait because the little girl doesn't want to be eclipsed by the new child just yet. He suggested that we use that day for a gradual reconnecting and a discussion about boundaries. When my mother arrived, Gary checked in with everyone to see how we were feeling after the last two days. My mother was feeling sorry for herself, but that made her irritated because I was the one with the damage. She felt sorry for herself because she didn't really have a life anymore. She wasn't the person she thought she was and she felt very alone. But she had spent a lot of time thinking about me and what I had suffered. Gary said she was going through a process of hearing it and processing it and then, she would have to grieve it. When he asked how Josh and I felt, we both said we felt positive and encouraged. Josh was glad I was able to articulate my concerns, pleased with my courage and strength, and pleased with my mother's response.

At this point, Gary addressed the issue of phone calls. He told my mother that in the past when I would call her a lot, especially as a visit neared, it wasn't driven by a healthy desire for contact, but by fear. He didn't want me to lapse back into that fearful pattern. He proposed that, since I wanted to reconnect with her, we start with a roughly designed weekly call. This was actually my idea and my mother wasn't happy with it. She said it sounded like a military regimen. Gary countered that it was an improvement over the past six months, to which she agreed. I said I didn't want it to be regulated like a military rule, but rather more natural. But calling every day or several times a day needed to stop. We decided to start gradually reconnecting by having a weekly phone call on Monday evenings, of course, reserving the right to call if there is something special or important or exciting.

Gary shifted the conversation to a discussion of boundaries. He told my mother that I've felt that I was just an extension of her and that there was a blurred sense of boundaries between us. He said my being her buddy, her helper, wasn't healthy. He never used the words *surrogate spouse*, but that was what he was alluding to. He said it's easy to make the kid a substitute in too many ways. He told her that I didn't need to be a child dealing with adult issues, enmeshment issues. I wanted to be connected, but I wanted to maintain my identity and not just be an extension of her. I wanted a healthy relationship, but I didn't want her in the middle of my marriage. When she expressed confusion about what I meant about her being in the middle of my marriage, I reminded her of the times she had asked about our sex life. Then she understood.

After that, Gary asked my mother about her relationship with her own mother. She talked about several things, including how over the last ten years, she and my grandmother had talked on the phone every evening. Gary noted that their relationship was somewhat unique, in that my grandmother was a widow and my mother wasn't married. But, he pointed out, he and his wife don't call their adult married children every day. He said it wouldn't be healthy for them to be overly intrusive in their children's lives. My mother admitted she felt uncomfortable with the phone call arrangement. She felt a sense of desperation. Gary told her that although she is desperately trying to clutch on to me, it will get better and she'll feel safer knowing there are good boundaries between us. We talked a little about visits to her house, and I asked if she could understand why I feared that house and why I feared coming without Josh. She said she could. Gary remarked that several missing pieces were now falling into place. Now she could understand why her friends' daughters would visit without their husbands, but I would not, And, Gary said, it wasn't because I don't love her, it was because I was working out my own demons and needed to feel safe.

In the subsequent session with Josh and me, Gary commented that the discussion that day had been a hard one for my mother because it addressed her neediness and her violation of boundaries. She admitted that some of her actions had been a frantic effort not to lose me. He warned me that when I deal with her I still need to be careful to keep my adult in charge. She won't stop being intrusive, needy, and manipulative just because we've had these talks. He cautioned me not to let my child get overly excited about the events of the week. Intellectually, my mother was signing on to what we were saying, but her personality structure was still the same. My child could easily become euphoric and forget that my adult needs to protect me.

We talked about the fact that she was feeling sorry for herself because she was realizing that she was the issue. We were challenging a lot of aspects of her life: her fantasy of our mother-daughter relationship, her view of her father, her fantasy of her own mental health. He quipped, "She thinks she's strong, but she's as weak as a noodle. She has lots of friends, but she's not transparent." He reiterated that I shouldn't worry about

CHAPTER 42: Face-To-Face

healing her. He didn't know how much she would change, but I would have a changed relationship because I have changed things. He likened her to the Wizard of Oz, not frightening after the curtain is pulled back. He advised me to protect myself and our baby with boundaries. There will always need to be boundaries. My forgiveness doesn't make the consequences go away.

We decided that the next day, Thursday, we would tell her that we were pregnant. That morning when I woke up, I panicked. I saw blood on my panties. I knew from what I'd read that spotting was normal, but I was scared. What if it was the beginning of a miscarriage? I called my doctor's office and left a message and I called a friend who had done in vitro fertilization and had started out carrying twins, but had lost one. She calmed me, encouraged me not to panic, but to rest, keep my feet up, try to stay calm, and wait to hear from my doctor. I did calm down, and I spent quite a bit of time praying.

When we arrived at Gary's office, Josh and I were able to talk to him before my mother got there. I was concerned. Should I still tell her or not? Gary made the point that a healthy relationship involves both the highs and the lows. Until now, I've tried to keep all bad news from my mother. That's the little girl wanting to protect Mother. And, he said, I was still pregnant. I needed to remember that. I wasn't having heavy bleeding nor was I having cramps. I was just spotting. So I decided to go ahead and tell.

When my mom got there, Gary started the session by asking the three of us how we felt about the week so far. We processed some things and Gary summarized his thoughts about the week. He reminded us that my mother had adequately expressed her sorrow over the things she had done and I had forgiven her and was at peace. He felt that the week, though painful, had been very productive. It was a long time needing to come. And, he admitted, I couldn't have done this even last year. He also talked about how Josh had added stability to the whole picture for me. My mother affirmed Josh too, saying it was obvious that he was perfect for me and that we complemented each other beautifully.

Then Gary said the ball was in my court and asked where I wanted to start. I looked at my mother and said to her, "There is something that I want to discuss today, but first I have to give you something." Out of my bag I pulled a grandma's photo book that I'd bought for my mother. The cover said, "Grandkids love you the best," and inside I had written,

"Mom, Congratulations Grandma! Love, Rochelle and Josh." I had also put a copy of the pictures of the three embryos in it. Handing it to her, I said, "I want to give you this because you're going to need it" and I waited for her response. She took the book and looked at it, puzzled, but I could tell the instant she understood. She looked at me and eagerly asked, "Really?" I nodded and she started crying. She jumped up and hugged both Josh and me, full of congratulations and joy. I then told her the story of how Josh and I had decided two years ago that we did want to try to have a child, all the way through the whole fertility process. She kept looking at the pictures and holding the book to her chest. Over and over, she told me how happy she was for us. And for her, too, because she wanted grandchildren so much. At one point, she said now she could understand why I couldn't think about getting pregnant and having a child before, when I was dealing with so much. Then she asked, "Do you think you'll ever trust me with your children?" I said, "I hope so." And Gary said, "That's what this week is all about. That's the goal."

After my mother left that day, Gary asked me to make a list of things I still wanted to address with her, either the next day, or in subsequent sessions several months from now. The three of us talked about a number of things, and I listed fifteen items in my journal.

1. I want to see her respect healthier boundaries.
2. I want to see her in therapy so she can be healthy.
3. She needs to deal with image—got to look good and strong on the outside; the idea that asking for help is a sign of weakness.
4. I don't want her being enmeshed with our child/children.
5. I don't want criticism and praise at the same time.
6. I don't want my children shamed.
7. I don't want them smothered.
8. She won't be the disciplinarian. I want her to respect/not undermine any discipline parameters Josh and I set up.
9. I will welcome suggestions, but I don't want her to be pushy.
10. I want her to have a healthy self-esteem that isn't based on image or externals.
11. I want her to deal with her narcissism. She sees everything from her own little world.
12. I don't want negativity or a critical attitude.

CHAPTER 42: FACE-TO-FACE

13. I have to be on my guard against her theology. It galled Jesus when people preached at others about a speck in their eye when they have a beam in their own eye, like she did when she left that page of guilting Scriptures. I don't trust her to have a healthy theology.
14. She needs to deal with her penchant for manipulation.
15. I would like to see her deal honestly with issues regarding her pregnancy, marriage and divorce, to be honest about her past.

We decided that Gary would address some of these issues with my mother the next day, particularly the issue of her seeking therapy. He said that would be better coming from him. Some of the other issues would best be discussed in a few months.

On Friday, Gary recapped the week. He reviewed the four major concerns that I had put on the table, my mother's responses and apologies, and my subsequent extensions of forgiveness. He said we had established truth and boundaries and the foundation for a new, healthier relationship. Then he addressed the question of where to go from here. He said that being able to revisit old hurts in a therapeutic context this week had freed me from my struggle of fearing my mother. Truth had prevailed. Now we could have healthy dialogue, and I would have my mother's support and prayers for our baby.

He then addressed my mother. He pointed out that this week hadn't been about doing therapy with her; it had been about dealing with my issues. He encouraged my mother to get individual therapy. He said, "That is hard for you because of your weakness mindset. You have probably cut yourself off from the feelings that would make you vulnerable. You need to address how you manage your world, which is that you try to control it. You need to put your own past on the table. You have hurts that you need to deal with over what your father did to Rochelle. You need to deal with your own marriage and divorce. Rochelle told me that you and her father made a pact never to tell her the truth. You need to deal with truth." He emphasized that trying to control the external image had made me a sick girl, and it was very unhealthy to try to make the outside look good without dealing with the inside. "You help other people, but you don't get help for yourself. You need to do this for yourself. You're not living the abundant life," he told her. He reminded her that she had asked if I would ever be able to trust her with our children. He told her she would enjoy her grandkids more if she got healthier. And he encouraged her with the knowledge that things do get better, wellness is possible, and he used me as an example. He gave her some suggestions on finding a good therapist and encouraged her to find out if the therapist had experience dealing with Axis II personality disorders, because her problems were in her personality structure. He explained how personality disorders develop. It starts out as a way we learn to protect ourselves, but then the very thing that protects us becomes our undoing. The very thing that protects you also insulates you from emotional closeness. If she got help, she wouldn't have to work so hard at trying to look good. Then Gary told us that he was proud of both of us. He was hoping for this outcome, but things had exceeded his expectations. He thanked Josh for his patience and for the support and courage he gave to me. Then, as Gary had done every day that week, he closed the session and the week with a prayer.

Josh and I had one final session with Gary after my mother left. He reiterated that we were way ahead of what he had expected, but he cautioned me not to get carried away. Her basic personality structure hadn't changed just because of this week. He had no doubt of her love for me, but he also had no doubt as to her level of dysfunction. He advised me to be on my guard. People like my mother take a blow and then start qualifying, justifying, and backtracking. But even if she did, the relationship would be different because I am different. I've seen that she is a paper-mache monster and that truth has won. He warned against letting my little girl go rushing to her rescue, but he praised me for handling myself as an adult during the week. I had protected the little girl and spoken truth. I had faced the biggest fear of my life and prevailed. He reminded me that she is a frail human being with tricks in her bag, and she would try to pull me into enmeshment. I needed to make sure that I didn't get so excited that the little girl wants to jump out and fix her, comfort her, and rescue her. She will have to grieve some things and forgive herself. He cautioned me not to let her pull me into therapy issues. If she tried, I needed to tell her that it's a therapy issue and she needed to discuss it with her therapist. It isn't my job to get my mother into therapy. It isn't about healing Mom. Whether she gets therapy is immaterial to our relationship. I will still have good boundaries. I'm not going to be her husband, her mother, her sister, or her therapist.

I told Gary that the week had brought about an incredible amount of healing for me. There would still be issues that I need to address with

CHAPTER 42: FACE-TO-FACE

my mother in the future, especially regarding boundaries with our baby and her involvement with her grandchild. We tentatively discussed scheduling another series of sessions in September or October before the baby is born.

We were almost finished, but before Josh and I left, we needed to tell Gary something important. I said, "We want you to know that if we have a son, his middle name is going to be Gary." He immediately put his hands to his heart and said, "You honor me. Wow! Thank you so much." Then I said, "Thank *you*, Gary."

43
The Big Picture

The Big Picture,
like watching a story
unfold
on a huge movie screen,
when before
you had only watched it
on a tiny
six-inch, black and white TV;
or,
like a photographer
focusing his lens,
adjusting the zoom,
and capturing
the whole scene
on film;
or,
like a detective,
finally figuring out
the last clue,
thus solving
the mystery;
or,
like someone putting together
a 3,000 piece puzzle,
starting with the corners
and borders,
slowly, painstakingly
filling in the picture
until finally,
after hours of
grueling work,

back aching from
bending over the pieces,
she picks up the
last piece
and snaps it into place.
The Big Picture.

The ultrasound I had on June 21 confirmed that I was carrying only one baby. I had started out carrying twins, but one of the babies had stopped growing. The doctor said that the bleeding I had was probably when I lost that one. But the other baby had a very strong heartbeat. Because of our ages, we were anxious about whether our child would be healthy. However, Josh and I decided not to do an amniocentesis or any other tests for birth defects. For one thing, miscarriage is a risk for all of the tests. For another, it wouldn't make any difference in our love for our child if we learned it had a birth defect. Our child is a gift from God regardless of its health. The final reason we decided not to do the tests was that I was tired of living controlled by my anxiety. Once we made the decision not to have the tests, I quit worrying about it. I prayed often for our child to be healthy, but the anxiety about it went away. I was not giving control to my anxiety. If our child were born with a defect, we would deal with it, but we would love our child regardless. I felt good about not giving my anxiety control.

Control

Life is a risk
with no guarantees,
full of trap doors and surprises,
both calm and rough seas.

I want to grasp hold
and cling to control.
I want all of my plans
to work perfectly to reach my goals.

But I've discovered in life
that it doesn't work this way,

CHAPTER 43: THE BIG PICTURE

there're too many things
out of my control each day.

That's frightening to me,
to think control is not there,
it gives me anxiety,
it gives me a scare.

But there's one thing I must remember
in this unsure world—
I don't have to be in control
as my life is unfurled.

As I give up control—
and this concept is so odd—
I'm really at peace knowing
life is controlled by our God.

God is the One who is in
control of this life.
He reigns supreme whether
there is serenity or strife.

And He will work good
out of whatever may be.
He can bring about good
out of trial, stress, tragedy.

So when I come up against
a situation where I feel out of control,
I need to remind myself that God is in charge
and that will give peace to my soul.

Things with my mother were going fairly well. We talked on the phone every Monday evening, and I actually enjoyed most of our conversations since the fear and uncomfortable feelings weren't lurking in the background. I was pretty sure my mother hadn't done anything about finding a therapist and getting into therapy because she spent most of her summer traveling. Then the school year started again, and the start of every school year finds my mother being incredibly busy. And, I realized what my mother had done. She had latched on to the coming baby and was excited about that. Knowing her, she had pushed aside everything else from the meetings in June and put it all on the back burner. We scheduled another series of meetings with my mother and Gary for a few days at the end of September. During those meetings, I wanted to address several issues: boundaries with both me and our child, Thanksgiving and Christmas, gift-giving, and a few others. I also wanted Gary to be able to remind her of her question—"Will you ever be able to trust me with your child?" If I could see that she is seeking help for her dysfunction, then I would be much more inclined to trust her with our child. Gary cautioned me to continue setting good boundaries with her.

Over the course of several months, I continued to lower the Risperdal in an effort to go off of it completely so that I could breastfeed. My mind was much more active, to be sure, but the depression wasn't a problem. And the anxiety, although present to some degree, was under control.

July 28 was the seventh anniversary of starting therapy with Gary. He said that the progress I'd made was unbelievable. He quipped, "The first time I met you, I thought, 'Oh my, there's a lot here,' and I was not wrong! But God has been good and you've come a long way." We talked about my book and how it has helped me to clarify things along the way. I documented the journey. He said that was important, because often you forget the journey, sort of like when a mother gives birth. The joy of the child takes away the memory of the pain. He said my story needed to be out there, because so many people need to know that this type of journey can be made victoriously. He also said that my book was unique because it was written as therapy progressed. I felt good about my book and all my progress, and I wondered if I were finished with it. Should I bring it to a close? Or were there some other things that needed to be addressed?

I had a conversation with Gary about the little girl and bedtime. Since Josh and I married, I've had issues at bedtime. I love bedtime, because Josh and I will lie there talking and praying for a good while each evening. That time is very special to me, but there are aspects of it that I hate. I don't want Josh to turn out the lights and go to sleep. So I stall. And it seems like the little girl came out at bedtime, because I would get what I call playful. Josh called it obnoxious. And it was interfering with

Chapter 43: The Big Picture

our sleep. Gary suggested I let the little girl talk to me about it—why does she stall? What's going on with her at bedtime? What is she wanting? Josh and I talked about it several times, and after one particularly frustrating evening of stalling, I sat down the next morning and had a conversation with her. I wrote with my left hand when she was talking.

Little Girl, I'd like to talk with you. Will you tell me what is going on when you stall at bedtime?

> I don't want to go to sleep.

I know you don't want to go to sleep, but **why** don't you want to go to sleep?

> 'Cause I get scared.

What scares you?

> The dark.

Why?

> 'Cause it's not safe.

Why isn't it safe?

> 'Cause sometimes he comes but she doesn't always come when I call her.

He, is that Papa?

> Yeah.

And she, is that Mommie?

> Yeah.

Why do you call her?

> 'Cause I'm scared.

Why doesn't she come?

> I don't know.

Do you call her real loud?

> No.

How do you call her?

> I whisper like this – Mommie! Mommie! Mommie! But she doesn't always come.

Why do you whisper?

> I don't want him to hear me.

What happens if he hears you?

> He comes in my room.

What does he do when he comes in your room?

> He tells me not to be scared.

Is that all?

> He touches me.

How do you feel when he touches you?

> Good, but scared.

Chapter 43: The Big Picture

Why does it scare you?

'Cause I can't tell or he'll die.

When he goes back to his room, what do you do?

I lie there being scared.

Little Girl, let me ask you this, when Mommie does hear you call, what happens?

She comes.

What does she do when she comes?

She makes me feel safe.

So you aren't scared when she comes in your room at night?

No. I'm scared before she comes in. I don't like the dark or the noises in the dark. And I don't like it when Papa comes in.

But those times when she does hear you whisper her name, she comes to your room and comforts you and makes the fear go away? Is that right?

Yeah.

Honey, let me ask you a question. Now, at night, at bedtime when you stall so much, are you still afraid that Papa is going to come in and hurt you?

I don't know.

Papa can't hurt you any more ever again. And the dark can't hurt you. You are safe in our house. The doors are locked, the dogs are good watchdogs, and Josh is there to protect you.

I know.

So why do you still stall so much?

> I don't know.

When you stall with Josh, what are you thinking?

> I don't want him to go to sleep and leave me alone.

Why not?

> 'Cause I'm scared to be alone.

Why?

> I already told you!

Okay, let me ask you another question. When you stall with Josh, why do you get obnoxious?

> I'm not obnoxious! Why does everybody tell me I'm obnoxious?!!

Okay, if you're not obnoxious, what are you?

> I'm playing!!

Why do you start playing at bedtime?

> 'Cause I don't want to go to sleep! And don't ask me why 'cause I already told you why!

Okay, how does it make you feel when Josh wants you to stop playing and let him go to sleep?

> It's not fair. I don't want to be left alone and when he wants me to stop playing I feel like y'all don't want me around anymore and it makes me mad and sad.

CHAPTER 43: THE BIG PICTURE

Honey, we still want you around, but it is important that Josh gets his sleep. It's important that you and I get our sleep. Can you understand that?

Yeah, but I don't want to be left out. I like to play. I feel happy when Josh plays with me.

I'm glad you feel happy. Could you play with Josh sometime other than bedtime?

Yeah, but that's when I feel most playful.

Honey, this is something that we're going to have to work on. We don't want you to feel left out, but we've all got to get our sleep. We'll work on this together. Can we talk about this some more later?

Yeah, okay.

Later that day I kept thinking about the little girl and I felt as though she had more to say. So I sat down at the computer. What came out was a letter from the little girl to Josh.

Josh,

I don't mean to make you mad at bedtime. I just want to be with you and Rochelle. I don't want to be left out. Bedtime with y'all is safe. I want to be safe. I don't want to be alone. Rochelle has changed a lot. She doesn't let me be in charge much anymore. She doesn't let me come around much anymore. And you don't want me to come around at bedtime. But I've got to come around because if I don't y'all will forget about me.

And now y'all are gonna have a baby. I wanted a baby, but I don't want to be left behind. You talk to the baby at night and sing to the baby but you don't want me there. I don't understand. I don't want to be left out. I don't know how to still be with y'all without being playful. That seems to be the only way anymore to get y'all to notice me. But you don't think I'm playful. You think I'm obnoxious. I'm not trying to be a pest. I just want you to love me. Please don't be mad at me. I'll try to not be a pest. But you have to help me. I'm just being playful. I don't want you and Rochelle to forget about me. I don't know any other way to be with y'all. I like to be playful. It's fun. Don't you like having fun together? I want y'all to still like me.

When the baby is born am I gonna be left out and forgotten? I don't want to be left out and forgotten. If y'all have a little girl, what about me? I thought I was the little girl. I just want to be with you and Rochelle. It is safe with you. That's why I like to be with you. And I like to play with you. Because you don't get mad at me like Mommie did. She would get mad and spank me, but you don't act like her. I keep on and on because I want to make sure you aren't like her. But now you don't want me to play with you anymore. I don't know how to play any other way. Can you teach me? I like to play with you. I like being playful. I don't want to have to stop that forever. I like to have fun. I don't know any other way to play. You have to teach me to play where you don't get tired of me. I don't want you to get tired of me. I want to be with you.

I like to play at bedtime. You make bedtime safe. But now you don't want me to play at bedtime. Josh I love you. Can you help me? Promise me you won't leave me out. Promise me you won't forget about me. Promise me you won't be mad at me. Promise me I'll still be the little girl.

Josh got teary-eyed when I read it to him. He was really touched and said we needed to find a way to include her so that the little girl doesn't feel left out. He also wondered if maybe, when I am stalling so much, the little girl just wants some attention. I thought about that idea and the next day started writing about it. But as I wrote, I realized some fears. I had babysat for a friend's three-year-old earlier that week and when I had to help her in the bathroom, I felt very uncomfortable. When I mentioned it to him, Gary said that because of what happened with me, things that are normal and uneventful for others are not normal for me, especially issues of privacy and sexuality. He said what happened is called transference. Transference, he explained, occurs when there is a situation that reminds me, even unconsciously, of my childhood. When that happens, I experience emotions that are similar to the emotions I experienced as a little girl. He said it may take a while for some transference issues to be

CHAPTER 43: THE BIG PICTURE

identified and worked through. He said that my discomfort was coming from the little girl. My adult is trustworthy, but the little girl is afraid. That is why the transference occurred. As I wrote about that event, other fears came out.

> I don't know why I stall so much. I said that bedtime and the dark wasn't safe. But I said that bedtime with Josh was safe. So I don't know why I stall so much. Josh said maybe I just want attention. Maybe that's it. I like being with Josh. When he turns out the light and goes to sleep I don't get to be with him anymore. Then it's just Rochelle. I like Josh better than Rochelle. Josh plays with me and he doesn't get mad at me. I know Rochelle doesn't get mad at me like she used to. But Josh is fun. Being with Rochelle is complicated. But not with Josh.

Little Girl, tell me what was going on with you on Wednesday when you felt uncomfortable when I was helping Emily pull up her panties after she went potty. Gary said the uncomfortable feeling was coming from you. He said to ask you why you felt uncomfortable and what you were thinking and feeling. He said to ask you why it felt dangerous. So, will you tell me?

> She didn't have her panties on. That's not safe. Panties protect. But she didn't have hers on. You had to put them on for her. How do I know you're gonna be safe with her? Little girls are dangerous because people hurt them. It felt dangerous because she couldn't protect herself. There wasn't anything there to protect her 'cause her panties were off.

I didn't hurt her, Little Girl. All I did was pull up her panties and help her get her shorts on. She was safe with me.

> I know. But it still felt scary. I don't like being with my panties off. And you know what else feels dangerous? Talking with Mommie about breastfeeding your baby. I know what that is. That's when you have to take your bra off and feed the baby with your booby. You and Josh were looking at stuff for that at the store yesterday. He couldn't help you 'cause he didn't

> know what to buy. But I don't want Mommie telling you what to buy or talking to you about it 'cause that doesn't feel safe. That's a private part. She doesn't do good with private parts. I don't want her talking about that with you. That's not safe.

Honey, when our baby is born, I am going to have to change his or her diaper. Josh will do that, too. And we'll have to give the baby a bath and clean his or her private parts because babies can't do that by themselves. And I'll have to help the baby do that for several years until he or she gets old enough to do it by himself. But I'll be safe with the baby. I promise, Little Girl, I won't hurt the baby. Can you trust me?

> I know what you are saying is true, but it's scary for me. It's uncomfortable. I don't want anything to happen. You say you won't hurt the baby and I believe you, but I'm still nervous. It just seems dangerous. I know babies are helpless and can't do things by themselves. I know you'll have to do things. But I don't want to be uncomfortable every time you take care of the baby. What can I do?

Little Girl, you can look at how I've been getting so well. I haven't hurt you in a long, long time. I promised you I wouldn't hurt you. I'm not going to hurt you and I will not hurt our baby. And I'm setting boundaries with Mother and acting in healthy ways, lots of healthy ways. Look at how well I've gotten. That should help you be able to trust me. And listen to Josh and Gary. They trust me. Follow their lead.

> I know you won't hurt the baby, but what if someone else does? I think that's what I worry about the most.

So do I, Little Girl. So do I.

That's something I've worried about for the last two years since we started trying to get pregnant. I can't imagine it ever happening, but what if we have a little girl and someday she hears about sexual abuse and she says Josh did something to her. He would never do anything like that. What if

CHAPTER 43: THE BIG PICTURE

someone puts thoughts in her head and she says that and it isn't true? What would I do? I know this is stupid to worry about because I can't fathom that ever happening because I know Josh, and I know he would never hurt our child, or any child. But what if someone else puts ideas into her head? We heard recently about a man who was falsely accused of child sexual abuse. Part of me felt sorry for him, but part of me knows that even though I believe him, I'm going to keep my child far away from him. What if someone influences our daughter and she makes claims that aren't true? How would I know if they were true or not? I feel like I'm betraying Josh by just thinking these things. He'd never do that. So why do I even worry about this. I don't worry about him doing anything. I worry about someone putting ideas into our child's head and causing her to make false claims. And that gets into a whole other realm. False claims versus truth. Being believed. Betraying self. I'm all mixed up about this. I've been thinking about this and worrying about it for two years now, but I haven't voiced it to Josh or Gary. I've been afraid to. I'm all mixed up. And now that I'm actually pregnant, I've been thinking about it a lot more. In the middle of September if we find out we're having a girl, I'll think about it even more. This is the one reason I don't want to have a girl. So what do I do with all this mixed up, confused thinking? Help me.

When I talked with Gary about what I'd written, he said my fears were coming from the little girl. I say in that last paragraph, "I know." My adult does know that it's not something to worry about. It's the little girl who is worried. He said it wasn't surprising that I was having these fears. He assured me that false claims of sexual abuse were very unusual. He said that in all his years of doing therapy with people, he'd only had one case like that and it was a teenage girl who was mad at her dad. He said false claims happen in highly dysfunctional families. Josh and I, he reassured me, have a healthy family and we're going to raise a healthy child. He reminded me about our discussion of control, and advised me not to let my anxiety get control here. He said one reason my mind was being more active and worrying was that I was off so much of my medication. The meds had repressed excessive thought; they had suppressed the anxiety. By being off so much of my medicine, I was seeing increased mental activity. Gary said I needed to work at identifying it and trying to control it. Say to my anxiety, "I'm on to you. You're not going to get control here." And he suggested that anything I'm worrying about that looks much past tomorrow or the next day is probably the anxiety. After we talked about it, my anxiety lessened and I quit worrying about my fears. I've noticed through the years that when I recognize the anxiety, voice it, and talk through it, it seems to lose its power. In other words, I am controlling it.

I was feeling quite well, my pregnancy was progressing well, I had the anxiety under control, I was continuing to lower the dosage of the Risperdal, and things seemed to be going fairly smoothly with my mother. On Tuesday, August 17, I had a good session with Gary. That evening Josh and I went to a bookstore, where a particular book caught my attention. I bought it, took it home and read the entire thing that evening. And it really affected me. It brought up the final core issues that I still needed to work through. It brought up a lot of pain. The next day I sat down and started typing.

I got a book at the bookstore, a novel about a teenager who had started having memories of childhood sexual abuse. She started cutting herself when she started having memories. It was a powerful book and really got to me. It made me realize that there are two core issues that I haven't dealt with yet.

First, is forgiving my grandfather. Only since last October have I really focused on my feelings toward my grandfather. Last fall I started getting angry at him. But the anger didn't get to the full-blown fury stage until February/March. That letter I wrote to Papa in March and the punching episodes I had about him were very powerful and full of rage. I asked at the end of that letter if you have to forgive someone who is dead. Josh and I were talking about forgiveness last night. The Bible makes it clear in Matthew 6 that if you don't forgive, you won't be forgiven. But Luke 17:1-4 talks about forgiveness, too. Jesus says there that if your brother sins against you **and repents**, you are to forgive him. That's a condition to forgiveness that Jesus doesn't say in Matthew 6. Are we really expected to forgive someone if they don't repent? Even God doesn't forgive without repentance. The Bible makes that very clear. Are we to be expected to be held to a higher standard than God? At the same time, I know that forgiveness will keep bitterness from growing in my heart. And forgiveness means not seeking vengeance. I can't seek vengeance on my grandfather because he's dead. So how do I forgive him? And does forgiveness mean anything else here? I mentioned to Josh that Jesus forgave those who

CHAPTER 43: THE BIG PICTURE

crucified Him. Josh pointed out that Jesus **asked God** to forgive them. Did God forgive them? Did God forgive them if they never repented and became Christians? Does God forgive without repentance, and if not, are we expected to do something that God doesn't do?

Obviously, my grandfather can't repent. He's dead. And I don't think he repented of the abuse before he died, because he kept on abusing me. My theory is that God knew he wasn't going to repent. He had given my grandfather plenty of opportunities. He was trying to get his attention with one heart attack after another. But the fifth one killed him, and my theory is that God knew he wasn't going to repent and that's why the fifth heart attack killed him. That's mine and Josh's theory. Don't know if it is right or not—perhaps. But regardless, I don't think my grandfather ever repented. So do I have to forgive him? And if I do, explain to me why I have to forgive him without repentance if God doesn't forgive without repentance. Of course, that issue aside, I can't keep hanging on to the bitterness and hatred and fury. But it is there.

In this novel I read, the father, her abuser, was incredibly wicked. He raped her from the time she was three until she was twelve. And when she was a little girl, he taught her to cut. He brainwashed her by having her cut herself and telling her that she would cut if she started to remember, she would cut to not tell, she would cut to forget, and if she told, she would cut to kill herself. Very different from my situation.

But there is one similarity. My grandfather taught me something, too. He taught me to masturbate. He didn't teach me to do that with malicious intent like the father in the novel did. But he did teach me to masturbate. And I used that to abuse myself. It's interesting that I had really bad flashbacks, intense and often, from September to March. The last one I had was the flashback of him masturbating me. After that, I haven't had any more since March. But that flashback was so disturbing to me because I realized where I had learned to masturbate. I have often thought, since that flashback, about the thousands of times that I masturbated over nearly twenty-five years. I carried so much shame and guilt because of all that.

The shame ate at me daily and nearly destroyed me. I was feeling shame even when I was ten years old. I described myself as shameful in the autobiography I wrote in fifth grade. And the shame and the masturbation were just horrific. I hurt myself so many times during the act of masturbating. I acted out so many times that I was being raped. And it was him! It all started with him! I hate him for that! I hate what he did to me! He nearly destroyed me. The shame and the guilt for all the years of masturbating used to grip me like the sharp talons of a demon. I blamed myself for all of that sickness and misery. But it was him!

Since I realized in March that he had taught me to masturbate, I've been so full of hatred and fury toward him. I've tried not to think about it or dwell on it, and I haven't let it out other than those two punching episodes and that letter I wrote him, but it's there. How can I forgive him for all he did to me? For all he caused me to do to myself? For all the shame? I've been angry at my mother and my book has had her as the focus for so much of it, but it all goes back to him. Even some of the issues I have with my mother go back to him. The physical abuse I experienced from her happened as a result of my acting out. My acting out happened as a result of the sexual abuse from him. It goes back to him! And my mother's image obsession and disregarding of my mental health probably go back to him, too. She said she didn't know where she got that philosophy from, but the same person who told me he would die if I told also raised her. She got it from him. Maybe some from my grandma, too, I don't know. But he started this whole mess of my life. Mom always told me I was a rotten kid. She thought I was rotten because of how I acted. And I acted the way I did because of what he was doing to me. It all goes back to him! I hate him!

I am full of bitterness and hatred and fury because of what he did to me. If I have to forgive to get rid of the bitterness and hatred, then I'll do it. How, I don't know. But it just seems so unfair. How does he deserve to be forgiven? He never repented. His wretched wickedness has affected me so deeply and so comprehensively that it makes me sick to think about it. And his wickedness still affects me. I've got all this transference going on in dealing with my own child and issues of protecting my own child. He is still affecting me. When will I stop being haunted by his ghost? I want to be free of him, but his presence and the consequences of his wickedness live with me daily. And even forgiving him doesn't mean that he stops affecting me. Oh God, please help me!

I said there were two core issues I haven't dealt with that the novel brought up for me. The second one has to do with my mother and her not protecting me. When we met with her in Gary's office, Gary pointed out that things were complicated for me as a child. Abuse was taking place and I felt very misunderstood. I was acting out and that was how I was calling for help, but instead of help, I got punished. Gary acknowledged that it hurt my mother deeply to realize that my acting out was a cry for help; but she didn't

CHAPTER 43: THE BIG PICTURE

help, she just made it worse. Those comments have sparked in me some deep thought. After reading this novel and seeing the weak, unprotecting mother character, I've been thinking even more about it. Gary's said to me numerous times that at some point I'm going to have to deal with the fact that my mother didn't protect me. But what I'm realizing now is that not only did she not protect me, she punished me instead. She just made things worse. And again, she scrubs her memory. She told us in Gary's office that she would only give me one swat when she spanked me. I have memories of way more than that. She tries to make herself look and sound good. One swat. Yeah, right. I'm crying out for help and she punishes me instead. And I felt like I deserved it. I felt like I was bad and depraved and wicked. Instead of helping me, she shamed me. She caused the shame dig in deeper because I felt I deserved to be punished. How many times did I cut to punish myself? How many times did I masturbate to punish myself? Too many to count. I felt like I deserved to be punished for all the years of masturbation and that was one reason I often cut. And the masturbation goes back to him. But the punishment mindset goes back to her. I was crying out for help. I was dying inside but I couldn't tell or he would die, so I was crying out for help in the only ways I knew how. But she didn't help. She punished me instead. But it wasn't just my behavior that was crying out. My body was crying out, too. I often had stomach aches in elementary school. And I wet the bed until I was a sophomore in high school. If those aren't cries for help, too, I don't know what is.

Why couldn't she see it? Did she not want to see it? Did she turn a blind eye to it? And her stupid mindset that seeking help for your problems is a sign of weakness! She thought she could handle the problems with me by herself. But she didn't handle them. She made them worse! I don't know that I can say that her behavior was wicked like my grandfather's, but it was abusive. And when I was in high school and wanted to go see that counselor because I was suicidal, she was so angry with me. She and my grandfather both created all these horrible problems for me and then she didn't want me to get help. If I don't call that wicked, what do I call it? How do I understand that? She told me in Gary's office that she didn't respect me for seeking help for my problems. Well, guess what, Mother? I don't respect you—for lots of reasons. I don't respect you for **not** seeking help. I don't respect you for punishing me when I was crying for help. I don't respect you for not protecting me from being sexually abused by your own father. I don't respect you for worrying so much about your stupid image.

I'm not sure what I do respect you for. It's hard to think of anything. And yet you had the nerve, the gall, to say to Josh and Gary and me that you didn't respect me for reaching out. Reaching out was the courageous thing to do. It was the intelligent thing to do, the right thing to do. How could someone not respect someone for that? And yet you didn't.

And I guess the biggest reason I don't respect her is because she didn't protect me. I've got to somehow deal with that. How could she not have known that something was wrong? Why did she ignore my cries for help? I couldn't tell her or he would die. But I needed help. I wanted help. Is it my fault she didn't help me because I didn't tell her plainly? I couldn't tell her plainly. He would die. I told her as best I could. And she didn't listen. In one of the conversations I had with the little girl last year, she said "Nobody listens to me. Nobody ever listens to me." My mother didn't listen to me. She listens to her friends and her students. Why couldn't she listen to her daughter? Why wouldn't she listen to me? Did she know back then? Did she suspect? I'll never know, because she scrubs her memory. Why didn't she listen to me? Why didn't she help me? She wants to know if I will ever trust her with my child. How can I? I couldn't trust her to care for me. What makes me think I'll ever be able to trust her to care for her grandchild? She didn't protect me—from him or from herself. What makes me think she'll protect my child? And here's another question. Can *I* protect my child?

Like I said, I've got some core issues I still need to deal with. There's still a deep, sharp pain in my heart. These are big things, core things. Gary told me a year ago that I still had some core issues that needed to be resolved, that I'm still traumatized, that I still don't have peace on some areas, that I still have unresolved pain. I didn't really understand what he was talking about then. Now I do. Now I know what the core issues are. How do I deal with them? How do I deal with them without it hurting so badly? And how long will it be before I am not so deeply affected by all of this? Will I ever get to the point that I don't live daily with the sorrow of having been an abused child? Will I look at my own child every day and see his or her precious life, and feel sorrow and regret for the life I never had, the childhood I never had? It's only about five months until our baby will be born. Our child is coming into a stable, healthy, nuclear family. Our child isn't going to have the dysfunction and sickness that existed in the family into which I was born. So, am I going to look at my child and her wonderful family, and feel sorrow for my inner child, for me? Josh will be the father to our child that I never had. I will be the mother to our child that I never

CHAPTER 43: THE BIG PICTURE

had. We will model God for our child, not abuse and abandonment. We will provide security and love, not fear and shame. It makes me glad for our child, for what he or she will have. But it makes me sad for me, for what I didn't have. Will I live the rest of my life still so affected by Mother and Grandfather? It's like I said in a poem back in February, "I want to be freed of his haunting. That is what I desire most."

After I read that piece to Josh, I started crying. We talked for a long time Wednesday evening about everything and I was weary. I wanted to talk to Gary and process everything, but I didn't have another session scheduled until Friday of the following week. I called his office on Wednesday evening and left him a message. He called me back on Thursday and told me that he was going to be traveling across the state on Friday and that we could talk then, while he was on the road. Thank God for cell phones! I called him Friday and read him the piece I had written. We focused on the first part of it, the part about my grandfather and forgiveness. He said a lot of the same things to me that he'd said last August when I was thinking about forgiveness in the context of my mother. He reminded me that God is just, and turning my grandfather over to God doesn't mean that justice won't occur. But God doesn't want us to have to carry the burden of bitterness around. The peace will come in trusting God to administer justice. Forgiveness doesn't mean he won't be punished. Forgiveness means I'm leaving it in God's hands. Forgiveness also doesn't mean that I have to give up my desire for justice. God knows and understands my hurt and anger about what happened. He understands my desire for justice. Gary encouraged me to be patient with myself; after all, it's only been recently that I've been able to acknowledge all that my grandfather had done. I understood all of what Gary was saying to me, but I was feeling so much hurt. After I got off the phone, I went down to Josh's office and talked to him for a while. That evening after dinner I cried for a long time. I was so full of pain. On Saturday I wrote about what I was thinking and feeling.

I've been really having a hard time since my session with Gary yesterday. Actually, since I read that book on Tuesday evening. But yesterday was really tough. I think I took about ten pages of notes during my session with Gary, and then I went down to Josh's office and talked to him for an hour and took five more pages of notes. I understand what Gary was telling me about God and justice and all. At least my adult understands. And I told Josh that the problem I'm having is not with God meting out justice if my grandfather never repented. If Papa never repented, God will punish him severely. I have no doubt of that. But what if he repented? What if, as he was having his last heart attack, he cried out to God, "I'm sorry God, please forgive me"? What then? What if he did that? How can he enjoy heaven after what he did? He hurt me so much! One thing Gary said yesterday was, "Why wouldn't we want his salvation?" I told him, "Because he hurt me so much." Not only did he hurt me, he caused me to sin. He taught me to masturbate. I hurt myself so badly with that for almost twenty-five years. Luke 17:1-2 says, "Jesus said to his disciples: 'Things that cause people to sin are bound to come, but woe to that person through whom they come. It would be better for him to be thrown into the sea with a millstone tied around his neck than for him to cause one of these little ones to sin.'" He caused me to sin. He caused one of God's little ones to sin. And Jesus says, "Woe to that person." If my grandfather had a death bed repentance, and then slipped into heaven, how is that woe? Josh said, first of all, God knows the heart. If there is true repentance, that is one thing, but if the person is repenting on his death bed just to try to avoid hell, well, God knows the heart. Josh also didn't think the little girl needs to be tormented by the thought that everything is hunky-dory with my grandfather. Josh said that if he had really repented, he didn't think that God would have taken his life, but would have given him the opportunity to confess and face the music. He said Satan's the one who offers the easy way out. Then he talked to me about something that Gary mentioned. Gary referenced 2 Thessalonians 2:11-12, which says that God sends a powerful delusion to those who refuse to love the truth but delight in wickedness so that they will believe the lie and not be able to repent, but will be condemned. Gary pointed out that there comes a point when a person can no longer repent. Josh said that there are some things a person can do that are so egregious that God doesn't let you repent. He referenced Romans 1 where Paul talks about the progression of sin. When people keep on sinning, eventually God gives them over to a depraved mind. They can no longer repent. Josh said that my grandfather abandoned natural relations and committed sin that was so egregious, so far beyond the pale, that Josh thinks God gave him over to his depraved mind. At least, that's what it seems happened according to Romans 1. He thinks that if God were going to save my grandfather in eternity because he repented, He would have punished him in this

CHAPTER 43: THE BIG PICTURE

life. Obviously, on this side of eternity, we don't know with 100 percent certainty, but based on what we do know, Josh said we don't have much reason to suspect that he died in a saved position. Gary mentioned that my grandfather, as the perpetrator, also lived with guilt and shame. Josh said, "Maybe so, but how much? When you keep violating your conscience, your conscience stops operating properly, at least in respect to that sin."

Of course, I talk about a possible death-bed repentance, but my grandfather's last heart attack happened in his sleep. He never regained consciousness. Josh told me that Gary is correct. I have to trust that God will do right. He reminded me of what Abraham said in Genesis 18:25, "Will not the Judge of all the earth do right?" I have to trust God to do what is right with respect to my grandfather. The little girl says that it's not fair that he would get to enjoy heaven after what he did. Josh said grace and mercy aren't fair, that's right, but my grandfather turned his back on God's grace when he turned his back on God's will. I guess the little girl is comforted by knowing that he probably didn't repent and that he's being punished. At least there's no evidence that he repented. And a part of me, a strong part, hopes he didn't. I want him to be punished. And then I feel guilty saying this because, as Gary said yesterday, "Why wouldn't we want his salvation?" And I have the same answer today that I had yesterday—because he hurt me so bad! He may not have been a literal monster, but he was a human being who did monstrous things. He wasn't just sick, he was wicked. And yes, he may have had his own struggles, but he didn't seek help for his struggles. Instead he turned his struggles into wicked, sinful, monstrous behavior toward me. And I wonder where my mother got her mindset that seeking help is a sign of weakness? It seems pretty obvious to me.

Anyway, I'm just having an incredibly hard time. I know that God's grace **can** reach a child molester, but I don't want it to reach him. I want **him** to be punished. I don't want him to be punished in Christ's blood. I want him personally to be punished. And I know that that desire puts me on precarious ground, because I **don't** want **me** to be punished personally. I want me to be punished in Christ's blood. But I am just full of so much hurt because of what my grandfather did. As Gary said, with my grandfather it gets personal. And that's where I am today—drowning in the hurt.

Last night after dinner, Josh and I were talking about the hurt. I told him I feel like I have come so far in respect to my mother, but with my grandfather, I feel like I am just starting. When I first began therapy with Gary, I wrote pages and pages about hurt. The hurt was staring me in the face and I couldn't think of anything else. But out of all those pages, very, very little was about the hurt my grandfather caused me. And I guess that's because I wasn't focusing on my grandfather much then. It's only been in the last year or so that I've really focused on him. And the hurt and anger toward him have only started recently. I started therapy with hurt and now, seven years later, I'm back to the same place. Josh said that, in dealing with the hurt, it's like I've had to go back in time. I've mentioned before that therapy has been like peeling away layers of an onion. I thought that dealing with my mother and my fear of her was the last layer. This week has shown me that it's not. It seems like the last layer is my grandfather and all the hurt he caused me. Last night I cried so hard when I was talking to Josh about how badly my grandfather hurt me. Josh said I was draining some of the pain. But there's still so much there.

He hurt me so bad! Image after image crosses my mind of the times I masturbated, the times I hurt myself doing it, the times I raped myself. My grandfather started a lifetime of self-abuse that nearly destroyed me. For almost twenty-five **years** I masturbated. And the shame of that ate away at my very soul. I hated myself. I tried to kill myself. I wanted to die so many times because of what I was doing. And he started it! And the cutting started because of him. The first time I cut was after I saw someone that sparked memories of the abuse. That's when the cutting started. Yes, I think the punishment mindset came from my mother because she punished me instead of helping me when I was crying out and acting out for help. But the first time I cut had so much to do with my grandfather. And every time I cut after I masturbated, which was very, very often, I was cutting because of my grandfather. I am so full of hatred for him and what he did to me. But I am also so full of pain and hurt.

Last night I got the portrait of the little girl, pointed to it and told Josh through clenched teeth, "Look at me! I was a child! I was just a little girl! I was a beautiful little girl and he destroyed me!" I think about that note my grandfather wrote me telling me that I was very, very precious and that he love, love, loved me. What a wicked lie! He hated me. I wasn't precious to him. I was an object, a plaything. His behavior showed that he hated me. He didn't love me. Love doesn't abuse. Love doesn't molest. Love doesn't ensnare someone in a vicious lie.

The hurt that I am feeling because of him threatens to overwhelm me. I feel like I am drowning in the hurt. I understand what Gary was saying about forgiveness, about giving it to God and trusting His justice. I do believe that God will do what is right, but how do I give all this to God when the pain of all the hurt is blinding me? Last night I cried so hard, I was so full of pain. I wanted to punch on my punching bag because I was so full of fury and hatred, but I didn't punch because of the baby. The longer I held back on punching, the more the fury and hatred turned to pain and I cried instead. I guess right now I am just consumed by the hurt and pain. I've got to deal with it. But it is so hard.

After I read what I had written to Josh on Saturday afternoon, I started crying again. The pain just kept coming. When I calmed down, I picked up my journal and wrote a poem.

A Man Named Foy

Maimed, abused, tormented—
that's what he did to my soul.
Hurt, pain, anguish—
to be free from that is my goal.

Blinded by pain, drowning in hurt,
that's where I'm at right now.
"I hope he burns in hell,"
is what my spirit growls.

His lust, his sin, his wickedness,
left me as a child full of shame.
Nearly destroyed by lies he spoke,
for years I felt I was to blame.

He wasn't punished in this life,
which is why I hope he is in the next,
yet **I've** had to live with the consequences
and that's left my heart and my spirit vexed.

It doesn't seem fair for him to escape
when I've had to live with such pain.
I'm the one who's had to live
with so much torment, storm and rain.

I know that God will do what is right,
I have to trust that truth,
I have to trust God rather than the lies
that were told to me in my youth.

Trusting, I feel a peace inside,
knowing justice will be served,
knowing that God will take care of him
and he'll get what he deserves.

But despite the peace of knowing this,
there's still such pain and grief.
I am drowning in the hurt he caused
and I cry out to God for relief.

I was sinned against and taught to sin,
and I was punished in this life,
for I have lived so many years
with pain and anguish and strife.

Oh God, I beg You, please dear Lord,
bring relief to my hurting soul,
take away the sorrow
that's left my spirit black as coal.

Let me see joy and gladness
for as many years as I have seen grief,
create in me a new heart, oh God,
take away the hurt, let me turn a new leaf.

Oh God, the grief wells up in me,
when I think about the damage he did.
He deceived me and taught me to hurt myself,
though I was just a little kid!

He sexually assaulted me,
and I in turn raped myself.

Chapter 43: The Big Picture

I tore out my heart, as he tore out my soul,
and I tossed it down on a shelf.

My heart lay there for twenty-five years,
bleeding and gasping for life,
until finally I got the help I craved,
and God also blessed me to be Josh's wife.

Through Gary and Josh, healing has come,
but there's still so much sorrow inside.
The hurt that he caused lives with me daily,
and I fear it will ever abide.

How can I bear the anguish I feel,
even in the midst of times of joy?
The shadows of childhood color everything,
all because of a man named Foy.

Though he's been dead for thirty-two years,
his ghost still haunts my mind.
And I'm haunted by the things I've done,
the sickness he left behind.

He didn't just abuse me once
and then from life his exit take.
No, the abuse went on for years and years,
first from him, then from me in his wake.

I've made such incredible progress,
but I've still so far to go.
I must deal with the hurt he caused me
if I am ever to be whole.

I need help to get past all the hurt
that he has in my life deployed.
Oh God, when will the pain ever end?
The pain from my grandfather named Foy.

After I wrote this poem and read it to Josh, I began to cry hard, as sobs broke loose from deep within. Waves of agony spewed out of me as the pain cut me like a knife. The anguish was almost blinding in its intensity, and my body ached from the heaving sobs that were coming from the depths of my soul. I cried out again and again, "Oh Josh, there's so much pain! It hurts so bad!" The pain in my heart threatened to overwhelm me as I sat there drowning in the hurt. Sunday was hard. Every song in church seemed to have a line that got to me. Josh said several things in his sermons that started me thinking about all the pain again.

That's where I am today—drowning in the hurt. I'm living my life, doing everyday things, going places, talking to people, eating, sleeping—and drowning. We watched an old scary monster movie last night and for a little while I actually forgot about the pain. But when the movie was over, it came flooding back in. I told Josh, "You want to know why I don't like monster movies? Because I've encountered real monsters. Not monsters that swallow you up like the Blob. Not monsters from the deep ready to devour virgin sacrifices like the Kraken. Not monsters poised to turn you to stone with one glance like Medusa. No, real monsters. Human monsters. Human beings who do the same monstrous things as the made-up monsters of legend and Hollywood. Human beings who do more monstrous things than the made-up monsters do. My grandfather was a monster. Like the Blob, he swallowed me up so completely that I became just like him, enacting upon myself the same monstrous acts that he first did to me. Like the Kraken, he devoured an innocent, virgin child. I trusted him and he laid me on his altar of self-gratification and sacrificed my purity. Like Medusa, he turned my heart into stone and I subsequently crumbled into a pile of rubble. That pile of rubble has slowly been pieced back together and rebuilt into a living human being again, but not without years of therapy and courage and labor. And anguish. I no longer do the same monstrous acts to myself that he first did to me, but I have to live with the memory of the things I did for twenty-five years. And I have to live with the consequences of what I did. And the consequences of what he did. And even though I have been reconstructed into a woman with life, there's one thing the monster of my grandfather did that can never be restored. He sacrificed my innocence, my purity, my spotless soul of childhood and I can never regain that. He permanently soiled the cleanness of a young girl's body with his dirty, vile behavior, and he left stains of shame and degradation on my soul. I can

Chapter 43: The Big Picture

never get back what he stole from me. He robbed me of my innocence. He robbed me of my childhood. And his monstrous behavior has left my heart and soul full of pain and anguish and anger. Forgiveness? For the sake of my sanity and my soul, I have to give the anger to God. I have to trust God to mete out justice. I can do that. I can trust God. But what do I do with all the pain? It is threatening to overwhelm me. I think the pain of what he did and the consequences of what he did hurt more than all the heartache I've had because of my mother. My grandfather is core. And at my core is deep, blinding pain. It hurts so badly. I'm drowning in the hurt.

Sunday night after we got home, I read to Josh what I had written about my grandfather being a monster and robbing me of my innocence. In Josh's sermon earlier that evening, he spoke about the betrayal price of thirty pieces of silver that Judas took to betray Jesus. I told Josh that my betrayal price was my innocence. Once again, I began sobbing. I couldn't hold back all of the pain and hurt. I told Josh that I was so thankful that God didn't allow me to have my memories years ago when I was still cutting. If I'd had to deal then with the pain I was feeling now, I would have cut myself permanently and committed suicide. I was so thankful that I wasn't feeling any desire to cut now. I was just feeling pain. Incredible pain. Unbelievable pain. I think it was stronger than any pain I had ever felt. I was seeing everything in my life with incredible clarity. It was all coming into focus. I saw my anger, the repression of memories, the depression, the masturbation, the cutting, my mother, my grandfather, the abuse, all the abuse—from him, from her, from me. I saw it all. It was all coming into focus.

I told Josh I could understand now. I understood why I cut. I understood why I masturbated. I understood the anger and the depression. It all made sense. And it all hurt. The pain was overwhelming and I writhed in anguish as I wept. Josh tried to calm me down. I would relax for a few moments, but then another wave would hit and I'd start sobbing uncontrollably all over again. Finally I told Josh, "I need to call Gary." It was about ten fifteen Sunday evening, but I knew Gary was a night owl, so I made the call.

As I talked to Gary, I sobbed. He acknowledged that I was grieving, and pointed out that so much had protected me from this pain through the years. For many years various defense mechanisms had protected me from the depth of my pain. He agreed that I had reached the very core.

He encouraged me to talk to my adult and my child and tell them we need to take a break. He encouraged me to lean on Josh for support. He mentioned that my being off so much of my medication right now wasn't helping, but this was all part of healing. "Actually," he said, "it's exciting. Healing is happening." He told me that the next day, Monday, he would be driving home from his trip and that we could again talk while he was on the road. Again, I thanked God for cell phones. By the time I got off the phone with him, I had calmed down. Josh and I talked a little longer and then we went to bed. Monday morning we went shopping for a crib, which helped keep my mind off of what was happening. That afternoon I talked to Gary.

I read Gary everything I had written since my session on Friday, including the poem and the monster analogy. I told him that for days now, images had been running through my head of all the things I had done to myself, how I had abused myself in ways that my grandfather had started. Josh had encouraged me to cling to God's forgiveness in order not to let the guilt affect me. But I told Gary that it wasn't guilt I was feeling, it was pain. Intense pain. The first thing Gary said to me was that I needed to set a time limit. I needed to restrict my journaling time to one hour a day. He had imposed that restriction on me three years ago when I was obsessing about my mother. He said that now, with the pain intruding on everything, I needed the same limitation. It would help keep me from drowning in the pain.

I was taking notes fast and furious because I didn't want to miss a word of what he was saying. "Up until this point, you've seen different parts of the picture. It was like a puzzle, but it didn't all fit together into a total picture. There were all these pieces—the self-harm, your mother, your grandfather, the little girl. I'm not sure all the pieces totally fit together until now. Now you're suddenly seeing the whole story. Our mind does that. It gives us parts. Everything you've written in the past was a part of it. Now you're seeing the whole picture. Until very recently, your mind hadn't let you in on all there was about your grandfather, but now your mind has yielded it up. Your mind doesn't do that unless it thinks you're able to cope. And you've already processed a lot of the individual pieces. Now you're dealing with the whole of it and with your grandfather. Now it's unified, and the whole impact of how horrific this was is crystal clear. I see what's happening here as positive, not negative. Healing is happening."

Chapter 43: The Big Picture

I asked him what I was supposed to do with all the pain. He told me that I have to experience it. He said healing comes when you deal with the reality of pain. The key, though, as much as possible, is to not give it license. That's why he advised me to put a time limit on my journaling. He acknowledged that I may not always be successful in shutting it off, but when I can, it communicates to my system that this is not life-and-death. He told me to remind the little girl that all this happened thirty-five years ago. This is historical. The pain is current, but the events are historical. The little girl is safe.

We talked about the pain and he recognized that in the past I couldn't deal with the enormity of it. It was why I had cut and why I had repressed the memories. It was why I used so many defense mechanisms. But it was a testimony of how God made our mind able to survive. It was a gift that I couldn't remember before. And now, he acknowledged, it was a gift that I'd been able to put all the pieces together. He talked about so many people he had worked with who weren't able to put all the pieces together. They could never really enjoy life. They suffer with chronic pain, chronic depression, lots of things. But I had stuck with therapy to the point that I've been able to complete the puzzle. Summing things up, he said, "The pain you are now suffering is also setting you free. It is setting you free from the things that almost consumed you. As you are seeing things, it's like you're looking at a wide screen and seeing the fullness of what happened to you. Everything suddenly makes sense. It is painful, but it makes sense. There may be details here and there that still need to come into focus, but you've got the whole picture. It's a sad, sad story. But it's also a story of victory, of healing. And the joy is right there in your belly. The fact that you are dealing with this pain before your child arrives is wonderful. This is last unfinished business so that then you can concentrate on the joy of motherhood."

I felt better after my session, calmer, peaceful. The pain was still there, but I was so glad to know that all the pieces had fallen into place. I finally understood things. I finally saw the big picture.

Now I Understand

Everything is falling into place. Gary was right; the pieces of the puzzle are all there. I drew a picture two years ago of the little girl as a puzzle, with several pieces missing. I entitled it "Missing Pieces Can't Hide the Truth" (see Chapter 28). The pieces are all there now. Now I see everything and I understand.

The repression of memories makes sense. How could I as a child deal with the incredible pain that has now come with the complete understanding of what my grandfather did? How could a child deal with the knowledge that she had been betrayed by every adult important to her? And after my grandfather died, as I continued his abuse by masturbating myself, I **had** to repress the memories. I had to, for the knowledge that I was abusing myself because of what he did, and in the same way that he did, would have been devastating to me. And quite possibly impossible for a child to understand and comprehend. So I repressed the memories.

All the years of addictive masturbation make sense. I was acting out what had happened to me as a child. My grandfather had first masturbated me and in so doing, had taught me how. And when he died, I continued it. I didn't have the ability as a child to handle all the sexuality that was being unfolded for me. I was confused, and in an effort to understand, I did it to myself. As Gary has said before, children often act out what has happened to them. For twenty-five years I acted out what had happened to me.

All the fantasies of being raped and all the times I acted out rape on myself make sense. Again, I was acting out what was done to me. What my grandfather did to me, according to the state penal code, was rape. It was Aggravated Sexual Assault. He didn't rape me with his penis, but he raped me with his fingers. And so, through the years, when I acted out that I was being raped, I was doing what he had done. And when I raped myself, I hurt myself both physically and emotionally. His actions may not have hurt me physically, but they hurt me emotionally. And mentally. And spiritually. For twenty-five years I was only acting out what he had already done.

The overwhelming depression that I lived with for the better part of twenty-five years makes sense. The depression itself was not only a reaction to everything I had gone through, it was also a defense mechanism. The depression kept me from really focusing on the pain, on the issues. It wasn't until Dr. Patel put me on the right medication to help control the depression that I was able to actually work in therapy. Before I was just barely surviving. The depression kept me from being able to think and process and analyze. It kept me from being able to remember why I was depressed in the first place. And although the medication has helped me immensely in being able to get past the depression, the years of therapy and uncovering the

CHAPTER 43: THE BIG PICTURE

trauma and putting the pieces together have kept it away. And will continue to keep it away, I'm confident.

All the suicidal thoughts and overtones and the attempt make sense. My grandfather told me that if I told, he would die. I didn't tell. But he died anyway. A child can't sort that out. So I felt like I had to die. I was dying inside. I couldn't deal with what I knew and the hurt I was feeling, so I wanted to die. I was hurt from many different fronts—my mother, my father, my grandfather, myself. If I could just kill myself, the hurt would go away, or so I thought. Suicide would have been a defense mechanism against feeling and working through all the pain. Thank God I never succeeded. Thank God that there was a fighter in me. I fought to stay alive.

The extreme anger I felt as a child that continued into adulthood makes sense. It kept the pain at bay. The emotion of anger kept the emotion of hurt from overwhelming me. I didn't understand what all the anger was about; I just knew I was angry. Of course, since I had repressed the memories, I didn't have the knowledge of why I was angry. I was just angry. But the anger makes sense. As long as I was angry at my mother, I didn't have to face the hurt that she had caused me. As long as I was angry at myself, I didn't have to face the hurt that I had caused myself. As long as I was angry at my grandfather, I didn't have to face the hurt that he had caused me. I was such an angry child and that anger originated with my grandfather. But even though I was angry, I couldn't admit to myself why I was so angry. I couldn't admit what had happened to me, because in my mind, if I told the truth, people would die. So I repressed the memories. But I didn't repress the anger. And the anger makes sense.

The cutting makes sense. For nine years I scraped myself raw. That escalated into full-blown cutting with razor blades. For nine years I scraped, then for three years I cut. In those twelve years, I turned the extreme anger I felt toward my mother and grandfather on myself and I cut. The rage that I felt toward myself for all the masturbation was expressed in the cutting. I cut to punish myself. I cut because I hated myself. I cut because I deserved to be all cut up. That's what I thought. And all the words I cut into my body make sense. I was trying to express the depth of my emotional pain. My body bore the marks of all the pain. The cutting was a defense mechanism, an attempt to keep it all in place and not fall apart. I was screaming on the inside, so I cut the terror and horror into my body. I use words to express myself. I've written a book using words expressing myself. Back then, I was writing the book on my body. My grandfather didn't teach me to cut, but he taught me to abuse myself. The cutting was my way of shrieking out the pain. It was my way of enacting the pain on myself. Just like I acted out rape, I acted out pain. And hurt. And confusion. And fear. The cutting was all of that. It makes sense.

The extreme anxiety I have suffered with for years makes sense. Anxiety is a God-given mechanism to keep you safe. Your fight-or-flight response kicks in when there is danger. Anxiety is when you get stuck there. I've been stuck in anxiety for years, but it makes sense. I wasn't safe as a child, not from my grandfather and not from my mother. My experience as a child caused me to get stuck in danger mode. And it has pervaded my life. I am constantly on the lookout to avoid danger. I am incredibly vigilant—about everything. That makes me a good strategist and planner, which can be good, but I recognize that the basis for it is my anxiety. And of course, anxiety is just a precursor to fear.

The incredible fear I have lived with makes sense. I was terrified that my grandfather would die when I was a little girl. He did die. So then I was terrified that my mother would die. And I was terrified of my mother. The physical abuse I suffered at her hands left me living in fear of her. As a little girl, I was strong-willed, which just made her punish me more. As I grew older, after my grandfather died and the sexual abuse stopped, I blocked that out and focused on my mother. And my fear of her grew. I became the dutiful daughter always seeking to meet her needs. I was afraid of making her mad. When I was a little girl and I made her mad, she would lash out at me and spank me in her rage. So it makes sense that later, as a teenager and young adult I was afraid of her anger and I lived in fear of her. But I was also afraid of her finding out bad things about me. Indeed, I lived in abject terror of that. Especially after I recanted. And I think that fear goes back to my grandfather. If he did tell me that she, too, would die if I told, then once I did tell and saw how angry she was at me, my fear just grew. And of course, the fear that started as a child grew out of proportion through the years, generalizing to many different things. As I said, the anxiety and fear are closely related. And they make sense.

The little girl makes sense. How could I grow up normally and have an integrated personality when my personality had been assaulted in childhood? I couldn't be whole until I had dealt with the very things that caused me to become fractured in the first place. I never developed multiple personalities, but I think I came awfully close. As a child, my reality

CHAPTER 43: THE BIG PICTURE

was very fractured; thus, I became fractured. The struggle I've had with trying to integrate my personality makes sense. I wasn't taught as a child how to deal with reality and emotions and fears. I wasn't taught truth. I lived with lies. My breaks with reality—the auditory hallucinations, the fugue experience—make sense. I couldn't face reality; it was too painful. It was easier to slip into psychosis. God blessed me with the wisdom of Dr. Patel and Gary to help me not stay there. It was so frightening when it was happening, but it makes sense.

My problems with my mother make sense. When Gary told me the first day of therapy that my mother was my problem, I didn't want to believe him. I guess with what he knew about the two of us after only one hour, his statement is understandable. Now, though, I think my mother and my grandfather **together** are the core. It started with my grandfather. But my mother was so dysfunctional and she didn't protect me. Since I had repressed the abuse, my anger at my mother for her not protecting me was masked by my anger at her for hundreds of other things. And all those things were legitimate reasons to be angry. But my anger at her started when my grandfather was abusing me and she wasn't protecting me. And the anger started when she was punishing me for acting out rather than helping me. And my fear of her started then, too. I don't have a clear memory, but I have a strong sense that my grandfather also told me that my mother would die, too, if I told. I have been protecting her all these years. It should have been her protecting me. But it didn't happen that way, and so the anger grew and the fear grew. My fear of her also started when she would lash out at me in anger. But also, my fear was part of my anger. If I acknowledged that I was angry at her for not protecting me, I would have to admit what my grandfather had done, and then she might die. So my anger at her was a defense mechanism against my fear of her. And my fear for her.

That makes my recanting make sense. I recanted because I couldn't handle living with her anger any longer. But I had told the secret. He said people would die if I told. I was afraid, in my unconscious, that she would die, too. I was living up to her image when I recanted. When I made the accusation about my grandfather, I betrayed the sick family system. The sick family system had made me sick. But I recanted because I was terrified that people would die. And of course, all that did was bring me closer to dying myself.

And the recovery of my memories makes sense. I first realized I was missing my memories in college, and I first started analyzing all the clues in 1992. When I was hospitalized in May that year, I had a ton of clues but no real memories. The only clear memories I had at that point were of the events surrounding my grandfather's death, the two recurring dreams I had as a child, and the memories of all the times I would dissociate and spiral up and float on the ceiling. Those few memories were clues. But the other clues I had were numerous. And it was the clues that led me to make the accusation. It wasn't until 2005, thirteen years later, that I started having memories of the abuse. And even then, the memories were sketchy and the flashbacks only lasted for about five months. But they were memories of my grandfather and they were flashbacks of inappropriate actions on his part. Then the flashbacks ceased with any regularity. From the end of 2005 until the beginning of 2009, I occasionally had memory flashes of my grandfather when Josh and I were being intimate, but they weren't very regular. In 2009 that all changed. I started really regaining my memories of the abuse, starting in February with the memory of him telling me he would die if I told. And from September 2009 until March 2010 I had an overwhelming number of flashbacks, very vivid and very detailed. I remembered the abuse. I remembered it all.

And my journey to remember makes sense. All along in my therapy, Gary said **if** I was going to remember, it would happen when the time was right, when I could handle the memories. He was correct. I couldn't have handled the intense memories I've had over the last year and a half any sooner. I wasn't healthy enough. I wasn't strong enough. If I had remembered everything while I was still cutting, I would have cut to kill myself. It would have overwhelmed me. If I had remembered everything before I had worked through so many of my issues with my mother, I would have betrayed myself again by recanting all over again. Or by totally denying the memories. I would have betrayed the little girl. I couldn't remember before now. I would have taken out the anger and the pain on myself. I would have continued to abuse myself. And the little girl would have gone into permanent hiding. I might very well have slipped completely into psychosis. My personality might very well have completely fractured into multiple personalities. I might never have gotten well. God was protecting me from myself, from all the pain and anguish, by not allowing me to remember sooner. He was protecting me until I was strong enough and healthy enough to handle the

CHAPTER 43: THE BIG PICTURE

memories and deal with them properly. God was guarding me. And I am thankful. It all makes sense.

Everything makes sense now. The years of anguish, the pain, the self-abuse, the anger, the fear, the crippling depression, the masturbation, the cutting. It all makes sense. He started sexually abusing me when I was six years old. That means that it has taken me almost thirty-five years to put all the pieces together. That's a long time to work on a puzzle.

So, where am I today? Well, I still haven't dealt with my emotions about my mother not protecting me. I guess that's what I'll work on with Gary next. And I'm still feeling incredible pain about what my grandfather did to me, and what I did to myself as a result of his abuse. I've calmed down and I don't feel like I'm drowning in the hurt like I was this past week. But the pain is still there and still very intense. As I continue to feel my feelings and talk through the pain, it will lessen. But I think that the pain will always be with me on some level. I will probably also have transference issues to work through when my own child is born, especially if we have a little girl. But I will work through them, because that's part of my healing. Can you have victorious pain? I guess so, because that's where I am. I'm in pain, but as Gary said, my story is also a story of victory and healing. I guess it's like my joy. I've still felt my joy all throughout the last three years since I found it, but it's been a sad joy. Quite the paradox, but that's how it is. Sad joy and victorious pain. That's me.

Josh said that the piece I had written was like a lawyer's closing argument, a summation statement. Gary agreed and reminded me that life, of course, goes on, but not with the intensity of all this other stuff. He asked me how the little girl felt about what I had written. I told him that she is saying, "Okay, now you understand." And Gary said if I understand, I can help her understand. She's had the reality of this pain all her life, but not the reality of the answers to put it all together. Now my adult can say to her, "It's okay. I understand. I'll take care of that. I'll take care of you." That will give peace and relief to the little girl.

Thinking about the joy and the victory reminded me of the passage in 1 Peter that talks about having inexpressible joy after having gone through trials. That's how I feel. I cannot express adequately the joy that I feel, precisely because it was born out of so much sorrow. Despite the sorrow, there is joy. Despite the pain, there is victory.

Inexpressible Joy

Joy is inexpressible joy
when it is born in the midst of pain,
for only there can the Father
turn your heart toward His again.

The joy that is born amongst pain,
it is deep and it suffereth long,
and it does not diminish or fade
though your world seems dark and all wrong.

For only that kind of joy
is what the Father wants in your heart,
for only that kind of joy
is the inexpressible joy that never will part.

Joy, the inexpressible joy,
is the joy born in my heart today
midst the pain of deep sorrow and grief,
it's the joy that will not fade away.

44

Victory

Victory,
like the man running
a marathon,
feet pounding the
burning pavement
mile after mile,
sweat pouring,
legs screaming for relief,
lungs gasping for air,
inching ever closer to his goal,
and finally,
depleted of all but his will,
crossing the finish line
a winner;
or,
like the mountain climber,
after days of
grueling toil,
twisted ankles,
bloodied hands,
bruised body,
and aching muscles,
finally reaching the summit,
celebrating his triumph
through exhausted cheers;
or,
like the battered army,
devoid of many of its
original soldiers,
lost to death,
beaten back

time and again,
yet each time surging forward
and regaining ground,
and finally overcoming
the foe,
winning the war,
and gaining their freedom.
Victory.

It's a fundamental truth that victory seldom comes without a cost. The cost is pain. I was achieving victory in my struggle for mental health, but not without incredible pain. As I lived with the reality of the pain that my grandfather caused me, I continued to think about the consequences of his actions. I thought about what his actions had caused me to do. And the pain grew.

Pain,
grows and builds with every
memory,
every understanding,
every moment of clarity.
Each flash of comprehension
into my life,
my childhood,
my struggle,
brings pain.
Years ago the pain
drove me to cut;
it drove me to contemplate
suicide.
It was agonizing.
Now, after years of
therapy,
and insight,
and arduous toil,
it still drives me,
but to other things.
It drives me to

CHAPTER 44: VICTORY

remember,
it drives me to
change,
it drives me to
create a new life
for myself
and for my family.
It is still agonizing.
Things are clear now,
crystal clear.
And that clarity
has brought about new levels of
pain.
It is a paradoxical pain.
There are elements of
victory
and healing
and triumph,
but that success is
intricately intertwined
with pain.
The pain will be with me
for the rest of my life.
It will lessen over time,
but it will still be there,
always reminding,
always exhorting me to
work
and labor
and strive
to heal and grow and change.
The pain of my childhood,
the pain of my life,
will not go away,
but will permeate
the rest of my years.
Over time,
lessening,

easing,
lightening,
but still hurting,
still causing me
pain.

On Saturday, August 28, the beginnings of a poem rumbled around in my brain. I finally sat down at the computer and started typing, but I realized pretty quickly that it wasn't a poem. It was something the little girl was writing, describing things from her perspective. She was sharing more memories, in four parts. The parts were memories, her perspective, from four different ages. The first, second, and fourth parts are included here. The third part is summarized.

The Little Girl's Perspective

Part 1, Age 7

I'm sitting in my room feeling weird.
Kinda good and bad at the same time.
Papa and I were playing our game again
and it was fun
and felt good,
but now I feel weird.
I wanted to play the game.
But I feel bad
because I can't tell anybody about the game
or he'll die.
That's what he told me—that he would die
if I told anyone what we were doing.
And he told me Mommie would die too.
It's a fun game,
but I don't understand it
because it's scary at the same time.
How can a game be fun if it's also
dangerous?
I feel bad.
I feel guilty like I shouldn't enjoy the game

CHAPTER 44: VICTORY

because he'll die
and Mommie will die
if anyone finds out about it.
It's our little secret game he says.
But why does it have to be a secret?
Is it because we play it without our clothes on?
Is that why it has to be a secret?
I thought these were private parts.
I'm confused.
It's fun to see what Papa's pee-pee can do.
It gets big and hard.
And sometimes it leaks stuff out.
Papa says not to worry about that
'cause when it does that he's won the game.
But I can't tell anyone.
He makes me kiss his pee-pee and touch it.
He touches me and puts his fingers inside of me.
It feels good when he touches me.
And sometimes when he's touching me
he makes me feel really good.
He makes me feel really, really good.
I've never felt that way before.
But it scares me at the same time because he'll die
and Mommie will die if I tell.
He always tells me that every time we play our game.
So how can I enjoy something that is so scary and dangerous?
Where is Mommie?
He says I can't even tell Mommie about our game.
Sometimes I don't like the game.
Sometimes I don't want to play 'cause it's dangerous and scary,
but he makes me play.
And when his pee-pee leaks out stuff he gets a scary look on his
    face.
But he says that's because he's so happy that he won the game.
But he doesn't look happy. He looks scary.
Sometimes when he is touching me I don't like it. 'Cause I feel so
    bad.
But I don't have to stay there if I don't like it.

I go up to the ceiling instead and stay up there.
I like floating on the ceiling. It feels safe up there.
My bedroom doesn't always feel safe.
I guess 'cause that's where we play the game and the game is dangerous.
Where is Mommie?
Can't she tell him not to play the game with me?
If it is dangerous, why doesn't she stop it?
If they'll die if I tell about it, why doesn't she stop the game?
I can't tell her 'cause he'll die if I do. Or she'll die.
But I don't want him to die. I don't want her to die.
But I don't always want to play the game either.
I like parts of the game, but parts of it I don't like.
And I wish Mommie would make him stop the parts I don't like.
But she doesn't know we are playing the game.
I tried to tell her without telling but she didn't listen.
It's hard to tell something when you can't tell.
But I don't act right.
I'm angry because I can't tell about the game.
And I'm scared 'cause the game is so dangerous.
What if he dies? It will be my fault.
Maybe I wet the bed all the time 'cause I'm so scared.
I wish I could smile happy, but I feel sad. And scared.
Mom and Papa and me went and got our picture made at a picture place.
I didn't like the picture. Nobody was smiling.
Doesn't Mommie see?
Why doesn't she look at me?
Why doesn't she listen?
But how can she listen when I don't tell her?
I can't tell her or they'll die.
But she should know.
She's my Mommie. She's supposed to know everything.
Why doesn't she know this?
Papa says he loves me. He says I am precious.
That's why he plays our special game with me.
But I don't feel precious. I feel scared.
Where is Mommie?

Chapter 44: Victory

Part 2, Age 11

Where is Mommie?
Oh no, she's coming. I have to stop.
I don't want to stop 'cause it feels good.
But she'll be mad at me if she sees what I'm doing.
Good, she stopped coming. I can keep going.
I love to touch myself the way I learned how.
It feels good.
But I feel so bad when I do it.
But I can't help myself.
I have to do it. I can't stop.

Part 3, Age 14

As I typed this section, I was having flashbacks to all the times I acted out being raped. I just typed what I was remembering. I started this kind of sexual acting out in my early teens. This section began with the little girl asking the question, "Where is Mommie?" But Mommie wasn't at home. She had gone out and the little girl was glad because she was then able to act out a scenario.

In this section the little girl pretended to be a guy who was going to rape a girl. I chose to summarize it rather than include it verbatim, because of the graphic content and language. The little girl, acting out the guy's role, tells the imaginary girl that he's going to rape her. References are made to the fact that the girl cannot protect herself. She can do nothing about it because she is a girl. The guy is in control and he's going to rape her hard enough that she'll scream out. He tells her she deserves to be raped. The language the little girl uses is very graphic and indicates that the rape is happening.

At that point in acting out of this type of scenario, I would turn the tables on myself. I would then take on the role of the girl being raped and masturbate violently. The little girl described perfectly what I would do and say as I acted out these scenarios. This section ends with the little girl realizing that Mommie has just pulled into the driveway. The violent masturbation episode is stopped by Mommie coming home. The little girl frantically tries to get out of the living room and get dressed before

Mommie comes in the door and catches her. But she says she cannot wait until Mommie is gone again, so she can act out another scenario.

Part 4, Age 40

Where was Mommie?
Why didn't she stop him?
Why did she let him hurt me?
Why did she let me hurt myself?
Oh, where was Mommie?

After I wrote this piece, or more accurately, after the little girl wrote this, I couldn't read it to Josh. Instead, I gave it to him to read, and after he read it I couldn't look at him. I was feeling so ashamed, particularly about the third section. We did talk about it some, but it was very difficult for me. I e-mailed Gary and told him that the little girl had written something that I wanted to discuss in my next session, but I wasn't sure that I could read it to him. I asked if I could e-mail it to him. He said I could. He wrote, "These are exciting and yet difficult days for you." So I e-mailed the piece to him. The next afternoon, I wrote a piece entitled "Memories of Shame." I am going to include parts of it here. Other parts are omitted due to the graphic content.

Memories of Shame

After I wrote, or more accurately, after the little girl wrote that piece from her perspective, I couldn't read it to Josh. There was too much shame. I could have read him the first two parts and the fourth part, but I couldn't have read him the third part. That's where all the shame was coming from. So he read it himself. Then when we were talking about it, I couldn't bring myself to look at him. And I asked him repeatedly, "Are you mad at me? Do you hate me?" I told him I hate myself for all I did to myself. I told him that there were two things about what I wrote that upset me.

First, as I was writing it, I remembered how the aggressive and violent aspect to much of my masturbation and acting out had actually aroused me. That's what brought so much shame. And that section the little girl wrote so accurately described how it was for me when I was acting out. I had flashbacks of those incidents as I typed. I just typed what I was seeing in my mind. And it described exactly what I did and said as I masturbated. Josh tried to help me understand that I was just a child acting out what was done to me, but I acted out scenarios like that from my early teens until my early thirties. If I remember correctly, the last time I acted out a rape scenario was sometime between when Josh and I started dating in January 2004 and when we got engaged on April 8, 2004. Of course, when we got engaged I stopped masturbating altogether. But I was thirty-four years old, obviously not a child acting out what was done to her. Not a child in age, but still very much a child emotionally. I finally told Josh to help me look at him. He gently lifted my chin and I met his gaze. He told me that there was nothing shameful now, that the shame I was feeling was a memory of the shame.

The second thing that upset me was what I had remembered about my personality. It seems that I had an aggressive male aspect of my personality. I can't tell you the number of times I acted out that I was a male. I was in early high school the first time I did this. Since March, when I first had the memory of my grandfather masturbating me, I have been flooded with memories of what I did to myself. The depth of emotional pain over what his actions caused me to do to myself has increased as I've been reminded of my actions. I never blocked all that out. Rather, I avoided thinking about it. Now I can't help but think about it. I had talked about these things with Gary before, but now I felt a drive to discuss them again in detail, like I need to purge myself of what I'd done. And as I remember these things, the shame of it is weighing me down. That and the pain. I'm not drowning in the hurt like I was last week, but there is just so much pain over what all I have done to myself. And I must deal with all of this stuff. Gary told me not to push it. Well, I'm not pushing it. It is just coming. I did take a break, like he said, but when I sat down to write, that piece from the little girl's perspective is what came out. It just came. I was just typing the flashbacks and everything she was saying.

And I can't get the flashbacks of what I did to myself to go out of my mind. Like all the flashbacks last fall of my grandfather and the abuse, they just keep coming. I feel so much shame about all that. Josh said he still loves me despite what all I did, but I just feel so shameful. How could I do that to myself? And I can't get the flashbacks of what I used to masturbate myself with to stop. When I was home alone, I would scour the house and garage for objects that even remotely resembled a penis and use them to rape myself as I masturbated. I used things that were so big and so hard that I actually tore myself and bled. If my grandfather had raped me with his penis, then I might be able to understand why I acted out all this stuff. But he didn't. He used his fingers to penetrate me, but he didn't rape me in the ways I acted out on myself. Why did my behavior go so far beyond what he ever did? What happened with that?

I also got involved with pornography. At first, when I was in middle school, my friend and I would sneak looks at her brother's Playboy magazines. Then later I would fantasize about what I had seen while I was masturbating. One time, while I was in high school, my mother brought home from work a Playgirl magazine picture that one of her fellow teachers had put in her locker as a practical joke. She actually showed it to me and laughed about it. How's that for responsible parenting? And some joke. What kind of joke is it when your daughter can still remember the picture twenty-five years later? What kind of joke is it when your daughter, after seeing the picture, fantasized about the guy in the picture as she was masturbating? Also in high school and in my twenties, I would steal some of my mother's slutty romance novels and read and reread the graphic sexual parts and masturbate at the same time. When I was in my twenties, there were times when I would go to a convenience store in a bad part of town to buy a Playgirl. I would keep it under my mattress and when my mother wasn't home I would look at the pictures and read it over and over again while I masturbated. Then later, when I was living on my own, I would go to pornographic websites and look at pictures and read articles while I masturbated. I've done all these things to myself.

There is so much shame. Josh reminded me that God has forgiven me for all of this, and I know He has, but the shame is still there. Ever since I had the flashback of my grandfather masturbating me, the memories of what I did to myself have been coming back with clarity and power. I don't do these things any more. I haven't in years. That's not who I am any more. But I have to live with the memories of what I did. I have to live with the memories of the shame. I know I'm getting healthier, but it seems like the healthier I get, the more I remember just how unhealthy and sick I really was.

Something else the little girl wrote upsets me. Over and over she asked the haunting question, "Where is Mommie?" In the section where she was seven years old, she wanted Mommie to help her and protect her and stop what was going on. But then in the sections when she was 11 and 14, she was asking where Mommie was because she didn't want Mommie to catch

CHAPTER 44: VICTORY

her at what she was doing. She knew Mommie would be furious with her and would shame her for what she was doing. I can remember so clearly all the times I would be masturbating and fantasizing, yet keeping one ear trained for any sound that Mommie had awakened and was coming over to my room. Or what about all the times I would masturbate in the bathtub? Mommie would barge into the bathroom without knocking, like she always did. I would shove myself back from the faucet so quickly and forcefully that water would slosh out of the tub. And of course, she would get mad about that and ask me what in the world was I doing. I'd lie and say I was moving the water back and forth with my body to regulate the temperature of the water. I never wanted her to catch me, and as far as I know, she never did. But in the piece I wrote yesterday, in the first part, the little girl wanted Mommie to know what was going on. She wanted Mommie to stop it. And she said that Mommie should know, but Mommie didn't. She didn't know what was happening to me and she didn't stop it. She didn't stop him from hurting me and she didn't stop me from hurting myself. I learned to hide things very well. I learned that from my grandfather. I mean, if people were going to die if I told, then I would become an expert at hiding. But the hiding made me sick and just fueled more dysfunction and sickness.

Where is Mommie? Hundreds of websites talk about protecting your child from sexual abuse. Hundreds of websites talk about the signs that your child might be being sexually abused. One of the biggest signs is sexual acting out. I was sexually acting out. Big time. All the times I acted out by myself, she never knew. And all the times I acted out sexually with guys, and that started when I was ten years old, she never knew. One time, on a church youth trip that my mother was one of the sponsors for, one of the guys and I were touching each other under a blanket in the back of the van. But she didn't know. Where was Mommie when all this acting out was going on? Why didn't she know?

Wow—I just had a powerful memory. A number of years ago, when I had come back to God, I wanted to have a celebration on the one year anniversary. Since it was going to be at my mom's house, where I was living, I thought I ought to fill her in on what the celebration was about. I took her out to eat and let her read a piece I had written. It talked generically about the sexual problems I'd had, mostly in reference to guys, not the masturbation. When she read it, her first angry question was, "Who knows about this?" Her second question, immediately after the first and just as angry, was, "Why didn't I know about this?" That's what I would like to know! Why didn't you know about this? Where were you when he was abusing me? Where were you when I was abusing myself? Why didn't you know about this?! Where is Mommie? Where was Mommie? Why weren't you protecting me? Why were you ignoring my cries for help? Why were you punishing me for crying out for help? Why weren't you listening to me? Why weren't you paying attention? Over the last two weeks, the pain of what my grandfather did to me and the pain of what I did to myself has been overwhelming. But now I'm starting to feel the depth of the pain I feel about Mommie not protecting me. Where was Mommie? Why didn't she protect me? The little girl wanted to know, "Where is Mommie?" That's a good question.

And really, there are two good questions I've asked here. One, of course, is "Where was Mommie?" But the second is this: how could I have acted out so much stuff that was so much worse than what my grandfather actually did to me? Like I said, I could understand me acting out all this stuff if he had actually raped me with his penis, but he didn't. At least I don't have any memories of that. So why did I act out all this stuff where I raped myself with makeshift penises? Why was my behavior so far beyond his? Why was my behavior so sick?

Like Josh said, God has forgiven me. But I still have to live with the memories of both my actions and my shame. There is more shame in what I've written about in this piece than anything else in my life, including the cutting.

Josh knew I had written something, and he asked if I wanted to read it to him. I told him I would read it to him after church that evening. When we got home that night, we sat down and I picked up the pages, but I had a hard time starting. I finally read it to him with a lot of pauses. I kept asking him throughout the piece, "Do you hate me?" He would reassure me that he loved me and I would keep reading. After I finished reading the piece, I broke down and wailed. I couldn't stop crying. I'd relax for a few seconds, then another wave of pain would hit me and I'd start weeping and wailing again. Once again, I was drowning in the pain. I wanted to call Gary at home, but it was too late in the evening. I finally calmed down. I called Gary's office and left him a message. I had an appointment with him on Wednesday, but that seemed so far away. The next morning, I saw that Gary had e-mailed me the night before. He had received and read the piece that the little girl had written from her perspective. He wrote,

CHAPTER 44: VICTORY

"The little girl is dealing with her struggle to understand shame, betrayal, and entrapment. We have a lot to talk about. Hang in there." Then a little while later Gary called me. He'd had a cancellation at ten o'clock that morning. I was so thankful because the grief was tearing me up inside and I needed to get it out.

Yesterday's session with Gary was hard. When I read him the piece, "Memories of Shame," I cried and cried when I got to the part about "Where is Mommie?" But we didn't really discuss that part of the piece. Twice now I've written about her not protecting me, and both times we have not discussed that issue. There've been other issues more fundamental. But I want to address the issue of her not protecting me and my pain about it. I think that is fundamental, too.

What we did discuss yesterday had to do with the little girl and my personality and the sexual addiction. Gary told me that what is going on is that I am bringing the two split-off parts of me together. He said I had a dual personality, not multiple personality disorder, but two parts to my personality that were split off from each other. On the one hand, there was the sick part who cut herself up with razor blades and was sexually addicted to abusive masturbation. On the other hand, there was the other part of me who went to church, prayed, loved God, and even went to Bible school to train for ministry. How could I sit in Bible class and then go home and cut and rape myself? How could I reconcile those two parts? I couldn't. So I split those two parts off from each other. There was no integration in my personality. Now, though, he said, integration was happening. He said what was happening with me was healthy. These two parts of me were coming together.

I realize how close I came to losing everything. My life, my sanity, my salvation, my future. If I hadn't gotten help, I would have continued on the path of self-destruction. My personality split could very easily have developed into multiple personalities. I could have continued to have breaks with reality. I may very well have committed suicide. I could have turned my back on God, concluding that He had turned His back on me. But none of that happened. And, of course, God didn't turn His back on me. He sent people to me to help me. He brought me many people through the years to counsel and strengthen me. And then, when I thought all hope was lost, He sent me Miss Penny, then Dr. Patel, then Gary, and finally Josh. These four people have sweated and prayed and labored for me. They have used their wisdom to help me. And God has worked through them to bring healing to me. And I am grateful.

The shame of what all I did, especially the shame of the sexual addiction, has always been powerful. I've lived with the shame since I was a little girl, and it grew stronger and stronger as I got deeper and deeper into the sexual addiction. Now, as I see clearly what I did to myself and what happened to me, I feel the shame still, but with a sense of understanding. The little girl had no control when the addiction started. She had been introduced to sexuality way before she should have been. As Gary pointed out so eloquently, my grandfather aroused things inside of me that should not have been aroused at that age. Those things should not have been awakened then. And my grandfather set in motion an out-of-control self-abusive addiction that started in childhood and persisted into adulthood. I became my own perpetrator. I wanted to know why my behavior went so far beyond what my grandfather did to me. Gary explained to me that that is the nature of an addiction. Any kind of addiction. It progresses deeper and deeper, and gets worse as time goes by. It takes more and more to satisfy the addiction. What started with my grandfather teaching me how to masturbate, progressed from me masturbating myself, to acting out scenarios of rape, to violent masturbation. Understanding the nature of an addiction helps me to understand my shame over what I did to myself. I'm just thankful that I am no longer enslaved by sexual addiction, nor the addiction to cutting. Over the last couple of weeks, I have come to understand all the shame I felt and where it all stemmed from. And I guess the understanding brings some peace. As I gain more insight into my past and my personality, like I said before, things makes sense. I don't like it. It isn't pleasant. In fact, the insight and understanding have brought about intense pain, but it makes sense. And in making sense of it, the shame doesn't seem to have as much power over me.

Everything Gary said yesterday makes sense. My personality is beginning to integrate. Healing is happening in incredible ways. Gary said that I am finally healthy enough to deal with all of this. He told me that what I am dealing with and processing right now is cataclysmic. The last two weeks have been a watershed experience for me, a crucial turning point in my healing. As I get the last bits of this infection out of me, the results will be a sense of freedom and relief. I am ready for that sense of freedom and relief. But right now I am left with the pain. I know the pain will lessen over time, but it will always be with me on some level. The pain

Chapter 44: Victory

of what my grandfather did to me will lessen. The pain of all I did to myself will lessen. The pain of what my mother did to me will lessen. As I continue to grieve over my life, the pain will become lighter and not so intense. But deep down, it will always be there. I hope that as the pain eases up, that I will be able to forgive, especially myself. I committed horrific acts of violence on myself. I need to be able to forgive myself for that. I think in time, I will.

My book has a bittersweet ending. On the one hand there is healing and triumph and victory. On the other hand there is pain. I have sad joy and victorious pain.

I became quite reflective thinking about everything that had happened over the last two weeks. I contemplated all I'd been through as a little girl. I pondered the depth of sickness and addiction in which I'd been entrapped. I meditated on the years of therapy and the healing that had taken place. I realized that, by the grace of God, I was a survivor. I had overcome. There was still a lot of pain, but the pain had brought victory.

When I talked to Gary a couple of days later, I was much calmer than I had been. I asked him about my mother not protecting me, and he pointed out that the little girl and my adult have different thoughts on the matter. The little girl feels betrayed. She is angry, she feels abused and wronged. My adult recognizes that my mother herself had not grown up. Although she'd had a baby, emotionally she was still a child herself. My adult recognizes that my mother didn't protect me like an adult should protect her child. My adult could explain what happened; I may not like it, but I could understand it. The little girl, on the other hand, may not want to hear the explanation. She is wounded and hurt and doesn't want what she perceives to be excuses. She's afraid that by explaining things that I will be excusing my mother and my grandfather. She's afraid that by explaining things that I will be invalidating her pain and telling her that she has no right to feel the way she does. But that's not true, and I need to communicate that to the little girl when she is ready to hear it. Eventually, he said, the little girl and my adult are going to have to communicate about all this in order for there to be peace inside about Mother and Grandfather.

A few days later, my mother came up for a visit over Labor Day weekend. The issue of her not protecting me came into focus as I realized with great clarity that I still couldn't trust her, not even to protect my own child.

Red Flags

Mom was here this weekend and red flags were popping up all over the place. The first flag had to do with boundaries. She constantly smothered me all the time, giving me no physical boundaries. She was always crowding me, whether in the church pew or the kitchen. She would get right up next to me in the kitchen while I was trying to work. She doesn't give me any space. She's that way with me and I know she'll be that way with our child.

And when I set boundaries, she ignored them. When I asked her to move down the pew Sunday morning, she did, and I put my Bible and purse on the seat between us. But as soon as Josh got up to preach, she pointed to my things and said, "Can you move this stuff to the other side of you?" I asked, "Why?" She said, "So I can scoot closer to you." I replied, "No," and turned my attention to the sermon. So she pouted. When she doesn't get her way, she pouts. So childish. An adult is supposed to teach a child not to be childish. What is her behavior going to teach our child?

She also constantly touched me. When I would hug her and start to pull away, she would ignore my boundary and hug tighter. When she was rubbing my back in the store, I had to ask her twice before she stopped, and then she only stopped because I moved away. And the worst was my stomach. I am really starting to show, and she kept wanting to touch my belly. The first time she put her hand flat on my belly, I picked it up and moved it off. She put it right back. I picked it up again and moved it off again. She put it right back. I picked it up yet again and moved it off and said, "You're as bad as some of the ladies at church." As she was putting her hand back, she said, "Yeah, but I'm your mother." I moved away from her so she couldn't touch me again. And Sunday night when I was in my recliner, she leaned over me, put her hands on my stomach, and started talking to the baby. "This is Mimi, Mimi. I want you to know the sound of Mimi's voice." I moved her hands and put my hands over my belly as a boundary to protect my stomach from her touching it. She just shoved my hands aside, kept touching and kept talking. I put my hands back over my belly and said I didn't like what she was doing. She just ignored me and said, "Well, I want my grandbaby to know her Mimi's touch, too." I was trapped in my chair and couldn't get away. She finally quit.

CHAPTER 44: VICTORY

And the whole time she was here, she kept wanting to take pictures of me. Right before she left, she wanted to take a picture of me in my pregnant T-shirt. I told her, "I don't want my picture made in this shirt." I had to repeat myself four times as she continued trying to take the picture, first from one angle, then another. Finally, after I firmly repeated myself the fourth time, she pouted off.

She totally ignores and violates my boundaries. And I've heard her use that line many times in the past, "Yeah, but I'm your mother." So, because she's my mother, that gives her the right to violate my boundaries? Apparently that's what she thinks. And I know she'll use that line on our child. "Yeah, but I'm your grandmother." She will violate any boundaries Josh and I set about our child, and she will violate any boundaries our child sets. And she's constantly asking me questions that have to do with my breasts, or with Josh's or my physical health, or with our financial situation. Things that are none of her business. She's so nosy and I know she will be nosy with our child, invading his or her space and being and life. Tons of red flags here.

Another red flag is how forgetful and oblivious she is. She is totally absorbed in herself and doesn't pay attention to what's going on around her. Lots of little things, but when you are watching a baby, you have to pay attention to the little things. I can't trust her to pay attention to our child in a healthy way.

But there are more red flags. She has poor judgment. She told me that when the weather gets cool, she wants me to come help her clean out her garage. When the weather gets cool, I'll be seven months pregnant! What business does a seven-months-pregnant lady have cleaning out a garage? I've cleaned out her garage many, many times and it is hard, physical labor. There's so much crap in there that you have to wiggle through tight spaces and really have good balance to keep from tripping over all the junk. Not something a big, pregnant lady can do very well. And then there's the lifting. Boxes and boxes and boxes. Like I'm supposed to be lifting heavy things! She has awful judgment! And I want her caring for my child? I don't think so! Last week she lost the key pad for her house alarm. She found it the next day laying in her yard. And that's not the first time it's happened. She is constantly losing things and forgetting things. I don't know how many times she has locked her keys in her car or locked herself out of her house. What if she does that while our child is in there? There's nothing safe about her!

And she's irresponsible. Sunday morning I asked her when she finished her tea to please put her mug in the dishwasher and start it. All she had to do was push a button. Got home from church and guess what? Dirty dishes! So I had to wash a few dishes before I could cook. No big deal. The big deal—and the red flag—is her irresponsibility. She did that with Grandma all the time. Grandma would ask her to do something for her and she'd say she would, but then she'd forget. After asking several times with the same result, Grandma would give up and do it herself. Often it was something that was dangerous or hard for Grandma to do. And I really want her taking care of my child? I don't think so! She told me when she was visiting a friend, she stepped right over a scorpion because she thought it was a twig. And I want her spending time alone with my child? Not!

The ultimate example of her irresponsibility and poor judgment happened on Saturday. We were getting ready to sit down for lunch and I noticed something white on the floor. I picked it up and saw it was a pill. It didn't look like one of mine or Josh's, so I handed it to my mother and asked her if it were hers. She took it, looked at it, and said, "I guess so. It might be." She kind of shrugged, popped it into her mouth, and swallowed it! She wasn't sure it was hers, but she swallowed it anyway! That is pathetic judgment! She didn't get up and check her pill container—she just swallowed it! And why was it on the floor in the first place?! Irresponsible! One of the dogs could have eaten it. Or what if the baby were here and crawling? Babies put everything into their mouths. It was a good-sized pill and could have gotten lodged in the baby's throat. Or if it had been swallowed, who knows what it could have done to the baby!! It could have been disastrous, and quite possibly deadly! And she wants to keep our child?! I don't think so! I wouldn't trust her to keep our child any farther than I could throw her. I wouldn't even trust her with our child for fifteen minutes. And Josh agrees. And I don't think any amount of therapy on her part will change her irresponsibility and poor judgment (assuming she'll ever get into therapy, which I doubt)!

What's scary is how she seems obsessed about certain things. Since she found out we were pregnant, I can't tell you the number of times she's said something to me about us leaving our baby with her whenever we travel. She's said it at least five times just this weekend. For one thing, why would we not take our child with us? We're a family and we want our friends to see our baby. And like we really want to drive three hours in the opposite direction just to drop off our kid at her house? But mainly, there's no way we will do that because we don't trust her. I'm not leaving our baby with her for fifteen minutes, much less for a week! There's no way!

CHAPTER 44: VICTORY

When we were in Gary's office she asked if I'd ever be able to trust her with our child. I said I hope so. But I don't see it happening. For one thing, she hasn't done anything about getting herself into therapy. And even if she did, I don't trust her to open up and really work on her issues. The only way I'd believe that her therapy was being effective is if she were in therapy with Gary because he already knows everything and wouldn't let her get away with her garbage. But therapy aside, what about her irresponsibility and her poor judgment? Those things won't change because of therapy. I'm really glad she came this weekend because it helped solidify some things for me. I've seen red flag after red flag and they are all pointing to one thing—she can't be trusted. I couldn't trust her to protect me when I was a child and I can't trust her to protect my child. Josh and I are in total agreement here. Our job is to protect our child from danger and we intend to do just that, which means we will have to protect our child from his or her grandmother. Because she can't be trusted!

And there's one more thing. She is obsessed with wanting us to have a little girl. She's told me that a hundred times. She goes gaga over the little girl clothes in the store; she refers to the baby as her granddaughter. If we have a girl, my mother is going to smother her and try to enmesh herself with her. In fact, the only thing she has said about us having a boy was really bizarre. We were in the store and were looking at potty seats for little kids, and she said, "If you have a boy, you need to train him to always pee sitting down so, when he grows up, his wife will be happy." That is just bizarre. If we have a girl, what will she teach our daughter about men? And if we have a boy, what will she teach our son about himself? She is so warped! Just another reason why I have no intention of leaving our child alone with her!

As she was getting ready to leave, she waited until Josh was out of the room and asked, "Did everything go okay with us this weekend?" I didn't know how to respond because I certainly didn't want to get into therapy issues. So I just kind of nodded my head and shrugged at the same time and halfheartedly said yeah. I wasn't forthright with her, but I couldn't honestly answer that question without opening up a can of worms, which I didn't want to do outside of Gary's office.

Like I said, this whole weekend has been one red flag after another. Conclusion: I don't trust her. I can't trust her. I never could. I couldn't trust her to protect me when I was a child and I don't trust her to protect my own child. As Josh said, "There is nothing about her that invites trust. She's irresponsible, undependable, scatterbrained, forgetful, clumsy, childish, and mentally ill. What else do you want?" Lots of red flags.

These are all things I intended to address with my mother in Gary's office at the end of September., but I didn't know if it would change anything, at least not on her part. I am changed, though, and I'll continue to change and heal and grow. In the middle of September, we found out that we were having a little girl. We decided to name her Anna Joy. As I've come to the final chapters of my book, I've realized that life will go on. And as my life goes on, I will be influencing a whole new generation. My generation was characterized by abuse and sickness, deception and danger. But the generation of my daughter will be characterized by wellness and safety. Josh and I are going to protect our little girl the way I wish I had been protected as a little girl. Knowing that gives me a sense of security and peace.

The last week in September we drove to meet with Gary and my mother for three days. Gary and Josh and I first planned out the meetings. I wanted to address the issue of not going to her house, Thanksgiving and Christmas, and physical touch. Gary framed each of those issues in the following terms: negative transference regarding her house, courage to state preferences, and boundaries/space/enmeshment. I also wanted to address the issue of boundaries regarding Anna, but Gary suggested we leave that discussion to a later meeting.

The issues of negative transference and preferences regarding Thanksgiving and Christmas were easy to deal with. The issues of boundaries, space, and enmeshment were another story. As we talked with my mother about these issues, I began to feel great fear. We were addressing some very core issues and it was terrifying to me. When my mother started talking about feeling rejected by me, my fear grew, but so did my anger. The last two days of sessions, I felt very exposed and vulnerable. After we left, my fear and anger continued to grow.

Rejection

Ever since we left the meetings with Gary on Friday, I've been feeling weird. Upset. Frustrated. I'm going to try to write about all of it and process it, but I'm afraid my thoughts aren't very cohesive right now. My thoughts are all over the place. I'll try to make sense and do the best I can.

CHAPTER 44: VICTORY

We had a friend from church drive with us on Wednesday so she could visit her parents for a couple of days. When Josh and I left on Friday, we talked about our sessions with my mother on the way to pick up our friend, but once we picked her up, we couldn't talk and process anymore. That was very frustrating to me. Our friend is a talker and that was good because it helped keep Josh awake once it got late. And since she and Josh were doing most of the talking, I did a lot of thinking. The fear that I had been feeling in our sessions on Thursday and Friday generalized into anxiety on the way home, especially once we were traveling after dark. And part of my anxiety was about the topics of conversation that were going on in the car.

Our friend, who used to be a teacher for at-risk kids, told us about many of her former students. She told us about one student and how his eyes were so frightening to her. It made me think about my grandfather's eyes and how frightening they were to me. She talked about these kids and I was thinking about my own situation. My situation was very different in many respects, but at the same time, very similar. Her stories reminded me of that movie, *Precious*. My situation was very different from hers, but frighteningly similar in many respects. My mother was like a sanitized version of the mother in the movie.

Then our friend told one story that really got to me. One good thing about it being dark was that she couldn't see my face and how I kept having to contort it up to keep from crying. I wanted to cry for the last five hours of the trip, but I held it in. She told about this middle school girl whose mother had held a gun to her head. My mother never held a gun to my head, never would, never would even think about such an awful thing. But she refused to get help for me in high school when I was holding a razor blade to my wrist. I asked Josh later, through my tears, "What's the difference?"

After we dropped our friend off at her house about midnight and were driving to our house, I started crying. I had been holding it in for five hours. I bawled all the way home, about fifteen minutes. I didn't know why I was crying, couldn't put my finger on a reason. I kept asking Josh to help me, but he didn't know what to do or how to help. When we got home I quit crying long enough to unload, unpack a few items, and get ready for bed. But once we got into bed, about 12:45 or so, I started crying all over again and I cried for about an hour. I wasn't just crying, I was wailing. All the hurt that I'd written about early on in my therapy with Gary was spilling out. Anger, too, but mostly hurt and pain.

I was hurting and in pain, first of all, because of some clarification I received. My mother confirmed for me that my grandfather used to pick me up from school and watch me until she and my grandmother got home from work. She confirmed that he did this when I was ages six, seven, and eight—the exact ages I have always thought the sexual abuse occurred. I guess it just brought me pain to hear confirmation so clearly, and to realize that what I had suspected (that much of the sexual abuse occurred in the afternoons after school when we were home alone) was true.

But the thing that upset me most was my mother's comments in Gary's office about rejection. I have no doubt that she has felt a lot of rejection in her life regarding my father and that other guy she dated whom she referred to. But she also talked about feeling rejected by me. And the reasons she gave had to do with pictures and physical touch. Because I don't have a picture of her in my house other than the one from the wedding, she felt rejected by me. Because I don't sit RIGHT next to her in church and put my arm around her anymore, she felt rejected by me. I told Josh Friday night that her reasons for feeling rejected by me seem so minor compared to all the reasons I've felt rejected by her my entire life! And yes, I'm sure she feels rejected by men. But don't most people in life experience rejection from a member of the opposite sex at some time or another? I think so. That's somewhat to be expected at some point in a person's life. But the rejection I experienced came from my mother! It's not supposed to be that way! I don't have time, nor do I need to go into all the ways I have felt rejected by her my entire life. I'll hit the high points. Try physical abuse. Try violation of my boundaries all over the place. Try calling me a rotten kid countless times. Try covert incest. Or enmeshment. Or expecting me to be an extension of her rather than letting me be my own person. Or how about the big ones? Not protecting me from being sexually abused when I was a little girl. Refusing to get help for me when I wanted to die. Refusing to acknowledge that I had serious mental health problems. Refusing to admit her mistakes and failings as a mother. What about all those things? She wants to talk about feeling rejected by me because I don't have her picture up and won't put my arm around her? What about how she has rejected me?! She wants to talk about feeling hurt because I don't have more pictures of her in my house? I could tell her a thing or two about hurt. I've written page after page of how I've been hurt by her!

And her refusal to get into therapy to help herself just feels like more rejection. She says I am the most important thing in the world to her, but

CHAPTER 44: VICTORY

she refuses to get help so that she can be healthy and we can have a healthy relationship. And every time I said something to her in Gary's office, her face and her reaction was one of shock and amazement. I violated your boundaries over Labor Day weekend? Impossible! I guilt you all the time? Never! You feel like you need to protect me? Preposterous! I'm passive-aggressive? Ridiculous! You feel like you can't have preferences with me? How silly! Everything was shock! She won't admit things! She said in her 2008 letter to me that she was stunned, appalled and perplexed that she had ever done anything to ever hurt me. She said that she had soul-searched, but still didn't know anything that she had ever done wrong! She is so self-deceptive! She even talked about how she tried to keep her friends when they were growing up from thinking she was a spoiled brat. She doesn't see that she still acts that way!

And she isn't buying in to anything Gary is saying to her about boundaries being healthy and not being about rejection. I can see it in her face. Trust me—I have spent almost forty-one years reading her and being intimately attuned to her every mood, facial expression, body movement, nuance. I've had to do that with her to keep myself safe, so I know when she is buying in to something or not. And she's not buying in to it. Gary told her that she wouldn't be at peace with this discussion unless she saw it as healthy. She doesn't, trust me. And that's one reason I had so much fear during the sessions.

Another reason I had so much fear was because everything I was telling her was greatly upsetting her. I could see it on her face and in her body language. My job has always been to protect her and make her happy, and I wasn't doing that. The little girl was screaming at me that it wasn't safe because I was making her upset and mad. I kept wanting to ask her, "Are you mad at me?" but I knew that Gary would click his pen at me if I did. My adult knew it wouldn't have been good to ask. But the little girl wanted to ask very badly. And then, of course, I wanted lunch time to be a time that I could reconnect and feel out the situation and feel safe again. It's like what Gary said about social workers going into homes where there is child abuse. They look to see who the child is with because the child is going to be with the abuser. It is the safest place. I **TOTALLY** understand that! That may be one reason why there has been so much enmeshment on MY part. I had to be enmeshed with her because that was where it was the safest. By being an extension of her, I was protected. The alternative was to risk experiencing her wrath if I branched out on my own. We didn't go to lunch with her on Friday and that felt so unsafe to me. That unsafe feeling just grew as we traveled home. I didn't feel safe all day.

Another reason I didn't feel safe was that she expressed her upset feelings and stuff and Gary didn't address them. He has said many times to me, and to her too, that these sessions are not about doing therapy with her, but about my issues, my healing. But both in June and this past week, every time my mother would talk about her issues, Gary never dealt with them or gave comfort or stuff like that. That was frightening to me. Why? Because in the past if she was upset, I would fall all over myself in an effort to comfort, appease, placate, soothe. Gary wasn't doing that. He wasn't soothing her at all. He would acknowledge what she was saying and then move right on. That upset my mother, I could tell. And in turn, it frightened me!

And somewhat related to Gary not soothing her was her comment on Friday that "there's no one to hold me and help me through it. I just have to do it." I wanted to say something, or I wanted Gary to say something, in response to that. That's how she feels, but that's not reality. If she would quit being so worried about image and reach out for help, she wouldn't have to go through it on her own. There are lots of people who would help her. She has friends, and there are plenty of resources in her church of 800 and her city of over a million people for her to get help. But she refuses to reach out! She refuses to crucify that stupid philosophy of hers that seeking help is a sign of weakness! She doesn't respect me because I did reach out! There's more rejection right there. If I hadn't reached out I would be dead at my own hand. So she would rather me suck it up and deal with it on my own and kill myself than reach out for help? That's what it sounds like to me! At least maybe then she could respect me!! If I told her that, she would deny it, but that's how it sounds. She would respect me if I dealt with it on my own, but not if I got help. And yet, when I was dealing with it on my own, I wanted to die. I was carving up my body with razor blades and masturbating in such a way that I was hurting and raping myself. So she can respect that, but not my being in therapy? What kind of warped, sick mother do I have?!

And then on Friday she made a statement that she felt worthless as a mother because she couldn't go back and undo things that she wouldn't have done if she'd had any idea of what it was doing to her child. She's right. She can't undo the things she's done, but she can try to change so she'll quit doing them. And yet that she refuses to do! She focuses on

CHAPTER 44: VICTORY

feeling worthless because she can't go backwards and fix things, yet she refuses to go forward and fix things! It doesn't matter how many times she meets with Gary and me or how many things we put on the table. It's not going to have an impact until she gets in therapy herself and starts dealing with her own issues. And yet she refuses to do that very thing! She is such a coward! And of course, she's not going to get help as long as she holds on to that destructive philosophy of hers! She's not buying in to what Gary's been telling her. I know that. And as long as she doesn't, she's going to stay sick. Gary tells me I'm getting healthy regardless of whether my mother ever gets healthy herself. But her refusal to get help for herself just feels like more rejection to me.

Gary told her she was codependent. He said that that word would bug her. Then he told Josh and me later that she **needed** me to be unhealthy so that she could feel safe, because my healthiness exposes her problems. I'm confused about that statement. How could she need me to be unhealthy when she refused to admit that I was unhealthy? That doesn't compute. Well, wait a minute, maybe it does.. If she admitted that I was unhealthy and got help for me, I would become healthy, and that would expose her. Okay, I see it now. That's why she didn't respect me for reaching out. She didn't respect me because my reaching out exposed her issues and her problems. So, I really do see the lie in her statement that I am the most important thing in the world to her. That's not true at all. The most important thing in the world to her is her. She would rather me be sick and dying inside and carving up my body with razor blades and losing my sanity (which almost happened) than admit that she has any problems. She's the most important thing in the world to her. Not me. It's more important for her to keep her glorious image of herself than for her daughter to live. And **SHE** wants to talk about rejection?! Gary says I rocked her foundations this week. Let me read her this paragraph. Let me read her this piece I'm writing. That'll rock her foundation. She doesn't care about me. She doesn't love me, not really. Not true love. She's absorbed with self-love and she loves me only for what she can get out of it for herself. That's why she is so enmeshed with me. She latched onto me like a parasite and sucked me dry for herself. When I reached out to others, she just sucked harder. When I reached out for help, she despised me and rejected me. I **HAVE** to protect Anna from her. Anna will be at my mother's mercy unless Josh and I protect her. And we will. **BY GOD, WE WILL!** I am *not* going to let my mother suck my daughter dry! I am ***not*** going to let her do to Anna what she did to me!

As I have been writing this piece, I've come to another understanding of why I fear her. She doesn't treat me as a mother should. She treats me like a spouse. She treats me like an extension of her. She treats me with disdain and disgust because I've sought help for my problems. She doesn't treat me with self-sacrificial love as a mother should treat her child. She treats me with selfish love, sucking me dry for everything she can get for herself. That kind of mother is a mother to be feared. And because I've been exposing her for who she really is, my fear is just growing. And so is the hurt and pain, because I've been realizing with great clarity how she really is toward me. When she snooped in my private writings, she told my grandmother that she found out what I really thought about her. Well, I am seeing what she really thinks about me. She thinks I don't have a right to exist outside of her. She thinks that I'm someone to be disrespected because I've sought help for my problems. She thinks that I'm a threat to her glorious, deceptive image of herself. And she would rather me stay sick and unhealthy and dying inside than have me to expose her failings. My mother has no strength of character. Rather than admit her own problems, she'd rather me be mentally ill and ignore it. I thank God that I had the strength of character to reach out for help. If I had listened to her, if I had trusted her, if I had bought into her philosophy, if I had allowed her to win, **I WOULD BE DEAD!** And she wants to talk about rejection because I won't put up her picture or put my arm around her in church? She thinks I'm rejecting her because I'm setting boundaries with her? She hasn't experienced rejection from me, not true rejection. Not the way she has rejected me. She would deny all this, no doubt. but it's true. And as I realize these things and write these things, the hurt and the pain just grow.

I wrote that piece on a Sunday afternoon, and that evening when I read it to Josh, all the hurt and pain and anger came pouring out as I cried. I asked Josh later if he had ever heard the term *primal scream*, because that's what it felt like I was doing. He agreed with me. I just kept wailing and couldn't seem to get control of myself. Finally, I told Josh through my tears that I wanted to call Gary. When he answered the phone, I couldn't stop crying. I managed to get out that I had written a piece about rejection and how I was so upset because I had realized that she would rather I stay sick and mentally ill than admit that she has problems. Gary worked at calming me down. He pointed out that her actions, while extremely hurtful to me, weren't intentional. I told him it didn't matter; it still hurt

CHAPTER 44: VICTORY

like hell. He agreed and told me that this last meeting with her was as momentous as the first because we exposed her games. He urged me to give my grief to the Lord for the evening, to take a walk to work off some of the excess adrenaline, and to take my sleeping medicine and get some sleep. He also said that my mother's system is the only one she knows how to operate under. She is terrified I'm going to leave her. She doesn't understand that truth is her friend. I was calmer after talking with Gary. I did what he suggested that evening and was able to get some sleep.

I had a regular session with Gary two days later. After I read him the piece I had written about rejection, I asked him point blank, "Am I right in what I wrote about her? Am I right in saying that she would rather me stay sick and mentally ill and dying inside than admit her failings?" He said I was. He did point out that it wasn't her intention, but that it was the result of her philosophy and her dysfunction. He reminded me that we hadn't played her games in the therapy sessions, we had confronted her on the covert incest (using a word she could understand – enmeshment), and it wasn't my job or his job to get her healthy. Our purpose, our goal, was to protect me—and to protect Anna. We would remind her of her need to get into therapy each time we meet with her, but that's her choice. Gary told me that he was very excited because I was staring the greatest fear of my life right in her face and I was surviving. And I've gotten out all of my anger and hurt and pain. Now I needed to think about our baby, enjoy life with Josh, and grow in my relationship with God. My adult needs to tell my little girl, "We are dealing with it." I am confronting the fears of my lifetime; I'm confronting all the anger and hurt; I'm confronting, and I'm surviving. Indeed, I am winning. We scheduled another series of sessions at the end of November to meet with my mother in which we would address the issue of protecting Anna and setting boundaries with my mother regarding her. But, Gary and Josh both noted, I have peeled away all the layers. Everything else is clean up. Everything else is practical, protecting issues. I would deal with transference issues as they arise. I would work on not being enmeshed with Anna. But I have faced my greatest fears, and I have survived. I can be at peace now. The little girl can be at peace.

Gary said if something is anchored at the bottom of the sea, and there is air in its lungs, it will rise. If the chains have been loosened, it will rise. That is God's plan for healing. It was like my memories coming when the time was right. Once the chains were loosed, the memories came. I thought a lot about that illustration, and I thought about what Gary had said regarding peace. I pondered the idea of victory and peace and how the two are closely related. I reflected on what I had written about victory coming only at the cost of pain. I began to feel a sense of peace pouring over me. When I did, I sat down in my chair and wrote a letter.

Dear Little Girl,

I know you were listening when Gary and I were talking. And you were listening as Josh and I were talking about protecting our child. I know you feel a sense of security knowing that Josh and I will protect Anna, even from Mother. Little Girl, I understand a lot of things and I can help you understand, too. But I don't know if you're ready to listen. Right now you may just want me to hold you and comfort you. Well, I want to do just that.

What happened to you was horrific, and it was not your fault. It shouldn't have happened. You were a beautiful, innocent little girl, and you were violated and abused and betrayed. You have lived with deep, profound shame for so long because of everything that happened to you, and because of the results of what happened. But honey, I am not ashamed of you. You do not have to live in shame any longer. I know you feel so much shame over the things that you did to yourself that I just continued into adulthood. But those things are in the past. God has forgiven us. We are washed clean. You know I don't do those things anymore. I haven't for a number of years. The chains of addiction are broken. We are not entrapped any longer. Instead, we are integrating and becoming whole. We are living a life of truth. We are experiencing victory.

I know you still hurt and are full of pain because of what Papa did to you and because of what Mommie did to you. There is absolutely no excuse for what they did. Papa will have to answer to God for what he did. And God is a just God. Mommie will have to answer, too. And hopefully Mommie will get into therapy herself and start to grow up, because really, she's an immature child who has never grown up. I pray for her that she will. She'll be so much happier and healthier if she does. But even if she doesn't, I will protect you. Josh and I will protect you and we will protect our daughter. You and Anna will be safe, regardless of what Mommie does.

Little Girl, as we grieve and cry over what happened to us, the pain will eventually lessen, I promise. The pain will always be there to some degree, but it won't hurt as bad. And you and I will continue to integrate into one healthy person. I want you to be at peace about things. I want me to be at peace about things. I think there is a peace that comes with seeing the big picture and understanding. As we continue to integrate, there will be peace. It's difficult to explain how there can be peace at the same time as pain, but it's true. I've said before that I have sad joy and victorious pain. Our peace is like that, too. There are all these hurts from our past, but there's a peace in knowing that God has redeemed us from our past. There's a peace in knowing that a **perfect** being—God—loves us and protects us and cares for us, even when our imperfect family didn't.

Little Girl, there is a peace in having overcome the past. I have labored diligently in therapy for over seven years now, trying to heal, trying to overcome, and I've been successful. There is victory in my life now. Pain, yes, but a victorious pain. And there is joy, too. And yes, it's a sad joy because it's a joy born out of sorrow. But it's based on truth, not circumstances. It won't go away, even if the circumstances get tough.

And now, Little Girl, I want there to be peace. I want to have peace and I want you to have peace. The peace that we can have came at a cost. We've paid a high price for our peace. It has taken years of courageous honesty, terrifying vulnerability, incredible sorrow, countless tears, and fearless self-examination to arrive at peace. A costly peace, but peace nonetheless.

And I'll continue to pay a high price for our peace, because I'll continue to hold myself up to the standard of God's Word to see where I am lacking, where I still need to heal and to change and to grow. I don't want to be complacent about the peace that I feel. I want to remain at peace—with myself, with you, and with God. Therefore, I will continue to examine myself. I'll continue to communicate with you. I'll continue to feel the pain and work through it. Little Girl, I promise you, I will never stop growing and healing. I owe it to myself. I owe it to you. I owe it to Anna. And Josh and I will protect Anna. We owe that to her. We owe that to you. Little Girl, I have come to a sense of peace and I hope, as time goes by, that I can help you understand things as I understand them, so that you, too, can feel that peace.

Little Girl, the first time I talked to you, I told you that it was okay and safe to cry. You have cried. We've cried together. As we've gone down this road, there have been so many tears. And Little Girl, it's been a long journey and we're still traveling. But the road we're traveling now is not as dangerous as the road we've traveled before. And you and I are not self-destructive as we were before. There is healing. There is health. There is joy and victory and peace. The joy is tinged with sadness, the victory is laced with pain, and the peace has come at a cost. Sad joy, painful victory, costly peace. The childhood we had was sad, there was a lot of pain, and the cost of your innocence was very high. That's why the joy and the victory and the peace I now have, have sorrowful aspects to them. But Little Girl, the joy born out of sorrow is real, it's lasting. The victory that was born out of pain is to be celebrated. The peace that came at a cost is comforting. We broke the chains. We survived. We are free.

I love you, Little Girl.

Love,
Rochelle

As I read the letter to Josh, my voice choked with emotion as I concluded with the words, "We broke the chains. We survived. We are free." It's taken thirty-five years of pain and struggle to break the chains of abuse and addiction and dysfunction, but the chains are loosed. They are broken and I am whole. Steven Curtis Chapman's song, "Beauty Will Rise," contains poignant lyrics. "But buried deep beneath all our broken dreams we have this hope—Out of these ashes, beauty will rise. We will dance among the ruins, we will see it with our own eyes. Out of this darkness, new light will shine, for we know joy is coming in the morning, in the morning. Beauty will rise.... It will take our breath away to see the beauty that is made out of these ashes, out of these ashes...."[11] My life was in ashes, in ruins, but God worked through many people and years of therapy to bring beauty out of the ashes. As Solomon wrote in Ecclesiastes 3:11, God "has made everything beautiful in its time." There is beauty in my life where once was grotesque ugliness. There is joy in my life where once was crippling depression. There is peace in my life where once was bitter conflict. There is victory in my life where once was crushing defeat. God has made everything beautiful in its time. It took thirty-five years, but now there is beauty. Now my life is beautiful, and Josh and I will create a beautiful life for our child.

45

Freedom

Freedom,
like a convict
pardoned,
a slave
emancipated,
a P.O.W.
freed,
given a second chance,
a new lease on life,
a new appreciation
for liberty;
or,
like a butterfly
coming out of
its cocoon,
unfolding its wings,
testing them out,
and flying off to bring
beauty to the world;
or,
like a magnificent eagle
who had been captured,
being released
back into its
native habitat,
spreading its
wings,
lifting off,
and soaring
high above all the
strife of

the world below,
gliding on the
wings of heaven,
unshackled,
unburdened,
free.
Freedom.

We scheduled another series of meetings with my mother and Gary for the Monday through Wednesday of Thanksgiving week. I was very concerned about these sessions with Gary and my mother, because we would be discussing boundaries regarding Anna. I knew this would really upset her, and after our sessions, she was supposed to come to our house for Thanksgiving. Gary reassured me that if I needed to change Thanksgiving plans, I could. We would see how the sessions went and play it by ear. As Thanksgiving week got closer, my anxiety and fear levels increased. Gary continually reminded me that all my significant people would be there with me—Josh, Anna, the little girl, and of course, Gary. As I waited for the week to arrive, while spending time online, I discovered a website I hadn't noticed before.

I found an amazing website last week called CovertIncest.org. I've been reading through the hundreds of posts people have made on this website, and I've been overwhelmed by the similarities to my own situation. I've known for a number of years now that my mother engaged in covert incest against me. Gary and I have talked about it on numerous occasions. But I always felt alone in that. I knew it existed because I had read two books on the subject—*Silently Seduced: When Parents Make Their Children Partners* and *The Emotional Incest Syndrome: What to Do When a Parent's Love Rules Your Life*. But I'd never met anyone else who had experienced it, especially not someone who had experienced same-sex covert incest, i.e. mother/daughter covert incest. Both books recognized that such a phenomenon exists, but neither focused on it, especially from the perspective of a single parent and her daughter. But on this website, I have read numerous women's accounts experiencing covert incest from their mothers. I'm not alone! There are other people out there who have gone through what I have gone through. True, there are things in their histories that are not in mine, but there are things in my history that are not

CHAPTER 45: FREEDOM

in theirs. Another find on this website has been to see how common it is for people to have experienced overt incest from one parent and covert incest from the other. Now granted, my overt incest was from my grandfather, not my father. But my grandfather was my father for the first nine years of my life, so I see it as the same. All in all, this website has been very beneficial to me. I am so thankful that I found it.

That said, let me mention some things that have been going on with me since I began reading on this website last week. First, my anger toward my mother is growing. As I read accounts on the website, I've been remembering more things from my childhood and adulthood that my mother did to me, with me, etc., that were quite inappropriate. As I remember these things, I've been checking them out with Josh. "Is this inappropriate? Is this covert incest?" And invariably his answer is yes. My mother was inappropriate with me in so many ways. It makes my skin crawl and my stomach flip. It feels so icky. And it is ongoing. The way she is obsessed with taking pictures of my pregnant body to put in her album just makes me want to puke! It's interesting to me that I've had so many memories of the abuse I suffered at the hands of my grandfather, but the memories of my childhood with my mother are just now, slowly, beginning to come into my awareness. And the memories start from adulthood and work back. I'm remembering inappropriate, incestuous actions on her part from the years I lived with her as an adult first. Only sketchy memories of her inappropriateness with me as a child are present at this point. Last March when I had the last flashback of my grandfather's abuse, I thought I had recovered my memories. But that's not a true statement. I have recovered part of my memories, the memories of the overt sexual abuse I suffered at the hands of my grandfather. But the memories of the abuse I suffered at my mother's hands have not been totally recovered. I have remembered some of the physical abuse, enough for me to finally admit that it *was* physical abuse. But the covert incest from childhood is just now starting to creep into my awareness. I thought I had blocked out my childhood solely because of my grandfather's abuse, but I'm realizing, over the last year or so, that his abuse was only part of why I blocked it out. My mother's abuse is a large part of it, and I am only beginning to acknowledge it. I've known for years that she had hurt me deeply, but it's only been over the last seven years that I've been able to acknowledge that she had abused me, both physically and emotionally (and covertly, sexually as well). And as I am acknowledging these things, my anger grows. I'm tired of dancing around things with her. I want it all out on the table. I say this, but I am still afraid. No, that's not accurate. I'm terrified to bring these things up to her, but it must be done. It must be done for the sake of my sanity and mental health. And for the protection of my own child.

That's been something I didn't expect. As the days go by, Anna is getting more and more active in my womb. She is moving and kicking and punching all the time and it is extremely exciting and wonderful to feel and behold! But every time I feel her moving inside of me, I think of my mother. I think of how I must protect my daughter from my mother. Then I think of myself as a little girl. I was once in my mother's womb, too. She felt me moving. She gave birth to me just as I will soon give birth to Anna. It overwhelms me with confusion as to how she could have gone through what I am going through with Anna and not be blown away by a protective instinct toward me. But she wasn't. Instead, she has spent her life exploiting me for her own uses and using me to meet her own needs, rather than meeting my needs. I see this powerfully now and I haven't given birth to Anna yet. I know that these thoughts are going to get even stronger once Anna is born, and especially as she grows older. I have read before that women who were abused in childhood, but blocked it out, often start having memories when their own child reaches the age they were when the abuse started. I can see that happening with me. I look at the portrait I have of me as a little girl, and I can see Anna in it and I am overwhelmed with a fierce desire to protect her. How could my mother not have protected me? How could she have, instead, used me and abused me? And then, as I became an adult, she refused to acknowledge my problems because she didn't want her own problems exposed. How utterly selfish! A mother is supposed to protect and nurture her child. A mother is supposed to put her child's needs first. A mother is supposed to do many things that my mother did not. I swear, with God as my witness, that **I WILL NOT BE LIKE MY MOTHER!**

I say all this thinking of what will transpire next week when we meet with Gary and my mother again. My anger is growing. Josh said I need to use my anger to fight my fear. But my fear is also growing. Which one will win out? Can I confront her on these things? Can I protect my daughter? Can I? I must. It's not an option. But I am afraid. I know I won't be alone. Gary will be there. Josh will be there. God will be there. Anna will be there, moving inside of me, reminding me of her presence and my need to protect her. My inner little girl will be there, terrified, but at the same time, cheering me on to stand up for myself and for her and for Anna. As Gary said when we found out we were having a little girl, "God has given you the opportunity to do things over. **This** little girl will be protected." The little girls in my life, my inner child and Anna, are who I am fighting for. They are the ones I am standing up to my mother for. And I will not let them down. I am afraid, I am terrified, but I will not let them down.

About a week before our sessions with my mother, I sat down at the computer and typed a letter to my mother. I wasn't sure I wanted to read it to her in Gary's office, or even if I'd be able to, but I was leaning toward it. I had two appointments with Gary the week before Thanksgiving week, and I read it to him during the first one. He told me it was the strongest I had ever put things to her. He said I made things very clear. At one point in the letter I used the word *narcissism*. Gary suggested that I take that word out. He said we didn't want to get into diagnosing her, even though he agreed with the diagnosis. He said it would be the one point she would come back to and argue about. Speaking from experience working with narcissists, he recommended I not use that word because narcissists typically have such poor insight into themselves and are extremely defensive about confrontation. He reasserted that our goal wasn't to create therapeutic insight into her problems. That would be for her to work on with her own therapist, if she ever gets one.

The second time I talked with Gary that week, we discussed the actual reading of the letter. I told Gary that I'd been reading it to Josh every day and he said that it was a good idea to desensitize myself to the letter by practicing reading it. I was very afraid of what her response would be. Gary assured me that she wouldn't like it, but we wouldn't be telling her these things for her to like them. We would be setting boundaries. He told me what he has told me many times over the years. She would eventually come around because I am all she has. He asked me why I wanted to read this to her. Did the little girl want to tell her off or did she want to be safe and have good boundaries? Or did she want to make Mother understand? Because, he said, she probably won't understand. And he repeated that it isn't my job to create therapeutic insight for her. I told him that the little girl needed to have these things said to Mother. In the past I have acquiesced, cowered, made excuses. But now, I needed to tell my mother these things in order for the little girl to be safe. I reminded Gary of something the little girl said in a conversation I'd had with her at the end of 2009: "I want you to tell her how she's hurt me. I want you to quit hiding. I want you to stand up to her. I want you to stand up for me. I want you to tell the truth about Papa. I want you to tell the truth about her. I want you to quit pretending that things are okay." That's what this letter was all about—telling her the truth about her. I had already told her the truth about Papa, and I had started telling her the truth about her. Now it was time to tell her the whole truth. No more hiding. No more cowering. No more pretending or lies. It was time for truth to be completely revealed.

We decided that when we started the sessions with my mother, Gary would introduce the boundary topics and then I would read the section of the letter that corresponded to that boundary. That way she would get it in chunks. But Gary reassured me that I would be able to read the entire letter. The letter said:

Dear Mom,

I've been thinking about writing this letter for a week or so, but haven't gotten the courage until now. Even so, I am scared to be writing this and terrified to read it to you. I'm not sure I can read it to you. If Josh or Gary read it to you, you'll get the letter nonetheless. But even with one of them reading it to you, I am still terrified.

I feel like we've been dancing around things in our meetings with Gary, especially in September, and I don't want that to happen in this next series of meetings. I'm tired of addressing things in Gary's office and you not generalizing the learning to other situations. If you were able to do that, you would have known intuitively from our discussion in September about touching that asking me how many bra sizes I've gone up was an inappropriate question. But inappropriate questions and such have been part of our relationship my entire life. I feel as if I don't have a right to have boundaries with my body with you because you have violated them my entire life. We talked before in Gary's office about all the times you wouldn't give me privacy, walked in on me in the bathroom, got angry when I wanted to close the bathroom door, wanted to see me naked, etc. My body has always seemed to be of great interest to you and that feels very, very icky to me. Even now, your obsession with taking pictures of my pregnant body and putting them in an album feels very icky, like I'm being violated. I've gone along with that obsession of yours for the last five months, but I haven't liked it. And it's got to stop.

CHAPTER 45: FREEDOM

Your seeming obsession with my body is the main reason why I have to set a boundary about something when Anna is born. I do not want you in the room when I am breastfeeding or anything connected with that. That's not safe. I don't want comments about my breasts or breastfeeding or anything like that. My breasts have always been fair game for you to comment about, and I hated it when you did. You would comment on how big they were, how much my husband someday would like them, how when I get old they're going to hang down, and so on. Your "fascination with my equipment," as Gary puts it, feels icky to me. And it's just weird. There are a lot of things over the years that were inappropriate, and I am tired of it. In a normal, healthy mother/daughter relationship, a pregnant daughter probably wouldn't have a problem with her mother putting her hand on her stomach, but I do. That's because we don't have a healthy mother/daughter relationship. It feels icky. And just because you ask permission doesn't mean I have to give it. You seem to think that because you ask permission that I must give it and I am being mean if I don't. I'm sorry if you think I'm being mean, but I have the right to say no. I have the right to set boundaries with you.

I have spent forty-one years reading you. I had to in order to be safe around you. I read your moods, your body language, etc., and I would adjust my actions to compensate or to appease or placate or soothe. One reason I was so scared during our last series of meetings was because I was reading your facial expressions and body language, and seeing was that you weren't buying in to what Gary was telling you about boundaries being healthy and you being unhealthy. But whether or not you're buying it, it's true.

I have always felt as if I was there to meet your needs, rather than the other way around. I felt it was my job to protect you. I felt it was my job to make you happy. That's one reason why writing this letter and reading it, or having it read to you, is so terrifying to me—I'm not making you happy with this. You would express disapproval, often subtly, if I didn't do things exactly the way you wanted me to do them. Over the last eight years, since I moved out, I have been getting healthier and trying to become my own person. But it has been incredibly difficult, because I've always felt like an extension of you, that I didn't have a right to my own life outside of you. The emotional abuse you inflicted on me has had me chained for many years. I felt like I didn't have the right to be my own person, have my own preferences. I've been afraid of you for many years and I still am. But that has to change. Indeed, it is changing. As I get healthier and stand up for myself with you, it's changing. But the fear is still there.

The bottom line is that you are toxic to me. Gary told me that several years ago, and it hasn't changed. When I spend time around you, it takes me days to get back to feeling normal afterward. That's not healthy. I worry and get anxious beforehand, as well. Again, not healthy. Spending a lot of time around you is incredibly difficult for me.

I have two things to say to you that you are going to be very unhappy about, angry about, upset about. But I have to say them. First of all, I am going to set a boundary about when Anna is born. I need that first week of her life to be as stress-free as possible in order for certain things, like breastfeeding, to go well. Having you at our house will not make it stress-free. Josh and I have discussed this, Gary and I have discussed this, and Josh and I have come to the decision that we do not want you to come until the first week is over. That will give Anna and me time to adjust to breastfeeding, and it will give Josh and me and Anna time to adjust to being a family without anyone else or any extra stress. Contrary to what you may think or what your friends may think, Anna is mine and Josh's child and that is the primary relationship that needs to be nurtured.

The second thing has to do with how much time you think you are going to spend with Anna. You have mentioned many times about us leaving Anna with you when we travel. You have mentioned many times that you are thinking of retiring and spending a week out of every month here. That's not going to happen. My mental health can't take that and I don't want Anna exposed to that much of your unhealthiness. Unless and until you get into some serious, intense, long-term therapy and start addressing your issues and getting healthy, your access to Anna is going to be limited. This is something that Josh and I are in total agreement on. We don't want to use Anna as a pawn to get you into therapy, but the fact remains that we do not trust you. You are very unhealthy and we don't trust you with our child as long as you remain unhealthy. We are not going to expose our child to your dysfunction. We are not going to let you repeat with Anna what you did with me.

You may think we are being unfair and mean and cruel and who knows what else. But, as one of my friends pointed out, there are consequences to your lifelong actions, and one of those consequences is limited access to your grandchild because we don't want your mental illness affecting her the way it has me.

CHAPTER 45: FREEDOM

You may hate me for saying all that I've said in this letter. You may threaten to cut me out of your will. You have done that before. You may decide that I am an awful, mean, unfair, cruel daughter. But I am saying all these things, and Josh and I are making these decisions because of **your** behavior. This letter is addressing the consequences of your behavior. Just like when you snooped on my computer and violated my boundaries, then you said that I meant to hurt you. That wasn't the case at all. You were hurt because of your **own** wrongdoing. You violated my boundaries. Same thing here. You may be very hurt by the content of this letter, but this letter is necessary because of **your** behavior. Josh and I are simply working to do what God has charged us to do—protect our child. I don't trust you with our child because you didn't protect me as a child, and because you were very unhealthy with me. We don't want that for Anna, and we will not let that happen. You asked me in June if I would ever trust you with our child. That is totally dependent on you and your behavior. If you seek help, start getting healthy, start addressing your mental illness, then maybe someday we'll be able to trust you with Anna. But right now, we do not.

In our last meetings in September, you spoke about feeling rejected by me. The reasons you gave were that I didn't have more pictures of you in my home and because I wouldn't sit right next to you in church and put my arm around you like I used to. You probably feel rejected by me because of the content of this letter. But let me point out a thing or two. One, I am working to develop a **healthy** relationship. Setting boundaries, as Gary has already told you, is not about rejection. It is about being healthy. Boundaries have been practically nonexistent in our family. That is unhealthy. Two, it is difficult for me to understand how you can feel rejected by me because I am setting boundaries to try to be healthy, when I feel as if you have rejected me my entire life. You didn't protect me from being sexually abused by your own father, but when I acted out because of the sexual abuse, you punished me abusively instead. You have spent years attempting to ignore my mental health problems. You point blank told me that you did not respect me for reaching out for help. A mother is supposed to be there for her child and help her. And yet, it seems as if you would rather I stay sick and unhealthy than for me to get healthy, because when I started getting healthy, I began to expose your problems. That is true rejection. You say I am the most important thing in the world to you, but I don't believe you. If I were, you would be actively taking steps to get healthy. And yet, it has been six months since Gary first recommended that you get into therapy and as far as I know, you have yet to do so.

One other thing. These meetings with Gary are not about working on your issues. They are about **my** therapy. They are about **me** getting healthy and well. They are about me standing up for myself and feeling safe. That's why Gary hasn't addressed your issues with you. That's for you to do with your therapist, if you ever bother to get one.

Saying all these things to you is incredibly frightening to me. Terrifying. Because I've always felt it was my job to protect you and make you happy and do whatever you wanted. That's because it seems that your relationship with me existed to meet your needs rather than my needs. It was as if I were trapped in a psychological marriage with you, that I was your surrogate spouse. I was always trying to please you, especially as I got older, and I never felt like I quite measured up. Because I was an extension of you, I felt like I was never seen as a separate human being with different needs, wants, preferences, and feelings from you. But I am a separate human being from you. I've been separating from you for the past eight years. But the consequences of living with you have been an incredibly difficult challenge to overcome. But I am overcoming. I am getting healthy. I'm protecting myself and my daughter. If you choose to get healthy, that's your choice. I can't make you do that, but I can set boundaries. There can be consequences. And there will be. My generation was characterized by abuse and sickness. That **WILL NOT** be repeated with my child!!

Whether you think so or not, I love you. If I didn't love you, I would have cut off contact years ago. But the fact that I'm going to so much trouble to try to work out our relationship shows that I do love you. And because I love you, I want you to get healthy. Part of getting healthy is facing the truth. I've been facing the truth about my life for the last seven years in therapy. It has been the most difficult thing I've ever done. But it's been worth it. And I'll continue to face the truth and get healthy, whether you ever do or not, because I need to be healthy. I need to be healthy for myself, for my husband, and for my daughter. These last seven years in therapy have helped me to finally start becoming the woman God always intended me to be. He doesn't want me to be mentally ill. He doesn't want me to be unhealthy. And He doesn't want you to be, either. So I will conclude with two things. One, you need to get help. Two, I love you.

Rochelle

CHAPTER 45: FREEDOM

When the first session with my mother started, Gary pointed out to her that one cannot be intimate with someone unless you know their hurts. What I would be telling her, he said, would hurt her, but that wasn't my intention. But in order for intimacy to be there, my hurts must be dealt with. He first mentioned the boundary about her taking pictures of my pregnant body. One thing that he pointed out to my mother was that all of the information we would be discussing must be processed in the context of my childhood—I was sexually violated by her father. If that hadn't happened things might be very different. When incest occurs, the survivor wants to protect her body. That's what I'm doing by setting the boundary about pictures.

I then read the section about not wanting her in the room while I am breastfeeding and about her touching my pregnant body. She came back with defensiveness about touching me. Gary told her that she was going to have to try to understand the ickiness that I feel about my body being violated, especially in the context of having been a victim of incest. Gary pointed out to my mother that I was reading these things to her with great fear. She expressed her shock over my fear of her, as she had done in previous sessions. Gary brought up the cutting and told my mother how I had gone to great lengths to hide my scars from her, and how I was petrified that she would find out. He acknowledged that it's hard for her to realize that she's the object of her child's greatest fear, but that fear needs to be brought out and dealt with.

I read and we discussed the section about me feeling as if I were there to meet her needs, and about me reading her moods, body language, etc., all the time. Gary explained to her that in abusive families, the other parent and the child are often enmeshed. This is what happened with my mother and me, and that's what developed the intense fear in me. He emphasized that the boundaries I was setting were coming out of the fear. As he put it, there is a fortress mentality for those who fear. He continually stressed to her the importance of me getting these things out in the open in order for me to be able to individuate from her. I have always felt as if it were my job to protect her, something children from broken or abusive families often feel, he said. But that's not my job. My job is to individuate, to separate from her. And that's why I'm setting these boundaries. He told her that she didn't have to agree with the boundaries, or even like them, but she must honor them.

He didn't let her respond during that session, but asked her to think about what I had said and what he'd said. He wanted her to be able to respond to me the next day in a non-defensive way, rather than being angry and defensive. He told me after she left that he was trying to get her to focus on her capacity to understand her daughter from my perspective. He said if she doesn't understand where I am, she would stay angry and wounded, and would continue to exhibit passive-aggressive anger toward me. As we processed what had happened in the session, I began to have a panic attack there in Gary's office. Once Josh and I left, the fear didn't subside. I told Josh that I was so terrified precisely because Gary didn't let her respond. I felt as if the little girl needed to "gauge the barometer" in order to feel safe. But Gary told me the next morning, before my mother arrived, that it's not healthy for me to go by her barometer, to be hooked to her moods. That is a way she has passive control over me. He said my safety is not in reading my mother. My safety is in my adult and in Josh and Gary. My future and my safety are not hinged on her anymore. He assured me that she is just like the Wizard of Oz, all huff and puff, but underneath a very small person, deeply insecure and deeply frightened. On the other hand, she is crafty, a showman, histrionic, and narcissistic. She hides behind what she wants others to see. She violates boundaries and has always done so, morally, ethically, religiously. She pushes the bounds. But, he reminded me, I'm going to have good boundaries. He point blank said he didn't like my mother's personality type. He said, "This kind of person gives me the ickies and we're not incestually related. I can see how icky it is for you. I can also see how others are drawn to it if they aren't perceptive enough to see through it." I was glad Gary was able to see through it! And I was glad I was able to see through it, finally. I was still very afraid, but I felt better.

When my mother arrived, Gary let her talk first and tell what she had thought about the previous evening. She had made lots of notes in her notebook and as she talked, I wrote down in my journal every possible word I could of what she was saying. I took nine pages of notes from what she said. First, she expressed her love for me and said that was the reason she was there. She admitted that, as she went through her notes from the day before, she realized many of her comments were "I, I, I," and she said she didn't want it to be all about her. She talked about feeling crushed and beaten to the ground to realize that her child was afraid of her. She expressed regret and sorrow over and over again, almost to excess. In fact, at one point she said that she would "lay flat on the floor groveling, asking for forgiveness." She talked about what a beautiful person I was and how much she admired me and was jealous of me. She did at times get defensive, saying that she had been willing to get a ticket to meet with us that very week when she got my letter back in February. We didn't bother to correct her on that or point out all of the excuses she gave back then. Then, in a further effort to defend herself, she said, "Do you remember when I did this? Do you remember when I did that?" But she then went back to begging for forgiveness, going on about how she never intended to hurt me, and saying how she should have been the one I felt the safest with.

When she finally finished, I was confused. I had expected denial and anger and who knows what else. Gary responded a little and then asked if we wanted a break. I think he could tell I was struggling, because he then asked if Josh and I would like to speak with him privately for a bit. After he sent my mother down the hall, I told him that now, after her response, I was afraid to read the rest of the letter. Gary gently chided me for trying to, once again, come to her rescue. He told me that she needs to be sorry. He acknowledged that she is hurt, but he reminded me that she is clever, too. He encouraged me to get the letter out there, read the rest of it in one fell swoop. Then we could piece together the damage. He told me, "Don't walk away from this. Get it on the table. It's very important that you communicate that you're going to protect Anna." So I decided I would read the rest of the letter when she returned to his office. While I was waiting with great trepidation for her to return, I read through the list of Scriptures I had typed out. I had written out two pages of Scriptures that were comforting and encouraging to me, Scriptures to combat fear and anxiety. I'd had the list sitting on the couch between Josh and me the entire time we had been meeting, both that day and the day before. As I read through them once again, the one that kept returning to my thoughts was from Psalm 86:16 where the Psalmist asks God to grant *His* strength to His servant. Over and over in my head I prayed that. "Lord, grant me *Your* strength to do this; grant me *Your* strength to read this letter; help me Lord!"

When she returned to Gary's office, I told her that I do forgive her, but reminded her that there are consequences and things that needed to be worked through. I sat there in silence for a few minutes, breathing heavily, licking my lips, trying to push the fear away, and praying for God's strength. Then, with a death grip on Josh's hand, I read the remainder of the letter. I couldn't look at her the entire time out of fear. But I did it. I read the letter. I said what needed to be said. When I finished reading, to my surprise, I relaxed my grip on Josh's hand and felt much calmer.

I could tell my mother was upset and somewhat in a state of shock. Gary emphasized to my mother that everything was now out on the table; she didn't need to be afraid of any more big bombshells coming from me. He summarized the boundaries that I'd established in the letter. Then he said, "Lynn, this was monumental for Rochelle to say these things to you. These things have been in her heart and have caused inordinate fear for a long time. We don't want your relationship forever hampered by fear. If she can say these things to you, the union between the two of you is not as weak as you think. The only way to lose it is to let Satan get in the middle. You know, of course, that you have your own wounds that need to be nursed. But this has been a good day. It's been a painful day, but good things come with pain. The joy of birth eases the memory of the pain." As Gary started to wrap things up for the day, my mother turned to a page in her notebook and showed it to Gary. She'd written down the names and numbers of three counselors in her city, names she had gotten from the Focus on the Family website. Gary told her to call them that afternoon and find out what their credentials were. He said if he knew what their credentials were, what their licenses were, then he would know which one would best be able to help my mother. I was amazed. She had actually done some research on counselors. We would have to wait and see what the next day brought to bear.

The rest of Tuesday, and as we arrived at Gary's office Wednesday morning, I was much more relaxed and calm. I told Gary that I'd like to express some compassion to my mother by saying that it must be tough to be told you are mentally ill and need therapy. I've always known I had problems and needed help. I wanted to tell her that even though therapy is tough, it's worth it. Gary cautioned me against that. He said the minute the little girl starts feeling compassion for Mommie, she yields up her boundaries. He said I wasn't un-toxic enough myself for him to know where the line is between rescuing and expressing compassion. Then he reminded me that just because she expressed sorrow and regret didn't mean that she wasn't still toxic to me. He gave me an analogy. "If you knew of a pedophile who was out of prison after ten years and was now a preacher, would you let him around your kid?" I replied, "Absolutely not."

He said, "Of course you wouldn't." Then he went on to say that my mother has some addictive tendencies like that that wouldn't change. Would they with intervention? Maybe some. But he warned that I'd have to have my eye on her and be the adult and enforce boundaries until the day she dies. He recognized that my child would like for her to ultimately be safe and trustworthy, but my adult knows I'd never be able to close both eyes with her. He told me that the little girl was like Charlie Brown with Lucy holding the football. He'd like to trust her, but he is a child and that's why he never learns. He always gives in and runs to kick the football, only to land flat on his back when Lucy pulls the football away. So, he said, I must keep my adult in charge.

When my mother arrived, Gary pointed out to her how much calmer and happier I seemed that day. He told my mother that one cannot share the happiness of life if one is terrified. He pointed out that the world says that if you deal with truth and fears there will be division and other bad things, but Jesus said the truth sets you free. He said, "If you understand her fears, you can understand her boundaries. Truth and love make fear go out the door." Then he contrasted for her Monday night versus Tuesday night for me. Monday night I was full of panic. But Tuesday night, after I had gotten the fear out on the table and spoken truth, the focus was on Anna and our future as I shared the DVD of my latest ultrasound/3-D ultrasound of Anna with dear friends.

My mother had spoken to three of the counselors. Gary coached her on what questions she needed to ask to clarify if they were experienced in working with people with personality disorders. He emphasized the advantage of a clinical psychologist. Then he talked to her about truth and how truth dispels fear. When truth is set forward, you can act with knowledge and knowledge always dispels fear. He talked about the boundaries and that they can be revisited as things progress. He acknowledged that right now she isn't happy with the boundaries, but she knows what to do about it. She told us that she feels like she's being punished and that I'm using her granddaughter as the ultimate punishment. Gary made it clear that this wasn't about punishment. It was about having good boundaries and being healthy. She said she felt as if she'd been involved in the pregnancy and now wasn't. Gary asked her, "Did she say she doesn't want you involved?" My mother admitted that I hadn't said that. Gary encouraged her not to let her fear cause her to curl up in a ball, not to overthink what I'd said, but to recognize that I'm just making sure that all the dysfunction doesn't pass on to Anna. As he closed out the session with my mother, he told her that she might find that things are really better now than they've ever been, and he encouraged her to do what it takes to become a trusted person in my eyes.

After she left, he cautioned me about becoming overly optimistic. He pointed out that her pathology didn't change just because we've had these meetings. Don't let down my guard, don't back track, don't undo what we have accomplished, don't lower my boundaries. Josh and I talked a lot about freedom as we drove home that day. I now have freedom as an adult. I am free from the fear of speaking truth to my mother. I am free to have an honest, healthy relationship with her. I am free to be myself. I now have freedom for the little girl. What she needed to say has now been said and the earth didn't stop, nothing blew up, and most importantly, I didn't let her down. Josh pointed out that with this last series of sessions I'd given the little girl the ultimate proof that my adult can be trusted.

This therapeutic journey of the last seven and a half years has given me much freedom—freedom from fear, from addictions (to masturbation and cutting), from self-deception, from other deception, from worrying and obsessing about what other people think, from self-destructive behaviors and thinking patterns, and from ignorance about the truth of my past. This therapeutic journey has also given me the freedom to love genuinely and unconditionally, to parent responsibly, to share openly, to speak honestly, to act courageously, and to be the woman God has always intended me to be.

Gary and I talked about freedom and how difficult the adjustment to it can be. For instance, someone who has been in prison for seventeen years and then is released deals with an incredible challenge to adjust to that freedom, but it can be done. I would have a tendency to want to slip back into anxiety. My mind will actually try to look for things to be anxious about, and I'd have to be on guard against that. Gary suggested that now I begin working on finishing my book, preparing for Anna's arrival, and thinking about ways other than my book that I could give back. He suggested that, after I finish this book, that I use my gift for writing to write books for children in dysfunctional families, or for girls who are wanting to cut, or maybe even start a website for people who are looking for true, wonderful healing. "After all," he quipped, "you have a PhD in cut-ology!" He said it would be like former drug users who get clean and then become drug counselors. There is something redemptive in that, that the suffering wasn't in vain. And, of course, that's what God said through the apostle Paul in Romans 8:28, "And we know that in all things God works for the good of those who love him, who have been called according to his purpose." No matter what Satan throws at us in this life, God can and will use it for good for those who love Him.

My sessions with Gary began to take on a different tone. The focus was no longer my mother or my fear. I began working on other, peripheral issues that needed addressing. I also began to focus on preparing for Anna's arrival in just a few short weeks. I was concerned about several things, including breastfeeding, and I discussed it with Josh and Gary. I guess, in essence, the focus of my therapy sessions became how to deal with the residue of my upbringing so that it didn't affect Anna's upbringing. After my conversation with Gary about breastfeeding, he suggested that I have a conversation with the little girl. As I listened to what she was saying and typed it, my eyes filled with tears of joy. When I read the conversation to Josh, he cried, too. It was so beautiful to me to see the depth of healing that has come into my life.

> I talked with Josh yesterday and with Gary today about the concerns I'm having about breastfeeding. I'm nervous about that more than anything, and I think it's not so much about the mechanics, although I am nervous about that and about it working. But I'm nervous about the idea of—how do I explain this?—breasts and mothers and daughters. I know that breastfeeding is the most natural thing in the world. It's the way God designed it. Women for millennia have been doing it. I was breastfeed. But what I'm uncomfortable about is that the thought of it feels very unsafe. Of course, I don't remember my experience with breastfeeding, but what I do remember about breasts and mothers isn't good. As Gary worded it not too long ago, my mother is fascinated with my equipment and she always has been, at least since I started developing in middle school. Her preoccupation with my breasts has always made me uncomfortable. And I know what Josh said is true, that with infants, there are no boundaries. But my experience as an older child, teenager, and adult was the same way—no boundaries between my mother and me when it came to my breasts. So how am I supposed to be comfortable about breastfeeding my own daughter when I'm so uncomfortable and conflicted about my own experiences between my mother and me and my breasts? Gary asked me if the idea of it felt too enmeshed or too close. Yes, I guess so. It just feels unsafe. And I'm not

sure who it is unsafe for. In other words, is it unsafe for me, the adult, for Anna, the child, or for the little girl, my inner child? Who is it unsafe for? And is it actually unsafe, or is that just a fear I have that is not grounded in reality? Gary told me to have a conversation about it with the little girl and see what she has to say about things. So I guess I'll try to do just that.

Little Girl, are you listening? I'd like to talk to you about when Anna is born. Will you talk to me?

> Yeah.

It's only a few more weeks until Anna is born.

> Yeah, I know.

Are you excited about it?

> I guess so.

I'm excited about it and I hope you will be, too. I think it's going to be a wonderful thing. I think you will have a wonderful time with Anna, especially as she gets older. Josh and I want you to re-experience your childhood as you watch us raise Anna. And this time it will be a good childhood.

> I want that too, but I'm worried.

What are you worried about?

> I'm not sure. Maybe that you won't love me anymore.

Oh, honey, of course I'll still love you. In fact, I'll probably love you even more.

> How can you do that if you love Anna?

That's easy, because I'll see you in Anna. I'll see you as the beautiful child you are as I see the beautiful child Anna is. I'll see her laugh and I'll think

CHAPTER 45: FREEDOM

of you. I'll see her learn to talk and walk and I'll think of you. I'll see her run into her daddy's arms and I'll think of how you never had that but always wanted that. And I hope when you see Anna run into Josh's arms, and you see Josh pick her up and swing her around and hold her and protect her that you will know that you now live in a safe and healthy family. You will always be safe here.

> That makes me cry.

Why does it make you cry?

> It makes me cry because I'm happy. Can you cry when you are happy?

Of course you can, honey. I'm glad that you are happy.

> Will Anna love me?

Yes, she will honey. I'll teach her as she is able to learn about you. She'll love you. And I'll teach her about healthy love.

> Do you know about healthy love?

Yes, Little Girl, I do. I've been learning about it for many years now.

> How did you learn?

I learned it from God's Word, the Bible. I learned it from Gary. He has taught me so much about healthy love. And I learned it from Josh. He has been a wonderful example of healthy love. It's because of God and Gary and Josh that I have learned how to love you and how to not hurt you.

> I'm glad you stopped hurting me.

I'm glad I did too.

> Will you hurt Anna?

No. Absolutely not. Never. Anna will be safe with me.

> How do you know?

Because I will do everything I can to keep her safe and because I will never stop learning and growing and getting healthy. I will be healthy myself so that I can be a healthy mommy.

> What does a healthy mommy do?

That's an excellent question, Little Girl. And I know why you asked it.

> You do?

Sure I do.

> Okay, why did I ask it?

Because you don't know what a healthy mommy looks like. You never had one.

> Will I ever have one?

I don't know, honey. Mother may never be healthy. Gary and I have told her that she needs to get help, but I don't know if she will. We can't make her get healthy, but I can be healthy. You can experience a healthy mommy by watching me with Anna. I will be a healthy mommy with Anna and you can watch me and see what a healthy mommy is supposed to do.

> Why does Anna get to have a healthy mommy and I don't? That's not fair.

You're right, it's not fair. And I don't have a good answer for that. The only answer I can give you is that Anna will have a healthy mommy because I have gotten healthy. I have worked incredibly hard to get healthy and to undo all the damage Mommie and Papa did to us. But I think that in a way, you will get to have a healthy mommy, just like Anna.

CHAPTER 45: FREEDOM

> How?

By watching how I am with Anna. And by seeing how I am with you now.

> I don't understand.

You are going to have to find a healthy mommy in me now, not in Mommie. Mommie isn't healthy. And she may never be. We can't force her to be. But I can be healthy. I can be a healthy mommy to Anna and I will be. And you will have to find out what a healthy mommy looks like and acts like by watching me with Anna. Does that make sense?

> I think so.

Honey, you said that you were worried. After what we've been talking about, are you still worried?

> Yeah.

What are you worried about?

> If you didn't have a healthy mommy how do you know how to be a healthy mommy? What if you mess up?

Oh, sweetie, I will mess up. I won't be perfect. But messing up is very different from being unhealthy. Because when I mess up, I will recognize it and admit it and apologize for it. And of course, I've already told you that I've been learning how to be healthy from God and Gary and Josh. You don't have to have been raised by a healthy mommy to know how to be a healthy mommy. I may have to work harder at it than other people, but I will. I will because I want Anna to have a healthy mommy and I want you to see what a healthy family is like.

> Will you do the things to Anna that Mommie did to me?

Absolutely not.

> Will you hit her?

No. I will never hit her, and I will never spank her out of anger or rage.

> Mommie spanked me a lot when she was mad at me when I was bad.

I know she did, honey, and I promise you, I will not spank Anna when I am angry. If I spank her, I will make sure that I am calm. And I'll be honest with you, Little Girl, I'm uncomfortable with any kind of spanking, but there may be times when it is needed. But I promise you, I will talk with Josh and Gary about that before the time ever arises and I will make good decisions about it. And honey, you aren't a bad little girl. Trust me, you're not. Do you believe me?

> Yeah, I believe you. Will you ignore Anna when she's trying to tell you something important?

Absolutely not.

> Will you punish her when it isn't her fault?

No.

> Will you make her feel icky?

Absolutely not. I will do my best to never make Anna feel icky. I will have good boundaries with her.

> Can you do that?

I will do my best.

> What about when she's a baby? Will you be safe with her?

Yes I will. I've explained something to you before, Little Girl, and I want to try and explain it again. There will be many times when Anna is little that Josh and I will have to do very personal, intimate things with Anna, like changing her diaper, bathing her, and breastfeeding her. But that's okay, it's safe, because she will be an infant. When babies are born, they can't do any of those things for themselves. But I promise you, when Anna gets old enough to do those things for herself, I will stop doing them for her.

Mommie stopped doing those things for me when I got older but that didn't stop making me feel icky.

That's because she was unhealthy. She didn't have good boundaries with you as you got older. To her, you were always an extension of her. She never weaned you.

What does weaned mean?

It means she never let you grow up. She wanted to keep you attached to her breast. She wanted to keep breastfeeding you once you got old enough that you didn't need it.

She didn't do that.

No, she didn't do that for real, but that's the way she treated you. She didn't want any boundaries between you and her, and she wanted it that way forever, just like there were no boundaries between you and her when you were an infant and a young child. That's why even now when she touches you or asks you personal questions, you get that icky feeling. Does that make sense?

Yeah, I think so.

You know, Little Girl, that I have been having a lot of uncomfortable feelings about breastfeeding Anna.

Yeah, I know.

I just realized something important, a huge difference between me breastfeeding Anna and our mother's unhealthy interest in my body.

What's that?

Well, when I breastfeed Anna, she will be interested in my breasts, not the other way around.

What do you mean?

Well, with our mother, she, the adult, was interested in my body, the child. Even once you grew up and I became an adult, she was still interested in my breasts. With us, it was a mother having an unhealthy obsession with her child's body. But when Anna is an infant and I am breastfeeding her, I won't have an unhealthy obsession about her breasts. She'll be the one with the obsession. She'll be obsessed with my breasts because that's where her food will come from. And it will be a healthy obsession because that's the way God designed it. And when she gets older, she'll grow out of that as she starts to eat solid food. I will wean her. I will let her grow up. I will let her stop breastfeeding. I won't try to keep her attached to me in unhealthy ways like our mother did with us. Does any of what I am saying make sense? I know it is kind of complicated and deep stuff, but I'm trying to say it in a way that you can understand.

I think I understand.

Tell me what you think I am saying.

It's okay for you to breastfeed Anna because it is healthy.

That's right. What else am I saying?

Mommie wasn't healthy with me because she wanted to keep me attached to her like I was when I was a baby.

That's exactly right! Little Girl, you are so smart!

I know.

Little Girl, when a baby breastfeeds, when they suck on their mommy's nipple it is called latching on. Anna will latch on to me, but when she is old enough to eat on her own, I will make sure to break the latch. And I will continue breaking it so she'll grow up healthy and wise. I promise you, Little

CHAPTER 45: FREEDOM

Girl, I won't make the same mistakes with Anna that our mother made with us. I promise you.

> Okay.

Little Girl, it's going to be so good for you when Anna is born. I've made a lot of promises to you tonight. I want you to promise me something.

> What?

When you see me playing with Anna, promise me that you'll remember that as I play with Anna, I'm also playing with you. Promise me that you'll think about how much I love you when you see how much I love Anna. And promise me that you won't forget that my love for Anna will only help my love for you grow that much more. Can you promise me that?

> Yeah, I can.

Little Girl, it's been two and a half years since I started paying attention to your dream. You always dreamed of growing up, getting married, staying married, and having a little girl who had a loving, faithful, protecting daddy. Am I right?

> Yeah.

But part of your dream, and you may not even know this, but part of your dream was to also grow up, get married, stay married, and **be** a loving, faithful, protecting mommy. I think I'm right about that, even if you never really understood that as a child. I think as you got older and started realizing and admitting to yourself that Mommie was unhealthy, you could understand that part of your dream. Does that make sense?

> I think so. But when I was a teenager I said I didn't want to have any kids. So maybe it doesn't make sense.

Oh, but it does, honey. You didn't want to have kids because you were beginning to see how unhealthy your family was and you didn't want to make the same mistakes. It just took many, many years for you to admit to yourself, for me to admit to myself, just how unhealthy Mommie really is. I mean, think about it. It's a very scary thing for a child to think that her mother is unhealthy and unsafe. It's easier to think of yourself as the bad child. You did that, didn't you?

> Yeah, I thought I was bad. But you keep telling me I'm not.

That's right, you're not. You are a precious, beautiful little girl. And Anna will be a precious, beautiful little girl. And together you can both see what a precious, beautiful family is supposed to be like. I will be the loving, faithful, protecting mommy to Anna that you never had. And you can experience what it should have been like through Anna. And Josh will be the loving, faithful, protecting daddy to Anna that you never had. And you can experience what that should have been like through Anna, too. You will finally have what you never had but always wanted as you allow yourself to grow up with Anna.

> Why does that make me sad?

Well, it makes you sad because it is sad. You never had what you wanted most of all. You never had what you needed. You never had what God wanted you to have. And Little Girl, make sure you understand me—none of that was your fault. The blame for that lies completely on Mommie and your father and Papa. It was **not** your fault. Do you believe that?

> I think so.

I hope you will keep believing that and believing it more and more. And I hope that even though you are sad, you will also find joy and happiness.

> I do. I am happy. I already told you that.

I'm so glad that you're happy, Little Girl. I want you to be happy. And I want you to be safe. I want those things for Anna, too. More than anything I want her to be happy and safe, both here on earth and later in heaven with God.

> That's what Mommie said about me. She said that her greatest wish was for me to be happy and to be with God.

CHAPTER 45: FREEDOM

That's true, she did say that, and I believe her.

> But if she wanted me to be happy, why did she make me so unhappy? I don't understand.

It's because she is so unhealthy. She wants you to be happy; I have no doubt about that. But she doesn't understand what true happiness is. She doesn't understand what joy is all about. But you do and I do. We've learned through our struggles over the years. We've learned that happiness comes from growing through trials. We've learned that happiness comes from facing truth, from telling the truth and living truth and loving truth. Mommie doesn't know that. Maybe she will one day. I don't know. But it isn't our job to make her happy. I know you have always thought it was your job to make her happy because that's what she taught you. But that's not true. That's a lie. The only person you can make happy is you, and the way that you make yourself happy is by doing things God's way. She doesn't do things God's way. That's why she is so unhappy and that's why she thinks it is your job to make her happy. Maybe she'll learn better. I don't know. But you and I are going to be happy regardless of what Mommie does. And I promise you, Little Girl, I will not expect Anna to make me happy. I will try to teach her what true happiness is all about. Josh and I both will work very hard to show Anna how to live God's way so that she can be happy. And I know one thing for sure.

> What?

I know that when I see Anna laughing in her daddy's arms, trusting him, loving him and learning from him and being protected by him, that it will all have been worth it. You will have been redeemed.

> What does that mean?

It means that you, my inner child, the little girl, will be **free**. You will be free to laugh and live and love safely and freely. You will no longer have to worry about everything that has worried you for so many years. Your scary, confusing childhood will no longer have to be reality for you. Reality will be the healthy family you now live in, the healthy family Anna will live in. You will be free to be a child, to laugh when Anna laughs, to play when she plays, to love with abandon as she will. You will be free from worrying about angry blows or terrifying touches or confusing messages. You will be free from fearing that someone will die if you tell the truth. As you see Anna learn about truth and learn how to tell the truth and learn how important and how wonderful truth is, you will be free from all the lies that were told you so many years ago. You'll be free, Little Girl. You'll be free.

> That makes me cry, too.

Are they happy tears?

> Yeah. Yeah, they're happy tears.

I'm so glad, Little Girl. You deserve to be happy. You deserve to be free. It makes me cry, too, Little Girl. Happy tears. I'm happy because you're happy. Because you're free.

> Rochelle?

Yeah?

> I love you.

I love you, too, Little Girl.

> And I love Josh, too.

I know you do. And he loves you.

> And I love Anna.

She loves you too.

> I'm glad Josh is the daddy. He's a good daddy.

I know he is, Little Girl. I know he is.

> And I love God, too.

CHAPTER 45: FREEDOM

And Little Girl, God loves you too, very much. In fact, He loved you before He ever created you. Before you ever started to grow, He loved you. Just like Josh and I love Anna even now while she is still in my tummy, that's how God has always loved you.

Rochelle?

Yeah?

I'm tired. Can we go to sleep?

Yes, we can, Little Girl. Yes, we can!

Anna's birth will be a rebirth for the little girl. And it will be a time of incredible joy for Josh and me. My Ob-Gyn recently told me that I was doing fantastic and that being pregnant seemed to be really good for me. He said I am actually healthier than many of his eighteen-year-old pregnant patients. What he doesn't know is that it isn't just about being healthy while I'm pregnant. It is about being healthy, period. He has watched me over the last four years and has seen me go from infertile to pregnant and doing so well. He told me that he has enjoyed watching me "blossom." What he doesn't realize is that the blossoming has been because I have been getting increasingly healthy. As I have worked through the pain and dysfunction and hurt of my past, I have grown into a healthy, vibrant woman. My Ob-Gyn sees it. Miss Penny sees it. Dr. Patel sees it. Gary sees it. Josh sees it. And I see it. I have gone from sick to healthy, from enslaved and addicted to free, from being full of despair to being full of hope, from true anguish to true joy! I owe so much to so many: Dr. Patel, for his medical knowledge and patience; Miss Penny, for her constant encouragement and love; Gary, for his vast wisdom, his perseverance, his incredible therapeutic skill, and his gentle guidance; Josh, for—Wow! How can I reduce what all he has done for me into a few words? I cannot. He truly is my joy, my strength, my leader, and my love. I owe so much to him. I owe so much to myself, as well, for my courage and perseverance in struggling through this incredibly difficult journey. And finally, I owe so much to God. He has been there with me since the day I was born, faithfully putting people in my path to help me, faithfully giving me strength from those people and from His Word, faithfully never giving up on me. Without Him, this journey to healing would have been impossible.

46
God

God?
like my
absent father,
abandoning,
uninvolved,
detached?
No.
God?
like my
controlling mother,
critical and condemning,
self-absorbed,
obsessed with image,
suffocating?
No.
God?
like my
deceitful grandfather,
abusing,
destroying,
shaming,
distorting?
No.
God,
like my
tender, compassionate
husband,
loving unconditionally,
faithful,
strengthening, supporting.
God.

Parents, and grandparents, are supposed to portray God to their children. Unfortunately, mine did not. But despite all the dysfunction, despite the distortions, despite the despair caused by years of living in such an unhealthy family system, I always kept coming back to God. Why? Well, I'm not sure. It certainly wasn't because of the way my family portrayed Him. Parents, and grandparents, are all-powerful to a child. A child sees his or her parents and typically makes the generalization that God must be like Mom and Dad. But in a situation like mine, where what is being modeled is abandonment, abuse, betrayal, control, criticism, and lies, it makes for a very distorted picture of God. The concept of God as Father was very difficult for me for many years. I knew that God was my Father and that I was His child. The Bible makes it clear that when I was baptized, I became His child. Yet picturing Him as a loving, faithful Father was still difficult. I once had a friend tell me not to judge God by the way my own family acted. Rather, judge God by the truth of what is said about Him in the Bible. So that was what I tried to do. The picture of God presented in the Bible is very different from the one that was presented to me by my family. But the picture of God in the Bible is the one that's true. The God of the Bible is faithful, even when you are going through struggles and difficulties. He is there helping you get through them. The God of the Bible is protective. He guards us and protects us from Satan's attacks. He gives us a way out from temptation. The God of the Bible is loving. He loves us so much that He provided a way for us to be rescued from our sins through the death of His Son, Jesus. The God of the Bible is patient. He is a God of second chances. And third and fourth and fifth chances. He is patient with us as we struggle through life. He wants us to trust Him to lead us. And the God of the Bible is gracious and kind to us. He has not left us in the dark, alone, without aide. He has given us the Bible, His Word, to guide us.

I think the Bible is the reason I always kept coming back to God. From a very young age, I read the Bible and memorized verses from it. I knew what the Bible said about God, and despite the picture I got from my family, I knew deep down that the Bible presented the accurate picture of God. It's good if someone models for us what God is like. But even if no one does, we can still get a correct view of God from the Bible. We can get a picture of what God is like by seeing what Jesus was like.

When I was a little girl, I had a recurring dream about Jesus. In my dream, I was in the jungle on a rope bridge. The rope bridge wound through the trees and as I tried to make my way over the bridge, there were fires and snakes and wild animals and all kind of dangers. It was incredibly difficult to keep from falling off the rope bridge. But every time I made it to the end. And at the end of the rope bridge, as it came out of the dangerous jungle, there was Jesus. He was bright and shining and strong and safe. I made it to Jesus every time. I loved this dream and whenever I had it I always felt safe and happy. The dream seemed to be a picture of life for me. It's a struggle getting through the jungle of life, but if you hang on and keep trying, Jesus is there at the end, waiting for you to bring you to safety and happiness and joy. In truth, Jesus is right there with you the entire way, helping you get to the end.

In my struggles, I clung to that dream. And I clung to the picture of God that I got from the Bible. I clung to verses like Hebrews 4:15–16 that told me that Jesus is able to sympathize with my weaknesses because He had been tempted in every way mankind is tempted, yet He was without sin. Because of that, the Bible says that we can "approach the throne of grace with confidence, so that we may receive mercy and find grace to help us in our time of need." I've had so many times of need in my life, and I did receive mercy and grace to help me. Remember the song I wrote about scars and how God understands scars because Jesus got scars in dying for us? That truth has sustained me. I have come to a deeper understanding of the gospel. Jesus had victorious pain. The peace that He bought for me at the cross was very costly. And the joy that God felt because mankind had been redeemed was tinged with sorrow over sin. Sad joy, painful victory, costly peace. God understands.

Psalm 34:18 says, "The Lord is close to the brokenhearted and saves those who are crushed in spirit." Depression, anxiety, mental illness, cutting, sexual abuse, physical abuse, sexual addiction, betrayal—all those things had broken my heart and crushed my spirit. But God was close to me and He saved me. He was close to me through His written Word; He was close to me through His people who helped me, people like Josh, Gary, Miss Penny and others who encouraged me and supported me through all my trials. And I had God's promise that if I tried to do things His way, the fear and shame that had plagued me all my life would be no more: "I sought the Lord, and he answered me; he delivered me from all my fears. Those who look to him are radiant; their faces are never covered with shame" (Psalm 34:4–5).

In one of Josh's sermons, he talked about why God allows us to suffer. One of the reasons he gave was that our suffering causes us to see our need for God. It helps us to learn to trust God. I realized something about my own situation. All my life, the little girl had longed for a daddy. She wanted what she never had. She wanted a daddy to love her, to cherish her, and most importantly, to protect her. She longed for a daddy to protect her from abusing grandfathers and dysfunctional mothers. So, all my life I have looked for father figures, but I needed to be looking for God, because He is the ultimate Father. God is my heavenly Father. He loves me. He cherishes me. And He protects me. He doesn't *insulate* me from suffering, but He protects me from myself. If I'll let Him. And He *uses* suffering. He uses suffering to help me grow and to help me learn to trust Him. God doesn't stop our suffering from happening, because He allows mankind to have free will. That means people are going to sin and hurt us. That means we are going to sin and hurt others. And hurt ourselves. But God uses all of our suffering to draw us to Him and to help us grow more and more into the image of Jesus. That is His ultimate goal for each and every person.

God never promises that life will be easy. In fact, Jesus says that we will have trouble in this world. But He also says to take heart, because He has overcome the world! When we lean on God and His Word and His people for support, we can have a much easier time of it. Easy? No, but easier. Everything I have gone through certainly hasn't been easy. But I recognize that were it not for God and His people who helped me, I would not be as healthy as I am today. In fact, I'd probably be dead. I still have healing and changing to do. I will need to do some healing and changing for the rest of my life. But I have mercy and grace to help me in my time of need.

God has truly blessed me in my life. He provided defense mechanisms for me as a child when I was faced with situations too frightening for a child to handle. He has given me people to help me along the way. He blessed me with Gary's wisdom and counsel, and He blessed me with Josh's love and strength. And now, He has blessed us with a child growing inside of me. I don't want to make the same mistakes that my family did. Josh and I will have a big responsibility when our daughter is born. We will have to model God for Anna. We will have to protect her. And we intend to do those very things. We will mess up and make mistakes, but we hope and pray that we'll do better than the last generation. Indeed, our future depends on it.

47
The Future

The Future,
like the depths
of the waters,
uncharted and
unexplored;
or,
like the
reaches of the
universe,
vast and
waiting to be
traversed;
or,
like a bold mountain,
daring the
climber
to scale and
conquer;
or,
like an expedition
into worlds unknown,
a journey
through life,
full of
excitement,
struggle,
discovery,
trial, and
joy.
The Future.

As I continue to have memories of my grandfather and the abuse I suffered at his hands, I continue to speak truth to myself. As I continue to come to grips with the pain that he caused me and the pain that I caused myself, I continue to speak truth. When I began this book, I had lots and lots of clues. Now I have the memories as well. Every day it seems, I remember something new, whether it has to do with my grandfather, or my mother, or just general memories from my childhood. And as I remember, I'm healing. As I speak truth to myself about what happened when I was a little girl, I'm healing. As I speak truth to myself about how my mother's dysfunction has affected me, I'm healing. As I speak truth to my mother, I'm healing. Whether she will ever deal with truth by seeking long-term, intense therapy for herself, I don't know, but I am still healing. I will be healing for the rest of my life.

My mother may or may not ever get healthy. Recently she brought up the possibility of getting into counseling. I just had to kind of laugh sadly as I listened to her say that she didn't know what to tell a counselor other than "my daughter's therapist thinks I have a personality disorder." She said she didn't understand why she needed counseling, because she looked at herself as a good person, not a bad person. I asked her, "Do you think I'm a bad person?" She replied, "No, of course not." I reminded her that I had been in therapy for seven and a half years. She quipped, "Yeah, but you had a reason to be. You had issues to work through." I told her that there were other reasons to be in therapy besides child abuse, and that it was a matter of getting healthy, to which she replied, "Yeah, but I don't think I'm unhealthy." After thirteen hours in Gary's office, two very pointed and detailed letters, and all of what Gary has told her, she still thinks she is healthy. She still deceives herself. When she was at our house for Christmas, she continued her same old dysfunctional behaviors. I called her on it. I told her she was being passive-aggressive. Josh and I caught her in an obvious lie and I called her on that, too. Of course, she denied lying. Even when I sent her an e-mail a week later telling her that I felt she owed me an apology for lying to me, she still denied it. But I confronted her. And I'll continue to confront her, because I'm not going to let her dysfunction negatively affect our daughter. I still have growing to do so that I don't let her sinful behavior affect me so strongly. As I continue to set boundaries with her, she will to have to realize that there are consequences to her actions. She doesn't like the boundaries, but I'll continue to set them. Once Anna is born and she realizes that Josh and

CHAPTER 47: THE FUTURE

I are serious about our boundaries, maybe then she'll get serious about getting healthy. I don't know, but I'm going to get healthy regardless of her actions. As Gary pointed out, my happiness and healing cannot be dependent on her. The foundation of my happiness and well-being are not based on what she does or doesn't do. I'll continue to get healthy and grow as I embrace the rest of my life.

The future holds out hope for many great things in my life. When our daughter is born, Josh and I will embark on the journey of parenthood. The prospect of being a mother is a sobering one. We have a great responsibility to model God for our child. We have a great responsibility to protect our daughter. Those tasks are ones that we'll undertake with much prayer and wise counsel. We are already praying daily for her and for ourselves as parents. If transference issues arise, I'll deal with them, because I want to be a healthy mother. I am awed by God's faithfulness and timing. He knew when in my healing I'd be healthy enough to be a good mother and healthy enough to protect my child, and He didn't allow me to become pregnant until that time. And I believe that the fact that we're having a little girl is something that God had His hand in as well. He's given me the opportunity to do things over. This little girl will be protected. This little girl will be loved unconditionally. This little girl will have a healthy family. I'll be able to witness what a little girl's life should be like. We will raise our daughter properly and my inner little girl will find healing in the process. And my inner child's dream—to grow up, get married, stay married, and have a child who has a loving, faithful, protective daddy—will be fulfilled. I am truly amazed at how God has worked in my life and to where He has brought me. And now, what a joy to think that in just a few short weeks, Josh and I will be holding our child for whom we hoped and prayed, our child for whom I have become healthy.

As I reread through my book for a final edit for my publisher, I am struck by how much I have changed since the early chapters. The destructive behaviors are gone, and so many of my faulty thinking patterns and emotional response patterns have changed. When I started therapy with Gary in 2003, I was convinced that I was crazy. I don't think that anymore. I think I am a woman who has had an incredible amount of hurt and pain in her life. I've been sinned against many times in my life by many different people, including myself. I've dealt with the pain and courageously faced the truth about my past, my family, and myself. I am still growing and learning and healing. I've been incredibly blessed by God with forgiveness and people to help and love me. I now have joy, victory, and peace—sad joy, painful victory, and costly peace. I have many scars in my life, but my scars are signs of healing. As I reflected on this book and my life, I sat down at the piano and wrote a song.

Listen

Verse 1 -   There's a peace that comes when you understand,
            when confusion is made clear,
            a costly peace, indeed it is,
            It's a peace I hold very dear.

Verse 2 -   There is joy that comes when you go through trial,
            when you struggle to survive,
            a sad joy, indeed it is,
            it's a joy that I am alive.

Verse 3 -   There is vict'ry that comes when you live through pain,
            when you work through all of your grief,
            a painful vict'ry, indeed it is,
            it's a vict'ry that brings relief.

Verse 4 -   There is freedom that comes when you break the chains,
            when you conquer all of your fear,
            a pure freedom, indeed it is,
            it's a freedom I hold very dear.

Bridge -   Sad joy, victorious pain, these are in my life.
            A costly peace has been attained as I've healed from pain
            that cut like a knife.

            I've had many scars in my life, scars that speak of pain.
            But my scars also speak of joy 'cause I've survived,
            I've broken the chains.

Ending -   Listen as my scars speak of joy.
            Listen as my scars speak of peace.

CHAPTER 47: THE FUTURE

> Listen as my scars speak of victory.
> Listen and be glad.

September 6, 2005, was the last time I cut. I began writing this book a few days later. At the time, I didn't know how it would turn out. That was over six years ago. Now, as 2011 winds down, I still don't know the whole story. My story will continue to be written each day that I live my life. However, the story of this book, which was written as I lived it, is over. My scars have spoken, and as I've allowed my scars to speak, I have grown healthier and stronger. My scars have spoken words of suffering and pain. My scars have spoken words of healing, renewal and restoration. I was self-destructive, and now I am not. I still have scars, physical and emotional, but now, instead of speaking to me of shame and fear and sorrow, they speak loudly of truth and triumph and joy.

Epilogue

Epilogue,
like beautiful strains
of music,
cadencing on notes
of sheer glory;
or,
like the happily-ever-after ending
to a fairy tale
full of villains and
dangers and woes;
or,
like the brilliant
sunset,
painting the sky at
day's end
with shades of
exquisite color;
or,
in my case,
like the closing of a door
on one chapter of life,
a chapter full of
pain and sorrow and fear,
and the opening of
another door
on a whole new
chapter of life,
a chapter full of
love and healing and joy.
Epilogue.

The third week in January, 2011, two and a half weeks early, our precious daughter, Anna Joy, was born. The instant they handed her to me, I knew that God had blessed us beyond measure. She was beautiful! And not only that, she was completely healthy! Our prayers had been answered many times over. Josh and I cried and prayed a prayer of thanksgiving to God within minutes of her birth. A day or two later, I gave Josh a card telling him that through him and through Anna, the little girl's dream had come true, and we both wept.

A few days after we came home from the hospital, Josh was holding Anna one evening and looking at her with an expression full of love. I could tell he was deep in thought, and it also appeared to me that he was tearing up, so I asked him what he was thinking. He choked out the words, "Gratitude for the moment and regret for the past." Then a few moments later, as he gazed at our precious child, he said, "I don't think I ever really knew what beauty was before this." We talked about how much God has blessed us with our daughter. He said God must have known how much we both needed this little girl to help us heal. And then, as I watched my amazing husband hold our newborn child, I heard him whisper through his tears, "I don't think I really realized just how much she was going to mean to me." At that moment, my love for my husband grew stronger than it had ever been before. Every time I see him with Anna, I love him even more. God truly has fulfilled my childhood dream through Josh and Anna.

The first several months after Anna was born were quite rough, as anyone who has had a newborn can understand. We had some breastfeeding issues, but I persevered through the struggles, despite the fact that I developed postpartum depression. Dr. Patel and my Ob-Gyn worked together to find the right medication for me, and things got much better. The struggles with the breastfeeding were due to a non-visible functional tongue-tie that Anna had, but we took steps to correct that. I ended up having to wean Anna when she was about four months old because my milk supply had dwindled down to almost nothing, despite taking numerous measures to help increase it. We were under quite a bit of stress those first few months, but God gave us the strength to get through it all.

I've been quite emotional at times, partially due to sleep-deprivation, partially due to hormones, partially due to the postpartum depression, but often due to the fact that I was constantly overwhelmed with gratitude and amazement at how far God had brought me. If someone had told me ten years ago that in ten years I would have achieved mental health, be married to an amazing man, and have a beautiful daughter, I wouldn't have believed them. And yet, that's where I am today. And every time I listen to Steven Curtis Chapman's, "Beauty Will Rise," I weep with joy. Out of the ashes of my life, beauty did rise. I am beautiful, my marriage is beautiful, and my daughter is beautiful. When my mother was here, she brought some of my baby pictures. Anna looks a lot like I did as a baby. Josh commented on how beautiful I was as a child.

The day after my mother left when she came to see Anna for the first time, I had a meltdown. I realized that when I was a child, I was as beautiful and innocent and pure as my precious daughter is right now. I also realized that they (my father, my mother and my grandfather) had marred me and soiled me. I wept with grief for what I'd lost and for what I'd never had. How could a father abandon his child? How could a grandfather molest his granddaughter? But the question that haunted me most was how could a mother mistreat and abuse her child? After only a short time of being a mother, my love for this child and my protective instincts toward her are incredibly strong. Holding my beautiful daughter, I cannot imagine ever telling her that she was a rotten kid. Gary told me that my feelings of grief may continue for a long time as we raise Anna in a healthy family. When I see what she has and realize very poignantly what I never had, I will grieve, but the grief will be tinged with the joy of seeing my daughter with her daddy—loved, cared for, protected. It will be laced with laughter as we raise our child in a healthy family. It will be marked with the peace of knowing that Anna is safe. Again, sad joy, victorious pain, costly peace.

And as Anna grows up, my inner child, the little girl, will be watching. She will be watching intently and seeing just what a healthy family really is like. She will be growing up in that healthy family vicariously through Anna. The little girl will be healing.

The dedication page of this book indicates that my journey to mental health was done for the little girls in my life. I became healthy for my inner child. She deserved to have me be healthy. Enough sickness and sin had affected her for years. But my daughter, the little girl that I gave birth to just a few short months ago, is the other little girl in my life. I became healthy for her. I will make mistakes as a mother. All mothers do, whether they are healthy or not. But the mistakes I will make won't be due to mental illness or major dysfunction, because I am no longer mentally ill. I am no longer dysfunctional. And Josh and I will protect Anna from those people who are, like my mother.

I recently found out that a friend's grandson had been sexually molested by a trusted family friend. I wept as she told me about it. I wept for the whole family, but mostly for that little boy. And as she told me about it, I looked down at the beautiful little girl in my arms and vowed once again to do everything in my power to keep her safe. I never want her to experience the things I had to suffer. I never want her to be affected by the sin and dysfunction of others the way I was. I never want her to have the scars I've had. When I speak, it is my scars that speak. When she speaks, I want her to speak unblemished, unmarred, unscarred. I want her to speak from a heart of purity and love and security. I want her life to be characterized by beauty and wellness and joy. I want her to be full of joy, just like her middle name.

Maybe one day I will write a sequel to this book—raising a child in a healthy family when you grew up in an unhealthy one, or something like that. I know I will continue to grieve over my own childhood. Gary has said that I may continue to experience flashbacks of the abuse I suffered at the hands of both my grandfather and my mother, especially as Anna gets to be the age I was when the abuse occurred. I know I will have transference issues to work through. And I *will* work through them. I'll deal with all of those things. That's what healthy people do. They deal with pain and trials in healthy ways.

My scars have spoken many words in this book, and I'll continue to let my scars speak as I protect my child, as I advocate for my daughter and for other children, as I encourage and support others who had dysfunctional childhoods. Maybe I'll write a book for children who are in abusive families. Maybe I'll work with the rape crisis center. Maybe I'll teach ladies' retreats and seminars on overcoming. Because that is what I have done. I have overcome. The title of my book is so appropriate because I did battle and I overcame. I am victorious and my reward is joy! I have walked away from the fight with scars, but also with a victory wreath—a precious family and a strong, abiding faith in God who has fought by my side the entire way. What greater joy could I have? Indeed, I cannot think of a greater joy than the joy that abides deep in my heart this very day.

Note from Josh

I hope you have found this book to be both powerful and encouraging—powerful, because this account of how abuse and mental illness can lead to cutting and other acts of self-destruction is so unusual (although I'm afraid it's more common than we think); encouraging, because it is ultimately a story of triumph and healing. It's difficult for me to assess the impact of this book on others, because I've been living in the middle of this story for a number of years now. As a result, I guess you could say I've gotten used to the unusual.

Even so, I think this book should be of great help to anyone with similar struggles. My wife writes with total honesty and, as she's very talented at expressing herself in words, she writes with great clarity. Consequently, I believe she's able to express what it's like to be a cutter, expose how such a condition can arise, and explain how she came to understand what was going on inside her and achieved mental health.

Anyone reading this book might well wonder, "Why did you ever marry a woman with so many problems?" That's a valid question, and the only answer I can give is that, although her problems were very real and very serious, there was obviously much more to her than just her problems or "issues." My wife is a wonderful human being—warm, caring, generous, sensitive to the needs of others. Despite her problems, early on in our relationship I discovered that we were very much alike in many ways. Indeed, it seemed to me that we were "soul mates." As the years have passed, I've never changed my mind or regretted our decision to marry.

I hope you've come to know my wife through this book. At the very least, I hope you have come to appreciate her courage. From the start, she has been determined to deal with her "baggage" and get well, no matter what it took or how hard it turned out to be. She has engaged in years of fearless self-examination, and that's the only reason this book ever came to be.

Although this isn't intended to be a "religious" book, I would be remiss were I to ignore the spiritual aspects of my wife's struggle to become healthy. Both my wife and I are Christians, and our respective worldviews are very much based upon the Bible. My wife credits God for her healing and rightly so. Her faith in God has been a tremendous source of strength as she's dealt with things about herself and her past that have scarred her greatly. While I don't think you have to be a Christian to obtain mental health, I do think it's a decided advantage, and so I hope you'll consider the claims of Christianity as you continue in your own personal struggle to become healthy.

Regardless of what you think about God or religion, I'd like to encourage you to seek outside help as you deal with your issues. My wife was blessed to find a gifted counselor and therapist, Gary, who has guided her on her journey to health. I frankly doubt she would have achieved her current level of progress without him. I also doubt that there are a lot of other "Garys" out there. Over the years, my wife went through any number of counselors before she found one who was truly able to help her. So, don't assume every therapist is equally competent and don't give up just because you aren't satisfied with your current professional.

Finally, I would advise you to be very careful in your dealings with your family of origin if, like my wife, you suspect your family is a big part of your problem. Dysfunctional families got that way for a reason, and they oftentimes are very resistant to honest introspection or the prospect of change. Try to assemble your own support group of friends and confidants who have no connection either to your family or your issues. If you have a loving spouse who supports you, even if he doesn't always understand you, then (as I'm sure you already know) you have a huge advantage. I hope and pray that reading this book has been helpful to you and that it will spur you on to do whatever you must to achieve the mental health God meant for you to have.

Acknowledgments

For some reason, this section seems incredibly difficult to write, maybe because after all I have been through, it seems trite to just say *thank you* to the people who have helped me along the way. And yet, *thank you* is precisely what needs to be said, so I shall endeavor to do just that.

Thank you:
To Brad Bevers at Lucid Books for seeing the potential in my manuscript. Thank you for being willing to publish my story.
To Marissa Torres for all your work on the production of the book. Thanks for being patient with all my emails!
To Terri Poss for the fabulous editing job you did! You took my lengthy, wordy manuscript and helped make it concise and accurate (it's still lengthy, though, but that's not your fault!).
To Paul Miller for designing such a powerful cover. It captured the essence of what I wish I had the talent to draw myself.
To Casey Cease for designing my website – it's really awesome!
To Lori, Glory, and Steve for using your incredible talents to help me bring my music to life!

Thank you:
To my many friends who supported me through my struggles, read my manuscript (or parts of it), counseled me, and most importantly, prayed for me. You know who you are. Your love and friendship have been invaluable in helping me to heal.

Thank you:
To Dr. Patel for using your great knowledge of medicine and the human mind to help me find the right combination of medications that would allow me to then do the hard work of

therapy. Your confidence and patience always helped put me at ease when I didn't know what to do. I'm glad you did!

Thank you:
To Terri for your love, friendship, and support. You always have encouraging words that lift my spirits. You have been like a mother to me—a *healthy* mother. Thank you for being my "mother in the faith."

Thank you:
To Gary for never giving up on me! Your patient wisdom and guidance brought me healing, your gentleness brought me peace, your faith and conviction brought me hope, and your commitment to truth brought me freedom. You saved my life, Gary. Thank you.

Thank you:
To my amazing husband. Your love and strength have given me the strength to go on so many times when I wanted to just give up. How many times have you held me as I cried? How many times have you tenderly told me words I desperately needed to hear? How many times have you talked and processed with me? How many times has your gentle humor brought joy to my heart? How many times can I say *thank you* before it is enough? I could never thank you enough! You truly are my joy, strength, leader, and love.

And finally, thank You:
To God my Father for loving me unconditionally even when I was trapped in sin and self-destruction. You loved me and forgave me, and You were so generous to me. You gave me childhood defense mechanisms to protect me. You gave me Your Word to guide me. You gave me many people to help me. You gave me a beautiful family to love and to love me. You gave me courage and endurance to enable me to fight for wellness. And You gave me Your Son, Jesus, to save me. Thank You.

Appendix A

Picture Title

Shackled By Chains	19
Impenetrable, Inescapable Fortress	20
Breaking Down the Wall	21
Deserving	23
Body Picture	24
All "The Junk"	35
More of "The Junk"	35
Yes & No, No & Yes	55
Holes	63
Is It Possible?	67
Beyond My Grasp	72
Hurt	92
Up & Down/Rage Slicing Through The Middle	94
Fear It!	96
Thoughts In My Brain	103
Isolation	109
Frightened	125
Breaking Through	147
Beginning To See	157
Is There A Monster Side of Mom?	161
Generations	164
Eyes Open, Walls Down, Fear Gone!	170
Fragile, Frightened, and Fractured	186

Elusive	186
Me	187
Why Is The Little Girl Hiding?	190
Portrait of Rochelle As A Little Girl	198
Missing Pieces Can't Hide The Truth	250
The Hug	292
Little	342
The Monster	386

Songs

Scars	43
Why Must This Thing Be?	63
I Cannot Understand	72
Break the Chains	76
Alone	109
O God	118
My Fears	125
Forty Years	350
Speaking Truth	394
The Chains of Childhood	413
Trust	441
I Want You, Lord	446
Listen	566

Appendix B

Scriptures To Combat Fear And Anxiety

Joshua 1:9 – Have I not commanded you? Be strong and courageous. Do not be terrified; do not be discouraged, for the Lord your God will be with you wherever you go.

Isaiah 41:10 – So do not fear, for I am with you; do not be dismayed, for I am your God. I will strengthen you and help you; I will uphold you with my righteous right hand.

Isaiah 42:3 – A bruised reed he will not break, and a smoldering wick he will not snuff out.

Zephaniah 3:17 – The Lord your God is with you, he is mighty to save. He will take great delight in you, he will quiet you with his love, he will rejoice over you with singing.

Romans 8:28 – And we know that in all things God works for the good of those who love him, who have been called according to his purpose.

1 Corinthians 10:13 – No temptation has seized you except what is common to man. And God is faithful; he will not let you be tempted beyond what you can bear. But when you are tempted, he will also provide a way out so that you can stand up under it.

Philippians 4:6-7 – Do not be anxious about anything, but in everything, by prayer and petition, with thanksgiving, present your requests to God. And the peace of God, which transcends all understanding, will guard your hearts and your minds in Christ Jesus.

2 Thessalonians 3:16 – Now may the Lord of peace himself give you peace at all times and in every way.

Hebrews 13:5b-6 – God has said, "Never will I leave you; never will I forsake you." So we say with confidence, "The Lord is my helper; I will not be afraid. What can man do to me?"

James 1:2-4 – Consider it pure joy, my brothers, whenever you face trials of many kinds, because you know that the testing of your faith develops perseverance. Perseverance must finish its work so that you may be mature and complete, not lacking anything.

1 Peter 5:7 – Cast all your anxiety on him because he cares for you.

1 John 4:4 – You, dear children, are from God and have overcome them, because the one who is in you is greater than the one who is in the world.

Psalm 9:9-10 – The Lord is a refuge for the oppressed, a stronghold in times of trouble. Those who know your name will trust in you, for you, Lord, have never forsaken those who seek you.

Psalm 10:14, 17-18 – But you, O God, do see trouble and grief; you consider it to take it in hand. The victim commits himself to you; you are the helper of the fatherless....You hear, O Lord, the desire of the afflicted; you encourage them, and you listen to their cry, defending the fatherless and the oppressed, in order that man, who is of the earth, may terrify no more.

Psalm 18:28b-29 – [M]y God turns my darkness into light. With your help I can advance against a troop; with my God I can scale a wall.

Psalm 23:1-4 – The Lord is my shepherd, I shall not be in want. He makes me lie down in green pastures, he leads me beside quiet waters, he restores my soul. He guides me in paths of righteousness for his name's sake. Even though I walk through the valley of the shadow of death, I will fear no evil, for you are with me; your rod and your staff, they comfort me.

Psalm 27:10 – Though my father and mother forsake me, the Lord will receive me.

Psalm 28:7 – The Lord is my strength and my shield; my heart trusts in him, and I am helped. My heart leaps for joy and I will give thanks to him in song.

Psalm 32:7 – You are my hiding place; you will protect me from trouble and surround me with songs of deliverance.

Psalm 34:17-19 – The righteous cry out, and the Lord hears them; he delivers them from all their troubles. The Lord is close to the brokenhearted and saves those who are crushed in spirit. A righteous man may have many troubles, but the Lord delivers him from them all...

Psalm 37:4 – Delight yourself in the Lord and he will give you the desires of your heart.

Psalm 55:22 – Cast your cares on the Lord and he will sustain you; he will never let the righteous fall.

Psalm 56:3-4 – When I am afraid, I will trust in you. In God, whose word I praise, in God I trust; I will not be afraid. What can mortal man do to me?

Psalm 73:25-26 – Whom have I in heaven but you? And earth has nothing I desire besides you. My flesh and my heart may fail, but God is the strength of my heart and my portion forever.

Psalm 86:16 – [G]rant your strength to your servant...

Psalm 94:19 – When anxiety was great within me, your consolation brought joy to my soul.

Psalm 119:28, 165 – My soul is weary with sorrow; strengthen me according to your word....Great peace have they who love your law, and nothing can make them stumble.

Appendix C

Suggested Reading

This is not an exhaustive list of books on these topics, nor is this list a complete list of all the books I have read on these subjects. These are just the books I have found to be most helpful, although I do not endorse all the opinions and/or beliefs held by the authors.

<u>Books About Borderline Personality Disorder</u>

Kreisman, Jerold J. *I Hate You – Don't Leave Me: Understanding The Borderline Personality.* New York: Avon Books, 1989.

Lawson, Christine Ann. *Understanding the Borderline Mother: Helping Her Children Transcend the Intense, Unpredictable, and Volatile Relationship.* Lanham, Maryland: Rowman & Littlefield Publishers, 2000.

Moskovitz, Richard. *Lost in the Mirror: An Inside Look at Borderline Personality Disorder.* 2nd Edition. Lanham, Maryland: Taylor Trade Publishing, 2001.

Reiland, Rachel. *Get Me Out of Here: My Recovery from Borderline Personality Disorder.* Center City, Minnesota: Hazelden Foundation, 2004.

<u>Books About Boundaries and Lies</u>

Cloud, Henry, & John Townsend. *Boundaries: When to Say Yes – When to Say No – To Take Control of Your Life.* Grand Rapids, Michigan: Zondervan, 1992.

Thurman, Chris. *The Lies We Believe*. Nashville: Thomas Nelson Publishers, 1999.

Thurman, Chris. *The Truths We Must Believe*. Nashville: Thomas Nelson Publishers, 1991

Books About Childhood Sexual Abuse/Trauma

Brand, Julie A. *A Mother's Touch: Surviving Mother-Daughter Sexual Abuse*. USA: Traafford Publishing, 2006.

Blume, E. Sue. *Secret Survivors: Uncovering Incest and Its Aftereffects in Women*. New York: Ballantine Books, 1990.

Carnes, Patrick J. *The Betrayal Bond: Breaking Free of Exploitive Relationships*. Deerfield Beach, FL: Health Communications, 1997.

Freyd, Jennifer J. *Betrayal Trauma: The Logic of Forgetting Childhood Abuse*. Cambridge, Massachusetts: Harvard University Press, 1996.

Books About Cutting

Kettlewell, Caroline. *Skin Game: A Memoir*. New York: St. Martin's Press, 1999.

Levenkron, Steven. *Cutting: Understanding and Overcoming Self-Mutilation*. New York: W. W. Norton, 1998.

Levenkron, Steven. *The Luckiest Girl in the World: A Novel*. New York: Penguin Books, 1997.

Miller, Dusty. *Women Who Hurt Themselves: A Book of Hope and Understanding*. New York: Basic Books, 1994.

Strong, Marilee. *A Bright Red Scream: Self-Mutilation and the Language of Pain*. New York: Penguin Books, 1998.

Books About Mothers/Parents

Adams, Kenneth M. *Silently Seduced: When Parents Make Their Children Partners: Understanding Covert Incest*. Deerfield Beach, Florida: Health Communications, 1991.

Brown, Nina W. *Children of the Self-Absorbed: A Grown-Up's Guide to Getting Over Narcissistic Parents*. Second Edition. Oakland, California: New Harbinger Publications, 2008.

Carder, Dave, et al. *Secrets of Your Family Tree: Healing for Adult Children of Dysfunctional Families*. Chicago: Moody Press, 1995.

Cloud, Henry, & John Townsend. *The Mom Factor*. Grand Rapids, Michigan: Zondervan, 1996.

Donaldson-Pressman, Stephanie, & Robert M. Pressman. *The Narcissistic Family: Diagnosis and Treatment*. San Francisco: Jossey-Bass, 1994.

Forward, Susan. *Emotional Blackmail: When the People in Your Life Use Fear, Obligation, and Guilt to Manipulate You*. New York: Harper Collins Publishers, 1997.

Forward, Susan. *Toxic Parents: Overcoming Their Hurtful Legacy and Reclaiming Your Life*. New York: Bantam Books, 1989.

Love, Patricia. *The Emotional Incest Syndrome: What to Do When a Parent's Love Rules Your Life*. New York: Bantam Books, 1990.

McBride, Karyl. *Will I Ever Be Good Enough? Healing the Daughters of Narcissistic Mothers*. New York: Free Press, 2008.

Endnotes

1. Marilee Strong, *A Bright Red Scream: Self-Mutilation and the Language of Pain*, (Toronto: Penguin Books, 1998), 64.
2. M. Scott Peck, *People of the Lie: The Hope for Healing Human Evil*, (New York: Touchstone, 1983), 33.
3. M. Scott Peck, 67.
4. Kenneth M. Adams, *Silently Seduced: When Parents Make Their Children Partners: Understanding Covert Incest*, (Deerfield Beach, FL: Health Communications, Inc., 1991), 9.
5. Kenneth M. Adams, Back Cover.
6. Kenneth M. Adams, 45-46.
7. Steven Levenkron, *The Luckiest Girl In The World*, (New York: Penguin Books, 1997), 16.
8. Susan Forward, *Toxic Parents: Overcoming Their Hurtful Legacy and Reclaiming Your Life*, (New York: Bantam Books, 1989), 124.
9. Amy Grant, *Home For Christmas*, "Grown-Up Christmas List," (Hollywood, CA: A&M Records), 1992.
10. Steven Curtis Chapman, *Beauty Will Rise*, "Faithful," (Brentwood, TN: Sparrow Records), 2009.
11. Steven Curtis Chapman, *Beauty Will Rise*, "Beauty Will Rise," (Brentwood, TN: Sparrow Records), 2009.

To contact the author, you can write her at
rochelle@scarsthatspeak.com

Also, please visit the website
to see Rochelle's full color artwork and to hear her music.
Scarsthatspeak.com

www.ingramcontent.com/pod-product-compliance
Lightning Source LLC
Chambersburg PA
CBHW030749250426
43673CB00058B/512